Hit of the Party

Hit of the Party

The Complete Planner for Children's Theme Birthday Parties

QUICK

EASY

INEXPENSIVE

FUN

A SIMPLE STEP-BY-STEP GUIDE TO GIVE CHILDREN THEIR
HAPPIEST BIRTHDAY PARTIES

WRITTEN AND ILLUSTRATED BY
AMY VANGSGARD

COOL HAND COMMUNICATIONS, INC.

©1994 by Amy Vangsgard
First Printing

COOL HAND COMMUNICATIONS, INC.
1098 NW. Boca Raton Boulevard
Suite #1
Boca Raton, FL 33432

Library of Congress #93-72927
ISBN: 1-56790-063-1

Printed in United States of America

Cover by Cheryl Nathan
Cover Photo by Susan Lakin
Author Photo by Kathryn Russell

◆　　◆　　◆　　◆　　◆　　◆　　◆

DEDICATED

TO MY LOVING HUSBAND, CHARLES

Acknowledgments

I would like to thank my daughters, Dawn and Natalie, for letting me try out so many games, crafts and recipes on them, modeling for my illustrations and being so patient with me while I work.

I would also like to thank my mom for all the birthday parties she gave me (especially the pink elephant cakes) and for making me feel so special as a child. And, I would like to thank my dad for encouraging me in whatever I do in life.

Finally, I would like to thank my book club and friends for all their encouragement in writing this book: Sandra Bieler, Anna Boorstin, Lisa Blaschke, Lockie Chapman, Judy Davidson, Denise Emanuel, Susan Garcia, Robin Gerber, Lee Jones, Marilyn Levin, Ria Levine, Stephanie Lowry, Lynette Mathis, Jean Osborne, and Linda Whittlesey.

Table Of Contents

INTRODUCTION

Welcome to the wonderful world of children's birthdays! Here, each party becomes a special memory for you and your children for the rest of your lives.

This book shows you how to create theme birthday celebrations that are fun, easy, inexpensive and don't require a lot of time or special skills. And it all starts when you and your child sit down together to decide on the theme for his or her birthday party.

PARTY-PLANNING MADE EASY

As you page through the book, you will see a wide variety of projects and activities, including:

- *Invitations and Thank-You Notes*
- *Party Menus*
- *Theme Birthday Cakes*
- *Decorations*
- *Loot Bags and Loot*
- *Activities*
- *Crafts*
- *Costumes*
- *Games*

There are more projects, games and activities in each chapter than you could possibly do at any one party. By picking and choosing, you and your child can create your own, very special birthday celebration.

PHOTOCOPY FUN!

Each chapter of this book has a theme party invitation, thank-you note, decorations, costumes and party favors that are designed to be photocopied. This not only saves you money, it helps you create a professional-looking party in very little time, with very little effort.

SPECIAL FEATURES

Every project for making invitations, decorations and favors lists an approximate completion time (for adults) to help you better budget your time. Many projects are designed for children to do as well. All activities (for children's games or crafts during the party) list the appropriate age range.

In every chapter, you will also find a number of helpful suggestions, identified by the following symbols:

TIMESAVER

When your time is limited, try these alternatives.

THE EXTRA TOUCH

Follow these suggestions when you have time to add a more personal touch or make something a little more special.

RECYCLER

These crafts and/or activities are designed to use recycled materials in order to help save the environment.

APPENDICES

There are four separate sections of the book that offer useful suggestions and additional party ideas for making food, decorating cakes, creating crafts and playing games.

APPENDIX A: RECIPES

All of the recipes presented in this section of the book are:
- Easy to make
- Fun to eat
- Designed to match party themes
- Made from children's favorite foods
- Divided into individual portions to make serving easier
- Nutritious

APPENDIX B: CAKE TIPS

In each chapter, there are two theme-related cake designs. Depending on how much time you have:
- You can make a pattern cake from scratch (or from a cake mix) and simply cut out the cake pattern, assemble the pieces, frost and decorate; or
- You can decorate a store-bought cake, saving time without sacrificing creativity

This section also contains:
- Guidelines to make baking and frosting cakes simpler and easier
- Creative shortcuts for decorating cakes and cupcakes
- Simple recipes for making your own cakes and frostings

APPENDIX C: CRAFT TIPS

This section contains numerous craft projects as well as helpful hints for all of the craft projects in the book, such as:
- Setting up a work area that is safe and efficient
- Tools and materials you will need to make projects go faster and easier
- Photocopying hints that will save time and money
- Photography and videotaping hints that will "save the memories"
- General instructions that can be used in craft projects for each theme party

APPENDIX D: GAMES

In addition to the many theme-related party games listed in each chapter, there are a number of traditional children's games suggested, which are located in this section. Most of the traditional games can be adapted to each theme birthday.

·—· ·—·

One final note...

A birthday party is a chance to give your child a special gift of love. Make your child feel special and loved and you will have given him or her the best birthday possible.

·—· ·—·

THE SEVEN " S's" TO SUCCESS

1. **S**tart planning early.
2. **S**hare party plans with the birthday child.
3. **S**horter and simpler parties work better.
4. **S**maller groups are easier to handle.
5. **S**chedules help the party run smoother.
6. **S**et up a party area that is safe and smart.
7. **S**ense of humor makes the party fun for everyone.

1. START PLANNING EARLY

The sooner you begin planning, the more time you will have to get everything done—and the more confident you will be about having a successful party. This "Party Countdown" will help you organize your time.

PARTY COUNTDOWN

FOUR-SIX WEEKS BEFORE THE PARTY:
1. Decide on a party theme.
2. Make a guest list.
3. Make a tentative schedule of party activities.
4. Decide which decorations and favors to make and which ones to buy.
5. List all supplies needed.
6. Photocopy invitations, decorations and favors.
7. Plan party menu.

TWO-THREE WEEKS BEFORE THE PARTY:
1. Make invitations.
2. Mail or drop off invitations.
3. Buy party supplies.
4. Start making party decorations and favors.
5. Order cake from bakery if you are not making your own.
6. Arrange for extra help.

ONE WEEK BEFORE THE PARTY:
1. Finish decorations and favors.
2. Confirm any orders placed for cake and/or party supplies.
3. Bake cake and freeze it, if making your own cake.
4. Make any other foods that can be made ahead of time and store foods in freezer.
5. Write out a final schedule of activities for the party.

TWO-THREE DAYS BEFORE THE PARTY:
1. Buy remaining food for the party.
2. Buy film and/or videotape.
3. Check batteries for cameras, flash units, and/or camcorders.
4. Get an exact guest count. Tally responses and call those who haven't responded.

ONE DAY BEFORE THE PARTY:
1. Finish decorating cake or pick up the cake from bakery. (To keep cake fresh, insert toothpicks along perimeter and in middle section of the cake, 1/2" deep. Cover loosely with foil or plastic wrap. Place in refrigerator.)
2. Child-proof party area.
3. Decorate any indoor areas of party. (Do not decorate outside area until the day of the party. Overnight weather can damage decorations.)
4. Prepare all "Do-Ahead" food.

THE DAY OF THE PARTY:

1. Prepare the rest of the food.
2. Decorate outside party area.
3. Mark the outside of the house or party area with balloons or a sign.
4. Keep your schedule of party activities handy.

HOW TO BUDGET YOUR TIME

TO DETERMINE HOW MUCH TIME YOU NEED TO WORK ON PARTY PREPARATIONS:

1. Make a list of which decorations, costumes, favors, recipes and party invitations you plan to make and which projects children will be making themselves.
2. Using the "estimated times" listed in each project, determine how long it will take to complete a project by using the following formula:

$$\frac{\text{ESTIMATED TIME PER ITEM} \quad X \quad \text{NUMBER OF GUESTS}}{\text{ESTIMATED TIME OF PROJECT}}$$

3. Estimates provided in the book for completing a project are based on an "average" adult skill level. When estimating how long it will take for children to complete a project, allow additional time, based on the age and skill level of the child.

HELPFUL HINTS FOR SAVING TIME:

1. Turn party preparations into a family project. If the birthday child and/or siblings are old enough to help, make some of the projects together—under your supervision—and have fun! Not only will you have less work to do, but your children will feel they helped make this birthday party a success.
2. Using the formula above, make a realistic estimate for how much preparation time is involved, and how much time you can devote to party preparation. Then budget your time. For example, if you only have 3 hours during the week to work on party projects, and you have estimated 6 hours of party preparation, you need to arrange your work schedule over two weeks.
3. Start early. It is much easier to find 15–30 minutes per evening than to make all of the projects on the last weekend (or night) before the party.
4. Make some of the items while you are doing other activities, like watching television or listening to the radio.
5. Save projects that require concentration for when children are asleep. You'll be amazed at how much faster and easier your work will go.
6. Consider "Timesaver" projects whenever possible.
7. Shop smart. Make a list of things you need and where you can get them. Then call stores ahead of time to check on availability and lowest prices.
8. Avoid extra shopping trips. Buy items for the party while doing everyday shopping or on your way to or from work.
9. Start collecting recycled materials as soon as you know what you will need. Ask family and/or friends to help.
10. After completing each project, store items in a safe area, away from curious little fingers.
11. Photocopy blank copies of the planning guides listed in the next few pages. Complete the information for each party to help organize your time before and during the party.

PROJECT PLANNING GUIDE

PROJECT TITLE	PAGE #	# ITEMS NEEDED	PROJECT LEADER	EST TIME COMPLETE	MATERIALS NEEDED

BIRTHDAY PARTY PLANNING GUIDE

PARTY DATE: _____ DAY OF WEEK: _____

TIME PARTY STARTS: _____ TIME PARTY ENDS: _____

BIRTHDAY PARTY THEME: _____

NUMBER OF GUESTS: _____ NUMBER OF INVITATIONS: _____

HELPERS

NAME: _____ PHONE: _____

NAME: _____ PHONE: _____

NAME: _____ PHONE: _____

GUESTS (CHILDREN)

NAME	ADDRESS	PHONE	PARENT	RSVP

GUESTS (ADULTS)

NAME	ADDRESS	PHONE(S)	RSVP

BIRTHDAY PARTY SHOPPING GUIDE

PHOTOCOPYING

NAME OF PROJECT	PAGE #	# OF COPIES	TYPE OF PAPER

SUPPLIES

❑ ENVELOPES

    NUMBER:_____

    SIZE: _____

❑ CANDLES

    NUMBER:_____

    COLOR: _____

❑ PLATES

    NUMBER:_____

    COLOR: _____

    SIZE: _____

❑ NAPKINS

    NUMBER:_____

    COLOR: _____

    SIZE: _____

❑ TABLECLOTH

    NUMBER:_____

    COLOR: _____

    SIZE: _____

❑ POSTAGE STAMPS

    NUMBER: _____

❑ MATCHES/LIGHTER

❑ FORKS/KNIVES/SPOONS

    NUMBER: _____

    COLOR: _____

❑ CUPS

    NUMBER: _____

    COLOR: _____

    SIZE:_____

❑ PLACEMATS

    NUMBER: _____

    COLOR: _____

DECORATIONS:

_____

_____

_____

_____

FAVORS:

_____

_____

_____

_____

ARTS AND CRAFTS SUPPLIES:

❑ ELASTIC CORD _____

❑ GLUE_____

❑ TRANSPARENT TAPE _____

❑ CRAYONS/MARKERS _____

_____

_____

❑ TRASHBAGS ❑ CAMERA TOOLS

SIZE: _____ STILL: _____ ❑ SCISSORS _____

COLOR: _____ VIDEO: _____ ❑ STAPLER _____

❑ FILM/VIDEO ❑ BATTERIES ❑ CRAFT KNIFE _____

NUMBER: _____ CAMERA: _____ ❑ HOLE PUNCH _____

TYPE: _____ VIDEO: _____ ❑ BALLOON PUMP _____

❑ LIGHTS ❑ EXTENSION CORDS _____

❑ MUSIC ❑ CASSETTE PLAYER _____

❑ RECORD PLAYER _____

_____ ❑ CD PLAYER _____

_____ ❑ RADIO _____

❑ RECYCLED MATERIALS ❑ PROPS FOR GAMES

_____ _____

_____ _____

_____ _____

_____ _____

_____ _____

_____ _____

_____

GROCERY LIST

❑ DRINKS ❑ EATS

_____ _____

_____ _____

_____ _____

_____ _____

_____ _____

_____ _____

_____ _____

_____ _____

_____ _____

_____ _____

_____

❑ ICE CREAM ❑ CAKE

_____ _____

_____ _____

2. SHARE PARTY PLANS WITH THE BIRTHDAY CHILD

Your birthday child will feel special and more involved when he or she is included in the party plans. Set some time aside to look through the book with your child, and let him or her choose the theme for the party. Children may change their mind several times, so start this process well before the party, and then make a deadline for the "final decision."

CHOOSE PARTY ELEMENTS TOGETHER:

1. As you and your child page through the theme chapter, select the menu, activities, decorations, favors, costumes and games he or she wants for the party.
2. You may have to "pull in the reins" a bit here, as children may want to do more than there is time for, or attempt activities inappropriate for their age.
3. Encourage siblings to share in the celebration so they will not feel jealous or excluded. Offer them special jobs to do before the party and important roles to play on the day of the party.

DISCUSS WITH YOUR CHILD WHICH FOODS HE OR SHE WANTS TO EAT:

1. Agree ahead of time to serve a nutritious selection of your child's favorite foods.
2. Include a variety of foods so even "fussy" eaters will have something to eat. (Keep in mind how tastes in foods differ from child to child and from one age to another.)
3. Try out recipes ahead of time.

DISCUSS WITH YOUR CHILD WHICH GAMES HE OR SHE WANTS TO PLAY:

1. Try out games ahead of time with your child—especially any that may be new.
2. Don't plan games that eliminate children from participating, such as "Simon Says."
3. Avoid competitive games where there is one winner. If you want competitive activities, plan team competitions, such as relay races.
4. Game prizes are not necessary. Enjoying the game is the best reward.
5. When selecting teams, don't let your child or other children pick team members. The pressure on choosers is unfair, and the order of selection often translates into hurt feelings. Instead, you may want to:
   - Pick names randomly out of a hat.
   - Line up children and have kids "count off." (Odd numbers are on one team; even numbers are on the other team.)

THINK TWICE ABOUT HIRING ENTERTAINMENT:

1. This book gives you alternatives to hiring entertainment—not only to save money, but to help make your child's birthday a more personal and meaningful celebration among family and friends.
2. If, however, your child has his or her heart set on having outside entertainment, chose the entertainment carefully. Here are a few guidelines that may help:
   - Plan the entertainment for the beginning of the party, when children are most alert. The program should start 1/2 hour after the party begins.
   - Make sure the entertainment is appropriate for your child's age group. Children 3 years of age and under can be terrified of clowns; children 5 years and under are generally too young to understand magic.
   - The length of the show should be no more than 20–30 minutes for children 4 years of age and under; and 30–45 minutes is long enough for children 5 years of age and older.
   - Get references first, or better yet, see the show yourself before the party.

MAKE FAMILY TRADITIONS A SPECIAL PART OF THE BIRTHDAY CELEBRATION:

1. It is important to share these traditions with family and friends or they may become lost over time.
2. If you don't have any family traditions associated with birthdays, maybe it's time to start some: a birthday banner for each member of the family, a special recipe, or a favorite game.

3. SHORTER AND SIMPLER PARTIES WORK BETTER

KEEP CHILDREN INTERESTED AND INVOLVED:

1. When planning the activities for your child's party, keep the activities simple—not too long and not too difficult—for each age group. Children can be overwhelmed by too much of anything, which can spoil the fun.
2. When completing your invitation, state exactly when the party starts *and* when the party ends. This not only gives everyone a specific timeframe for the party, but it tells parents exactly when to pick up their children.
3. If serving lunch, state on the invitation when lunch will be served.
4. The activities in this book have been rated according to age, based on general interests and skill levels. These ratings are intended only as a guideline, as individual interests and abilities vary widely among children.
5. Older children can handle longer parties, but even they have their limits. Here are some suggested guidelines for each age group:

PARTY LENGTH GUIDELINES

AGE (IN YEARS)	LENGTH OF PARTY
1	Based on the infant's nap time
2–3	1–1 1/2 hours
4–5	2–2 1/2 hours
6–7	2–3 hours
8–10	3–3 1/2 hours

BIRTHDAY PARTY ACTIVITY GUIDE

AGE	ACTIVITY GUIDELINES
1	• Children are too young to participate in any structured activities • Party is mainly for child's family and friends of the family
2–3	• A loosely-structured party works best • Children more often "parallel play" rather than play together • Some simple activities that are appropriate are: bean bag toss; follow-the-leader; puppet shows; simple clay or gluing crafts • Most children still need a parent present at the party • Non-competitive games work best
4–5	• Most children have developed an interest in costumes • Some of the simpler games can be played because social skills are more developed • Most children no longer need a parent present at the party
6–7	• Children much more aggressive in activities • Most children eager for more complex games • Relay races are popular
8–9	• Children may want "all-girl" or "all-boy" parties • Children complete games at a more rapid rate • Children enjoy games more than favors and costumes • Avoid activities that might be considered "babyish"

4. SMALL GROUPS ARE EASIER TO HANDLE

THE SMALLER THE GROUP, THE EASIER IT IS TO KEEP EVERY-THING UNDER CONTROL:

1. The number of children you invite is based on your child's age. Small children tend to be overwhelmed by large numbers of people.
2. A general rule for children under 6 years of age is that the number of guests should equal the age of the child.
3. Children 6 years and older can handle as many as 10–12 guests, as long as *you* can.
4. If you do decide to invite a large group of children, like a school class or a club, don't exclude anyone as this can be hurtful to those who are left out.

SPACE CAN BE A LIMITING FACTOR:

1. Be realistic about how many children will fit in your party area. A backyard party generally offers more room than an indoor party and less possibility of breakage—as long as weather permits.
2. Parks offer even more room, but there is less privacy and more problems with decorating and bringing food to the party area.

EXTRA HELP CAN ALSO AFFECT THE SIZE OF YOUR PARTY:

1. The more help you have, the easier it will be to hold a larger party.
2. This does not mean you need to hire professional help. You can always ask relatives, friends or parents of your child's guests. (If you offer to help out at *their* parties, you can get the help you need and at the same time, you can start a nice tradition.)
3. If you can't get enough help in these ways, you can always hire inexpensive but reliable help—like a teenager in the neighborhood or your regular baby-sitter.

5. SCHEDULES HELP THE PARTY RUN SMOOTHER

SCHEDULES SHOULD BE USED AS GUIDELINES

Make a list of the party activities with the birthday child, and then use the "Party Schedule" and "Scheduling Guidelines" to help you plan your schedule.

During the party, it may be necessary to change your schedule. For instance, if an activity isn't going well, you may want to cut it short. There's no reason to keep it going, "just because it's on the schedule." On the other hand, if something is working well, you may want to extend the time. Making your schedule work means following your basic plan, while at the same time, remaining open to change.

PARTY SCHEDULE

ARRIVAL ACTIVITIES   TIME

_____   _____

_____   _____

_____   _____

_____   _____

_____   _____

MAIN ACTIVITIES   TIME

_____   _____

_____   _____

_____   _____

_____   _____

_____   _____

_____   _____

_____   _____

_____   _____

_____   _____

_____   _____

REFRESHMENTS   TIME

_____   _____

_____   _____

_____   _____

CONCLUDING ACTIVITIES   TIME

_____   _____

_____   _____

_____   _____

_____   _____

SCHEDULING GUIDELINES

THE GREETING:

Make each child feel welcome the moment he or she walks in.

1. Greet children by name or give each child a "theme name" according to the theme of the party, such as:
    - "Astronaut Amanda"
    - "Brian the Brontosaurus"
    - "Cowgirl Katie"
2. This is a good time to give each child a theme costume for the party, such as:
    - Space helmet
    - Pirate's eye patch
    - Fairy wings
3. You might also want to give each child one of the theme party favors during this time, such as:
    - Safari binoculars
    - Bumble bee kazoo

It is generally during the "Greeting" portion of the party that you accept gifts from your guests. Put the gifts away from curious fingers until it is time to open presents.

ARRIVAL ACTIVITIES (10–30 MINUTES):

Since children will not all arrive at the same time, start with an activity that can be joined quickly and easily, without disrupting the fun. Make sure any late arrivals feel welcome and join the arrival activity as soon as possible. Here are a few suggestions:

1. **Play Structures**
    These include play areas created from appliance boxes, play equipment and assorted items on hand that can be designed and decorated to match the party theme.
2. **Crafts**
    Independent activities for children to create favors or costumes that are part of the theme.
3. **Face Make-Up**
    This is always a popular activity and can immediately make children feel part of the party theme. Some children may not want to participate, but they will want to watch.
4. **Photographs**
    Children are usually freshest at the beginning of the party, as are their costumes and make-up. Take individual photographs of each child behind a theme party backdrop or somewhere in a party setting. If you use a Polaroid® camera, your photograph can lead children directly to one of the theme photo-craft activities, which are part of every chapter.

MAIN ACTIVITIES (20–45 MINUTES):

Begin your main group activity when most of your guests have arrived. (Don't wait too long for late arrivals, you may run out of time for some of the activities or projects you planned.)

This is the longest portion of the party, when everyone has a chance to participate.

1. **Vary the pace of activities.**
    Start with the more active games, like the treasure hunt or running relay races. After 2–3 such games, have everyone "cool down" with some of the quieter activities, such as the guessing games, story-telling or crafts, especially if you plan to serve refreshments next.
2. **Have extra games planned.**
    No matter how carefully you structure activities, it is a good idea to have a few additional games ready to play, in case children finish sooner or become bored.

REFRESHMENTS (15–30 MINUTES):

Whatever you decide to serve, keep in mind that the birthday cake will be the climax of the party.

1. Have a set time for serving the cake and try to stick to it. This will help your party stay on schedule.
2. Don't feel as if you have to provide a full meal. Sometimes, snacks are just fine. Or, you may want to serve just cake and ice cream, especially if you have the party in the late afternoon.
3. Take advantage of the quiet time. While your guests are eating, you may want to have some quiet activity, such as reading a story to the children or performing a puppet show.

CONCLUDING ACTIVITIES (15–30 MINUTES):

This is a good time to open presents. Older children may want to present their gifts to the birthday child themselves. With younger children, you may just want to skip opening presents, as small ones often want to keep the presents they gave.

1. Have someone make a list of who has given which gift. This will help you write your "Thank-You" notes.
2. Hand out loot bags as your guests are walking out the door. If you distribute the hand-out loot bags during the party, children may get their bags mixed up and begin to fight over what belongs to whom. (Don't forget to put the loot bags in a box or bag by the door—out of reach but in sight—so you won't forget to hand them out.)
3. Schedule "wind down" activities, such as:
   - **Coloring activities**
     Photocopy some of the theme illustrations from the book and provide children with crayons, markers and a place to color until it is time for them to leave.
   - **Sing-alongs**
     This is a fun activity that children can enjoy until it's time for them to leave.
4. When the party is over, don't rush to clean up. Sit down and talk with your child about how much fun the party was. This will help avoid "post-party letdown," and ease him or her back into everyday life.

6. SET UP A PARTY AREA THAT IS SAFE AND SMART

Part of the secret to a well-organized party is setting up an efficient party area. Start by reviewing your party schedule, and imagine how each of the activities will flow from one area to the next. Anticipate what you will need in each area, and get these items ready ahead of time. Here are some suggestions:

TABLES:

1. Most adult-size tables are too tall for small children to sit comfortably. To make a child-size table, you first need a table top. Use a door, a large sheet of 3/4" plywood, or a folding table with the legs folded up.
2. Place the table top on a base approximately 20" high. You might want to use crates, boxes, buckets or end tables as a base or "legs."
3. To keep the table top from "rocking," use same-size units on each end.

CHILD-SIZE CHAIRS:

1. Inexpensive, molded plastic chairs can be purchased at many discount stores.
2. If you don't have extra chairs, ask your guests if they have child-size chairs they can bring from home.

TRASHCANS:

1. Have at least two empty trashcans, along with separate recycle trashbins, around the party area.
2. Remove lids to make tossing trash that much easier.
3. Put at least one empty trashcan near the eating area and another near the area where you will be opening presents, if these areas are separate.

PRESENT BOX (OR BASKET):

1. Decorate a box or laundry basket and place it near the front door. As guests arrive, have them put their gifts in the "present box."
2. Keep the "present box" away from the party area until it is time to open presents. Then carry the box to the appropriate area and open the presents.
3. After the gifts have been opened, put them back in the basket (along with a list of who gave which gift).

CAMERA AND FILM:

1. If you are going to take pictures and/or videotape the party, make sure your camera is loaded and ready.
2. Keep extra film and/or videotape handy.

CRAFT AND GAME SUPPLIES:

1. Place craft supplies in several containers so children will not have to reach over each other or squabble over supplies.
2. Place all game supplies in a box ready to use.

PAPER TOWELS AND CLOTHS:

1. Don't get upset over spills and messes—you are bound to have some.
2. Have towels and cloths placed in several locations in the party area to make clean-up easier.

TAKE CARE OF THE HOUSEHOLD PETS:

1. If you have pets, make sure they are kept out of the way during the party.
2. Place animals in a safe location to protect both the pets and your guests.

BREAKABLE AND DANGEROUS OBJECTS:

1. Remove temptation before an accident happens.
2. Lock-up anything breakable or dangerous.
3. Close-off restricted areas, and make it clear that no one is allowed in those areas.
4. Your house and yard are probably already safety-proof for the age level of your children and their friends. But it is still a good idea to go over the party area with safety in mind.
5. Some of the items parents often overlook, especially in backyard parties are:
   - Charcoal lighter fluid
   - Garden chemicals
   - Gardening tools/equipment
6. If the party is to be held outdoors, rake the lawn to make sure there are no sharp objects hidden in the grass.
7. Don't forget to child-proof the bathroom.

BALLOON WARNINGS:

1. Small children can swallow and suffocate on deflated or broken balloons.
2. If you have balloons at a party, make sure balloons stay inflated. Remove any deflated or broken balloons immediately.
3. Do not take metallic balloons outside. If they take flight, metallic balloons can get caught in power lines and cause serious problems.

PARTY DAY CHECKLIST

- ❑ Child-proof party area
- ❑ Finish decorating
- ❑ Set party table
- ❑ Mark outside of the house or party area
- ❑ Complete food preparations
- ❑ Secure family pet
- ❑ Assign duties to each of the helpers
- ❑ Set out trashcans and trashbags
- ❑ Place paper towels in eating and work areas
- ❑ Camera/film/batteries
- ❑ Cassette/compact disc player
- ❑ Cassette tapes/compact discs
- ❑ Set out first-aid kit
- ❑ Set out craft supplies
- ❑ Set out game supplies
- ❑ Have basket/box ready for presents
- ❑ Have loot bags ready
- ❑ Candles
- ❑ Matches
- ❑ _____
- ❑ _____
- ❑ _____
- ❑ _____
- ❑ _____
- ❑ _____
- ❑ _____
- ❑ _____
- ❑ _____
- ❑ _____
- ❑ _____
- ❑ _____

7. SENSE OF HUMOR MAKES IT FUN FOR EVERYONE

Don't feel as if everything has to be "perfect" or just as you planned. Expect the unexpected. This is a party, so don't let "the little things" get in the way of having a good time.

COPING WITH THE PROBLEM CHILD:
1. Be prepared to deal with a problem child.
2. Some children may get overexcited or overstimulated at your party and act out. The best way to deal with a problem child is to avoid any public confrontation.
3. If the problem child's parent is not present to intervene, separate the child from the rest of the group and let him or her know that you have certain rules about party behavior, and that you expect everyone to follow those rules.
4. If the child continues to misbehave, ask him or her politely to "stop it," explaining that bad behavior ruins the party for everyone else.
5. Some problem children might behave better if given a special task to do.

HELPING THE SHY CHILD:
1. If a child is shy or is having trouble joining in, give him or her an alternative activity or special place to observe.
2. Be encouraging, but don't force a shy child to participate. Your job is not to change them, but to help them adapt so the party keeps moving smoothly.

WHEN THE BIRTHDAY CHILD IS A PROBLEM:
1. Sometimes, the birthday child gets overexcited or overstimulated.
2. Other times, the birthday child gets disappointed that his/her "Big Day" isn't all that he/she imagined it to be.
3. Whatever the reason, there are specific ways to prevent such problems from developing at your child's birthday party:
    *   Let the birthday child go first in all games and activities.
    *   Always serve food to the birthday child first, especially the birthday cake.
    *   Make sure you have enough help so you can spend time with the birthday child.
    *   Siblings may cause problems out of jealousy or lack of attention. Give older siblings specific jobs to do, and arrange help in attending to the younger ones.
    *   Don't make the mistake of giving more attention to the siblings than to the birthday child.
    *   Unless your child is exceptionally good about sharing, close-off the child's bedroom or toy area so that none of the other children can play with the birthday child's things. If you want to set out some toys for the guests, ask your child to select a few toys that would be okay to share. Place these toys in the party area for guests to use.

STORMY WEATHER:
1. Have an indoor alternative in case the weather forces you inside.
2. Plan a few "backup" activities that can be played indoors as well as outdoors.

EMERGENCY SITUATIONS:
1. Have a fully-stocked, first-aid kit on hand, as well as a fresh supply of ice cubes.
2. Know how to use the age-appropriate methods to overcome choking.

DON'T GET CAUGHT SHORT:
1. Have extra food, games, costumes and prizes. You never know who will decide to "bring a guest," and you certainly wouldn't want to hurt that child's feelings.
2. Children may also lose or damage costumes, favors, and prizes. So, be prepared with extra supplies of each.

HAVE FUN AT YOUR CHILD'S PARTY:
1. No matter how hectic it gets, this party should be fun for you, too.

Teddy Bear Picnic Party

CHAPTER 1

Somewhere in the forest, teddy bears are looking for their honey pots and honey bees are busy making honey. It's a lovely day and they are all getting together to celebrate your birthday. Pack your baskets full of treats and let's go on a teddy bear picnic.

ILLUSTRATION 1-01

TEDDY BEAR PICNIC INVITATION

Estimated Time: 2–3 minutes each

Let this lovable teddy bear welcome your guests to a teddy bear picnic. Kids will delight in seeing the bear trying to catch the bee.

WHAT YOU NEED:

- Illustration 1–03 "Teddy Bear Picnic Invitation" (page 39)
- Copier paper (white, pink or yellow)
- Envelopes (3 5/8" x 6 1/2")
- Scissors
- Felt-tip pen (black)
- Crayons, markers and/or colored pencils ❦

❦ Optional

ILLUSTRATION 1-02

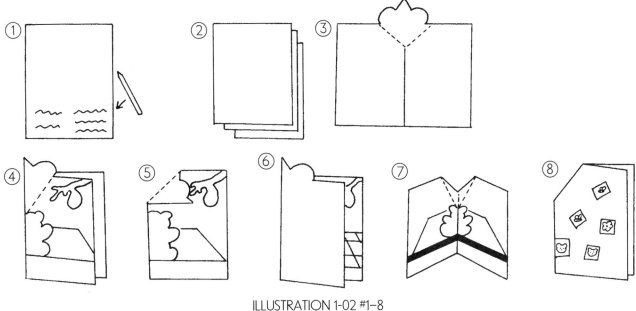

ILLUSTRATION 1-02 #1–8

WHAT YOU DO:

1. Make one photocopy of Illustration 1–03. This is your "master copy." Fill out all party information with felt-tip pen on the master copy (Illustration 1–02 #1).
2. Photocopy as many invitations as needed (Illustration 1–02 #2).
3. Color invitation, if desired.
4. Cut out invitation along outer lines (Illustration 1–02 #3).
5. Fold invitation in half so that illustration is facing outward, and make a sharp crease along fold line (Illustration 1–02 #4).
6. Fold over corner along dotted line (Illustration 1–02 #5), making a sharp crease along fold line.
7. Open invitation and fold so illustration faces inward, (Illustration 1–02 #6), then press along fold line.
8. Pull "bee" inward, tucking it into center of invitation; close invitation and press along all fold lines (Illustrations 1–02 #7 and 1–02 #8).
9. Open and close invitation and watch the bear try to catch the bee! (Illustration 1-02)

👉 THE EXTRA TOUCH

- Glue "Teddy Bear Picnic Stickers" (page 31) to front of invitation and to seal envelope.

TEDDY BEAR THANK-YOU NOTE

The "Teddy Bear Picnic Thank-You Note" (Illustration 1–04) is on the same page as the "Teddy Bear Picnic Invitation." When you photocopy the invitation, you will also be copying the thank-you note. Simply cut out the thank-you note, and write your personal message in the space provided.

Estimated Time: 1 minute each

MENU

Pack your little bears and bees a scrumptious lunch in individual picnic baskets. Wrap foods separately in clear or colored plastic wrap (or recloseable bags) to keep fresh. Include a "Teddy Bear Straw" (page 27) and a napkin in each basket. When it comes time to serve lunch, just hand each child his/her own basket. (See "Picnic Basket" in **CRAFT TIPS** (page 350) for an easy-to-make basket or use paper lunch bags if you are short of time.) Choose foods from each group, and follow the recipes on the pages listed below.

DRINKS:

Honey Bee Punch ....Page 312
Berry Beary Punch ....Page 312

EATS:

Biscuit Sandwiches (Use teddy bear cookie cutter) ....Page 325
Teddy Bear Smackers ....Page 323
Bear Claws ....Page 329
Beary Crunchy Critters ....Page 331
Honey Bee Treats ....Page 332
Peach Blossoms ....Page 320
Cookie Puppets (Use teddy bear cookie cutter) ....Page 329
Trail mix ....Page 333
Small boxes of raisins
Individually wrapped servings of cheese
Individual portions of fruit snacks (teddy bear)
Strawberries and grapes served in recloseable plastic bags

CAKE AND ICE CREAM:

Teddy Bear Cake ....Page 25
The Bears and the Bees Picnic Cake ....Page 26
Teddy Bear Ice Creams ....Page 336
Flower Pot Ice Creams ....Page 339

 THE EXTRA TOUCH

- Serve your punch in a large pot, jug or cooler, decorated with some "Honey Bees." Photocopy Illustration 1-17 or 1-18 to make the bees, (pages 42 and 43) and make a sign that says "Honey."
- Children may enjoy eating lunch on a picnic blanket rather than at a table.

TEDDY BEAR CAKE

Estimated time: 1–1 1/2 hours

Your guests will love this teddy bear cake—it tastes beary, beary good!

INGREDIENTS:

1   "Basic Cake" recipe in Appendix A, on pages 343 and 344; or use your favorite box cake mix

1   "Chocolate Frosting" recipe in Appendix A, on page 345; or use 1 can of your favorite canned chocolate frosting

1   "Buttercream Frosting" recipe in Appendix A, on page 345; or use a can of your favorite canned buttercream frosting

2   Chocolate mint patties (round), approximately 1 1/2" diameter

1 oz.   Unsweetened baking chocolate

2 c.   Flaked coconut

1   Marshmallow (cut in half)

1/2 c.   Chocolate chips

1   Licorice whip (red)

     Food coloring (red)

     13" x 18" tray or foil-covered board

     Illustration 1-05 "Teddy Bear Cake Pattern" (page 40)

ILLUSTRATION 1-06

DIRECTIONS:

1. Prepare and bake cake in two 8" round cake pans as directed in recipe or cake package.
2. Cool cake completely on wire rack.
3. Wrap in plastic wrap and freeze cake at least 45 minutes. (Freezing the cake does not affect its flavor and makes it easier to work with. It also enables you to make the cake ahead of time, to help balance your work load for the party.)
4. Trace Illustration 1–05 "Teddy Bear Cake Pattern" on wax paper. Cut out wax paper pattern into sections and reassemble on top of one cake round.
5. Using long knife, cut cake into sections along pattern (Illustration 1–06 #1).
6. Assemble sections on tray into shape of a teddy bear (Illustration 1–06 #2).
7. Tint buttercream frosting pink by adding a few drops of red food coloring and mix until color is uniform.
8. Frost connecting sections of cake with pink frosting.
9. Spread pink frosting in a circle to form bear's "muzzle," and use pink frosting to make two half-moon shapes, forming the inside of bear's "ears" (Illustration 1–06).

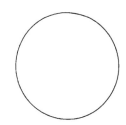

ILLUSTRATION 1-06 #1

10. Frost top and sides of "bow" with pink frosting.
11. Frost top and sides of remaining bear with chocolate frosting.
12. Melt unsweetened chocolate in a double boiler or in a microwave oven. (If using microwave oven, heat until chocolate just starts to bubble.)
13. Stir coconut and melted chocolate together in a bowl.
14. Sprinkle coconut evenly over top and sides of chocolate frosting, gently pressing coconut into cake.
15. Press one chocolate mint into pink circle to create "nose," and one mint into center of "bow."
16. Press marshmallow halves into bear's face to form "eyes." Dip two chocolate chips into chocolate frosting and place in centers of marshmallows to form "pupils."
17. Cut licorice whip into two, 2" pieces and place on pink circle to form bear's "mouth."
18. Place chocolate chips on pink bow to make polka dots.

ILLUSTRATION 1-06 #2

THE BEARS AND THE BEES PICNIC CAKE

Estimated time: 20–30 minutes

Here's a quick way to decorate a store bought cake—and one your guests will be buzzing about.

INGREDIENTS:

1	Frosted store-bought cake (round or rectangular)
24	Candy corns
24	Candy-coated chocolates (brown)
1–2	Licorice whips (red or black)
1 c.	Flaked coconut
1	Doll table
	Toy bears (one or more)
	Food coloring (green)

DIRECTIONS:

ILLUSTRATION 1-07

1. Place frosted cake on plate or serving platter.
2. Make "bees" around the side of the cake by pushing two candy-coated chocolates side-by-side into frosting, wherever you want bees on cake (Illustration 1–07).
3. To make bee's "wings," place two candy corns between two chocolates, with pointed end headed toward the bee's body (Illustration 1–07 #1).
4. To make bee's "antennae," cut licorice whips into 1/2" pieces and place two at the top of the bee's "head."
5. Place coconut in bowl and tint green by mixing with a few drops of green food coloring.
6. Sprinkle green coconut on top of cake and around bottom edge to make "grass."
7. Arrange doll table and teddy bears on top of cake.

ILLUSTRATION 1-07 #1

👉 THE EXTRA TOUCH

- Add doll tablecloth, dishes and other "picnic accessories" for your teddy bears.
- To add foliage to picnic scene, use mint leaves and/or gumdrops.

DECORATIONS

It doesn't take much to create a teddy bear picnic setting. A few decorations and the whole party area will come alive with bears and bees. You can use decorations as craft activities at your party. Or, save money by giving some of these decorations out as favors in your loot bags.

PARTY STREAMERS

Estimated time: 1–2 minutes per streamer

Select one (or more) of the streamers suggested below, and follow the directions for "Party Streamers" in **CRAFT TIPS** (page 349).

- **Flower Streamer** Pattern CT-01 (page 361)
  Use bright colors of crepé paper.
- **Doll Streamer** Pattern CT-02 (page 359)
  Use bright colors of crepé paper.
- **Teddy Bear Streamer** Pattern CT-07 (page 360)
  Use bright colors of crepé paper.

⏰ TIMESAVER

- Hang crepé paper streamers (in pre-packaged rolls) around party area.

BEE BALLOONS

Estimated time: 2–3 minutes each

This project may be completed ahead of time as a decoration or during the party as a craft.

WHAT YOU NEED:

- Illustration 1–09 "Bee Wings" (page 41)
- Copier paper (white or yellow)
- 7" or 9" yellow or light-colored balloon
- Wide-tipped, felt marker (black)
- Scissors
- Pencil
- Hole punch
- Yarn or string

ILLUSTRATION 1-08

WHAT YOU DO:

1. Photocopy Illustration 1–09 onto copier paper.
2. Cut out "bee wings."
3. Fold "bee wings" in half and punch hole into center of wings (Illustration 1–08 #1).
4. Inflate balloon and knot end.
5. Using marker, draw rings around bottom half of balloon (Illustration 1–08 #2).
6. Pull knotted end of balloon through hole in wings (Illustration 1–08).
7. Tie string to knot and hang balloons in party area.

ILLUSTRATION 1-08 #1–2

ILLUSTRATION 1-10

TEDDY BEAR STRAWS

Estimated time: 1–2 minutes each

Make your own "Teddy Bear Straws" (Illustration 1–10) and watch children giggle as they sip those delicious drinks. Use Illustration 1–11 "Teddy Bear" (page 44) and follow directions for "Drinking Straws" in **CRAFT TIPS** (page 353).

TEDDY BEAR SUCKERS

Estimated time: 1–2 minutes each

Make your own "Teddy Bear Suckers." (Illustration 1–12) Use Illustration 1–11 "Teddy Bear" (page 44) and follow directions for "Party Suckers" in **CRAFT TIPS** (page 353).

ILLUSTRATION 1-12

💡 MORE DECORATING IDEAS...

- Create a swarm of bees by tying bee balloons on a long string and placing a beehive piñata (page 30) in the center .
- Use stuffed teddy bears to decorate table and/or party area.
- Cover table with butcher paper and make "Paw Prints" left by all those hungry bears. Follow directions for "Paw Print Tablecloth" in **CRAFT TIPS** (page 353).
- Make placemats by having children glue "Teddy Bear Picnic Stickers"(page 31) onto 9" x 12" sheet of construction paper. Provide crayons for children to color placemats, if desired.
- Buy flowering plants in inexpensive pony packs. Pot each one in a paper cup, with guest's name written on outside, and use as place marker. Then give away as a party favor.

- Hang kites from ceiling or trees. See "Bee Kite" (page 31).
- Tie a helium balloon to each stuffed teddy bear and place throughout party area.
- Make "Honey Jars" by filling baby food jars with honey. Decorate by tying a square of fabric to top of jar. Write "Honey" on self-stick labels and place on side of jar.
- Photocopy Illustration 1-17 or 1-18 "Honey Bees" (pages 42 and 43), cut out and hang from strings suspended in party area.
- Photocopy Illustration 1-01 "Teddy Bear Cake" (page 22) and hang on outside of front door or at front of party area to greet guests.
- Photocopy Illustration 1-33 "Bear Paws" (page 43), cut out and tape on walkway leading to front door or party area.

LOOT BAGS

Select one (or more) of the following loot bags and follow the directions for "Loot Bags" in **CRAFT TIPS** (page 350).

- **Picnic Basket** (page 350)
- **Sticker Bag** (page 350)
  Use Illustration 1-29 "Teddy Bear Picnic Stickers" (page 44).
- **Treasure Box** (page 351)
  Use Illustration 1-29 "Teddy Bear Picnic Stickers" (page 44).
- **Honey Pot**
  Use a small sand pail and write "Honey" on outside with a permanent marker.

LOOT BAG "LOOT"

Looking for something to put in those loot bags? Here are some creative suggestions you can make, or if you are short of time, you can buy.

LOOT YOU CAN MAKE:
- **Teddy Bear Picnic Stickers** (page 31)
- **Teddy Bear Straws** (page 27)
- **Teddy Bear Suckers** (page 27)
- **Teddy Bear Polaroid® Photo Frame** (page 30)
- **Paw Puppets** (page 33)
- **Honey Bee Kazoo** (page 32)
- **Beary Crunchy Critters** (page 331)
- **Cookie Puppets** (page 329) Use teddy bear cookie cutter.
- **Honey Jars** (top section of this page)

LOOT YOU CAN BUY:
Teddy bears are very popular and can be found as:
- Stickers
- Small stuffed animals
- Costume jewelry, fashion accessories
- Stationery, pencils/pens
- Rubber stamps
- Small story books about bears
- Teddy bear graham crackers
- Teddy bear fruit snacks
- Gummi bears
- Bit-o'-Honey® candy bars

ACTIVITIES

Your guests will be romping around like teddy bears and buzzing about like bees.

Don't feel as if you have to do all of these activities—there isn't enough time at any party. Discuss with the birthday child which ones he or she would like to do and plan your party activities accordingly.

ARRIVAL ACTIVITY

As each child arrives, let him/her pick a special name, as in "Penny the Pooh Bear," "Honeybee Henry," "Bryan the Bear," "Christina the Cub," and the like. Announce their name with a little fanfare.

BEEHIVE OR BEAR CAVE

Recommended for all ages

WHAT YOU NEED:

- Illustration 1–17 or 1–18 "Honey Bees" (pages 42 and 43)
- Copier paper (yellow or white)
- Card table or dining table
- Blankets
- Duct tape or cloth-backed masking tape
- Transparent or "double-stick" tape
- Scissors

WHAT YOU DO:

1. Photocopy Illustration 1–17 or 1–18 "Honey Bees" onto copier paper.
2. Cut out bee designs.
3. Cover table with blankets, leaving an opening for the "door" of the hive or cave. Secure blankets in place with duct tape (Illustration 1–16).
4. Using double-stick tape or transparent tape (rolled on itself), tape back of bees to blanket.

ILLUSTRATION 1-16

 THE EXTRA TOUCH

- Use potted house plants to suggest foliage.
- Add extra tables and chairs to make a larger hive or cave.
- Tie "Bee Balloons" to hive or cave.
- Place stuffed teddy bears on and around hive or cave.

↻ BEEHIVE PHOTO BACKDROP

Recommended for all ages

Use Illustration 1–19 "Beehive Photo Backdrop Pattern" and follow the directions for "Photo Backdrop" in **CRAFT TIPS** (page 354) to give children and their parents the best party favor they can have—a memorable "Teddy Bear Picnic Snapshot."

You can take a Polaroid® photograph and hand it out at the party (see "Polaroid® Photo Frame below), or you can use a 35 mm camera and send a photo along with your thank-you note.

 THE EXTRA TOUCH

- Glue "Honey Bees" (this page) to your photo backdrop.

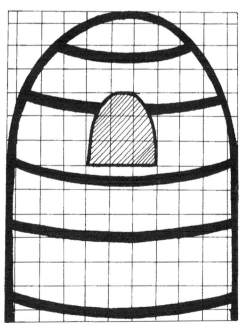

ILLUSTRATION 1-19

TEDDY BEAR POLAROID® PHOTO FRAME

Recommended for all ages

Hand out these wonderful memories at the party using a Polaroid® photo and follow the directions for "Polaroid® Photo Frame" in **CRAFT TIPS** (page 357).

 THE EXTRA TOUCH
- Glue "Teddy Bear Picnic Stickers" (page 31) on photo frame (Illustration 1-20).

ILLUSTRATION 1-20

↻ PUPPET SHOW

Recommended for all ages

What better way to entertain your guests than with puppets. Make your own puppet theater by cutting out the bottom of a tissue box and covering it with wrapping paper.

ILLUSTRATION 1-21

PUPPET SHOW IDEAS:
- The "Paw Puppets" (page 33) make good "players," or use your child's favorite puppets to star in the show.
- Adapt a scene from a popular book, such as *Winnie the Pooh, Goldilocks and the Three Bears* or make up your own bear or bee stories.
- Depending on the age of your children, you may want to have the birthday child and your guests participate by working the puppets while you tell the story.
- Have children make up their own story and act it out with puppets.
- A good time to present the show is while children are eating or just before the meal. Keep the program short (maximum of 10 minutes).

BEEHIVE PIÑATA

Estimated time: 30–45 minutes

WHAT YOU NEED:
- Illustration 1–17 or 1–18 "Honey Bees" (pages 42 and 43)
- Copier paper (yellow)
- Large paper grocery bag
- Full sheet of newspaper
- Rope or cord (minimum 18'–20')
- Three sheets of 9" x 12" construction paper (yellow)
- One sheet of 5" x 5" construction paper (black)
- 3' of ribbon (approximately 1" wide)
- Scissors
- White glue
- Prizes (wrapped candy, peanuts in the shell, small boxes of raisins, small toys)

ILLUSTRATION 1-22

WHAT YOU DO:
1. Photocopy Illustration 1–17 or 1-18 "Honey Bees" onto copier paper.
2. Tear newspaper into pieces and crumple each piece.
3. Open paper bag and fill with prizes and crumpled pieces of newspaper.
4. Gather top of bag together and tie ribbon around top (Illustration 1–22 #1).
5. Cut yellow construction paper into 3" wide strips and fringe edges (Illustration 1–22 #2).
6. Glue paper strips all around bag (Illustration 1–22 #3).
7. Make entrance to beehive by cutting out arch-shaped "door." Start with a 5" x 5" square of black construction paper and round-off one side of square (Illustration 1–22 #4).
8. Glue "door" to front of bag (Illustration 1–22).

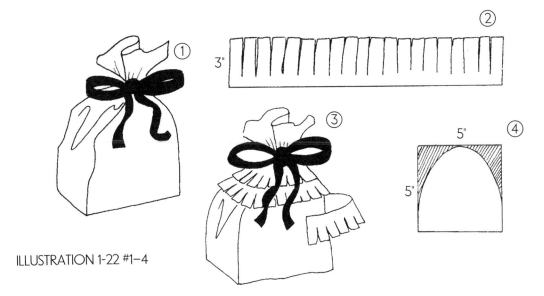

ILLUSTRATION 1-22 #1-4

9. Cut out paper bees and glue on bag.
10. Tie one end of rope around top of hive, and loop other end over a tree limb, beam or other support.
11. Pull on rope to make piñata move up and down as children try to hit it.
12. See "Piñata Fun" in **GAMES** (page 368) for safety suggestions when playing with piñatas.

CRAFTS

Children will have fun making these crafts as a group activity during the party or you can make these crafts yourself ahead of time and save money on party favors. Select one or two of the crafts for your party from the following list. Don't feel as if you have to make all of them—there just isn't enough time!

TEDDY BEAR PICNIC STICKERS

Recommended age: 3 and older for gluing
5 and older for cutting and gluing

Make your own party stickers for children to use in various crafts and activities in this chapter. Use Illustration 1–29 "Teddy Bear Picnic Stickers" (page 44) and follow directions for "Party Stickers" in **CRAFT TIPS** (page 352).

You could also make "Flower Stickers" for the Teddy Bear Picnic Party. Use Illustration 10–19 "Flower Stickers" (page 260), and follow directions for "Party Stickers" in **CRAFT TIPS** (page 352).

BEE KITE

Recommended age: 5 and older

WHAT YOU NEED:
- Illustration 1–30 "Bee Hat" (page 42)
- Copier paper (yellow or white)
- 9" paper plate
- 7'–8' crepé paper streamers (yellow)
- String or yarn (36")
- Scissors (child-safe)
- White glue
- Hole punch
- Crayons, markers and/or paint ❀

ILLUSTRATION 1-24

❀ Optional

WHAT YOU DO:

Before the party:

1. Photocopy Illustration 1–30 "Bee Hat" onto copier paper.

During the party:

2. Cut out bee's head and glue onto bottom of plate.
3. Color or paint kite, if desired.
4. Cut crepé paper streamer into 6–8 separate lengths, each approximately 12"–15" long.
5. Staple or glue one end of each streamer around rim of plate.
6. Punch a hole on opposite sides of plate.
7. Tie ends of string or yarn through holes in plate (Illustration 1–24).
8. When kite is dry, children can hold onto middle of string and run with kite or swing kite in circles.

 ## THE EXTRA TOUCH

- Glue "Teddy Bear Picnic Stickers" (page 31) to kite.
- Photocopy "Honey Bees" (Illustration 1-17 or 1-18 pages 42 or 43). Cut out bees and glue to the ends of the streamer.

 HONEY BEE KAZOO

Recommended age: 6 and older

WHAT YOU NEED:

- "Teddy Bear Picnic Stickers" (page 31)
- Copier paper (white or brightly-colored)
- Cardboard toilet paper tube
- Wax paper
- Construction paper (yellow or bright colors)
- Rubberband
- Crayons and/or markers
- White glue
- Hole punch
- Ruler

ILLUSTRATION 1-25

WHAT YOU DO:

Before the party:

1. Cut wax paper into 3 1/2" circles (one circle for each kazoo).
2. Cut construction paper into 4 1/2" x 6" rectangles (one rectangle for each kazoo).

During the party:

3. Glue construction paper around toilet paper tube (Illustration 1–25 #1).
4. Glue on stickers and color, if desired.
5. Using hole punch, make a hole near top of tube (Illustration 1–25 #2).
6. Wrap wax paper circle over end of tube (same end with punched hole) and glue in place (Illustration 1–25).
7. Wrap rubberband tightly over wax paper (Illustration 1–25).
8. To use kazoo, simply put mouth to open end and hum.

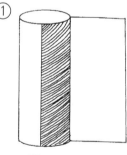

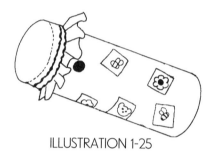

ILLUSTRATION 1-25 #1-2

PAW PUPPETS

Recommended age: 5 and older

ILLUSTRATION 1-26

WHAT YOU NEED:

- Illustration 1–27 "Paw Puppets" (page 45)
- Copier paper or copier card stock (white or bright colors) ❀
- Scissors (child-safe)
- Craft knife (adult use only)
- Crayons, markers and/or colored pencils

___

❀ Card stock is preferred for this project.

WHAT YOU DO:

Before the party:
1. Photocopy Illustration 1–27 "Paw Puppets" onto copier paper or card stock.
2. Carefully cut out finger holes with craft knife.

During the party:
3. Color puppets, if desired.
4. Cut out each puppet along outer lines.
5. To use puppets, place index and middle fingers through holes.

☞ THE EXTRA TOUCH

- Tie a set of the puppets together with ribbon as a take-home favor.

BEE HAT OR BEAR HAT

Recommended age: 5 and older

WHAT YOU NEED:

- Illustration 1–30 "Bee Hat" (page 42) or Illustration 1–31 "Bear Hat" (page 44)
- Copier paper or copier card stock (white, yellow or pink) ❀
- One 14" length of elastic cord (or one 14" length of yarn)
- Scissors (child-safe)
- Hole punch or sharp pencil
- Markers, crayons and/or colored pencils ❀❀
- Transparent tape ❀❀

___

❀ Card stock is preferred for this project.

❀❀ Optional

ILLUSTRATION 1-28

WHAT YOU DO:

Before the party:
1. Photocopy Illustration 1–30 "Bee Hat" or Illustration 1–31 "Bear Hat" onto copier paper or card stock.
2. If using copier paper, reinforce holes with transparent tape before punching holes.

During the party:
3. Color hat, if desired.
4. Cut out around hat pattern.
5. Punch a hole in both ends of headband, as marked on illustration.
6. Tie one end of elastic cord through one hole in headband.
7. Thread other end of cord through other hole in headband and adjust length to fit child's head; then knot cord in place (Illustrations 1-28 and 1-29).

ILLUSTRATION 1-29

BEAR PAWS

Recommended age: 5 and older

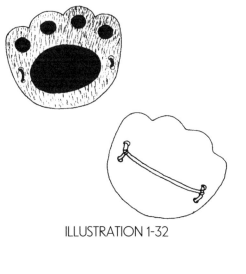

WHAT YOU NEED:
- Illustration 1–33 "Bear Paws" (page 43)
- Copier card stock (white or pink)
- Two 7" lengths of elastic cord (or two 7" lengths of yarn)
- Scissors (child-safe)
- Hole punch or sharp pencil

WHAT YOU DO:
Before the party:
1. Photocopy Illustration 1–33 "Bear Paw" onto card stock.

During the party:
2. Cut out around paw patterns.
3. Punch a hole in both sides of paws, as marked on illustration.
4. Tie one end of elastic cord through one hole in each paw.
5. Thread other end of cord through other hole in paw and adjust length to fit child's hand; then knot cord in place (Illustration 1-32).

ILLUSTRATION 1-32

BEE WINGS

Recommended age: 5 and older

WHAT YOU NEED:
- Illustration 1–09 "Bee Wings" (page 41)
- Copier paper or copier card stock (white or yellow) ❊
- Two 18" lengths of elastic cord (or two 18" lengths of yarn)
- Hole punch
- Scissors (child-safe)
- Pencil
- Glue, glitter and/or sequins ❊❊
- Crayons, markers and/or colored pencils ❊❊

❊ Card stock is preferred for this project.

❊❊ Optional

ILLUSTRATION 1-34

WHAT YOU DO:
Before the party:
1. Photocopy Illustration 1–09 "Bee Wings" onto copier paper or card stock.

During the party:
2. Color wings, if desired.
3. Cut out wings.
4. Fold wings in half (Illustration 1–34 #1).
5. Punch outer holes in wings near fold line (Illustration 1–34 #1).
6. Decorate wings with glue, glitter and/or sequins, if desired.
7. Open wings and tie one end of elastic cord through each top hole in wings.
8. Thread other end of cord through each bottom hole in wing and adjust length to fit child; then knot cord in place (Illustration 1–34 #2).

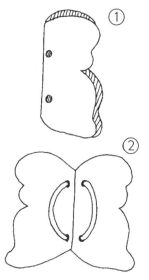

ILLUSTRATION 1-34 #1–2

GAMES

Select several of the games for your party from the following list. Don't feel as if you have to play all of them, but you should plan for a few extra games. Here are some unique games for your Teddy Bear Picnic Party.

BEELINE

Recommended age: 2–5 years of age

How about a twist on the traditional game of "Follow the Leader?" Try this!

WHAT YOU NEED:
- "Honey Bee Kazoos" (page 32)

HOW TO PLAY:
1. Have children line up in single file (birthday child first).
2. Give each child a "Honey Bee Kazoo" and tell children they are all bees.
3. Leader takes bees on a journey, humming or "buzzing" along the way.
4. Bees must follow leader wherever he/she goes, and they must buzz the very same tune or make the same sound the leader makes along the way.
5. Allow children to make one complete path and then change leaders.

PAW PAW BALLOON TOSS

Recommended age: 4 years and older
Children can use their "bear" hands to play, or add "Bear Paws" for more fun.

WHAT YOU NEED:
- One set of "Bear Paws" for each child (page 34) ❀
- Balloons (inflated)
- String or a bag of white flour

_____
❀ Optional

HOW TO PLAY:
1. Draw a line that divides the play area into two equal sections. (To make the line, lay string or pour a thin line of flour onto the ground.)
2. Divide children into two equal teams, and have each team stand on opposite sides of the line.
3. Give each team an equal number of balloons, at least one balloon per child.
4. Each team tries to hit the balloons from their side to the other side of the line.
5. Set a time limit for the game, and the team with the least number of balloons on their side of the line wins.

HANGING BALLOONS

Recommended age: 1 1/2 to 5 years of age
Children can use the "Bear Paws" or their "bear" hands.

WHAT YOU NEED:
- "Bee Balloons" (page 27)
- Rope or string
- One set of "Bear Paws" for each child (page 34) ❀

_____
❀ Optional

HOW TO PLAY:
1. Hang balloons at different lengths along a rope or string.
2. Some balloons should be easy to reach and others should hang just high enough so that children have to jump to reach them.
3. Let children bat at the balloons with their "Bear paws" or "bear" hands.

HONEY HUNT

Recommended age: 3 years and older

WHAT YOU NEED:
- Loot Bags (page 28), one for each child.
- Candies or small favors as loot
- Yellow tissue paper
- Transparent tape

HOW TO PLAY:
1. Wrap loot in yellow tissue paper.
2. Hide the loot or "honey" throughout party area.
3. Have children search for their "honey" and gather their goods in a loot bag.

BEAR BANDIT

Recommended age: 5 years and older

WHAT YOU NEED:
- One "Bee Bean Bag" (page 37) for each child

HOW TO PLAY:
1. Mark off a game area with start/finish line on one side and two equal piles of "Bee Bean Bags" 15'–20' away.
2. Select one child (birthday child to start) to be the "bear." Divide the rest of children into two equal teams of "bees."
3. Have each team line up (single file) behind the start/finish line. Each player in line runs to the "Bee Bean Bags," picks up a bag and runs back across the start/finish line. He/she then lines up at the end of the team line, holding his/her "Bee Bean Bag."
4. The only obstacle stopping the children is the "bear." The "bear" waits anywhere between the start/finish line and the "Bee Bean Bags," trying to tag the "bees" as they run back and forth across the field. If the bear does tag the bee, the bee has to start over.
5. The first team with all players standing in line, holding their own "Bee Bean Bag," wins the game.
6. If time allows, trade off who plays the bear.

PIN THE BEE ON THE HIVE

Recommended age: 3 years and older

WHAT YOU NEED:
- "Beehive Photo Backdrop" (page 29)
- Illustration 1-17 and 1-18 "Honey Bees" (page 42 and page 43)
- Copier paper (yellow)
- 1 piece of cardboard (at least 10" x 10")
- Duct tape (at least 2" wide)
- Masking tape or double-stick tape
- Pencil
- Blindfold

HOW TO PLAY:
1. Photocopy Illustration 1–17 or 1-18 "Honey Bees" onto yellow copier paper, and cut out each bee.
2. With duct tape, secure piece of cardboard to back of hive, covering "hole."
3. Place beehive on one side of game area and have children line up (single file) at least 5 feet away.
4. Write names of each child on front of "Honey Bee" and place a piece of masking tape rolled on itself (or double-stick tape) on back of "Honey Bee."
5. Blindfold first person in line (birthday child first) and turn child 2–3 times. Then hand child his/her "Honey Bee" and tell him/her to place bee in entrance of hive.

- Instead of making a backdrop, you can tape a 8" x 8" square of black construction paper to a wall to play the game.

BEE BAG TOSS

Recommended age: 3 years and older

Follow the directions for "Bean Bag Toss" in **GAMES** (page 364), using the "Beehive Backdrop" as the game board.

WHAT YOU NEED:

- "Beehive Photo Backdrop" (page 29)
- Bean Bags in **GAMES** (page 364)
- Wide-tipped, permanent ink marker (black)
- Pipe cleaners

ILLUSTRATION 1-38 #1

HOW TO PLAY:

1. Make "Beehive Photo Backdrop".
2. To turn "Bean Bags" into "Bee Bags," fold down top of sock and wrap pipe cleaner around knot, twisting pipe cleaner to secure in place (Illustration 1–38 #1).
3. With black marker, draw two large dots to form "eyes," and make black stripes on "body" (Illustration 1–38 #2).

MORE GAMES...

It's always a good idea to plan some extra party games. Here are some standard party games, adapted for your Teddy Bear Picnic Party. Specific directions for these games are listed in **APPENDIX D: GAMES**, beginning on page 363.

ILLUSTRATION 1-38 #2

PORRIDGE TOSS

Recommended age: 3 years and older

Follow the directions for "Party Game Toss" in **GAMES** (page 367). Tell children that they are tossing their peanuts or candy into three bowls of porridge.

THREE BEARS' MUSICAL CHAIRS

Recommended age: 4 years and older

Follow directions for "Fun Time Musical Chairs" in **GAMES** (page 366). Tell children that they are all teddy bears, looking for a place to sit down and eat their honey!

BUZZ, BUZZ, BEE

Recommended age: 4 years and older

Follow the directions for "Duck, Duck, Goose" in **GAMES** (page 365). Have one child be the "bear" (birthday child first), and have bear walk around the outside of the circle, tapping each child on the head or shoulder lightly, saying, "buzz." When bear wants someone to be "It," bear taps that child and says "bee."

BEE STING TAG

Recommended age: 5 years and older

Follow the directions for "Freeze Tag" in **GAMES** (page 366).

BEAR'S BUFF

Recommended age: 5 years and older

Follow the directions for "Blindman's Buff" in **GAMES** (page 364). Have children make growling bear sounds to scare "It."

WHO HAS THE BEE?

Recommended age: 5 years and older

Follow the directions for "Who Has It?" in **GAMES** (page 371). Have children use a "Bee Bag" (page 37) to play the game.

BUZZING BUMBLE BEE

Recommended age: 3 years and older

Follow the directions for "Hot Potato" in **GAMES** (page 366). Have children use a "Bee Bag" (page 37) to play the game.

BOUNCING BEAR

Recommended age: 2–5 years of age

Follow the directions for "Trampoline" in **GAMES** (page 371). Have children use a stuffed teddy bear to play the game.

SWARM

Recommended age: 5 years and older

Follow the directions for "Blob" in **GAMES** (page 365).

SAVE THE QUEEN/KING BEE FROM THE BEAR

Recommended age: 5–9 years of age

Follow the directions for "Save the Prince/Princess from the Dragon" in **GAMES** (page 369). Have one child (birthday child) play the queen/king of the hive and another play the hungry bear.

ILLUSTRATION 1-04

Teddy Bear Picnic

For _____ Time _____

Birthday Party Place _____

Date _____

P.S.V.P.

ILLUSTRATION 1-03

ILLUSTRATION 1-05

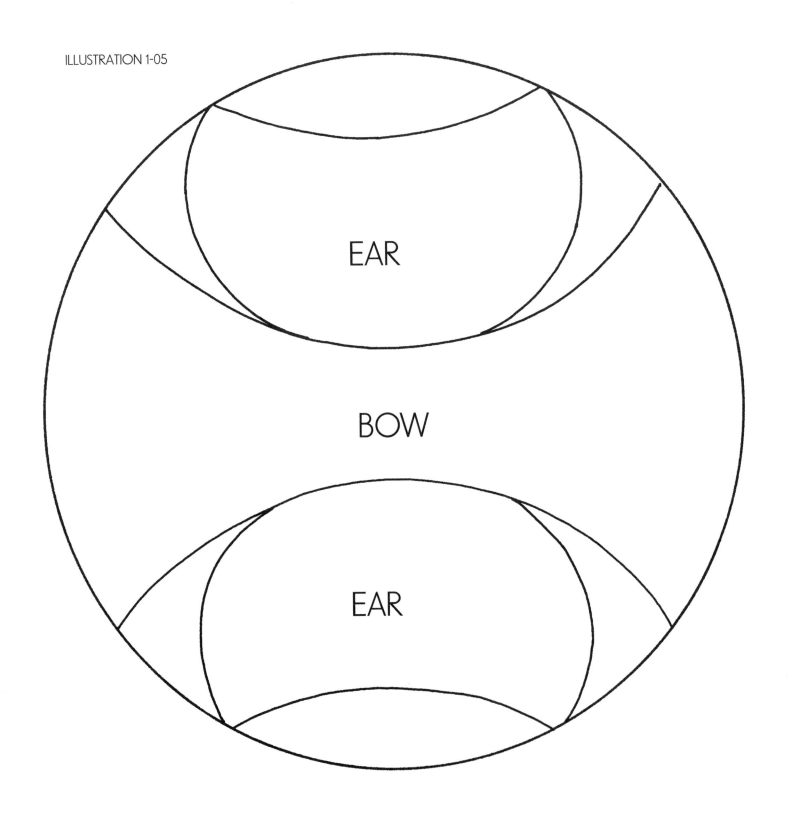

EAR

BOW

EAR

ILLUSTRATION 1-09

ILLUSTRATION
1-30

ILLUSTRATION
1-17

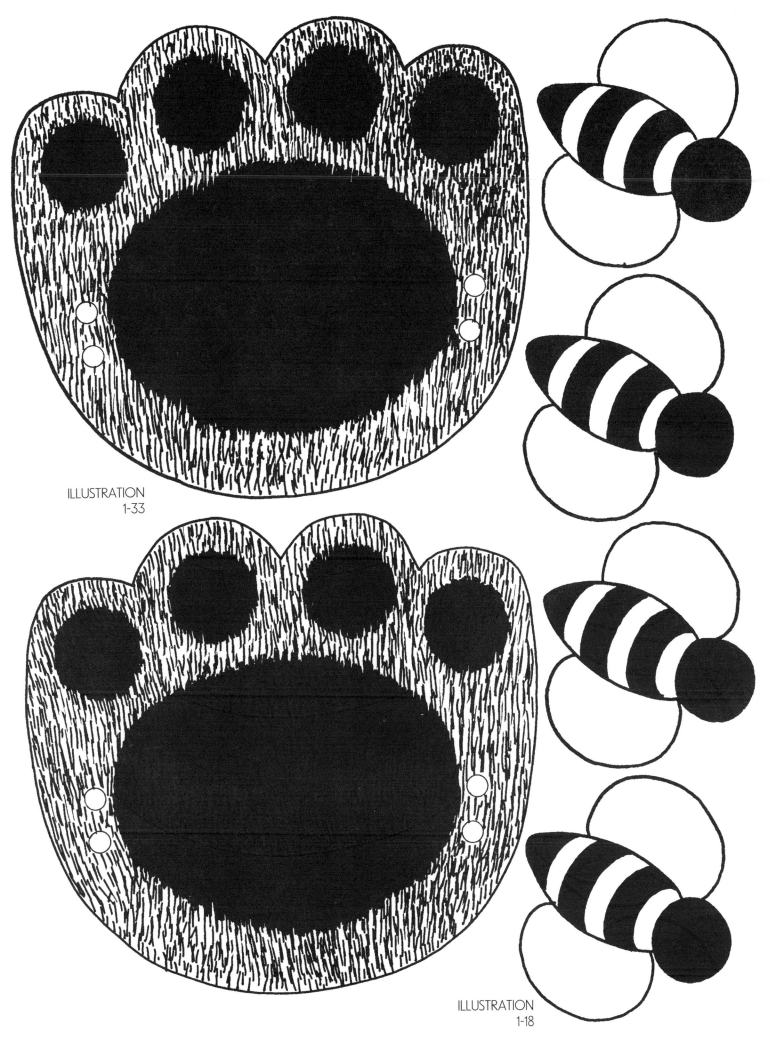

ILLUSTRATION
1-33

ILLUSTRATION
1-18

TEDDY BEAR PICNIC PARTY

43

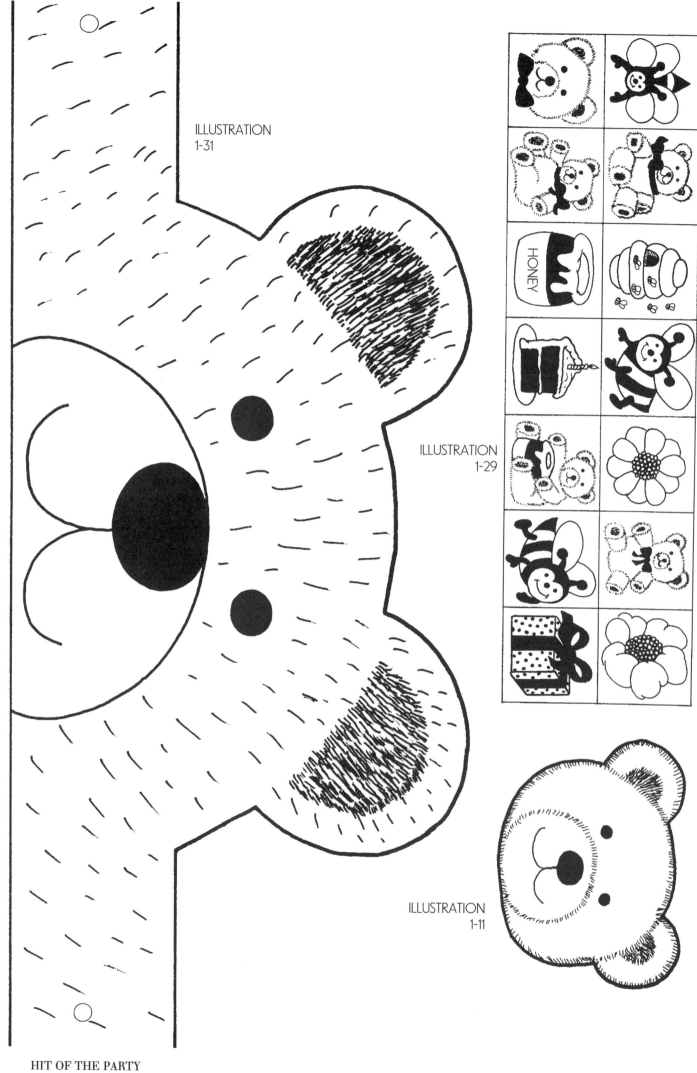

ILLUSTRATION
1-31

ILLUSTRATION
1-29

HONEY

ILLUSTRATION
1-11

ILLUSTRATION 1-27

Fairy Tale Party or ... Knights of the Round Table

CHAPTER 2

Once upon a time, Kings and Queens ruled the land, dragons roamed the forests and fairies granted wishes. There was a special kind of magic in the air. You can have that same magic as you turn your child's special birthday into a Fairy Tale Party.

ILLUSTRATION 2-01

FAIRY TALE PARTY

CASTLE INVITATION

Estimated time: 2–3 minutes each

The fun starts when your friends get an invitation and start opening the castle doors. They won't be able to wait for your party to begin.

WHAT YOU NEED:

- Illustration 2–03 "Castle Invitation" (page 68)
- Copier paper or copier card stock (white or bright colors) ❀
- Envelopes (3 5/8" x 6 1/2")
- Scissors
- Craft knife (adult use only)
- Crayons, markers and/or colored pencils ❀❀

❀ Card stock works better for this project.

❀❀ Optional

WHAT YOU DO:

1. Using Illustration 2–03 "Castle Invitation," photocopy as many invitations as needed (Illustration 2–02 #1).
2. Color invitation, if desired.
3. With scissors, cut out invitation (Illustration 2–02 #2).
4. Using craft knife, cut open "doors" along dotted lines. Fold "doors" downward forming a "hinge." (Illustration 2–02 #3).
5. Fold invitation in half (Illustration 2–02 #4).
6. Write in specific party information behind each door (Illustration 2–02 #5).
   Be sure to include the date; time; place; RSVP (telephone number) and who the party is for.

ILLUSTRATION 2-02

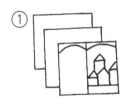   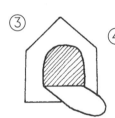 

ILLUSTRATION 2-02 #1–5

👉 THE EXTRA TOUCH

- Glue "Coat of Arms Stickers" (page 57) to seal envelope.

*NOTE: If your child would rather have a **"Knights of the Round Table"** party instead of a "Fairy Tale" party—no problem! The title of the "Castle Invitation" can be easily changed. Here's how:*

1. Photocopy Illustration 2–03 "Castle Invitation" onto copier paper.
2. Cut out "Knights of the Round Table" title and glue it over the "Fairy Tale" title.
3. Prepare invitation as outlined above.

CASTLE THANK-YOU NOTE

The "Castle Thank-You Note" (Illustration 2–04) is on the same page as the "Castle Invitation." When you photocopy the invitation, you will also be copying the "thank-you" note. Simply cut out the "thank-you" note and write your personal message in the space provided.

Estimated time: 1 minute each

MENU

Make a magical medieval feast! Here are a few mouth-watering ideas for your royal guests. Choose foods from each group, and follow the recipes on the pages listed below.

DRINKS:

EATS:

CAKE AND ICE CREAM:

THE DRAGON CAKE

Estimated time: 1–1 1/2 hours

INGREDIENTS:

1 "Basic Cake" recipe in Appendix A on pages 343 and 344; or use your favorite box cake mix
2 "Buttercream Frosting" recipe in Appendix A on page 345; or two cans of your favorite canned frosting
1 Marshmallow (cut in half)
1 c. Candy corn
5 Gumdrops
1/2 c. Chocolate chips
1 Licorice twist (red)
Food coloring (green)
13" x 18" tray or foil-covered board
Illustrations 2–06 #1 and 2–06 #2 "Dragon Cake Patterns" (page 69 and 70)

DIRECTIONS:

1. Prepare and bake cake in two 8" round cake pans as directed in recipe or cake package.
2. Cool cake completely on wire rack.
3. Wrap in plastic wrap and freeze cake at least 45 minutes. (Freezing the cake does not affect its flavor and makes it easier to work with. It also enables you to make the cake ahead of time, to help balance your work load.)
4. Trace Illustrations 2–06 #1 and 2–06 #2 "Dragon Cake Patterns," on wax paper. Cut out wax paper patterns into sections and reassemble on top of each cake round.

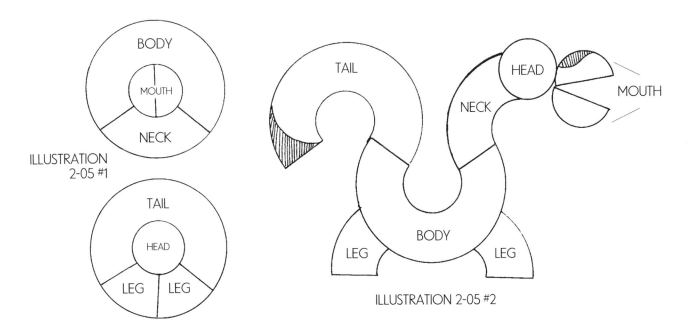

ILLUSTRATION
2-05 #1

ILLUSTRATION 2-05 #2

5. Using long knife, cut cake into sections along patterns (Illustrations 2–05 #1).

6. Assemble sections on tray into shape of a dragon (Illustration 2–05 #2).

7. Tint frosting green by adding drops of green food coloring and mix until color is uniform.

8. Frost connecting sections of cake with green frosting.

9. Trim off shaded areas (Illustration 2–05 #2).

10. Frost top and sides of entire cake.

11. Push candy corns along top edge of dragon to make "scales."

12. Place a marshmallow half on its head to form an "eye."

13. Dip chocolate chip in frosting and place on "eyeball" to form "pupil."

14. Use one gumdrop for a "nostril."

15. Cut a 4" piece of licorice twist and fray it on the end by making a few cuts. Push unfrayed end into dragon's "mouth."

16. Push gumdrops on tops of dragon's feet to form "toe nails."

17. Decorate dragon's body with chocolate chips.

THE CASTLE CAKE

Estimated time: 20–30 minutes

Children and adults will "ooh!" and "ahh!" when they see this incredible cake. You may want to have your child help with some of the decorating.

INGREDIENTS:

1   Frosted store-bought cake (1/4 sheet) ✿
1   Buttercream frosting recipe in Appendix A (page 345) or
    1/2 cup canned frosting
4   Sugar ice cream cones
4   Flat-bottom ice cream cones
4   Wafer cookies
4   Drinking straws
    Gumdrops, coated-chocolate candies or other small candies
    Food coloring
    Colored sprinkles
    13" x 18" tray or foil-covered board

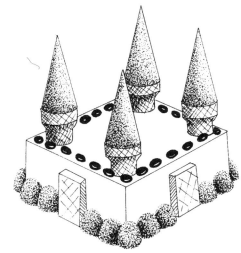

ILLUSTRATION 2-07

✿ without decorative flowers or trim

DIRECTIONS:

1. Cover flat-bottom ice cream cones with frosting.
2. Make a pilot hole (about 1" deep) in each corner of the cake.
3. Place one frosted, flat-bottom cone in each corner of cake. (Push a drinking straw through the bottom of each flat-bottom cone and into cake for stability.)
4. Frost sugar ice cream cones with frosting and shake colored sprinkles on icing.
5. Place sugar ice cream cones on top of flat-bottom cones and use frosting to "set" sugar cones in place (Illustration 2-07).
6. Place a wafer cookie on each side of cake to make "doors" of castle.
7. Add gumdrops or other candies to trim castle.

 THE EXTRA TOUCH

- To make a center tower, stack one flat-bottom cone on top of a second flat-bottom cone, which has been placed upside down on cake.
- Add paper "flags," glued to toothpicks, and insert into the tip of the sugar cone. (Before frosting cone, cut off tip of cone to allow a place for toothpick to be inserted.)
- Add as many frosted cookies and small candies to fit your idea of what a "Fairy Tale Castle" should look like.
- See "Castle Cake" (page 48) for more ideas.

DECORATIONS

Choose your favorite of these simple decorations and create a magical fantasy world by hanging stars, moons, banners, shields and streamers. You can use decorations as craft activities at your party. Or, save money by giving some of these decorations out as favors in your loot bags.

PARTY STREAMERS

Estimated time: 1–2 minutes per streamer

Select one (or more) of the streamers suggested below, and follow the directions for "Party Streamers" in **CRAFT TIPS** (page 349).

- **Flower Streamer** Pattern CT–01 (page 361)
  Use bright or pastel colors of crepé paper.
- **Star Streamer** Pattern CT–03 (page 360)
  Use bright colors of crepé paper.
- **Triangle Streamer** Pattern CT–05 (page 361)
  Use bright colors of crepé paper.

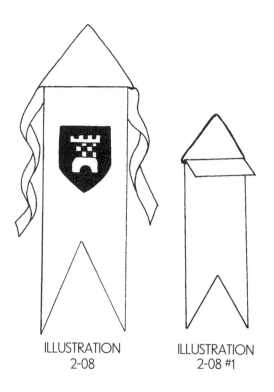

ILLUSTRATION 2-08

ILLUSTRATION 2-08 #1

 TIMESAVER

- Hang crepé paper streamers (in pre-packaged rolls) around party area.

MEDIEVAL BANNERS

Estimated time: 5–8 minutes each

WHAT YOU NEED:

- Illustration 2–09 "Medieval Banners" (page 71)
- Copier paper or copier card stock (white or bright colors)
- String or yarn (at least 18" in length)
- Transparent tape
- White glue
- Scissors
- Crepé paper streamers ✿

✿ Optional

WHAT YOU DO:

1. Photocopy Illustration 2–09 "Medieval Banners" onto copier paper.
2. Cut out banner.
3. To hang banner, fold 1" of top edge toward back of the banner. Place string or yarn along fold line, and glue or tape folded edge over string or yarn (Illustration 2–08 #1).
4. Decorate banner with crepé paper streamers, if desired.

JACK AND THE BEANSTALK DRINKING STRAWS

Estimated time: 1–2 minutes each

Make your own "Jack and the Beanstalk Drinking Straws" (Illustration 2-10). Use Illustration 2–11 "Jack and the Beanstalk Drinking Straw" (page 72) and follow directions for "Drinking Straws" in **CRAFT TIPS** (page 353).

ILLUSTRATION 2-10

ILLUSTRATION 2-12

💡 MORE DECORATING IDEAS...

- Sprinkle confetti along walkways or on party tables to make area look as if it has been covered with "fairy dust."
- Decorate party area with Christmas lights.
- Hang "Stars and Moon" (page 226) to give castle a magical look.
- Make placemats by having children glue "Coat of Arms Stickers"(page 57) onto 9" x 12" sheet of construction paper. Provide crayons, markers and/or colored pencils for children to color placemats, if desired.
- Make a "Castle Centerpiece" (Illustration 2-12) out of empty cartons, boxes, cardboard tubes, etc. Cover cartons and boxes with construction paper or brown paper bags. Assemble cartons and boxes to make castle. Decorate with construction paper to form turrets, flags and banners. Cut out a drawbridge, folding the bottom to form a "hinge." Draw or paint details if desired.
- Make "Magic Balloons" by gluing glitter and gummed stars on balloons (pages 226 and 227).
- Create your own drawbridge for guests as they enter the front door or party area. Place a wooden plank (at least 12" wide) in front of door or on walkway.
- Photocopy "Castle Cake" illustration 2-01 (page 48) and place on front door.
- Make a sign on front door or at front of party area that says, "[Birthday Child's Name] Castle."

LOOT BAGS

Select one (or more) of the following loot bags and follow the directions for "Loot Bags" in **CRAFT TIPS** (page 350).

- **Sticker Bag** (page 350)
  Use Illustration 2-28 "Coat of Arms Stickers" (page 72).
- **Treasure Box** (page 351)
  Use Illustration 2-28 "Coat of Arms Stickers" (page 72).
- **Magic Bag** (page 351)

LOOT BAG "LOOT"

Looking for something to put in those loot bags? Here are some creative suggestions you can make, or if you are short on time, you can buy.

LOOT YOU CAN MAKE:
- **Coat of Arms Stickers** (page 57)
- **Magic Stickers** (page 232)
- **Flower Stickers** (page 252)
- **Jack in the Beanstalk Drinking Straw** (page 53)
- **Jack's Bean Garden** (page 58)
- **Fairy Tale Polaroid® Photo Frame** (page 56)
- **Magic Wand** (in "Fairy Costume" page 58)
- **Sock Puppets** (page 57)
- **Fairy Tale Stick Puppets** (page 57)
- **Cookie Puppets** (page 329)
- **Golden Nuggets** (page 333)

LOOT YOU CAN BUY:
- Gummed stars
- Small fairy tale books
- Glitter puff paints
- Gumdrops (wrapped in tissue paper or colored plastic wrap tied with a ribbon)
- Toothbrush/toothpaste sets
- Crayons or colored pencils (to color stickers and/or stick puppets)
- Toy figures (horses, knights, fairies)
- Kaleidoscopes
- Magic tricks (packaged)

ACTIVITIES

It's time to have your fairy tale come true. Don't feel as if you have to do all of these activities—there isn't enough time at any party. Discuss with your child which ones he or she would like do and plan your party activities accordingly.

ARRIVAL ACTIVITY

As each child arrives, let him/her pick a special name, as in "Duke Dan of Beachwood Drive," "Queen Emma," "Lady Linda of Rossmore," or "King Gerald of Iowa." Announce their name with a little fanfare or mock trumpeting.

↻ FAIRY TALE CASTLE

Estimated time: 1–1 1/2 hours

With a recycled appliance box, and a little imagination, you can create an activity center with many uses (Illustration 2-14 Page 55). For instance, children can play in the "Fairy Tale Castle" while other guests arrive. The "Castle" also doubles as a "Puppet Theater," where you can stage some of your favorite fairy tales stories during the party. After the party, your child will continue to enjoy the "Castle" and "Puppet Theater."

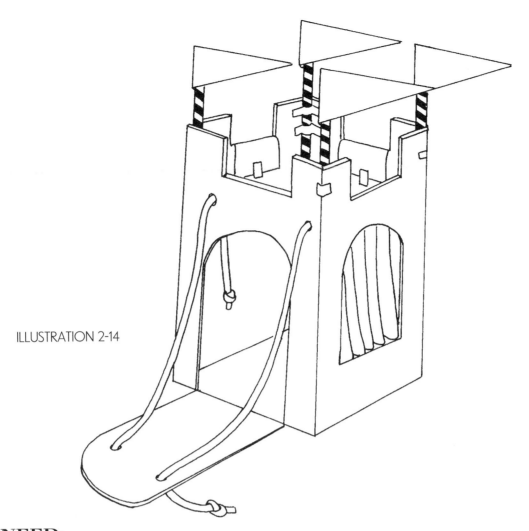

ILLUSTRATION 2-14

WHAT YOU NEED:

- Large cardboard box (refrigerator/large appliance)
- Scissors
- Craft knife (adult use only)
- Ruler
- Pencil
- Rope
- Duct tape or cloth-backed masking tape
- Cardboard wrapping paper tube or newspaper rolls ❀
- Fabric or towel (large enough to cover any window)

❀ Directions for making newspaper rolls are in **CRAFT TIPS** (page 355).

WHAT YOU DO:

1. Cut open door and fold down making a "hinge" for a drawbridge. (When cutting cardboard, follow the directions "Cardboard Play Structures" in **CRAFT TIPS** page 355.)
2. Cut out a window on one side.
3. Cut notches along top of the box to make "lookouts." (You don't need to cut the sections out completely. Just cut flaps and fold flaps inward. Tape flaps to inside of castle to strengthen walls of box.)
4. Make 2 holes (about 1/2" in diameter) toward top of drawbridge, and 2 more holes (same size) in wall just above drawbridge (Illustration 2–14).
5. Thread rope through both sets of holes, and tie knot at each end to secure rope in place.
6. Take a piece of fabric or towel, slightly larger than window, and tape to inside of window, as a curtain for castle.
7. Decorate with flags taped to cardboard tubes or newspaper rolls.

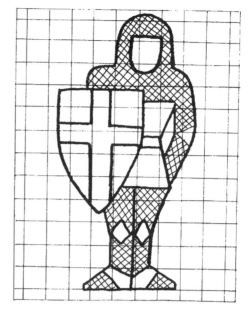

ILLUSTRATION 2-16 #1   ILLUSTRATION 2-16 #2

⟳ FAIRY OR KNIGHT PHOTO BACKDROP

Recommended for all ages

Use Illustration 2–16 #1 "Fairy Photo Backdrop Pattern" or Illustration 2–16 #2 "Knight Photo Backdrop Pattern" and follow the directions for "Photo Backdrop" in **CRAFT TIPS** (page 354) to give children and their parents the best party favor they can have—a memorable "Fairy Tale Snapshot."

You can take a Polaroid® photograph and hand it out at the party (see "Polaroid® Photo Frame" below), or you can use a 35 mm camera and send a photo along with your thank-you note.

FAIRY TALE POLAROID® PHOTO FRAME

Recommended for all ages

Hand out these wonderful memories at the party by using a Polaroid® photo and follow the directions for "Polaroid® Photo Frame" in **CRAFT TIPS** (page 357).

☞ THE EXTRA TOUCH

- Decorate frames with gummed stars, "Coat of Arms Stickers" (page 57), "Magic Stickers" (page 232) and/or with glue and glitter. (Illustration 2-17)

ILLUSTRATION 2-17

PUPPET SHOW

What better way to tell a fairy tale than with puppets. Use the "Fairy Tale Castle" as your "Puppet Theater." Simply close the drawbridge and use the curtained window as your stage.

Here are some "puppet show" suggestions:

1. The "Fairy Tale Stick Puppets" (page 57), "Sock Puppets" (page 57) or "Pop-up Clown" (page 187) will make good players, or use your child's favorite puppets to star in the show. Select a favorite fairy tale to read and act it out.
2. Depending on the age of children, you may want to have the birthday child and your guests participate by working the puppets while you tell the story.
3. Have children make up their own story and act it out with puppets.
4. A good time to present the show is while the children are eating or just before the meal. Keep the program short (around 10 minutes).

CRAFTS

Children will have fun making these crafts as a group activity during the party or you can make these crafts yourself ahead of time and save money on party favors. Select one or two of the crafts for your party from the following list. Don't feel as if you have to make all of them—there just isn't enough time.

COAT OF ARMS STICKERS

Recommended age: 3 and older for gluing
5 and older for cutting and gluing

Make your own party stickers for children to use in various crafts and activities in this chapter. Use Illustration 2–18 "Coat of Arms Stickers" (page 72) and follow directions for "Party Stickers" in **CRAFT TIPS** (page 352).

You could also make "Flower Stickers" or "Magic Stickers" for the Fairy Tale Party. Use Illustration 10–19 "Flower Stickers" (page 260) or 9-26 "Magic Stickers" (page 241), and follow directions for "Party Stickers" in **CRAFT TIPS** (page 352).

FAIRY TALE STICK PUPPETS

Recommended age: 4 and older

WHAT YOU NEED:
- Illustrations 2–20 #1, 2–20 #2 and 2–20 #3 "Stick Puppets" (page 73)
- Scissors (child-safe)
- Copier paper or copier card stock (white or bright colors) ❀
- Craft sticks or drinking straws
- Transparent tape
- Colored pencils, crayons and/or markers ❀❀

❀ Card stock works better for this project.

❀❀ Optional

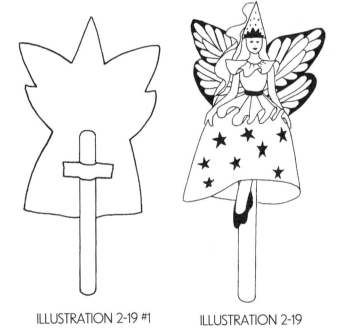

ILLUSTRATION 2-19 #1   ILLUSTRATION 2-19

WHAT YOU DO:
Before the party:
1. Photocopy Illustrations 2–20 #1, 2–20 #2 and 2–20 #3 onto copier paper or copier card stock.

During the party:
2. Color puppets, if desired.
3. Cut along outer lines of illustration.
4. Tape stick or straw to back of puppet (Illustration 2–19 #1).

SOCK PUPPETS

Recommended age: 4 and older

WHAT YOU NEED:
- 1 sock for each puppet
  (Cotton socks are preferred as glue sticks to cotton better than synthetic materials. Use same-size sock as the children wear so children's hands won't be "swallowed up" by their own puppet.)
- White glue or tacky glue
- Scissors (child-safe)
- Felt (red or pink)
- Buttons, fake eyes, sequins, felt/fabric scraps, yarn, feathers, fabric notions, ribbon, pom poms and other scraps to add character

WHAT YOU DO:

Before the party:

1. Precut felt into an oval shape, approximately 1 1/2"–2" wide and 3"–5" long. One oval for each sock puppet.
2. Slip sock over hand so thumb is in the "heel" and fingers are in "toes" of sock.
3. The natural cavity formed by the thumb and fingers is the "mouth" of the sock puppet. Glue felt oval into this cavity, forming inside of "mouth." (Illustration 2-21)

During the party:

4. Glue various fabric notions and scraps to create "eyes," "nose," "ears," "hair" and other features or accessories of favorite fairy tale character.
5. Let glue dry completely before attempting to play with puppets. (Do this craft at the beginning of party, so there is time for puppets to dry before guests go home.)

ILLUSTRATION 2-21

JACK'S BEAN GARDEN

Recommended age: 3 and older

THIS IS WHAT YOU NEED:

- "Jack and the Beanstalk Drinking Straws" (page 53)
- One drinking cup (8 ounces)
- One package of dried beans (16 ounces)
- Easy access to water (small watering can or additional drinking cups filled with water)
- Ordinary garden dirt or planting soil

WHAT YOU DO:

Before the party:

1. Soak beans overnight. This will help beans sprout faster.
2. Fill cups with dirt.

During the party:

3. Place 3–4 beans on surface of dirt.
4. Press beans about one inch (1") into dirt.
5. Moisten dirt with water.
6. Insert "Drinking Straw" into dirt (Illustration 2-22).
7. Explain how to take care of the bean garden so children can actually see their own garden grow. Tell youngsters (and their parents) to keep the bean garden moist, but not wet, and in a warm area that is not in direct sunlight.

Beans will sprout within a few days, and the vines will start to grow up around the straw. After sprouting, place garden in a sunny window or outside in direct sunlight.

ILLUSTRATION 2-22

FAIRY COSTUME

In medieval times, fairy princesses wore cone-shaped hats that were said to have magical powers! See what happens to your royal guests as they don these wonderful creations.

Recommended age: 5 and older

WHAT YOU NEED:

- Illustration 2–22 "Fairy Costume" (page 74)
- Copier paper or copier card stock (white or bright colors) ❀
- One 14" length of elastic cord (or one 14" length of yarn)
- Scissors (child-safe)
- Hole punch or sharp pencil

- Drinking straw
- Transparent tape
- Glue, glitter and sequins ❀❀
- Crayons, markers and/or colored pencils ❀❀

❀ Card stock works better for this projects.

❀❀ Optional

WHAT YOU DO:

Before the party:

1. Photocopy Illustration 2–22 "Fairy Costume" onto copier paper or card stock.
2. If using copier paper, reinforce area around holes with transparent tape.

During the party:

3. Cut out around hat.
4. Children can use crayons, markers and/or colored pencils to color hat and star or glue on sequins and/or glitter.
5. Punch a hole in both ends of headband, as marked on hat.
6. Tie one end of elastic cord through one hole in headband.
7. Thread other end of cord through other hole in headband and adjust length to fit child's head; then knot cord in place.
8. To make fairy "wand," tape straw to back of star.

ILLUSTRATION 2-23 #1   ILLUSTRATION 2-23 #2

THE EXTRA TOUCH
- Make a princess veil by stapling a long piece of tissue to top of "Fairy Hat."
- Wrap thin ribbon (paper or cloth, approximately 1/4" wide) around straw and tape in place, and/or add additional ribbon as streamers (Illustration 2–23 #2).
- Make a princess collar from "Clown Costume" (page 189).

FAIRY WINGS

Recommended age: 5 and older

WHAT YOU NEED:
- Illustration 1–09 "Fairy Wings" (page 41)
- Copier paper or copier card stock (white or yellow) ❀
- Two 18" lengths of elastic cord (or two 18" lengths of yarn)
- Hole punch
- Scissors (child-safe)
- Pencil
- Glue, glitter and/or sequins ❀❀
- Crayons, markers and/or colored pencils ❀❀

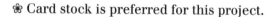

❀ Card stock is preferred for this project.

ILLUSTRATION 2-24

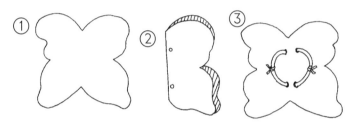

ILLUSTRATION 2-25 #1-3

❀❀ Optional

WHAT YOU DO:
Before the party:
1. Photocopy Illustration 1–09 "Fairy Wings" onto copier paper or card stock.
During the party:
2. Cut out wings (Illustration 2–25 #1).
3. Fold wings in half (Illustration 2–25 #2).
4. Punch outer holes in wings near fold line (Illustration 2–25 #2).
5. Color wings, if desired.
6. Decorate wings with glue, glitter and/or sequins, if desired.
7. Open wings and tie one end of elastic cord through each of the upper holes in wings.
8. Thread other end of cord through each bottom hole in wing and adjust length to fit child; then knot cord in place (Illustration 2–25 #3).

THE KNIGHT'S HELMET

Recommended age: 6 and older

WHAT YOU NEED:
- Illustration 2–25 "Knight's Helmet" (page 75)
- Copier paper or copier card stock (white or bright colors) ❀
- Two brass brads
- One 14" length of elastic cord (or one 14" length of yarn)
- Scissors (child-safe)
- Hole punch or sharp pencil
- Transparent tape ❀❀

❀ Card stock is preferred for this project.
❀❀ Optional

ILLUSTRATION 2-26

WHAT YOU DO:

Before the party:

1. Photocopy Illustration 2–25 "Knight's Helmet" onto copier paper or card stock.
2. If using copier paper, reinforce area around holes with transparent tape and then punch holes.

During the party:

3. Cut out around visor and headband.
4. Punch holes in ends of both visor and headband, as marked on illustration.
5. Position hole of one end of visor directly over one of the inner holes of headband (Illustration 2–26 #1).
6. Insert brass brad through both holes in step #5 and flatten tines outward to secure in place.
7. Repeat same steps for other end of visor.
8. Tie one end of elastic cord through one of the outer holes in headband.
9. Thread other end of cord through other outer hole in headband and adjust length to fit child's head; then knot cord in place.

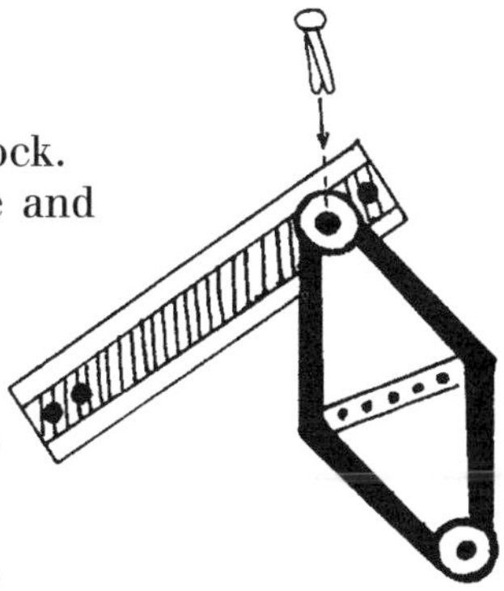

ILLUSTRATION 2-26 #1

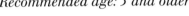STICK HORSE

Recommended age: 5 and older

WHAT YOU NEED:

*   Illustration 2–26 "Stick Horse" (page 72)
*   Cardboard (wrapping paper) tube or "Newspaper Rolls" ✿
*   Copier paper or copier card stock (white or bright colors)
*   Scissors (child-safe)
*   White glue
*   Crayon, colored pencils and/or markers ✿✿

✿ See "Newspaper Rolls" in **CRAFT TIPS** (page 355)

✿✿ Optional

ILLUSTRATION 2-27

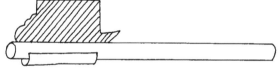

ILLUSTRATION 2-27 #1

WHAT YOU DO:

Before the party:

1. Photocopy Illustration 2–26 "Stick Horse."

During the party:

2. Color horse head, if desired.
3. Cut out horse head.
4. Place glue on back of horse head. Wrap horse head around one end of the tube or roll (Illustration 2–27 #1).

SHIELDS

Recommended age: 6 years and older

WHAT YOU NEED:

*   Illustration 2–09 "Banners" (page 71)
*   One paper plate (per shield)
*   Copier paper (white or bright colors)
*   Poster board
*   Masking tape
*   White glue
*   Scissors (child-safe)
*   Crayons, markers and/or colored pencils ✿

✿ Optional

WHAT YOU DO:

Before the party:
1. Photocopy Illustration 2–09 "Banners."
2. Cut poster board into 1" x 8" strips (one for each shield).

During the party:
3. Color paper plate and shields, if desired.
4. Cut out around shield patterns.
5. Glue one shield to underside of paper plate.
6. Make 1 1/2" folds at both ends of cardboard strip and bend folds under strip (Illustration 2–29 #1).
7. Tape tabs of cardboard strip on top side of plate (Illustration 2–29 #2).

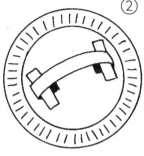
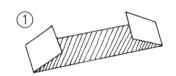

ILLUSTRATION 2-29 #1   ILLUSTRATION 2-29 #2

GAMES

Select several of the games for your party from the following list. Don't feel as if you have to play all of them. But you should plan for a few extra games. Here are some unique games for your Fairy Tale/Knights of the Round Table Party.

JOUSTING

Recommended age: 6 years and older

Here's a good way to let those rambunctious knights vent some of their pent-up energy.

WHAT YOU NEED:
- Two "Shields" (page 61) ❁
- Two cardboard wrapping paper tubes or newspaper rolls ❁❁

- Two sponges or piece of foam rubber (approximately 4" x 6")
- Two socks
- Two large rubberbands or one roll of duct tape
- Six cardboard boxes (with lids taped shut)
  Two large boxes—same size
  Two medium boxes—same size
  Two small boxes—same size

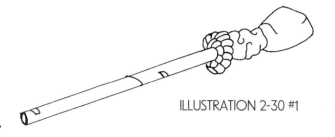

ILLUSTRATION 2-30 #1

❀ Optional

❀❀ See "Newspaper Rolls" in **CRAFT TIPS** (page 355).

WHAT YOU DO:

1. Make lance by first covering end of cardboard tube or newspaper roll with sponge.
2. Put sock over sponge and tube.
3. Secure sock in place with rubberband or duct tape (Illustration 2-30 #1).

HOW TO PLAY:

1. Divide children into two relay teams, and line teams up (single file) behind a starting line (birthday child first).
2. Stack boxes into two piles, one pile opposite each team, 15–20 feet away from starting line. Place large box on bottom, medium box in the middle and small box on top (Illustration 2-30–#2).
3. Have first player in each line run toward their team's pile of boxes and "joust" or knock down the stack with lance. After child knocks down all boxes, he/she returns to team, hands over lance and shield to next child in line and stands at end of line. (Restack boxes after each turn.)
4. The first team to have all players complete their turns, wins.

FAIRIES OR KNIGHTS ON HORSES

Recommended age: 2–5 years of age

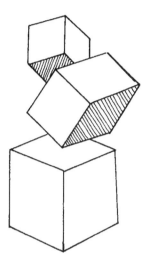

ILLUSTRATION 2-30 #2

Young children love the traditional game of "Follow the Leader." This game can be played either as "Fairies" or "Knights on Horses." Give each child a medieval stick horse—and have a lot of fun.

WHAT YOU NEED:

- One "Stick Horse" (page 61) for each child

HOW TO PLAY:

1. Give each child his/her own stick horse.
2. Whichever game you choose, select a King/Queen to be leader (birthday child first).
3. Explain to children that the King or Queen must ride to the castle, and everyone must follow the King/Queen to the castle, no matter where he/she travels.

LEAPING FROG PRINCE

Recommended age: 5 years and older

HOW TO PLAY:

1. Divide children into two relay teams, and line them up (single file) at a starting line.
2. Explain to children that at one time they were all princes and princesses. But an evil witch has cast a spell on them and turned

them all into frogs. Now, they are lost in a forest. If, however, they can make their way back to their castle, they will turn back into princes and princesses.

3. Locate the "castle" or finish line at least 15–20 feet from the starting line.
4. The first player on each team takes a standing broad jump (like a frog would) and, wherever he/she lands, grabs his/her ankles, and remains in a crouched position.
5. The second player takes a running start and leaps or vaults over the first crouched frog. As the second player lands, he/she assumes the same crouched position, and waits for the third player to leap over him/her.
6. This continues until the entire team has leapfrogged its way to the castle.

THE SEARCH FOR THE HOLY GRAIL

Recommended age: 6 years and older

You may want to start this game by explaining a little about the legend of the Holy Grail. Avoid lengthy details. For example, you may want to say simply that in medieval times (or in the times of fairy tale kings and queens), King Arthur and his "Knights of the Round Table" spent many years searching for "The Holy Grail," which was a special cup with magical powers.

WHAT YOU NEED:
- 2 paper cups
- Aluminum foil
- One 9" x 12" (or larger) sheet of heavy construction paper or lightweight poster board (any color)
- Transparent or masking tape
- White glue
- Sequins and/or glitter ❀

❀ Optional

WHAT YOU DO:
1. To make the Holy Grail, take two paper cups and glue or tape bottoms of both cups together.
2. Cover cups with aluminum foil, gluing down foil edges.
3. Decorate cup by gluing on sequins and/or glitter (Illustration 2–32 #1).
4. Hide the Holy Grail in an out-of-the-way spot, and write the exact location of Holy Grail on piece of construction paper (Illustration 2–32 #2). (Draw a map of its location for an older group on a piece of construction paper showing location of Holy Grail).
5. Cut construction paper into a puzzle of 8–10 different shapes.
6. Hide pieces of puzzle in different locations. (Pieces should be visible but not obvious.)

HOW TO PLAY:
1. Explain to children that they have just been appointed to serve King Arthur as Knights of the Round Table, and that their mission is to find the Holy Grail.
2. Then tell children that directions for (or a map of) the location of the Holy Grail have been made into a puzzle, and that the pieces of the puzzle have been hidden.
3. Give children boundaries of your hiding areas, and tell them that everyone must look for the pieces of the puzzle.
4. Once they find a puzzle piece, they must bring it to the "castle," a central area (like the party table) where you will start putting the puzzle back together.
   (If possible, try to get a round table for the "castle.")
5. Play game until children figure out where Holy Grail is hidden.
6. Emphasize team effort in this game, as children learn to work together.

ILLUSTRATION 2-32 #1   ILLUSTRATION 2-32 #2

WILLIAM TELL

Recommended age: 7 years and older

Legend has it that William Tell was such an accurate bowman, he agreed to split an apple resting on top of his own son's head. Fortunately, his son lived to tell the tale.

HOW TO PLAY:

1. Divide children into two relay teams, and give each team an apple.
2. Mark a starting line for relay race, and a turn-around point—a tree or a chair—between 15–20' from starting line.
3. Explain to children that each player must balance an apple on his/her head, and walk as fast as he/she can to turn-around point and back. The first team to have all players complete the race, wins.
4. Make sure children understand they cannot hold the apple while walking. If apple falls, player must stop, place apple back on head, and continue race. Anyone caught holding the apple will have to start his/her turn over.

QUEST FOR THE MAGIC CASTLE
OR
FIRE-BREATHING DRAGON

Recommended age: 4 years and older

WHAT YOU NEED:

- Feathers
- Rings
- Bags of confetti
- Sprigs of leaves
- Ropes (medium weight, approximately 12" in length)
- Stars (from "Stars and the Moon," page 226)
- Whistles

HOW TO PLAY:

1. Tell children that they are on a quest or journey to reach the "Magic Castle" or "Fire-Breathing Dragon," and when they get there, they will feast on "Dragon Cake" or "Castle Cake." However, before they can reach the castle or dragon, they must travel through the "Mystery Forest," where they will encounter goblins, witches and monsters who will try to keep them from reaching the castle or dragon— and keep the cake for themselves.
2. Ask older children (or adults) to be goblins, witches or monsters, so all of the birthday guests will have a chance to play the game.
3. Depending on the size of your group, give each child one or more of the items listed above. Explain that these items all have magic powers that will work in different ways to overcome any trouble they may have with goblins, witches or monsters.
4. Here are suggestions for the powers each of your magical items might have:
   - Feathers will give children the power to fly
   - Rings will give children the power to become invisible

- Confetti can be a magic "fairy dust" that can turn an enemy into a harmless frog
- A sprig of leaves can grow a forest around an enemy—as long as that enemy doesn't eat trees
- Ropes can be used to tie enemies up—especially those with lots of hands
- Stars can fool an enemy into thinking it is nighttime and to stay underground
- Whistles can be used to deafen enemies whose hearing is vital to their survival

5. Encourage children to work together, using their arsenal of magical powers to overcome the enemies they encounter.
6. There are many different scenarios you can dream up as you and the children journey to the castle. (Have someone else bring out the cake, plates and utensils while you are out on your quest. The cake should be set up in an area that children can't see, so the surprise has more impact.)

MORE GAMES...

It's always a good idea to plan some extra party games. Here are some standard party games, adapted for your Fairy Tale/Knights of the Round Table Party. Specific directions for these games are listed in **APPENDIX D: GAMES**, beginning on page 363.

↻ FAIRY TALE/KNIGHTS BEAN BAG TOSS

Recommended age: 3 years and older

Follow the directions for "Bean Bag Toss" in **GAMES** (page 364). Use "Fairy or Knight Photo Backdrop" (page 56) as theme backdrop.

SAVE THE PRINCE/PRINCESS FROM THE DRAGON

Recommended age: 5 years and older

Follow directions for "Save the Prince/Princess from the Dragon" in **GAMES** (page 369).

CATCH THE DRAGON'S TAIL

Recommended age: 5 years and older

Follow the directions for "Catch the Tail" in **GAMES** (page 365), using a "dragon" as the theme for the game.

WHO HAS THE MAGIC WAND?

Recommended age: 5 years and older

Follow the directions for "Who Has It?" in **GAMES** (page 371), using a "magic wand" (in "Fairy Costume" page 58) as the theme for the game.

FAIRY TALE MEMORY GAME

Recommended age: 8 years and older

Follow the directions for "Memory Game" in **GAMES** (page 367), using objects that deal with fairy tales as theme objects for the game.

KING ARTHUR'S SEARCH FOR THE BURIED TREASURE

Recommended age: 3 years and older

Follow the directions for "Searching for Buried Treasure" in **GAMES** (page 369), using pennies to play the game.

DRAGON TAG

Recommended age: 6 years and older

Follow the directions for "Tag" in **GAMES** (page 371), using a "dragon" as "It" to play the game.

FAIRY/WIZARD FREEZE TAG

Recommended age: 5 years and older

Follow the directions for "Freeze Tag" in **GAMES** (page 366), using a "magic wand" (in "Fairy Costume" page 58) to play the game.

ILLUSTRATION 2-04

ILLUSTRATION 2-03

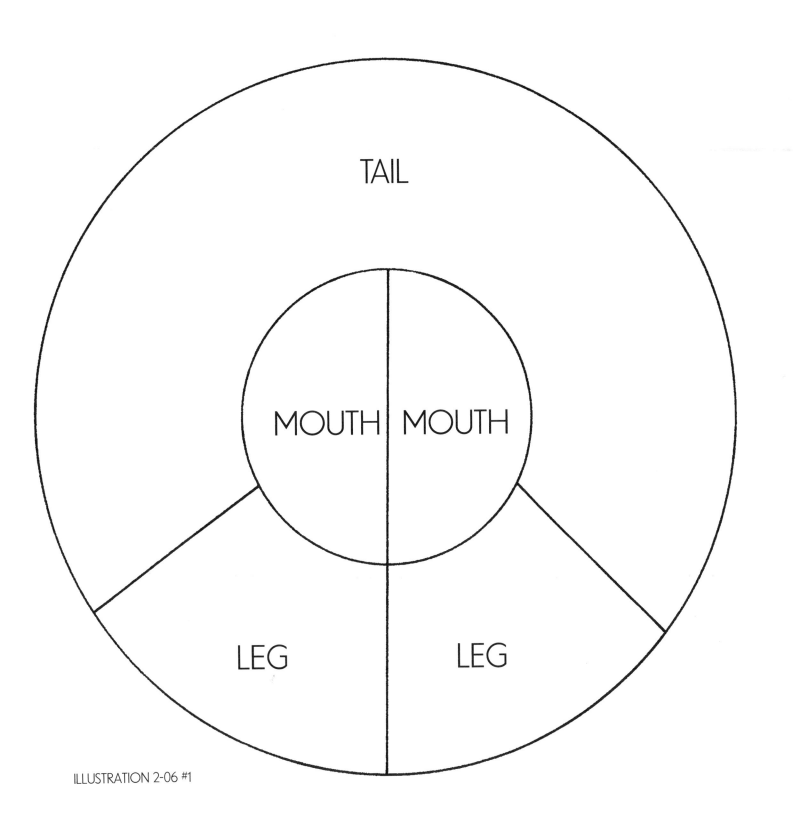

ILLUSTRATION 2-06 #1

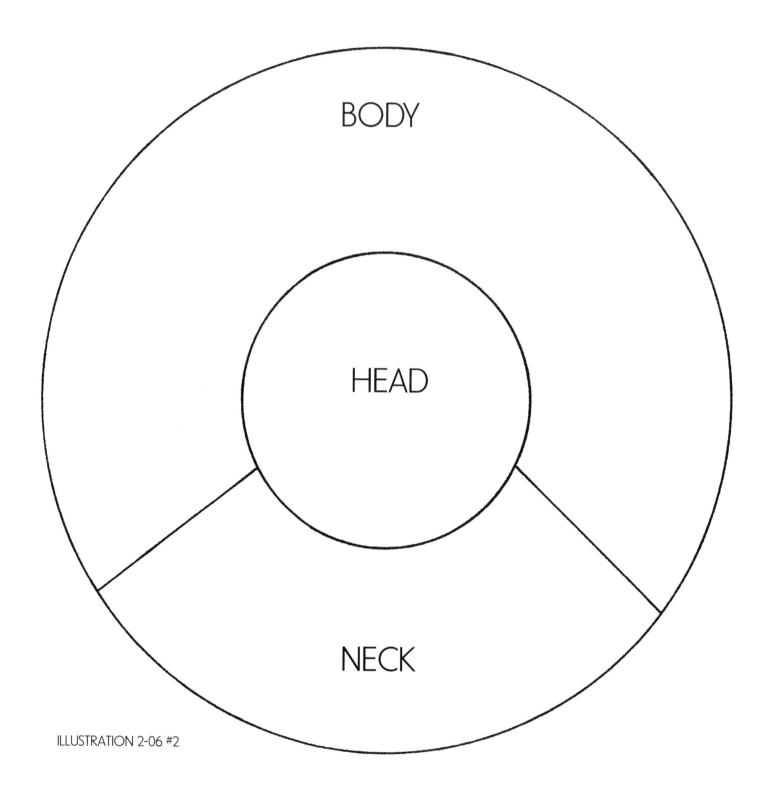

BODY

HEAD

NECK

ILLUSTRATION 2-06 #2

ILLUSTRATION 2-09

ILLUSTRATION
2-18

ILLUSTRATION
2-26

ILLUSTRATION 2-11

ILLUSTRATION
2-20 #2

ILLUSTRATION
2-20 #1

ILLUSTRATION
2-20 #3

ILLUSTRATION 2-22

ILLUSTRATION 2-25

CHAPTER 3

Jungle Safari

Deep in the dark jungle live exotic animals of all colors, shapes and sizes. Monkeys swing on vines, birds call from trees, and tigers lurk in the bushes. Take your child on an unforgettable adventure, complete with all of the sights, sounds, and even tastes of a jungle safari.

ILLUSTRATION 3-01

Jungle Safari Party

JUNGLE SAFARI INVITATION

Estimated Time: 3–4 minutes each

WHAT YOU NEED:

- Illustration 3–03 "Jungle Safari Invitation" (page 96)
- Copier paper (white, green or beige)
- Envelopes (3 5/8" x 6 1/2")
- Scissors
- Felt-tip pen (black)
- Crayons, markers and/or colored pencils ❀

❀ Optional

ILLUSTRATION 3-02

WHAT YOU DO:

1. Make one photocopy of Illustration 3–03. This is your "master copy." Fill out all party information with felt-tip pen on master copy (Illustration 3–02 #1).
2. Photocopy as many invitations as needed (Illustration 3–02 #2).
3. Color invitation, if desired.
4. Cut out invitation (Illustration 3–02 #3).

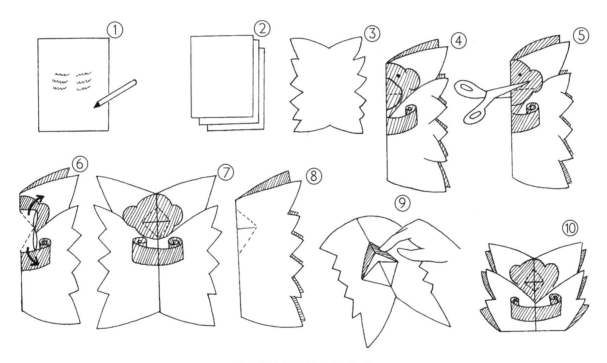

ILLUSTRATION 3-02 #1-10

5. Fold invitation in half, lengthwise, with design on outside (Illustration 3–02 #4).
6. With scissors, cut along dotted line (Illustration 3–02 #5).
7. Fold back flaps, making sharp creases, to form two triangles (Illustration 3–02 #6).
8. Fold flaps back to original position and open invitation (Illustration 3–02 #7).
9. Fold invitation so design is on the inside (Illustration 3–02 #8).
10. Holding paper so it looks like a tent, put finger on top triangle and push down. Then, pinch two folded edges of top triangle so that triangle is pushed through to other side of paper (Illustration 3–02 #9).
11. Perform same step for bottom triangle as in top triangle.
12. Fold invitation in half, widthwise, with design on outside (Illustration 3–02 #10).
13. Open and close invitation and see monkey talk!

- Glue on "Safari Stickers" (page 87) to seal envelope.

JUNGLE SAFARI PARTY THANK-YOU NOTE

Estimated time: 1 minute each

The "Jungle Safari Party Thank-You Note" (Illustration 3–04) is on page 97. Photocopy as many thank-you notes as you need for your "wild" guests. Simply cut out thank-you note with scissors and write your personal message in space provided.

MENU

Create your own tropical treats for those hungry animals of yours. Choose foods from each group, and follow the recipes on the pages listed below.

DRINKS:

EATS:

CAKE AND ICE CREAM:

MONKEY CAKE

Estimated time: 1–1 1/2 hours

Your kids will go "ape" over the this tasty treat.

INGREDIENTS:

1	"Basic Cake" recipe in Appendix A, on pages 343 and 344; or use your favorite box cake mix
2	"Chocolate Frosting" recipes in Appendix A, on page 345; or 2 cans of your favorite canned frosting
1/2 c.	"Buttercream Frosting" (page 345); or 1/2 cup of your favorite vanilla canned frosting
3	Chocolate cookies—3" in diameter
1 1/2 oz.	Unsweetened baking chocolate (1 1/2 squares)
3 c.	Flaked coconut
1	Marshmallow (cut in half)
2	Chocolate chips
1	Licorice whip (red)
	Red food coloring
	13" x 18" tray or foil-covered board
	Illustrations 3–05 #1 and 3–05 #2 "Monkey Cake Patterns" (pages 98 and 99)

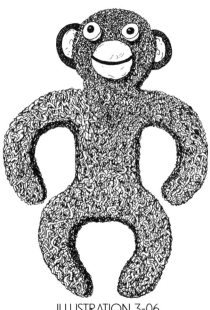

ILLUSTRATION 3-06

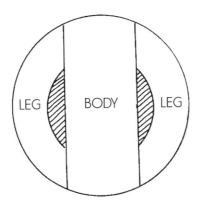 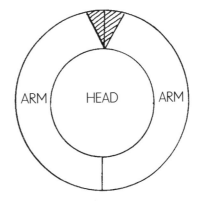

ILLUSTRATION 3–06 #1

DIRECTIONS:

1. Prepare and bake cake in two 8" round cake pans as directed in recipe or cake package.
2. Cool cake completely on wire rack.
3. Wrap in plastic wrap and freeze cake at least 45 minutes. (Freezing the cake does not affect its flavor and makes it easier to work with. It also enables you to make the cake ahead of time, to help balance your work load for the party.)
4. Trace Illustrations 3–05 #1 and 3–05 #2 "Monkey Cake Patterns," on wax paper. Cut out wax paper patterns into sections and reassemble on top of each cake round.
5. Using long knife, cut cake into sections (Illustration 3–06 #1).
6. Assemble sections on tray into shape of a monkey (Illustration 3–06 #2).
7. Frost connecting sections of cake with chocolate frosting.
8. Frost top and sides of entire cake.
9. Melt unsweetened chocolate in double boiler or microwave oven. (If using microwave oven, heat until chocolate just starts to bubble.)
10. Stir coconut and melted chocolate together in a bowl.
11. Sprinkle coconut evenly over top and sides of cake, gently pressing coconut into cake.
12. Tint white frosting pink by adding a few drops of red food coloring and mix until color is uniform.
13. Frost top of one cookie with pink frosting.
14. Place pink frosted cookie on monkey's head to create "mouth" (Illustration 3–06).
15. Lay licorice whip across "mouth" to form a smile (Illustration 3–06).
16. Push two chocolate cookies into side of head to form "ears" (Illustration 3–06).
17. Frost inside of ears with pink frosting (Illustration 3–06).
18. Press marshmallow halves into monkey's "head" to form "eyes" (Illustration 3–06).
19. Place two chocolate chips in centers of marshmallow "eyes," using a dab of chocolate frosting to hold in place.

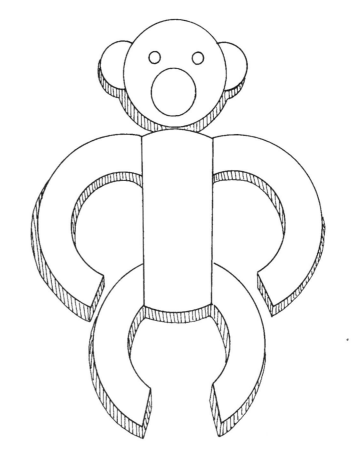

ILLUSTRATION 3–06 #2

 # THE SAFARI CAKE

Estimated time: Approximately 20–30 minutes

You can get a store-bought cake, and decorate it yourself with cookies and candies to create an entire jungle fantasy.

INGREDIENTS:

1	Frosted store-bought cake (round or rectangular)
	Animal cookies or plastic toy animals (at least 1 animal for each child)
1/2 c.	Gummi worms
1 c.	Gumdrops or chocolate-covered malt balls
1 bunch	Mint leaves
1 c.	Flaked coconut
	Green food coloring

ILLUSTRATION 3-07

DIRECTIONS:

1. Place frosted cake on plate or serving platter.
2. Mix flaked coconut with few drops of green food coloring in bowl. Use tinted coconut for "grass" on top of cake.
3. Press animal cookies or plastic toy animals into top of cake, arranging groups of animals in a "jungle scene."
4. Use mint leaves to create "trees" and "bushes" around animals.
5. Use gummi worms to form tropical plants.
6. Gumdrops or malt balls can be used for rocks and boulders.
7. Trim bottom of cake with gumdrops or malt balls.

☞ THE EXTRA TOUCH

- Add "palm trees" and/or "mountains." See "Treasure Island Cake" (page 132).

DECORATIONS

By adding a few of these simple decorations, you can transform any party area into the wilds of the jungle. Children will enter the "jungle" and think that they are truly on a safari. You can use decorations as craft activities at your party. Or, save money by giving some of these decorations out as favors for your loot bags.

PARTY STREAMERS

Estimated time: 1–2 minutes per streamer

Select one (or more) of the streamers suggested below, and follow the directions for "Party Streamers" in **CRAFT TIPS** (page 349).

- **Flower Streamer** Pattern CT-01 (page 361)
  Use bright colors of crepé paper.
- **Leaf Streamer** Pattern CT-06 (page 362)
  Use green crepé paper.

⏰ TIMESAVER

- Hang crepé paper streamers (in pre-packaged rolls) around party area.

THE SWINGING MONKEY

Estimated time: 3 minutes each

This project can be completed ahead of time as a decoration or during the party as a craft.

WHAT YOU NEED:

- Illustration 3–08 "The Swinging Monkey" (page 100)
- Copier paper or copier card stock (white, brown or beige)❀
- Scissors
- String, crepé paper or "Leaf Streamer" (See "Party Streamers" above)

❀ Card stock is preferred for this project.

WHAT YOU DO:

1. Photocopy Illustration 3–08 "Swinging Monkey" onto copier paper or card stock.
2. Cut out around monkey.
3. Cut a slit along dotted lines on each "hand."
4. Hang on crepé paper, string or "Leaf Streamers" by bending slits back and threading string between slits.

ILLUSTRATION 3-09

MONKEY STRAWS

Estimated time: 1–2 minutes each

Make your own "Monkey Straws." (Illustration 3-10) Use Illustration 3–11 "Monkey" (page 97) and follow directions for "Drinking Straws" in **CRAFT TIPS** (page 353).

ILLUSTRATION 3-12

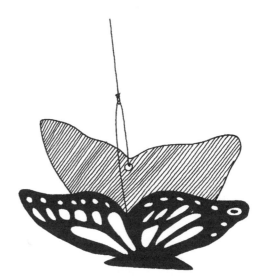

ILLUSTRATION 3-10

MONKEY SUCKERS

Estimated time: 1–2 minutes each

Make your own "Monkey Suckers." (Illustration 3-12) Use Illustration 3–11 "Monkey" (page 97) and follow directions for "Party Suckers" in **CRAFT TIPS** (page 353).

💡 MORE DECORATING IDEAS...

- Place potted plants around party area to give a lush, tropical look.
- Hang "Flying Butterfly" (page 89) around party area by attaching string to the wings (Illustration 3-13).
- Cover party table with butcher paper and make "Paw Print Tablecloth" in **CRAFT TIPS** (page 353).
- Make placemats by photocopying Illustration 3-31 "Bird Hat"(page 103) onto copier paper (white or bright colors). Provide crayons for children to color placemats, if desired.
- Make placemats by having children glue "Safari Stickers" (page 87) onto 9" x 12" sheet of construction paper. Provide crayons, markers and/or colored pencils for children to color placemats, if desired.
- Place stuffed jungle animals or hang posters of jungle animals around party area.
- Photocopy "Monkey Cake" illustration 3-01 (page 78) and tape on front door or front of party area.

ILLUSTRATION 3-13

LOOT BAGS

Select one (or more) of the following loot bags and follow the directions for "Loot Bags" in **CRAFT TIPS** (page 350).

- **Sticker Bag** (page 350)
  Use Illustration 3-21 "Safari Stickers" (page 101).
- **Treasure Box** (page 351)
  Use Illustration 3-21 "Safari Stickers" (page 101).
- **Mask Bag** (page 351)
  Use Illustration 3-31 "Bird Mask" (page 103).

LOOT BAG "LOOT"

Looking for something to put in those loot bags? Here are some creative suggestions you can make, or if you are short of time, you can buy.

LOOT YOU CAN MAKE:

- **Safari Stickers** (page 87)
- **Monkey Straws** (page 83)
- **Monkey Suckers** (page 83)
- **Jungle Safari Polaroid® Photo Frame** (page 86)
- **Safari Binoculars** (page 88)
- **Safari Camera** (page 88)
- **Crunchy Critters** (page 331)
- **Cookie Puppets** (page 329) Use animal cookie cutters.
- **Animal Smackers** (page 323)
- **Trail Mix** (page 333)

LOOT YOU CAN BUY:

- Plastic animals
- Stuffed animals
- Animal stickers
- Binoculars
- Rubber stamps (jungle animals)
- Small books about jungle animals or the environment
- Box of animal crackers
- Crayons or colored pencils (to color stickers)

ACTIVITIES

Get your gear and let's go on a safari! Don't feel as if you have to do all of these activities—there isn't enough time at any party. Discuss with your child which ones he or she would like do and plan your party activities accordingly.

ARRIVAL ACTIVITY

As guests arrive, let each child pick an animal that he/she wants to be. Announce the guest's name with the appropriate animal sounds, and have children roar, squawk, trumpet, or hoot as they make their entrance.

ILLUSTRATION 3-16

⟳ JUNGLE SAFARI OBSTACLE COURSE

Recommended for all ages

This is a wonderful, hands-on experience for children and a great way to welcome your guests to participate in the jungle experience. Kids will love to climb through, jump over, slide down, peer into, and crawl under the "jungle" you have created. Each obstacle course will be different, depending on how you put it together, how large your party area is, and what items you have available.

WHAT YOU NEED:
- Recycled appliance box(es) (large enough for children to crawl through)
- Chairs (sturdy enough for children to climb on)
- Cushions
- Old tires
- Outdoor playground equipment
- Wooden shelving boards (1/2" by 10" or 12" wide, and at least 6' in length)

WHAT YOU DO:

1. Using whatever materials you have around your house, arrange a "jungle" for the children to climb over, under and through.

 THE EXTRA TOUCH

*   You can incorporate a photo backdrop into your obstacle course. See "Safari Photo Backdrop" below.
*   Tape "Leaf Streamer" (page 82), "Swinging Monkey" (page 82) and "Flying Butterfly" (page 89) to different parts of the "Jungle Safari Obstacle Course."
*   Draw or paint pictures of jungle foliage and animals.

SAFARI PHOTO BACKDROP

Recommended for all ages

Use Illustration 3–17 "Monkey" or Illustration 3–18 "Tiger" and follow the directions for "Photo Backdrop" in **CRAFT TIPS** (page 354) to give children and their parents the best party favor they can have—a memorable "Jungle Safari Snapshot."

You can take a Polaroid® photograph and hand it out at the party (see "Polaroid® Photo Frame" below), or you can use a 35 mm camera and send a photo along with your thank-you note.

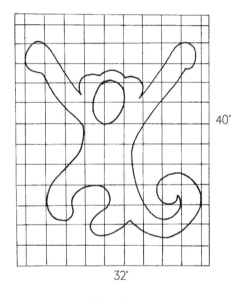

ILLUSTRATION 3-17

ILLUSTRATION 3-18

JUNGLE SAFARI POLAROID® PHOTO FRAME

Recommended for all ages

Hand out these wonderful memories at the party by using a Polaroid® photo (Illustration 3-19) and follow the directions for "Polaroid® Photo Frame" in **CRAFT TIPS** (page 357).

THE EXTRA TOUCH

*   Photocopy (Illustration 3-21) "Safari Stickers" (page 101). (Reduce to half-size. Cut out and glue on frame.)
*   Color "Photo Frame" with crayons and/or markers.
*   Glue construction paper leaves on "Photo Frame" (Illustration 3-19).

ILLUSTRATION 3-19

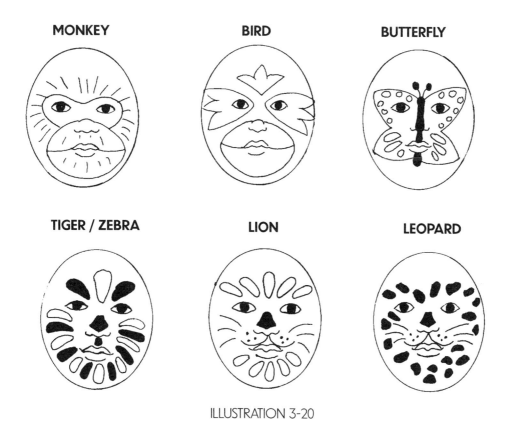

MONKEY   BIRD   BUTTERFLY

TIGER / ZEBRA   LION   LEOPARD

ILLUSTRATION 3-20

ANIMAL FACE PAINTING
(Non-Toxic Make-Up)

Recommended age: 3 and older

Use Illustration 3–20 "Animal Face Painting" as a source of ideas and follow the directions for "Face Painting Make-Up" in **CRAFT TIPS** (page 354).

CRAFTS

Children will have fun making these crafts as a group activity during the party or you can make these crafts yourself ahead of time and save money on party favors. Select one or two crafts for your party from the following list.

SAFARI STICKERS

Recommended age: 3 and older for gluing
5 and older for cutting and gluing

Make your own party stickers for children to use in various crafts and activities in this chapter. Use Illustration 3–21 "Safari Stickers" (page 101) and follow directions for "Party Stickers" in **CRAFT TIPS** (page 352).

⟳ SAFARI BINOCULARS

Recommended age: 5 and older

WHAT YOU NEED:
- 2 toilet paper tubes
- String or yarn (approximately 28" in length)
- Masking tape
- Hole punch
- Scissors (child-safe)

WHAT YOU DO:
During the party:
1. Tape two toilet paper tubes together, side-by-side.
2. Punch single hole on outside at one end of each tube (Illustration 3–22) #1.
3. Tie ends of string or yarn through holes of binoculars, forming neck strap.

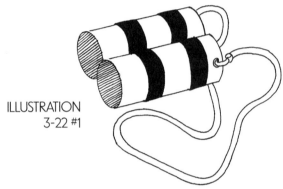

ILLUSTRATION
3-22 #1

ILLUSTRATION 3-22

⟳ SAFARI CAMERA

Recommended age: 5 years and older

WHAT YOU NEED:
- One 3-ounce or 6-ounce gelatin box; or one 4 oz. "variety pack" cold cereal box
- Construction paper (at least two contrasting colors)
- Hole punch
- Scissors (child-safe)
- White glue
- String or yarn (approximately 28" in length)
- Button or plastic bottle cap
- One set of "Safari Stickers" (page 87) for each camera

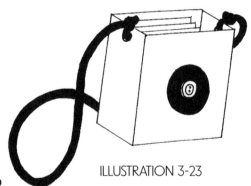

ILLUSTRATION 3-23

WHAT YOU DO:
Before the party:
1. Cut off top of each box.
2. Cut out a piece of construction paper large enough to wrap around each box.
3. Cut a 1 1/2" circle out of construction paper (one for each camera).

During the party:
4. Glue construction paper around outside of box.
5. With hole punch, make hole on each side of box, approximately 1/4" from top.
6. To make neck strap, tie ends of string or yarn through holes of box.
7. Glue circle in center of one side of box, where you want to place the "lens."
8. Glue button or bottle cap in center of circle to make the "lens."
9. Place a set of "Safari Stickers" inside the camera body and take your guests on a photographic safari. Children "photograph" an animal in the jungle and pull out its picture from the camera.

FLYING BUTTERFLY

Recommended age: 5 years and older

WHAT YOU NEED:

- Illustration 1–09 "Flying Butterfly" (Page 41)
- Copier paper or copier card stock (white bright colors)
- Scissors (child-safe)
- Paper hole punch
- One 8" length of elastic cord (or one 8" length of yarn)
- Crayons, colored pencils, or markers ✿

✿ Optional

ILLUSTRATION 3-24

WHAT YOU DO:

Before the party:
1. Photocopy Illustration 1–09 onto copier paper or copier card stock.

During the party:
2. Color butterfly, if desired.
3. Cut out butterfly.
4. Punch out two inner holes in wings, as marked on illustration.
5. Loop cord through inner holes of wings (Illustration 3-24).
6. Tie two ends of cord together, adjusting length to fit child's wrist.
7. As children raise and lower their wrist, the giant butterfly actually "flies" through the jungle.

ANIMAL SNOUTS

Recommended age: 6 and older

WHAT YOU NEED:

- Illustration 3–25 "Animal Snouts" (page 97)
- Copier card stock (white or bright colors)
- Scissors (child-safe)
- Stapler
- Hole punch
- One 20" length of elastic cord (or one 20" length of yarn)
- Markers, crayons, and/or paint and brushes ✿

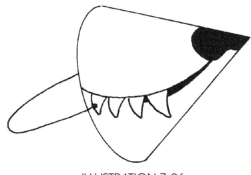

✿ Optional

ILLUSTRATION 3-26

WHAT YOU DO:

Before the party:
1. Photocopy Illustration 3–25 onto copier card stock.

During the party:
2. Color snout, if desired.
3. Cut out animal snout.
4. Bend and staple animal snout to form cone shape of snout (Illustration 3-26 #1).
5. Punch holes in snout, as marked on illustration.
6. Tie one end of elastic cord through one hole in snout.
7. Thread other end of cord through other hole in snout and adjust length to fit child's head; then knot cord in place.

ILLUSTRATION 3-26 #1

EGG CARTON JUNGLE ANIMALS

Recommended age: 5 years and older

WHAT YOU NEED:

- Egg cartons (at least 1 carton for every 2 children) ✿
- White glue
- Transparent tape
- Scissors (child-safe)
- Paints, brushes and/or markers
- Fabric scraps, felt scraps, yarn, string, buttons, feathers, fake eyes, pom poms and construction paper
- Pipe cleaners

─────────
✿ Cardboard cartons are easier to cut and glue than styrofoam cartons

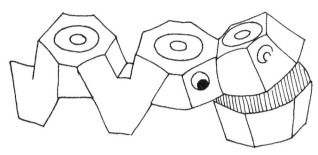

ILLUSTRATION 3-27 #1

WHAT YOU DO:

Before the party:

1. Cut egg cartons into individual cups or groupings for main body parts, such as the head, shoulders, and rear end. Encourage children to create their own animals, either real or imaginary. (Older children can cut their own egg cartons.)

During the party:

2. Color egg carton sections with paint or markers.
3. Tape or glue pipe cleaners on cardboard to make limbs, necks and tails.
4. Glue on fabric scraps, felt scraps, yarn, string, buttons, feathers, fake eyes, construction paper and pom poms to give each animal its own character.

ILLUSTRATION 3-27 #2

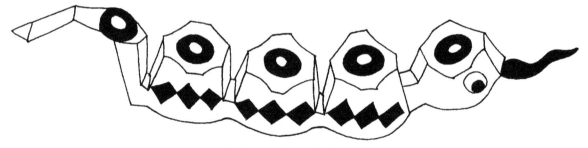

ILLUSTRATION 3-27 #3

MONKEY HAT

Recommended age: 6 years

WHAT YOU NEED:

- Illustration 3–29 "Monkey Hat" (page 102)
- Copier paper or copier card stock (brown, beige, pink or white) ✿
- Stapler
- One 14" length of elastic cord (or one 14" length of yarn)
- Scissors (child-safe)
- Hole punch
- Crayons, markers and/or colored pencils ✿✿
- Transparent tape ✿✿

─────────
✿ Card stock is preferred for this project.
✿✿ Optional

ILLUSTRATION 3-28

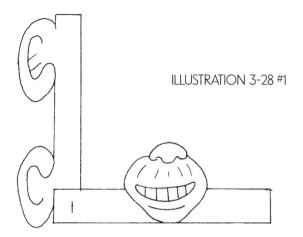

ILLUSTRATION 3-28 #1

WHAT YOU DO:

Before the party:
1. Photocopy Illustration 3–29 onto copier paper or copier card stock.
2. If using copier paper, reinforce holes with transparent tape before punching holes.

During the party:
3. Color hat, if desired.
4. Cut out top headband (with ears), and front headband (with mouth).
5. Place two headbands at right angles to one another, and staple in place. Then bend bands and staple other side together (Illustration 3–28 and 3–28 #1).
6. Punch a hole in both headbands where they meet, as marked on illustration.
7. Tie one end of elastic cord through one hole in headband.
8. Thread other end of cord through other hole in headband and adjust length to fit child's head; then knot cord in place.

BIRD HAT OR BIRD MASK

Recommended age: 5 years and older

WHAT YOU NEED:

- Illustration 3–31 "Bird Hat/Mask" (page 103)
- Copier paper or copier card stock (white or bright colors) ❀
- One 14" length of elastic cord (or one 14" length of yarn)
- Scissors (child-safe)
- Hole punch or sharp pencil
- Markers, crayons and/or colored pencils ❀
- Transparent tape ❀
- Craft knife (adult use only) ❀

❀ Optional

WHAT YOU DO:

Before the party:
1. Photocopy Illustration 3–31 onto copier paper or card stock.
2. If using copier paper, reinforce holes with transparent tape before punching holes.

During the party:
3. Color hat, if desired.
4. Cut out hat.
5. Punch hole in ends of headband, as marked on illustration.
6. Tie one end of elastic cord through one hole in headband.
7. Thread other end of cord through other hole in headband and adjust length to fit child's head; then knot cord in place.
8. You can turn your "Bird Hat" into a "Bird Mask" by cutting out eye holes with craft knife.

ILLUSTRATION 3-30

GAMES

Select several of the games for your party from the following list. Don't feel as if you have to play all of them—there just isn't enough time. But you should plan for a few extra games. Here are some unique games for your Jungle Safari party.

ANIMALS IN THE JUNGLE

Recommended age: 2–5 years of age

Here is a twist on the traditional game of "Follow the Leader."

WHAT YOU NEED:

- 1 set of "Safari Stickers" (page 87)

HOW TO PLAY:

1. Place stickers in a bag or box, and have children close their eyes and pick one sticker to start game. (Make sure you have at least as many stickers as guests so no one will be left out.)
2. After everyone has a sticker, have children line up (single file) with birthday child at head of line.
3. Tell children that this is a game of "Follow the Leader," but a very special kind of leader—an animal leader.
4. Ask birthday child to tell everyone what animal he or she is—and how that animal walks, talks and acts.
5. Then explain that everyone in line has to walk, talk and act like the leader's "animal."
6. Set a course for the leader to take his/her animals through the jungle.
7. After the group has completed the course, have leader move to back of line and have next person in line be the new leader.
8. Continue game until everyone has had a turn as leader.

ANIMAL CHARADES

Recommended age: 4 years and older

Here is a twist on the traditional game of "charades."

WHAT YOU NEED:

- 1 set of "Safari Stickers" (page 87)

HOW TO PLAY:

1. Place stickers in a bag or box and have birthday child pick a sticker to start game. (Make sure you have at least as many stickers as guests so no one will be left out.)
2. Tell birthday child not to tell or show anyone which animal he/she picked.
3. Take card from the birthday child and tell him/her to walk and talk like the animal.
4. Ask children to guess name of the animal.
5. The child who guesses correctly picks the next animal.
6. Make sure everyone who wants to participate gets a turn.

PIN THE ANIMAL IN THE JUNGLE

Recommended age: 3 years and older

WHAT YOU NEED:

- Illustration 3–21 "Safari Stickers" (page 87)
- Copier paper or copier card stock (white)
- Scissors
- Butcher paper or poster board (green or white)
- Masking tape or double-stick tape
- Pencil
- Blindfold
- White glue or transparent tape
- Crayons, markers and/or colored pencils ❋

ILLUSTRATION 3-32

❋ Optional

HOW TO PLAY:

Before the party:

1. Photocopy Illustration 3–21 onto copier paper, so there is at least one sticker per guest, plus one set of stickers to make the "game board."
2. Cut out one "sticker" for each child.
3. Cut out one set of "Safari Stickers" for the game board.
4. To make the game board, glue or tape a complete set the stickers onto butcher paper or poster board and make your own jungle "landscape."
5. Use crayons, markers and/or colored pencils to add vines, trees, bushes, exotic flowers and other elements to your jungle landscape, if desired.
6. Tape game board to wall in party area.

During the party:

7. Have children line up (single file) at least five feet away.
8. Place stickers in a bag and have each child pull out one sticker.
9. Write each child's name on the front of the "Safari Sticker" and place a piece of double-stick tape or masking tape rolled on itself on back of sticker.
10. Tell children to look at the jungle landscape and to find the animal that matches their sticker.
11. Blindfold the birthday child first and turn him or her 2–3 times. Then tell the child to place the "Safari Sticker" on top of the matching animal on the map.
12. See who can get their animal sticker closest to its mate.

SWING YOUR TRUNKS

Recommended age: 6 years and older

WHAT YOU NEED:

- 2 bowls of nuts in their shells (20 nuts per bowl)
- 2 empty bowls

HOW TO PLAY:

1. Divide children into 2 relay teams, and have teams line up, facing each other.
2. Place a bowl of nuts next to the first person in each line, and place an empty bowl next to the last person in each line.
3. Tell children that they are all "elephants," and that they will be using their "trunks" to pass nuts from one team member to the next.
4. The first player picks up a nut and holds it in his/her clasped hands, which are outstretched to look like a "trunk." The player then swings his/her "trunk" and passes the nut into the outstretched hands of the next "elephant" in line, who in turn, passes the nut down the line to the last person, who drops the nut into the empty bowl.
5. The first team to pass all of the nuts to the end of the line, wins.

ANIMAL RELAY RACES

*Recommended age: 7 years and old*er

This game can be hilariously funny. It also gives the birthday child a chance to be the center of attention.

HOW TO PLAY:

1. Mark a start/finish line and a turn-around point (like a tree or a chair) approximately 15–20 feet from starting line.
2. Divide children into two relay teams and have them line up (single file) behind start/finish line.
3. Explain to children that at the signal, "Go!", the first member of each relay team runs to the turn-around point and back As they cross the start/finish line, they must tag the next player in line.
4. What makes this race special is that the birthday child does not run. Instead, he/she calls out the name of an animal and demonstrates how it runs. All players must run the race as if they were that animal. They complete the course running on all fours, flapping arms like a bird, crawling on hands and knees or slithering like a snake.
5. To add more fun, birthday child may call out a different animal at any time, even while runners are in the middle of the course.
6. The first team to have all players complete the race, wins.

ANIMAL TREASURE HUNT

Recommended age: 4 years and older

This game helps children understand the need to protect animals and to ensure the survival of endangered species.

WHAT YOU NEED:
- 1 set of "Safari Stickers" (page 87)
- "Safari Binoculars" (page 88) ✣

✣ Optional

HOW TO PLAY:
1. Before starting game, have someone usher children into a separate section of party area, where they can't see you, and hide stickers in and around game area.
2. After stickers have been hidden, bring children into game area and explain that they have just been asked to protect certain animal groups or "species" in the jungle. But in order to protect them, tell children that they must find the animals and take it to a preserve.
3. Give children boundaries for their hunt and hold up a sticker so they know what they are looking for.
4. Children must bring the sticker to the "preserve," which could be a central area or special table (like the party table with the birthday cake just waiting to be devoured).
5. Play game until all animals have been "saved."
6. Emphasize team effort in this game, as children work together to look for and save the animals.

ELEPHANT WALK

Recommended age: 5 years and older

HOW TO PLAY:
1. Mark a start/finish line and a turn-around point (like a tree or a chair) approximately 15–20 feet from starting line.
2. Divide children into two teams and have them line up (single file) behind start/finish line.
3. The first child in each line extends one arm outward as a "trunk" and the other arm back through his/her legs as a "tail" (Illustration 3-34).
4. The second child holds the first child's tail with his/her "trunk" and extends his/her arm back through the legs for the third person to hold.
5. Continue arranging the line until each person has extended his/her "trunk" to hold the "tail" in front of him/her.
6. At the signal, the race begins and the "elephants" walk, as a team, from the start line to the turn-around point, and back to the finish line.
7. "Elephants" must keep hold of one another's tail throughout the race.
8. The first team to cross the finish line, wins.

ILLUSTRATION 3-34

MORE GAMES...

It's always a good idea to plan some extra party games. Here are some standard party games, adapted for your Jungle Safari Party. Specific directions for these games are listed in **APPENDIX D: GAMES**, beginning on page 363.

↻ FEED THE WILD ANIMAL

Recommended age: 3 years and older

Follow the directions for "Bean Bag Toss" in **GAMES** (page 364). Use "Monkey or Tiger Photo Backdrop" (page 86) as theme backdrop.

MONKEY, MONKEY, WHERE IS YOUR BANANA?

Recommended age: 5 years and older

Follow the directions for "Who Has It?" in **GAMES** (page 371). Use a banana for the theme object and have one child sit in the middle of the circle to play the "monkey." (The birthday child should be first to lead.)

WILD ANIMAL'S BUFF

Recommended age: 5 years and older

Follow directions for "Blindman's Buff" in **GAMES** (page 364) and have other players move around "It," making wild animal sounds.

JUNGLE ANIMAL EXTINCTION

Recommended age: 5 years and older

Follow directions for "Sardines" in **GAMES** (page 369) and have players choose to be an animal (perhaps an endangered species) to participate in the game.

JUNGLE ANIMAL SCRAMBLE

Recommended age: 6 years and older

Follow directions for "Animal Scramble" in **GAMES** (page 364). Use "Safari Stickers" (page 87) to play the game.

THE HERD!

Recommended age: 5 years and older

Follow directions for "Blob" in **GAMES** (page 365), using the theme of an animal herd to play the game.

TIGER TAG

Recommended age: 6 years and older

Follow directions for "Tag" in **GAMES** (page 371), using "tigers" (or birthday child's favorite jungle animal) as it to play the game.

SLIPPERY BANANA

Recommended age: 3 years and older

Follow directions for "Hot Potato" in **GAMES** (page 366), using a banana as the game object. (It might be a good idea to have some extra bananas on hand.)

CATCH THE SNAKE'S TAIL

Recommended age: 5 years and older

Follow directions for "Catch the Tail" in **GAMES** (page 365), using a "snake" as the theme animal for the game.

for _____
time _____
date _____

Place _____

r.s.v.p. _____

Party

Safari

Jungle

ILLUSTRATION 3-03

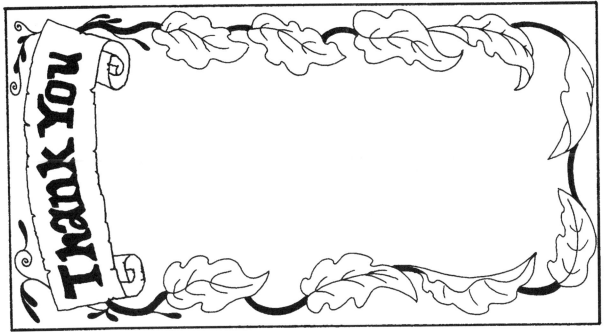

ILLUSTRATION
3-04

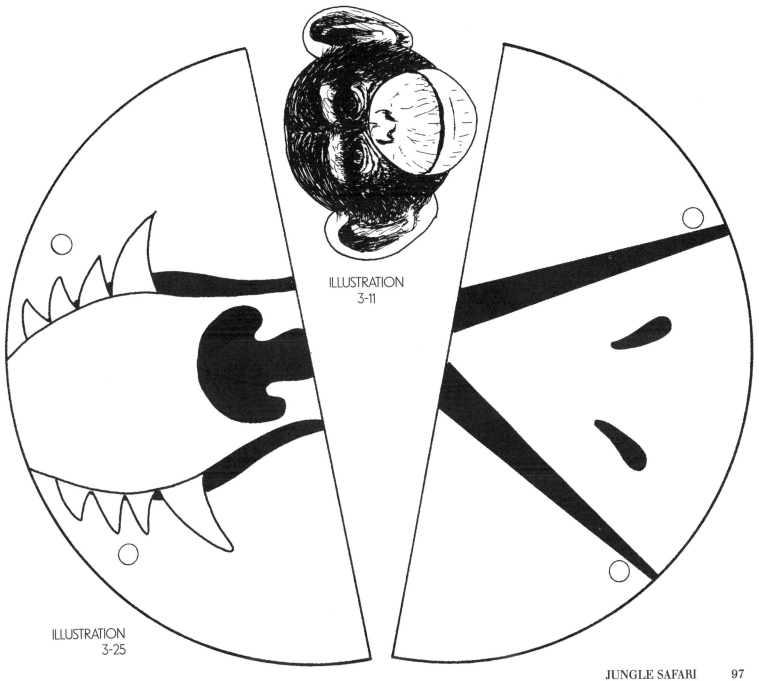

ILLUSTRATION
3-11

ILLUSTRATION
3-25

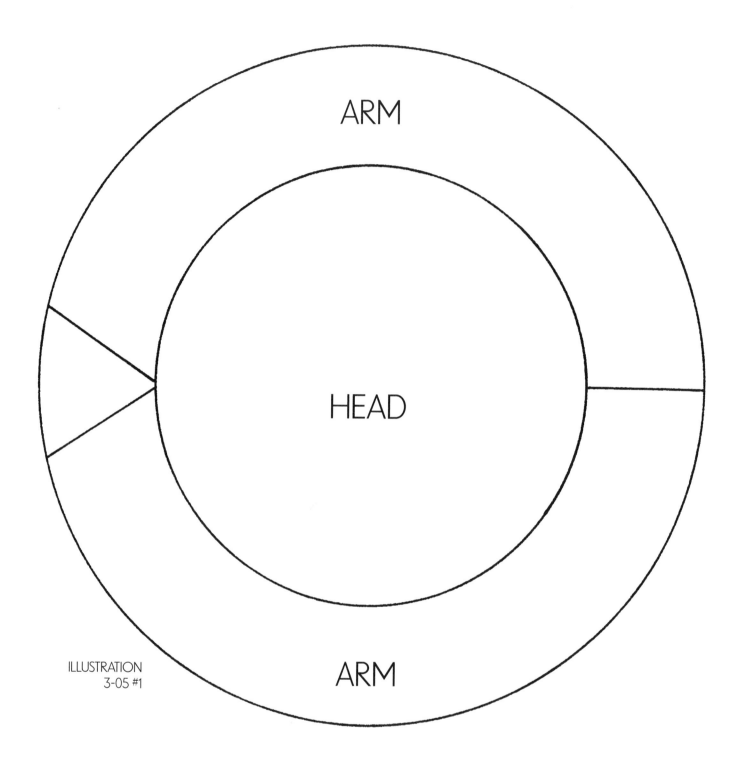

ARM

HEAD

ARM

ILLUSTRATION
3-05 #1

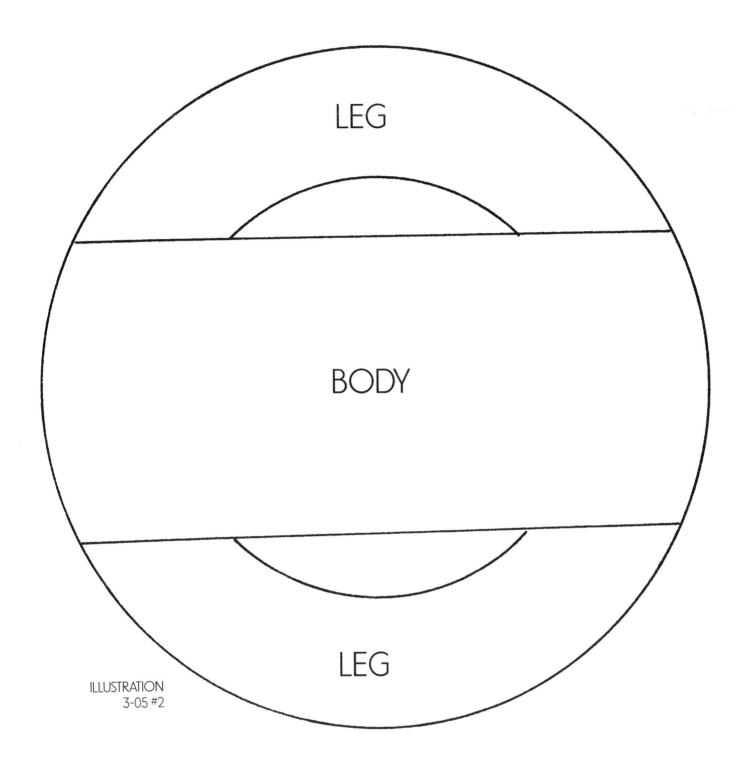

LEG

BODY

LEG

ILLUSTRATION
3-05 #2

ILLUSTRATION 3-08

ILLUSTRATION 3-21

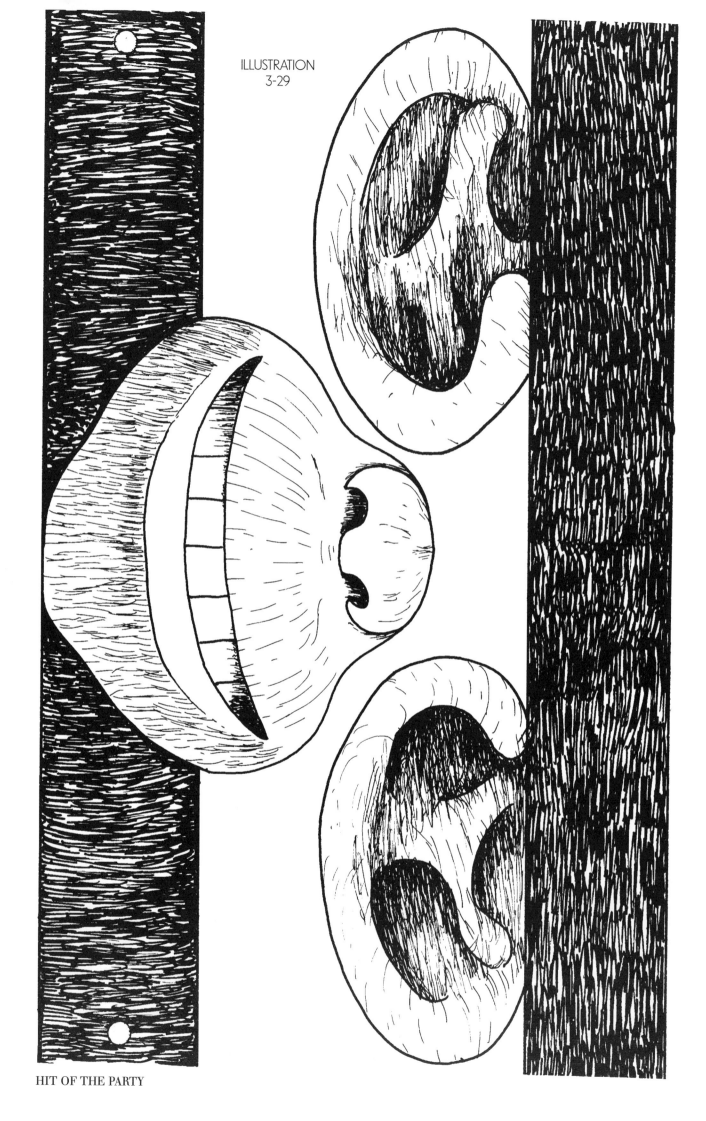

ILLUSTRATION
3-29

ILLUSTRATION
3-31

Wild West Party

CHAPTER 4

Way out West, in the days of old, when cowboys rode the range and Indians hunted buffalo, it was a rough 'n' ready time. Are you ready for a rootin', tootin' good time at a Wild West Party? Saddle up!

ILLUSTRATION 4-01

WILD WEST INVITATION

Estimated Time: 2–3 minutes each

You won't need a posse to round up your guests. Just lasso them with this invitation!

WHAT YOU NEED:

- Illustration 4–03 "Wild West Invitation" (page 123)
- Copier paper (white, pink or beige)
- Envelopes (3 5/8" x 6 1/2")
- Scissors
- Felt-tip pen (black)
- Crayons, markers and/or colored pencils ✿

———————

✿ Optional

ILLUSTRATION 4-02

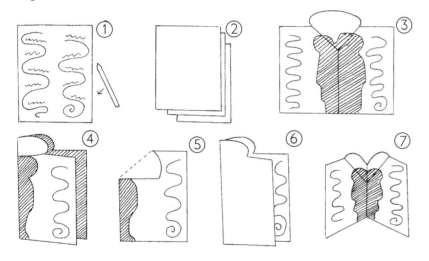

ILLUSTRATION
4-02 #1-7

WHAT YOU DO:

1. Make one photocopy of Illustration 4–03. This is your "master copy." Fill out all party information with felt-tip pen on master copy (Illustration 4–02 #1).
2. Photocopy as many invitations as needed (Illustration 4–02 #2).
3. Color invitation, if desired.
4. Cut out invitation along outer line (Illustration 4–02 #3).
5. Fold invitation in half so illustration is facing outward, and make a sharp crease along fold line (Illustration 4–02 #4).
6. Fold over corner along dotted line (Illustration 4–02 #5), making sharp crease along fold line.
7. Open invitation and fold along fold line so illustration faces inward (Illustration 4–02 #6).
8. Pull "lasso" inward, tucking it into center of invitation (Illustration 4–02 #7), pressing along all fold lines.
9. Open and close invitation and watch lasso pop out!

☞ THE EXTRA TOUCH

- Glue "Wild West Stickers" (page 115) to the front of invitation and to seal envelope.

WILD WEST THANK-YOU NOTE

Estimated Time: 1 minute each

The "Wild West Thank-You Note," Illustration 4–04, is on page 124. Simply photocopy the thank-you note and write your personal message in the space provided.

MENU

Come and get it! Call your guests to the chuck wagon for a genuine taste of the Old West. You might want to serve the food in pie tins or "Covered Wagons" (page 110) for a rustic effect. Choose foods from each group, and follow the recipes on the pages listed below.

DRINKS:

EATS:

CAKE AND ICE CREAM:

HORSE CAKE

Estimated time: 1–1/2 hours

Your rough 'n' ready rustlers will be hungry enough to eat a horse! And when they see this cake, your guests will be chomping at the bit for a bite.

INGREDIENTS:

1	"Basic Cake" recipe in Appendix A, on pages 343 and 344; or use your favorite box cake mix
1	"Chocolate Frosting" recipe in Appendix A, on page 345; or 1 can of your favorite canned frosting
1	"Buttercream Frosting" recipe in Appendix A, on page 345; or 1 can of your favorite canned frosting
1 oz.	Unsweetened baking chocolate (1 square)
2 c.	Flaked coconut
1	Marshmallow (cut in half)
1	Chocolate chip
1	Gumdrop
3	Licorice twists (red)
1	Licorice whip (red)
	13" x 18" tray or foil-covered board
	Illustration 4–05 "Horse Cake Pattern" (page 125)

ILLUSTRATION 4-06

DIRECTIONS:

1. Prepare and bake cake in 9" x 13" pan as directed in recipe or cake package.
2. Cool cake completely on wire rack.
3. Wrap in plastic wrap and freeze cake at least 45 minutes. (Freezing the cake does not affect its flavor and makes it easier to work with. It also enables you to make the cake ahead of time, to help balance your work load for the party.)

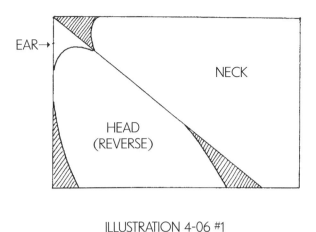

ILLUSTRATION 4-06 #1

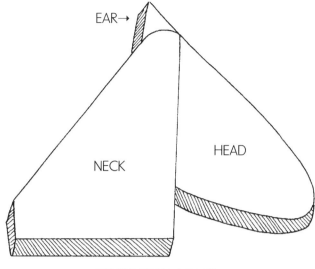

ILLUSTRATION 4-06 #2

4. Trace Illustration 4–05 "Horse Cake Pattern," on wax paper. Extend lines 1" on cake pattern as indicated by arrows.
5. Cut out wax paper pattern into sections and reassemble on top of cake.
6. Using long knife, cut cake into sections by following pattern (Illustration 4–06 #1).
7. Assemble sections on tray into shape of horse's head. Flop front of horse's head to make it face correct direction (Illustration 4–06 #2).
8. Frost connecting sections of cake with chocolate frosting.
9. Frost top and sides of chocolate sections of cake (Illustration 4–06).
10. Melt unsweetened chocolate in double boiler or microwave oven. (If using microwave oven, heat until chocolate just starts to bubble.)
11. Stir coconut and melted chocolate together in a bowl.
12. Sprinkle coconut evenly over chocolate sections of cake, gently pressing coconut into cake.
13. Frost white sections of cake, making broad strokes with knife to form "mane."
14. Cut licorice twists to make "bridle" (Illustration 4–06).
15. Push marshmallow half into head to create "eye" (Illustration 4–06).
16. Place chocolate chip into center of marshmallow "eye" using dab of chocolate frosting to hold in place.
17. Press piece of licorice whip into head to create "mouth" (Illustration 4–06).
18. Press gumdrop into nose to form "nostril" (Illustration 4–06).

⏰ POWWOW CAKE

Estimated time: 20–30 minutes

This will really get kids dancing and whooping it up for your very own Powwow.

INGREDIENTS:

1	Frosted store-bought cake (round or rectangular) ✿
1 c.	Flaked coconut
3–4	Plastic teepees
3–6	Plastic Indians and horses
6–8	Pretzel sticks
1 pkg.	Licorice twists
1/2 c.	Gumdrops
	Green food coloring

✿ without decorative flowers or trim

ILLUSTRATION 4-07

DIRECTIONS:

1. Place frosted cake on a plate or serving platter.
2. Mix flaked coconut in bowl with a few drops of green food coloring. Sprinkle tinted coconut on top of cake to make grass (Illustration 4-07).
3. Cut licorice twists into sections, approximately 3"–5" in length.
4. Push licorice twist pieces into side of cake, forming a zig-zag pattern around cake.
5. Push one gumdrop into center of each pattern.
6. Place plastic teepees, Indians and horses on top of cake to create Indian village scene.
7. Build a campfire out of pretzel sticks.

 THE EXTRA TOUCH

- Instead of decorating the top of cake with plastic teepees, use sugar cones to create your own, edible teepees. Follow the directions for "Teepee Ice Creams" in **RECIPES** (page 338), but do not fill cones with ice cream.

DECORATIONS

Create the look of the Old West with a few, simple materials and a little imagination. Make decorations as craft activities at your party. Or, save money by giving some of these decorations out as favors in your loot bags.

PARTY STREAMERS

Estimated time: 1–2 minutes per streamer

Select one (or more) of the streamers suggested below, and follow the directions for "Party Streamers" in **CRAFT TIPS** (page 349).

- **Star Streamer** Pattern CT-03 (page 360)
  Use red, white and/or blue crepé paper.
- **Triangle Streamer** Pattern CT-05 (page 361)
  Use red, white and/or blue crepé paper.

↻COVERED WAGONS

Estimated time: 6–8 minutes each

This project can be completed ahead of time, or used as a craft activity during the party.

WHAT YOU NEED:

- Illustration 4–09 "Wagon Wheels" (page 126)
- Copier paper or copier card stock (white or red)
- Shoe box or tissue box ✽
- Large brown paper (grocery) bag (one for every two wagons)
- 8 1/2" x 11" sheet of paper (white)
- Scissors
- Pencil
- White glue
- Transparent tape

✽ If using a tissue box, cut off the top of box completely before starting project.

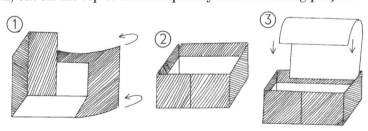

ILLUSTRATION 4-08 #1-3

WHAT YOU DO:

1. Photocopy Illustration 4–09 onto copier paper or card stock.
2. Cut open grocery bag and cut in half, lengthwise.
3. Wrap paper around outside of box (Illustration 4–08 #1).
4. Fold down edges and glue or tape in place (Illustration 4–08 #2).
5. Cut out wheels.
6. Glue wheels to sides of box with bottom of wheel even with the bottom of the box.
7. Glue or tape short sides of white paper to inside of box so that the end of paper is 1/2" from top of the box (Illustration 4–08 #3).

 THE EXTRA TOUCH

To make wheels so that they actually turn:

1. Cut out cardboard circles same size as wheels and glue wheels onto cardboard circles.
2. Place each wheel so that it is 1/2" lower than bottom of box.
3. Using a nail, punch a hole in center of each wheel and into the box. Fasten wheels with brads and move 'em out!

INDIAN TEEPEES

Estimated time: 2–3 minutes each

Make an Indian village out of paper and straws. This project can be done ahead of time as a decoration or during the party as a craft.

WHAT YOU NEED:

- Illustration 4–10 "Teepees" (page 126)
- Copier paper or copier card stock (white or beige) ❀
- 3 drinking straws
- Scissors
- Stapler
- Markers and/or crayons ❀❀

❀ Card stock is preferred for this project.

❀❀ Optional

ILLUSTRATION 4-11

WHAT YOU DO:

1. Photocopy Illustration 4–10 onto copier paper or card stock.
2. Cut out teepee along dotted lines.
3. Bend ends of teepee together and staple into cone shape. (Illustration 4–11 #1).
4. Cut a slit along dotted line, and fold back to make flap (Illustration 4–11).
5. Insert 3 straws into top of teepee to create "poles."

ILLUSTRATION 4-11 #1

ILLUSTRATION 4-12

HORSE STRAWS

Estimated time: 1–2 minutes each

Bring your horse to water (or punch) and make him drink it! Use Illustration 4–13 "Horse" (page 126) and follow directions for "Drinking Straws" in **CRAFT TIPS** (page 353).

HORSE SUCKERS

Estimated time: 1–2 minutes each

Make your own "Horse Suckers." (Illustration 4-14) Use Illustration 4–13 "Horse" (page 126) and follow directions for "Party Suckers" in **CRAFT TIPS** (page 353).

ILLUSTRATION 4-14

💡 MORE DECORATING IDEAS...

- Use a gingham tablecloth on the party table.
- If you live in an area where bales of hay are easy to get, place a few around party area and use as seats for guests.
- Make placemats by photocopying Illustration 4-30 "Indian Headdress" (page 127) onto copier paper (white or bright colors). Provide crayons for children to color placemats, if desired.
- Make placemats by having children glue "Wild West Stickers"(page 115) onto 9" x 12" sheet of construction paper. Provide crayons, markers and/or colored pencils for children to color placemats, if desired.
- Place plastic cowboys and Indians in center of table or at each place setting.
- Here are a few suggestions for making cardboard signs at your party:
  - Randy's Ranch
  - George's Gulch
  - Tina's Trail
  - Sally's Saloon
  - Carl's Corral
  - Dodge City
  - Silver Dollar Saloon
  - Wild West Show
  - O.K. Corral
  - Boothill
- Photocopy "Horse Cake" Illustration 4-01 (page 106) and tape to front door or front of party area to greet guests as they enter the party.

LOOT BAGS

Select one (or more) of the following loot bags and follow the directions for "Loot Bags" in **CRAFT TIPS** (page 350).

- **Sticker Bag** (page 350)
  Use Illustration 4-24 "Wild West Stickers" (page 123).
- **Treasure Box** (page 351)
  Use Illustration 4-24 "Wild West Stickers" (page 123).
- **Hat Bag** (page 351)
  Use Illustration 4-33 "Sheriff's Hat" (page 128).
- **Covered Wagon** (page 110)

LOOT BAG "LOOT"

Looking for something to put in those loot bags? Here are some creative suggestions you can make, or if you are short of time, you can buy.

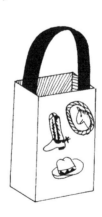

LOOT YOU CAN MAKE:

- **Wild West Stickers** (page 115)
- **Horse Straws** (page 111)
- **Horse Suckers** (page 112)
- **Wild West Polaroid® Photo Frame** (page 114)
- **Sheriff Badge** (page 118)
- **Wild West Finger Puppets** (page 116)
- **Indian Drum** (page 116)
- **Indian Bead Necklace** (page 117)
- **Trail Mix** (page 333)
- **Sheriff Cookie Badges** (page 329)
- **Golden Nuggets** (page 333)
- **Crunchy Critters** (page 331)

LOOT YOU CAN BUY:

- Plastic sets of cowboys, Indians and horses
- Bandannas
- Sheriff badges
- Indian drums
- Trail mix
- Small books about the Old West
- Harmonicas
- Toy guitars
  [NOTE: It is not a good idea to give out toy guns at a party, as some parents may object.]

ACTIVITIES

Ready for a rootin', tootin' good time?

Don't feel as if you have to do all of these activities—there isn't enough time at any party. Discuss with your child which ones he or she would like to do, and plan your party activities accordingly.

ARRIVAL ACTIVITY

As each child arrives, let him/her pick a special name, as in "Sheriff Sean," "Chief Charles," "Calamity Karen," "Wild Bill Hickok," and the like. Announce their name with a little fanfare.

↻ THE WILD WEST TOWN

Recommended for all ages

Recreate the Old West with recycled materials and a little imagination. Children will enjoy playing out scenes from the Wild West in their very own town while waiting for the other guests to arrive. Your child will enjoy playing in the Wild West Town after the day's events.

WHAT YOU NEED:

- Large cardboard box (refrigerator/large appliance)
- Scissors
- Craft knife (adult use only)
- Ruler
- Pencil
- Duct tape or cloth-backed masking tape
- 4–6 wooden dowels
- Crayons, markers and/or poster paints ✿

✿ Optional

WHAT YOU DO:

1. Draw door(s) and window(s) where you want them.
2. Cut all openings with craft knife. (For suggestions in cutting cardboard, see "Cardboard Play Structures" in **CRAFT TIPS** on page 355.)
3. Reinforce "hinges" for doors and shutters with duct tape.
4. Make a sign out of any leftover cardboard, which could read "Sally's Saloon," "Dawn's General Store," "Dodge City Jail," or any other name you wish.
5. To make bars in jail window, place wooden dowels an equal distance apart on inside of window and secure with duct tape.
6. Paint or draw wooden slats, knotholes or bullet holes on outside of building and paint or draw furniture on inside of building.

⟳WANTED POSTER PHOTO BACKDROP

Recommended for all ages

Use Illustration 4–19 "Wanted Poster Photo Backdrop Pattern" and follow the directions for "Photo Backdrop" in **CRAFT TIPS** (page 354) to give children and their parents the best party favor they can have—a memorable "Wild West Snapshot."

You can take a Polaroid® photograph and hand it out at the party (see "Polaroid® Photo Frame below), or you can use a 35 mm camera and send a photo along with your thank-you note.

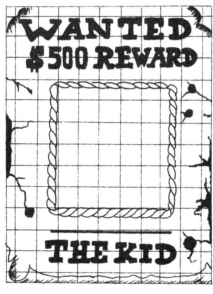

ILLUSTRATION 4-19

ILLUSTRATION 4-20

WILD WEST POLAROID® PHOTO FRAME

Recommended for all ages

Hand out these wonderful memories at the party by using a Polaroid® photo and follow the directions for "Polaroid® Photo Frame" in **CRAFT TIPS** (page 357).

 ☞ THE EXTRA TOUCH

- Color with crayons, markers and/or colored pencils.
- Decorate the frames with "Wild West Stickers" (page 115) or gummed stars (Illustration 4-20).

INDIAN FACE PAINTING
(Non-Toxic Make-Up)

Recommended age: 3 and older

Use Illustration 4–21 "Indian Face Painting" as examples and follow the directions for "Face Painting Make-Up" in **CRAFT TIPS** (page 354).

ILLUSTRATION 4-21

⟳ WILD WEST THEATER

What better way to entertain your guests than with puppets. Make your own puppet theater by cutting out bottom of a tissue box and cover the tissue box with wrapping paper (Illustration 4-22). Use "Finger Puppets" (page 116) as players.

Older children may enjoy making their own plays for each other or for younger siblings and friends.

ILLUSTRATION 4-22

OLD WEST SING-ALONG

Recommended age: 4 and older

In the days of the Old West, the cowboys sat around the campfire and sang their favorite songs. Use your own instruments or make your own "Indian Drum" (page 116) and/or "Spoons" below. Here are some suggested songs.

"Home on the Range"   "She'll be Comin' 'Round the Mountain"
"My Darling Clementine"   "Pony Boy (Girl)"
"Get Along Little Doggies"   "Streets of Laredo"
"Happy Trails"

SPOONS

Recommended age: 5 and older

Create the sound of a galloping horse with this old-time musical instrument.

WHAT YOU NEED:

*   Two metal spoons

WHAT YOU DO:

1. Hold first spoon between thumb and forefinger with top of spoon facing thumb.
2. Hold second spoon between forefinger and middle finger with top of spoon facing middle finger (Illustration 4-23).
3. Slap front of second spoon on leg to make spoons click together.

CRAFTS

Children will have fun making these crafts as a group activity during the party, or you can make these yourself ahead of time and save money on party favors. Select one or two of the crafts for your party from the following list.

WILD WEST STICKERS

ILLUSTRATION 4-23

Recommended age: 3 and older for gluing
5 and older for cutting and gluing

Make your own party stickers for children to use in various crafts and activities in this chapter. Use Illustration 4–24 "Wild West Stickers" (page 123), and follow directions for "Party Stickers" in **CRAFT TIPS** (page 352).

INDIAN DRUM

Recommended age: 5 and older
What Powwow would be complete without drums!

WHAT YOU NEED:
- Illustration 4–26 "Indian Drum Design" (page 124)
- Copier paper (white or bright colors)
- Empty can, with label removed (16 fluid ounce)
- Masking tape (approximately 1" wide)
- Two drinking straws or two unsharpened pencils
- Scissors (child-safe)
- White glue
- Crayons, markers and/or colored pencils ✿

✿ Optional

ILLUSTRATION 4–25

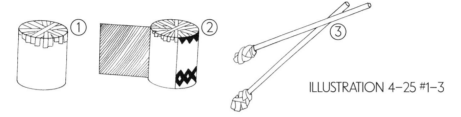

ILLUSTRATION 4–25 #1–3

WHAT YOU DO:
Before the party:
1. Photocopy Illustration 4–26 onto copier paper.

During the party:
2. Cover top of can completely with masking tape by overlapping individual strips of tape across top of can (Illustration 4–25 #1).
3. Color illustration, if desired.
4. Cut out Indian drum illustration along outer lines.
5. Glue illustration around outside of can (Illustration 4–25 #2).
   [NOTE: Indian drum illustration was designed to fit height of standard 16 ounce can. Some trimming may be necessary for other-than-standard sizes.]
6. To make drumsticks, cover ends of two drinking straws with masking tape until a rounded end is formed; or use eraser end of two unsharpened pencils (Illustration 4–25 #3).
7. If you put this favor in a loot bag, use a rubberband to keep drumsticks and drum together.

WILD WEST FINGER PUPPETS

Recommended age: 5 and older
Finger puppets are a great craft activity. Have children make a set of five puppets, one for each finger, and watch kids put on their own Wild West Puppet Shows (Illustration 4-27).

WHAT YOU NEED:
- Illustration 4–28 "Wild West Finger Puppets" (page 124)
- Copier paper or copier card stock (white or bright colors) ✿
- Scissors (child-safe)
- White glue or transparent tape
- Crayons, markers and/or colored pencils ✿✿

✿ Card stock is preferred for this project.

✿✿ Optional

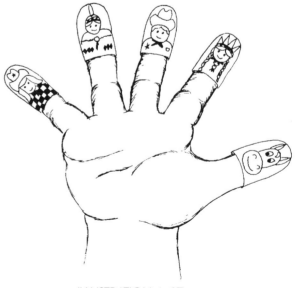

ILLUSTRATION 4–27

WHAT YOU DO:

Before the party:

1. Photocopy Illustration 4–28 onto copier paper or card stock.

During the party:

2. Color puppets, if desired.
3. Cut out each puppet along outer lines.
4. Glue or tape ends of tabs together (Illustration 4–27 #1), adjusting size to fit child's fingers.

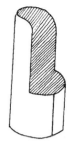

 THE EXTRA TOUCH

- Tie a set of puppets together with a ribbon as a take-home favor.

ILLUSTRATION
4-27 #1

INDIAN HEADDRESS

Recommended age: 5 and older

WHAT YOU NEED:

- Illustration 4–30 "Indian Headdress" (page 127)
- Copier paper or copier card stock (white or bright colors)
- One 14" length of elastic cord (or one 14" length of yarn)
- Scissors (child-safe)
- Hole punch or sharp pencil
- Crayons, markers, colored pencils ❀
- Transparent tape ❀

❀ Optional

WHAT YOU DO:

Before the party:

1. Photocopy Illustration 4–30 onto copier paper or card stock.
2. If using copier paper, reinforce holes with transparent tape before punching holes.

During the party:

3. Color headdress, if desired.
4. Cut out around headdress.
5. Punch a hole in ends of tabs, as marked on headdress.
6. Tie one end of elastic cord through one hole in headband.
7. Thread other end of cord through other hole in headband and adjust length to fit child's head; then knot cord in place.

INDIAN BEAD NECKLACE

Recommended age: 6 and older

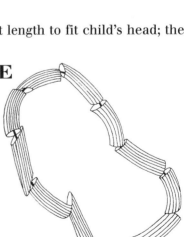

WHAT YOU NEED:

- Hollow pasta
- Inexpensive beads
- Plastic, colored drinking straws (cut into 1/4"–1" lengths)
- Shoe lace or 1/4" ribbon
- Cupcake tin, egg carton or small bowls
- Food coloring

WHAT YOU DO:

Before the party:

1. Color pasta at least one day before party. To do so, add 4–5 drops of food coloring to 1 cup of water. Use more food coloring for a deeper color.
2. With slotted spoon or strainer, dip pasta in water and stir 30–60 seconds or until evenly coated.
3. Place wet pasta on paper towel to dry overnight.

During the party:

4. Use cupcake tin, egg carton and/or small bowls to divide beads, pasta and straw sections into separate containers.
5. Place containers in work area and have children use shoe laces or ribbons to string necklaces.

SHERIFF'S HAT AND BADGE

Recommended age: 6 and older

WHAT YOU NEED:

- Illustration 4–33 "Sheriff's Hat" and "Badge" (page 128)
- Copier paper or copier card stock (white or bright colors) ❊
- One 14" piece of elastic cord (or one 14" length of yarn)
- Scissors (child-safe)
- Craft knife (adult use only)
- Hole punch or sharp pencil
- Safety pin
- Transparent tape
- Glue, glitter and/or sequins ❊❊
- Crayons, markers and/or colored pencils ❊❊

_____

❊ Card stock works better for this project.

❊❊ Optional

WHAT YOU DO:

Before the party:
1. Photocopy Illustration 4–33 "Sheriff's Hat" and "Badge" onto copier paper or card stock.
2. If using copier paper, reinforce area around holes with transparent tape.
3. Using craft knife, cut along dotted line on hat.

During the party:
4. Color hat and star, if desired.
5. Cut out around hat and star patterns with scissors.
6. Glue on sequins and/or glitter, if desired.
7. Punch a hole in both ends of headband, as marked on hat.
8. Slip band through slits in hat (Illustration 4-32 #1).
9. Tie one end of elastic cord through one end in headband.
10. Thread other end of cord through other hole in headband and adjust length to fit child's head; then knot cord in place.
11. To make "Sheriff's Badge," tape safety pin to back of star.

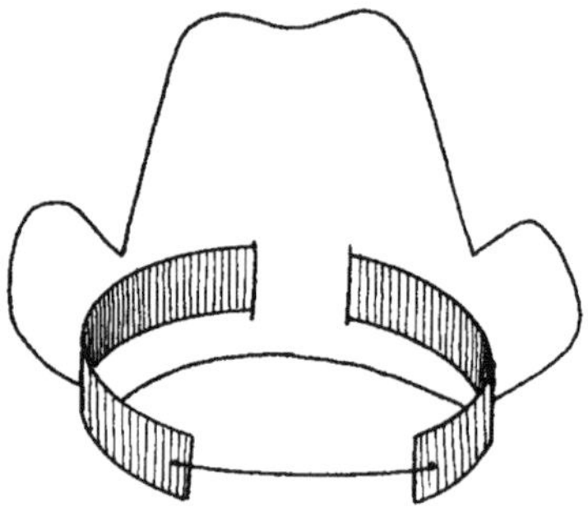

GAMES

Select several of the games for your party from the following list. Don't feel as if you have to play all of them—there just isn't time. But you should plan for a few extra games. Here are some unique games for your Wild West Party.

ILLUSTRATION 4-32 #1

ROUNDUP RING TOSS

Recommended age: 4 years and older

WHAT YOU NEED:

- One chair (folding or straight-back)
- One blanket
- String
- Two brooms or wooden dowels (at least 1/2" in diameter and 4' long)
- One large paper grocery bag
- One wide-tipped, felt marker (black)
- Five feet of heavy rope (1/4"–1/2" in diameter)
- Duct tape
- Scissors

ILLUSTRATION 4-34

ILLUSTRATION 4-34 #1-3

HOW TO MAKE THE BULL:

1. Tie broom handles or wooden dowels together with string in an "X" pattern to form "horns" of "bull" (Illustration 4–34 #1).
2. Place crossed sticks against chair so "horns" lean across seat and against back of chair.
3. Tie crossed sticks with string firmly to seat so they won't slip.
4. Lay paper bag flat, and using Illustration 4–34 (page 118) as a guide, draw picture of a bull on one side of bag. [NOTE: The top of the drawing, or the "ears" of the bull, should point toward the bottom of the bag.]
5. Place bag over wooden "horns," and mark where "horns" touch inside bottom of bag.
6. Cut 2 holes in bottom of bag so wooden "horns" can poke through bag.
7. Slip bag over wooden "horns" and down back of chair (Illustration 4–34 #2).
8. Drape blanket over chair to suggest bull's "hide." [NOTE: You may want to use safety pins to hold the blanket in place.]
9. Cut rope into 4 pieces, each 15" in length.
10. To make lassos, bring ends of each piece of rope together to form a circle. With duct tape, tape ends together (Illustration 4–34 #3).

HOW TO PLAY:

Before the party:
1. Have birthday child try to "lasso" the "bull," by tossing lassos over "horns."
2. Based on child's ability, establish a comfortable "playing distance" for your child's age group.

During the party:
3. To play, have children form a single line, with birthday child first.
4. Each player takes a turn (4 tosses) to see how many times he/she can lasso bull.

PIN THE BADGE ON THE SHERIFF

Recommended age: 3 years and older

WHAT YOU NEED:

- Large sheet of butcher paper
- Illustration 4-33 "Sheriff's Badge" (page 128)
- Copier paper (white or yellow)
- Masking tape or double-stick tape
- Pencil
- Blindfold
- Scissors
- Poster paints or crayons ✿

✿ Optional

HOW TO PLAY:

Before the party:
1. Photocopy Illustration 4–33 "Sheriff's Badge" onto copier paper (one for each guest), and cut out each badge.
2. Make a body tracing of birthday child on butcher paper. Cut out tracing and draw on a cowboy/cowgirl hat, vest, leggings, boots and "Sheriff Badge."
3. The birthday child might want to color the body tracing.

During the party:
4. Write each child's name on front of "Sheriff's Badge" and place piece of masking tape rolled on itself (or double-stick tape) on back of badge.
5. Blindfold first in line (birthday child first) and turn child 2–3 times. Then hand child his/her "Sheriff's Badge" and tell him/her to place badge on top of badge on sheriff.

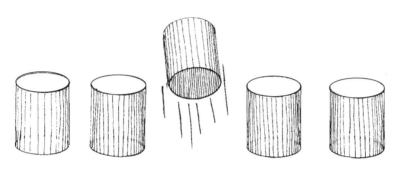

↻ WILD WEST TARGET PRACTICE

Recommended age: 3 years and older

WHAT YOU NEED:
- 5 empty soda cans
- 1 table (at least 3 feet in length)
- Dry beans (at least 1 pound)
- Children's socks (8–12 individual socks)

HOW TO PLAY:

Before the party:
1. Fill socks half-full with beans, and tie a knot at end of sock (Illustration 4–36 #1).
2. Set up soda cans on table and have birthday child try to knock cans down with bean bags.
3. Based on birthday child's ability, establish a comfortable "playing distance" for your child's age group.

ILLUSTRATION 4-36 #1

During the party:
4. Have children form a single line, with birthday child first.
5. Each player takes a turn (5 tosses) to see how many cans he/she can knock down.

FEATHER RACE

Recommended age: 6 years and older

Based on an authentic Native American game for children, the "Feather Race" promotes agility and speed in a fun activity.

WHAT YOU NEED:
- 2 paper plates
- 2 feathers

HOW TO PLAY:

1. Divide children into two relay teams, and give each team a plate and a feather.
2. Mark start/finish line for relay race, and a turn-around point, like a tree or a chair, 15–20' from the start/finish line.
3. Each player must place the feather on the plate, and walk as fast as he/she can, from the start/finish line to the turn-around point and back, balancing the feather on the plate. The first team to have all players complete the race, wins.
4. Children cannot hold feather while walking. If feather falls, player must stop, place feather back on the plate and continue the race. Anyone caught holding the feather will have to start his/her turn over.

PONY EXPRESS

Recommended age: 6 years and older

WHAT YOU NEED:

* Bean bags (page 120) used as "Pony Express Mail Bags"

HOW TO PLAY:

Before the party:

1. Make bean bags by following the directions listed in the "Target Practice" Activity. (One bag for each child.)

During the party:

2. Mark off game area so there is a start/finish line on one side and two equal piles of "Mail Bags," at least 20 feet away, on the opposite side of play area.
3. Select one child (birthday child first) to be the "Bandit." Then divide children into two equal teams of "Pony Express Riders."
4. Have each team line up behind start/finish line and point out to them which is their pile of "Mail Bags."
5. The first person in line runs as quickly as he/she can to the pile of "Mail Bags," picks up one bag and runs quickly back to the start/finish line. "Riders" wait at end of line, holding his/her "Mail Bag."
6. The only thing that could stop "Riders" is the "Bandit." "Bandit" will try to tag "Riders" as they make their way to and from "Mail Bag" pile. If "Bandit" does tag "Rider," then "Rider" has to start over.
7. The first team to have all "Riders" in line holding "Mail Bags," wins.
8. If time allows, trade off who plays next "Bandit."

ROUNDUP TIME

Recommended age: 6 years and older

WHAT YOU NEED:

* 2 brooms
* String or a bag of white flour
* 1 balloon per team, with each team having a different-colored balloon ❧

❧ Keep an extra supply of balloons on hand as some of your "cattle" may end up a little flat.

HOW TO PLAY:

1. Set up an obstacle course in party area, using boxes, chairs, bushes, trees, etc.
2. Mark path of obstacle course using string or flour.
3. Divide children into two teams, and line up both teams at "start," with birthday child at head of one line.
4. First player in each line uses a broom to herd balloon(s) (or "cattle") through course (or "cattle drive").
5. Each player must herd balloon through entire course to complete his/her turn. The first team to finish course wins. (Older children may find the game more challenging with 2 or even 3 balloons per turn.)
6. If a player's balloon should "pop" during his/her turn, player must return to start line, get another balloon ("cow") and start again.

RIDE 'EM COWBOYS/COWGIRLS

Recommended age: 2–5 years of age

WHAT YOU NEED:

- 1 "Stick Horse" (page 61) for each child
- Obstacle course or "Western Trail" (See "Roundup Time," page 121)

HOW TO PLAY:

1. Establish a play area for a "Follow-the-Leader" game.
2. Give each child his/her own stick horse.
3. Select a leader. (Let birthday child be first leader, but everyone should get a turn.)
4. Leader must ride the "Western Trail," and everyone must follow leader.

MORE GAMES...

It's always a good idea to plan some extra party games. Here are some standard party games, adapted for your Wild West Party. Specific directions for these games are listed in **APPENDIX D: GAMES**, beginning on page 363.

WILD WEST BEAN BAG TOSS

Recommended age: 3 years and older

Follow the directions for "Bean Bag Toss" in **GAMES** (page 364). Use "Wanted Poster Photo Backdrop" (page 114) as theme backdrop.

WILD WEST MUSICAL CHAIRS

Recommended age: 4 years and older

Follow the directions for "Fun Time Musical Chairs" in **GAMES** (page 366) and use "Country Western" music in playing the game.

CATCH THE HORSE BY THE TAIL

Recommended age: 5 years and older

Follow the directions for "Catch the Tail" in **GAMES** (page 365), and use a horse theme to play the game.

WILD WEST MEMORY GAME

Recommended age: 8 years and older

Follow the directions for "Memory Game" in **GAMES** (page 367), using wild west objects (toy cowboys, Indians, horses, cows, etc.) to play the game.

MINING FOR GOLD

Recommended age: 3 years and older

Follow the directions for "Searching for Buried Treasure" in **GAMES** (page 369), using pennies to play the game.

WESTERN CHANGE RELAY RACE

Recommended age: 6 years and older

Follow the directions for "Quick Change Relay Race" in **GAMES** (page 368), using cowboy/cowgirl outfits to play the game.

OLD WEST TARGET PRACTICE

Recommended age: 4 years and older

Follow the directions for "Squirt Ball" in **GAMES** (page 370).

Good Luck

Wild West Party

for

place

date

range

time

ILLUSTRATION 4-24

ILLUSTRATION 4-03

ILLUSTRATION 4-26

ILLUSTRATION 4-28

ILLUSTRATION 4-04

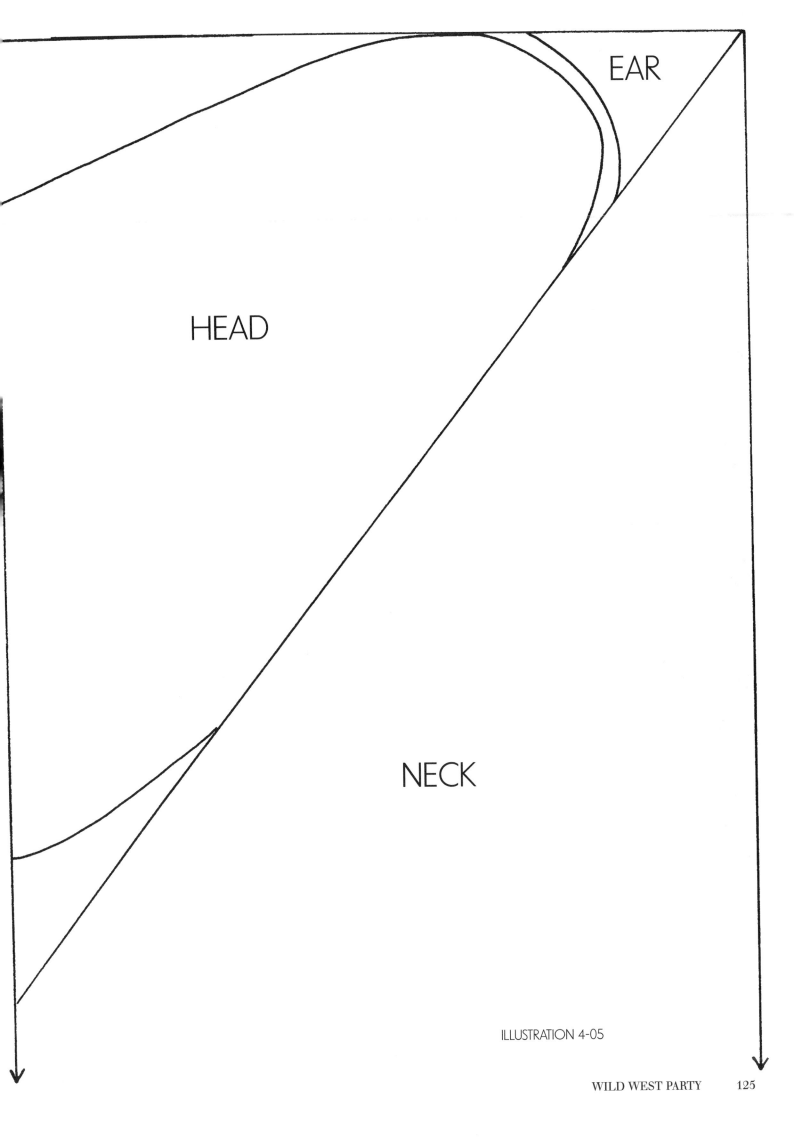

EAR

HEAD

NECK

ILLUSTRATION 4-05

ILLUSTRATION
4-09

ILLUSTRATION
4-13

ILLUSTRATION
4-10

ILLUSTRATION 4-30

ILLUSTRATION 4-33

Pirate Party

CHAPTER 5

It's time to sail the Seven Seas for an exciting adventure. We will be landing on "Treasure Island" for your birthday party, where we will search for wondrous gifts and delicious foods. Hop on board!

ILLUSTRATION 5-01

TREASURE MAP INVITATION

Estimated Time: 2–3 minutes each

Send out real treasure maps to your guests! They will sail into the party, ready for a fun-filled adventure.

WHAT YOU NEED:

- Illustration 5–03 "Treasure Map Invitation" (page 148)
- Copier paper (white or tan)
- Envelopes (4 1/8" x 9 1/2")
- Scissors
- Sponge
- Coffee (1 cup is more than enough) ❀
- Felt-tip pen (black)
- Crayons, markers and/or colored pencils ❀

ILLUSTRATION 5–02

❀ Optional

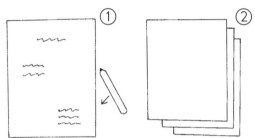 

ILLUSTRATION 5–02 #1–4

WHAT YOU DO:

1. Make one photocopy of Illustration 5–03. This is your "master copy." Fill out party information with felt-tip pen on master copy (Illustration 5–02 #1).
2. Photocopy as many invitations as needed (Illustration 5–02 #2).
3. Cut out invitation with scissors along outer line (Illustration 5–02 #3).
4. Give invitation an "aged" or "buried" look by using the following method:
   a) Crumple invitation;
   b) Dip sponge in coffee and stain invitation by blotting or spattering coffee over surface.
5. Color invitation, if desired.
6. Roll up invitation widthwise (as a scroll) and place in envelope (Illustration 5–02 #4).

 THE EXTRA TOUCH

- Tie scrolled invitation with string or ribbon.
- Glue "Pirate Flag Stickers" (page 139) to seal envelope.

PIRATE THANK-YOU NOTE

The "Pirate Thank-You Note," Illustration 5–04, is on page 150. Simply photocopy Illustration 5–04 and cut out the thank-you note. Then write your personal message in the space provided.

Estimated Time: 1 minute each

MENU

Join the crew at the captain's table, but mind your manners, or you'll be walking the plank. Choose foods from each group, and follow the recipes on the pages listed below.

DRINKS:

Yo! Ho! Pirate Punch ....Page 314
Mermaid's Delight ....Page 314

EATS:

CAKE AND ICE CREAM:

TREASURE ISLAND CAKE

The greatest treasure of all is the birthday cake. Dig into this Treasure Island for a real treat.

Estimated time: 1–1 1/2 hours

INGREDIENTS:

1	"Basic Cake" recipe in Appendix A, on pages 343 and 344; or use your favorite box cake mix
2	Buttercream Frosting" recipes in Appendix A, on page 345; or use 2 cans of your favorite canned frosting
3	Sugar cones
4	Square-shaped cookies (approximately 1 1/2" x 1 1/2")
1 c.	Gummi worms
2	Soft-centered, chilled chocolate bars (at least 4" in length)
1/4 c.	Chocolate coins or other small candies
1 c.	Gumdrops
1	Licorice whip or twist (black)
	Green and blue food coloring
	Toothpicks
	13" x 18" tray or foil-covered board
	Illustration 5–05 "Treasure Island Cake Pattern" (page 149)

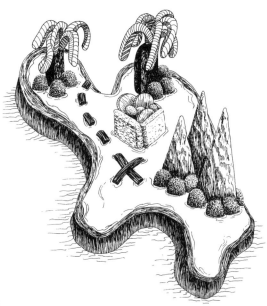

ILLUSTRATION 5–06

DIRECTIONS:

1. Prepare and bake cake in 9" x 13" cake pan as directed in recipe or cake package.
2. Cool cake completely on wire rack.
3. Wrap in plastic wrap and freeze cake at least 45 minutes. (Freezing cake does not affect its flavor and makes it easier to work with. It also enables you to make cake ahead of time, to help balance work load for the party.)
4. Trace Illustration 5–05 "Treasure Island Cake Pattern" on wax paper. Extend lines 1" on cake pattern as indicated by arrows.
5. Cut out wax paper pattern into sections and reassemble on top of cake.
6. Using long knife, cut cake into sections by following pattern (Illustration 5–06 #1).

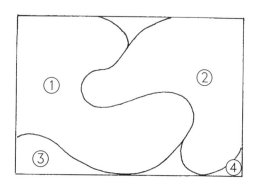

ILLUSTRATION 5–06 #1

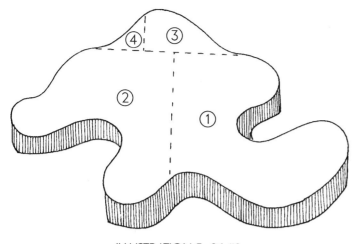

ILLUSTRATION 5-06 #2

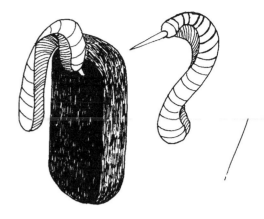

ILLUSTRATION 5-06 #3

7. Assemble sections on a tray into shape of an island (Illustration 5–06 #2).
8. Divide buttercream frosting into 2 separate bowls. Tint 1 bowl green and 1 bowl blue by adding a few drops of food coloring and mix until color is uniform.
9. Frost connecting sections of cake with blue frosting.
10. Frost sides and 1/2" of top perimeter or "shore" of island with blue frosting.
11. Frost remaining top surface of island with green frosting.
12. To make "palm tree," use 4–5 gummi worms for fronds and one chocolate bar for trunk. Insert toothpicks halfway into each gummi worm, and place other end of each toothpick into chocolate bar (Illustration 5–06 #3).
13. Make pilot hole (about 1" deep) into surface of cake, wherever you want a palm tree to go and push "trunk" (chocolate bar) into hole.
14. To make "mountains," push sugar cones into cake (Illustration 5–06).
15. Frost mountains green.
16. To make "treasure chest," insert 4 cookies into cake to form a box. Fill treasure chest with chocolate coins or other small candies.
17. To make "path to treasure chest," and the "X" that marks the spot, cut up licorice and place on surface of cake (Illustration 5–06).
18 Use gumdrops to suggest foliage and landscaping for island.

 THE EXTRA TOUCH

- Add mint leaves to suggest additional foliage around island and mixed nuts to suggest rocks and boulders.
- Make "mountains" into "Never-Land Teepees" by following directions in "Teepee Ice Creams" **RECIPES** (page 338), except do not fill cones with ice cream.
- Add plastic pirate figures.

⏰ **PIRATE SHIP CAKE**

Estimated time: 20–30 minutes

A pirate ship has just arrived for your birthday celebration—filled with a bounty of treasures from far-off lands.

INGREDIENTS:

1	Chocolate-frosted, store-bought cake (round) ❀
1 roll	Lifesavers® (white)
2 doz.	Pretzel sticks
3	Wooden skewers or 1/4" dowels (10"–12" in length)
1	8 1/2" x 11" sheet of construction paper (white)
	White glue
	"Pirate Flag Stickers" (page 139)

ILLUSTRATION 5-07

❀ without decorative flowers or trim

WHAT YOU DO:

1. Place frosted cake on plate or serving platter.
2. To make the main sail, cut construction paper in half (widthwise) to form 2 equal pieces 8 1/2" x 5 1/2" (Illustration 5–07 #1).
3. To make front and back sails, cut one of the 8 1/2" x 5 1/2" of paper diagonally (Illustration 5–07 #1).
4. Cut two slits in each sail, as shown in Illustration 5-07.
5. Insert a skewer or dowel through slit in each sail to form a "mast."
6. Push masts into surface of cake to form main sail as well as front and back sails (Illustration 5–07).
7. Glue "Pirate's Flag" to top of center mast.
8. With a fork, draw horizontal lines around side of cake, forming wooden slats of ship.
9. Push Lifesavers® into sides of cake to form "portholes."
10. Place pretzels evenly-spaced around top perimeter of cake to suggest ship's "riggings."

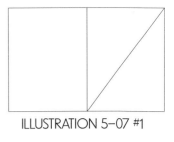

ILLUSTRATION 5–07 #1

[NOTE: Remove sails just before lighting candles, or paper sails could catch fire.]

 THE EXTRA TOUCH

- Make the "treasure chest" (from the "Treasure Island Cake," page 132), and place on the ship's main deck.
- Add plastic pirate figures to top of cake.

DECORATIONS

Ahoy, landlubbers! Transform your party area into a pirate cove fit for the likes of Captain Hook or Long John Silver. Save money by using some of these decorations as favors in your loot bags.

PARTY STREAMERS

Estimated time: 1–2 minutes per streamer

Select one (or more) of the streamers suggested below, and follow the directions for "Party Streamers" in **CRAFT TIPS** (page 349).
- **Wave Streamer** Pattern CT–04 (page 359)
  Use blue crepé paper.
- **Triangle Streamer** Pattern CT–05 (page 361)
  Use red and/or black crepé paper.

 TIMESAVER

- Hang crepé paper streamers (in pre-packaged rolls) around party area.

 PIRATE FLAG

Estimated time: 3–5 minutes each

WHAT YOU NEED:

- Illustration 5–09 "Pirate Flag" (page 153)
- Copier paper (white)
- Cardboard wrapping paper tubes; newspaper rolls ❀ or wooden dowels
- Transparent tape
- White glue
- Scissors

❀ For directions on making "Newspaper Rolls" see **CRAFT TIPS** (page 355).

WHAT YOU DO:

1. Photocopy Illustration 5–09: "Pirate Flag" onto copier paper.
2. Cut out flag.
3. To hang flag, wrap top end of paper around cardboard tube, rolled newspaper or wooden dowel and glue in place (5-08 #1).

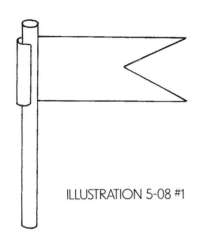

ILLUSTRATION 5-08 #1

PIRATE SOAP BOAT

Estimated time: 3–4 minutes each

This project can be completed ahead of time or during the party as a craft activity.

WHAT YOU NEED:

- Bar of soap ✿
- Craft stick
- 4" x 6" sheets of construction paper (white or bright colors)
- Scissors
- Craft knife (adult use only)
- Hammer
- "Pirate Flag Stickers" (page 139)

_____

✿ You will need a brand that floats. (Pure Ivory® Soap is one such brand.)

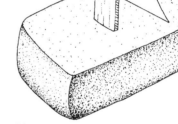

ILLUSTRATION 5-10

WHAT YOU DO:

1. To make sail, cut 2 slits in each sheet of construction paper with craft knife (Illustration 5–10).
2. To make mast, use hammer to pound craft stick into center of soap.
3. Slip "sail" over "mast" (Illustration 5–10).
4. Glue pirate flag on top of mast.
5. Place ships on table top. Have one for each child to take home as a favor.

PIRATE STRAWS

Estimated time: 1–2 minutes each

Sit down, mateys, and share a drink with one of these thirsty pirates. Use Illustration 5–12 "Pirate" (page 153) and follow directions for "Drinking Straws" in **CRAFT TIPS** (page 353).

PIRATE SUCKERS

Estimated time: 1–2 minutes each

Make your own "Pirate Suckers." (Illustration 5–13). Use Illustration 5–12 "Pirate" (page 153) and follow directions for "Party Sucker" in **CRAFT TIPS** (page 353).

ILLUSTRATION 5-11

ILLUSTRATION 5-13

⚙ MORE DECORATING IDEAS...

- Make placemats by photocopying illustration 5-22 "Captain Hook Marionette"(page 151) onto copier paper (white or bright colors). Provide crayons for children to color placemats, if desired.
- Make placemats by gluing "Pirate Flag Stickers" (page 139) onto 9" x 12" sheet of construction paper. Provide crayons, markers and/or colored pencils for children to color placemats, if desired.
- Cover party table with butcher paper and draw a treasure map. Provide crayons for guests to color in detail.
- If you have an old trunk lying about, fill it with old clothes and place costume jewelry, goblets, candlesticks, chocolate gold coins, and other "treasures."
- Make a pirate dummy by covering the bristle end of a broom with a paper bag and draw a pirate face on bag (Illustration 5-14). Stuff old clothes with newspaper and pull clothes over stick end of broom. Add "Pirate Costume" (page 141), and "Hook" (page 142).
- Photocopy "Treasure Island Cake" illustration 5-01 (page 130) and tape to front door or front of party area to greet guests.

ILLUSTRATION 5–14

LOOT BAGS

Select one (or more) of the following loot bags and follow the directions for "Loot Bags" in **CRAFT TIPS** (page 350).

- **Sticker Bag** (page 350)
  Use illustration 5-20 "Pirate Flag Stickers" on page 153.
- **Treasure Box** (page 351)
  Use illustration 5-20 "Pirate Flag Stickers" on page 153.
- **Hat Bag** (page 351)
  Use illustration 5-26 "Captain's Hat" on page 152.

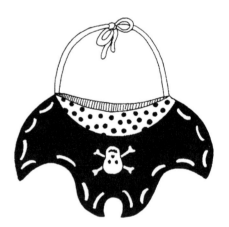

LOOT BAG "LOOT"

Looking for something to put in those loot bags? Here are some creative suggestions you can make, or if you are short of time, you can buy.

LOOT YOU CAN MAKE:
- **Pirate Flag Stickers** (page 139)
- **Pirate Straws** (page 135)
- **Pirate Suckers** (page 135)
- **Pirate Polaroid® Photo Frame** (page 138)
- **Pirate Patch** (in Pirate's Costume page 141)
- **Telescope** (page 297)
- **Mustache** (in Pirate's Costume page 141)
- **Parrot Puppet** (page 140)
- **Pirate Soap Boat** (page 135)
- **Hook** (page 142)
- **Golden Nuggets** (page 333)

LOOT YOU CAN BUY:

- Chocolate gold coins
- Fake Jewelry
- Bandannas
- Eye patches
- Small boats
- Small candies that look like jewels (gumdrops or jelly beans)
- Pirate hook
- Treasure box
- Kaleidoscopes
- Shiny pennies ❧

❧ Shine up old pennies by soaking them with a solution of (1/2 cup) vinegar and (4 Tbs.) salt.

[NOTE: It may not be a good idea to give out toy swords at a party, as some parents might be offended.]

ACTIVITIES

Let the fun begin!

Don't feel as if you have to do all of these activities—there isn't enough time at any party. Discuss with your child which ones he or she would like to do and plan your party activities accordingly.

ARRIVAL ACTIVITY

As each child arrives, let him/her pick a special name, as in "Captain Nick," "Long Dawn Silver," "Bobby the Bluebeard," "Pam the Pirate," and the like. Announce each name with a little fanfare.

 PIRATE SHIP

Recommended for all ages

WHAT YOU NEED:

- "Pirate Flag" (page 134)
- Large cardboard box (refrigerator/large appliance)
- Scissors
- Craft knife (adult use only)
- Ruler
- Pencil
- Duct tape or cloth-backed masking tape
- Broom or wooden dowel (at least 46" in length)
- Wooden dowel (approximately 18" in length)
- One sheet of 22" x 28" poster board (white)

WHAT YOU DO:

1. Draw a deck and porthole(s) where you want them (Illustration 5–17).
2. Using craft knife, cut out deck and porthole(s). For suggestions in cutting cardboard, see "Cardboard Play Structures" in **CRAFT TIPS** (page 355).

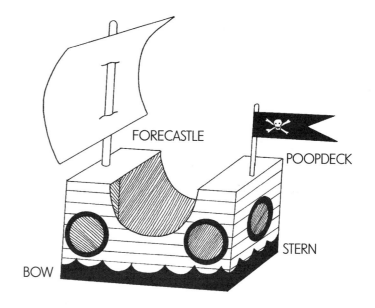

ILLUSTRATION 5-17

3. Use broom or longer wooden dowel to make the "mast." To set "mast," cut a hole (equal to diameter of broom handle or dowel) in "forecastle" (or front deck), approximately 1/2" from side of box.
4. Push broom handle or dowel up through hole (or drop dowel down hole), making sure bristles or bottom of dowel rest squarely on bottom of box.
5. With duct tape, secure broom or dowel in place (Illustration 5–17 #1).
6. Use poster board to make sail by cutting two 3" slits (Illustration 5–17), and thread mast through sail.

7. Use shorter wooden dowel for "flag pole." To set pole, cut a hole (equal to diameter of dowel) toward ship's "stern" in "poop deck" (or rear deck), approximately 1/2" from "stern."
8. Drop dowel down hole and make sure bottom of dowel rests just above porthole.
9. With duct tape, secure dowel in place (Illustration 5–17 #2).
10. Tape "Pirate Flag" to flag pole.

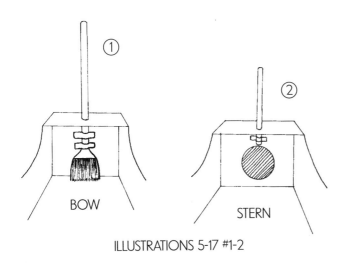

ILLUSTRATIONS 5-17 #1-2

ILLUSTRATION 5-18

 THE EXTRA TOUCH

- Use crayons, markers and/or poster paints to make wooden slats, portholes or "bounding waves" on outside of ship.

PIRATE PHOTO BACKDROP

Recommended for all ages

Use Illustration 5–18 "Pirate Photo Backdrop Pattern" and follow the directions for "Photo Backdrop" in **CRAFT TIPS** (page 354) to give children and their parents the best party favor they can have—a memorable "Pirate Snapshot."

You can take a Polaroid® photograph and hand it out at the party (see "Polaroid® Photo Frame below), or you can use a 35 mm camera and send the photo along with your thank-you note.

PIRATE POLAROID® PHOTO FRAME

Recommended for all ages

Hand out these wonderful memories at the party by using a Polaroid® photo and follow the directions for "Polaroid® Photo Frame" in **CRAFT TIPS** (page 357).

 THE EXTRA TOUCH

- Color with crayons, markers and/or colored pencils.
- Glue on "Pirate Flag Stickers" (page 139).
- Glue on glitter, sequins or fake jewels, yarn or string.

ILLUSTRATION 5-19

PUPPET SHOW

Recommended for all ages

What better way to tell a tale of adventure on the high seas than with puppets. Turn the "Pirate Ship" into a "Puppet Theater." Use one of the decks or the rear porthole of the "Pirate Ship" for the stage of your "Puppet Theater."

Here are some "Puppet Show" suggestions:
1. The "Captain Hook Marionette" (this page), the "Parrot Puppet" (page 140) will make good "players;" or use your child's favorite puppets to star in the show.
2. Adapt a scene from a popular book, such as *Peter Pan* or *Treasure Island*, or make up your own tale from the high seas.
3. Depending on the age of your children, you may want to have birthday child and your guests participate by working the puppets while you tell the story.
4. Have children make up their own story and act it out with the puppets.
5. A good time to present the show is while the children are eating or just before the meal. Keep the program short (around 10 minutes).

CRAFTS

Children will have fun making these crafts as a group activity during the party or you can make these crafts yourself ahead of time and save money on party favors. Select one or two of the crafts for your party from the following list.

PIRATE FLAG STICKERS

Recommended age: 3 and older for gluing
5 and older for cutting and gluing

Make your own party stickers for children to use in various crafts and activities in this chapter. Use Illustration 5–20 "Pirate Flag Stickers" (page 153) and follow directions for "Party Stickers" in **CRAFT TIPS** (page 352).

You could also make "Under-the-Sea Stickers" for the Pirate Party. Use Illustration 11–22 "Under-the-Sea Stickers" (page 281), and follow directions for "Party Stickers" in **CRAFT TIPS** (page 352).

CAPTAIN HOOK MARIONETTE

Recommended age: 5 and older

WHAT YOU NEED:
- Illustration 5–22 "Captain Hook" (page 151)
- Copier paper or copier card stock (white)
- Cardboard tube (paper towel) or drinking straw
- Two 10" pieces of string or yarn
- Scissors (child-safe)
- Transparent tape
- Crayons, markers and/or colored pencils ❀

❀ Optional

WHAT YOU DO:
Before the party:
1. Photocopy Illustration 5–22 "Captain Hook" onto copier paper or card stock.

During the party:
2. Color "Captain Hook," if desired.
3. Cut out illustration.
4. Tape each piece of string or yarn to back of Captain's hands (Illustration 5–21).
5. Tie strings to cardboard tube (Illustration 5–21).
6. To make Captain Hook move, hold marionette by middle of tube and rotate ends of tube up and down and/or side to side.

ILLUSTRATION 5-21

PARROT PUPPET

Recommended age: 7 and older

WHAT YOU NEED:

- Illustration 5–24 "Parrot Puppet" (page 150)
- Copier paper or copier card stock (bright colors)
- Cardboard tube (toilet paper)
- One pipe cleaner (cut in half)
- Hole punch
- White glue
- Scissors
- Transparent tape
- Safety pin
- Crayons, markers and/or colored pencils ❀

❀ Optional

ILLUSTRATION 5-23

WHAT YOU DO:

Before the party:

1. Photocopy Illustration 5–24 onto copier paper or card stock.

During the party:

2. Color parrot, if desired.
3. Cut out all four parts of parrot.
4. Glue parrot's body to cardboard tube (Illustration 5–23 #1). Trim cardboard tube even with parrot's body.
5. To make "beak," fold both sections of beak along dotted lines (Illustration 5–23 #2).
6. Glue both upper and lower sections of beak to parrot's "body" (Illustration 5–23).
7. Using hole punch, punch five holes in parrot's body as marked on illustration.
8. To make "feet," thread one pipe cleaner half through one set of paired holes at front of parrot's body (Illustration 5–23 #3).
9. Twist pipe cleaner into a knot to hold "foot" in place. Then curl ends of pipe cleaner to form "claws" (Illustration 5-23 #4).
10. Repeat Steps #8 and #9 to make other parrot foot.
11. Glue "tail feather" to back of body (Illustration 5–23).
12. To fasten onto child's shoulder, push safety pin through hole at back of parrot and pin to child's shirt or sweater.

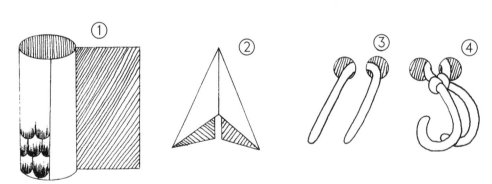

ILLUSTRATION 5-23 #1-4

👉 THE EXTRA TOUCH

- Turn your "Parrot" into a "stick puppet" by gluing or taping a craft stick inside the tube.

PIRATE COSTUME

Recommended age: 5 and older

WHAT YOU NEED:

- Illustration 5–26 "Pirate Costume" (page 152)
- Copier paper or copier card stock (white) ❀
- One 14" length of elastic cord or one 14" length of yarn (for hat)
- One 20" length of elastic cord or one 20" length of yarn (for patch)
- Scissors (child-safe)
- Craft knife (adult use only)
- Hole punch or sharp pencil
- Crayons, markers, colored pencils ❀❀
- Transparent tape or double-stick tape

❀ Card stock is preferred for this project.

❀❀ Optional

WHAT YOU DO:

Before the party:

1. Photocopy Illustration 5–26 "Pirate Costume" onto copier paper or card stock.
2. Using the craft knife, make slits on hat and patch along dotted lines as indicated in illustration. (If using copier paper instead of card stock, you will have to reinforce holes with transparent tape before punching holes.)

During the party:

3. Color costume, if desired.
4. Cut out hat, band, patch and mustache.
5. To make hat, insert band through slits on hat (Illustration 5–25 #1).
6. Punch a hole in ends of headband, as marked on illustration.
7. Tie one end of elastic cord through one hole in headband.
8. Thread other end of cord through other hole in headband and adjust length to fit child's head; then knot cord in place.
9. To make patch, insert elastic through slits on patch and adjust length to fit child's head; then knot cord in place (Illustration 5–25 #2).
10. To make mustache, pull off a 1" piece of double-stick tape or a 2" piece of transparent tape rolled on itself, with "sticky" side out (Illustration 5–25 #3).
11. Place tape on back of mustache (Illustration 5–25 #4).
12. Stick mustache under child's nose.

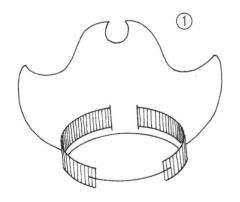
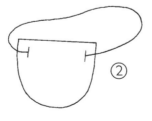

ILLUSTRATION 5-25 #1-4

HOOK

Recommended age: 5 and older

WHAT YOU NEED:
- Illustration 5–28 "Hook" (page 150)
- Copier card stock (yellow or white)
- Paper drinking cup (8 ounces)
- Scissors (child-safe)
- Craft knife (adult use only)
- Transparent tape
- Craft stick or drinking straw

WHAT YOU DO:
Before the party:
1. Photocopy Illustration 5–28 onto copier card stock.
2. With craft knife, make slit (approximately 1 1/2" in length) in bottom of drinking cup (Illustration 5–27 #1).

During the party:
3. With scissors, cut out hook pattern.
4. Tape craft stick (or straw) to base of hook (Illustration 5–27 #2).
5. Insert stick (or straw) and base of hook through slit of cup (Illustration 5–27 #2).
6. To wear hook, child places hand in cup, and holds stick.

ILLUSTRATION 5-27

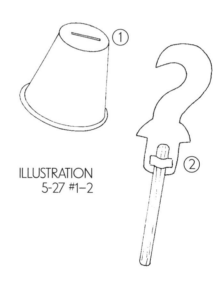

ILLUSTRATION
5-27 #1–2

PETER PAN HAT

Recommended age: 5 and older

WHAT YOU NEED:
- Illustration 5–30 "Peter Pan Hat" (page 154)
- Copier paper or copier card stock (white or green) ✤
- One 20" length of elastic cord (or one 20" length of yarn)
- Scissors (child-safe)
- Hole punch
- Transparent tape

✤ Card stock works better for this project.

WHAT YOU DO:
Before the party:
1. Photocopy Illustration 5–30 "Peter Pan Hat" onto copier paper or card stock.

2. If using copier paper, reinforce holes with transparent tape before punching holes.

During the party:
3. Color hat and feather, if desired.
4. Cut out hat and feather.
5. Bring two ends of hat together and staple into cone shape (Illustration 5–29 #1)
6. Staple feather to hat.
7. Punch two holes in hat, as marked on illustration.
8. Tie one end of elastic cord through one hole in hat.
9. Thread other end of cord through other hole in hat and adjust length to fit child's head; then knot cord in place.

ILLUSTRATION
5-29 #1

GAMES

Select several of the games for your party from the following list. Don't feel as if you have to play all of them—there just isn't time. But you should plan for a few extra games. Here are some unique games for your Pirate Party.

PIN THE "X" ON THE TREASURE MAP

Recommended age: 3 years and older

WHAT YOU NEED:
- Illustration 5–32 "X" (page 153)
- Copier paper (white)
- One sheet of 22" x 28" lightweight poster board or butcher paper (white)
- Masking tape or double-stick tape
- Pencil
- Wide-tipped, felt marker or crayon (black)
- Blindfold

HOW TO PLAY:
Before the party:
1. Photocopy Illustration 5–32 "X" onto copier paper (one for each child), and cut out each "X".
2. With black marker or crayon, draw a "treasure map" on poster board or butcher paper.
3. Using Illustration 5–32 as a pattern, trace an "X" on the map to mark location of the treasure, and where children need to pin their "X".

During the party:
4. Place "treasure map" on one side of game area and have children line up (single file), at least five feet away.
5. Write each child's name on the front of the "X" and place a piece of double-stick tape or masking tape rolled on itself on back of "X".
6. Blindfold first player in line (birthday child) and turn child 2–3 times. Then hand child his/her "X" and tell him/her to place the "X" on top of the "X-Marks-the-Spot" on the map.

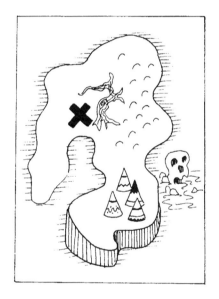

WALK THE PLANK

Recommend age: 3 years and older

WHAT YOU NEED:
- One piece of wood 1" x 6" x 8' (knotty pine)
- Blindfold ✤
- Book ✤

✤ Optional

HOW TO PLAY:

During the party:

1. Place piece of wood on the ground (open lawn area is best) and tell children that the wood is a "Pirate's Plank," and that they must walk from one end to the other, and back again, without falling into the "water," which is full of crocodiles and sharks!

2. Have birthday child start game by standing at one end of plank and have other children line up around plank—at least 3 feet away.

3. Tell children to act like sharks and crocodiles, growling and snapping at the plank-walker. They can't touch the plank-walker, but they can try to scare him/her into falling into the "water."

4. Let everyone have a chance to "Walk the Plank."

5. To increase the challenge and fun for older groups, try these variations:
   Ages 5–7:   Blindfold plank-walkers
   Ages 8 and older: Blindfold plank-walkers and/or balance a book on their heads

RAID THE PIRATE SHIP

Recommended age: 5 years and older

WHAT YOU NEED:
- Balloons (inflated)
- String or bag of flour

HOW TO PLAY:

1. Draw a line down middle of play area using string or by dripping a line of flour.

2. Divide children into two groups on opposite sides of the line.

3. Place an equal number of balloons on each side, at least one balloon per child.

4. Tell children that they are members of two different pirate crews, each with a "bounty" of treasures, as represented by balloons.

5. The object is to raid the other pirates' treasures by crossing into the other pirates' territory and take treasures (balloons) to their own side, or "ship."

6. The trick is, no one can use their hands. Pirates must take their treasure by using only their feet. (Have adults monitor the game and "remind" players to use only their feet.)
7. Tell pirates that they have five minutes to "raid." The team with the most balloons at end of game, wins.

PIRATE COVE

Recommended age: 5 years and older

WHAT YOU NEED:
- Chairs (one less than the number of players)

HOW TO PLAY:
1. Place chairs throughout game area (outside yards work best).
2. Select one player (birthday child first) to be "It," and ask rest of children to sit on chairs.
3. Explain to children that "It" is a pirate ship, looking for a pirate cove or a safe place to anchor. The other children are also pirate ships, who have found a pirate cove (the chairs) and are safely anchored.
4. "It" then goes from cove to cove and says, "Can I anchor my ship?" The cove says, "No!", and "It" goes to another cove, asking the same question, and getting the same response.
5. At any point during his/her turn, "It" can say, "All ships out!" When he/she does, everyone must get off their chair and find another cove. During the scramble, "It" tries to find his/her own cove (sit on a chair). The child left without a cove (chair) after all are seated, is "It" for the next round.

TICK-TOCK FIND THE CROC

Recommended age: 2–5 years of age

WHAT YOU NEED:
- Kitchen timer

HOW TO PLAY:
1. Take children away from game area for a few minutes while someone hides a kitchen timer in the game area. (Make sure you wind up timer before hiding it.)
2. Bring children into game area and tell them a crocodile is hiding somewhere. Fortunately, that crocodile has swallowed a clock and the only way anyone can find him is by listening for the "tick-tock" of the croc's clock. (Children must be very quiet so they can hear the clock.)
3. Whoever finds the clock gets to hide it in the next round.

CAPTAIN HOOK'S TREASURE MAP

Recommended age: 6 years and older

In this game, children use a map to find a treasure that has been hidden. Treasure can be a bag of candy (enough for everyone) or a box containing all of the loot bags for your guests.

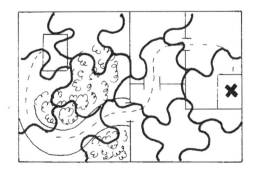

WHAT YOU NEED:
- One 9" x 12" (or larger) sheet of construction paper or lightweight poster board (bright colors)
- Treasure (object to be found)
- Transparent tape
- Scissors
- Felt marker or crayon (black)

HOW TO PLAY:
Before the party:
1. Decide where you will hide the treasure. Pick a hard-to-find location outside the immediate party area.
2. Using a marker or crayon and construction paper or poster board, draw a map showing where the treasure is located. Use obvious landmarks on the map to help orient players to the "lay of the land."
3. Then cut map into a puzzle of at least 10 different shapes.
4. Hide the treasure in secret location, then hide pieces of puzzle in different locations throughout game area. (Pieces should be visible, but not obvious.)

During the party:
5. To start game, tell children that there is a treasure hidden in a secret location, and that a map of the location has been scattered around the party area. Only by finding that map, and putting it together, can they ever hope to find the buried treasure.
6. Provide children with a work surface (party table), and a roll of transparent tape, so they can assemble their treasure map. Emphasize team effort.
7. Once puzzle has been taped together, and location of treasure has been determined, the entire group can follow the map and claim their treasure.

MORE GAMES...

It's always a good idea to plan some extra party games. Here are some standard party games, adapted for your Pirate Party. Specific directions for these games are listed in **APPENDIX D: GAMES**, beginning on page 363.

↻ FEED THE SHARK

Recommended age: 3 years and older

Follow the directions for "Bean Bag Toss" in **GAMES** (page 364). Use "Shark Photo Backdrop" (page 271) as theme backdrop. Turn bean bags into a fish by drawing "eyes" and a "mouth" on each bag with black ink marker.

PIRATE TREASURE MEMORY GAME

Recommended age: 8 years and older

Follow the directions for "Memory Game" in **GAMES** (page 367), using pirate toys and small treasures as objects for the game.

PIRATE'S SEARCH FOR THE BURIED TREASURE

Recommended age: 3 years and older

Follow the directions for "Searching for Buried Treasure" in **GAMES** (page 369), using shiny pennies as objects for the game.

SAVE PETER PAN/TIGER LILLY FROM CAPTAIN HOOK

Recommended age: 5 years and older

Follow the directions for "Save the Prince/Princess from the Dragon" in **GAMES** (page 369), using Peter Pan characters for the theme.

DROP THE COINS IN THE BOTTLE

Recommended age: 4 years and older

Follow the directions for "Drop the Clothespins in the Bottle" in **GAMES** (page 365), using shiny pennies as the object for the game. (To learn how to shine up old pennies, see "The Extra Touch" on page 370.)

CATCH THE CROC BY THE TAIL

Recommended age: 5 years and older

Follow the directions for "Catch the Tail" in **GAMES** (page 365), using a crocodile as the theme animal.

PIRATE COSTUME RELAY RACE

Recommended age: 6 years and older

Follow the directions for "Quick Change Relay Race" in **GAMES** (page 368), using colorful striped clothes, scarves, black hats, eye patches, and other clothing that suggest pirate outfits.

ILLUSTRATION 5-03

148   HIT OF THE PARTY

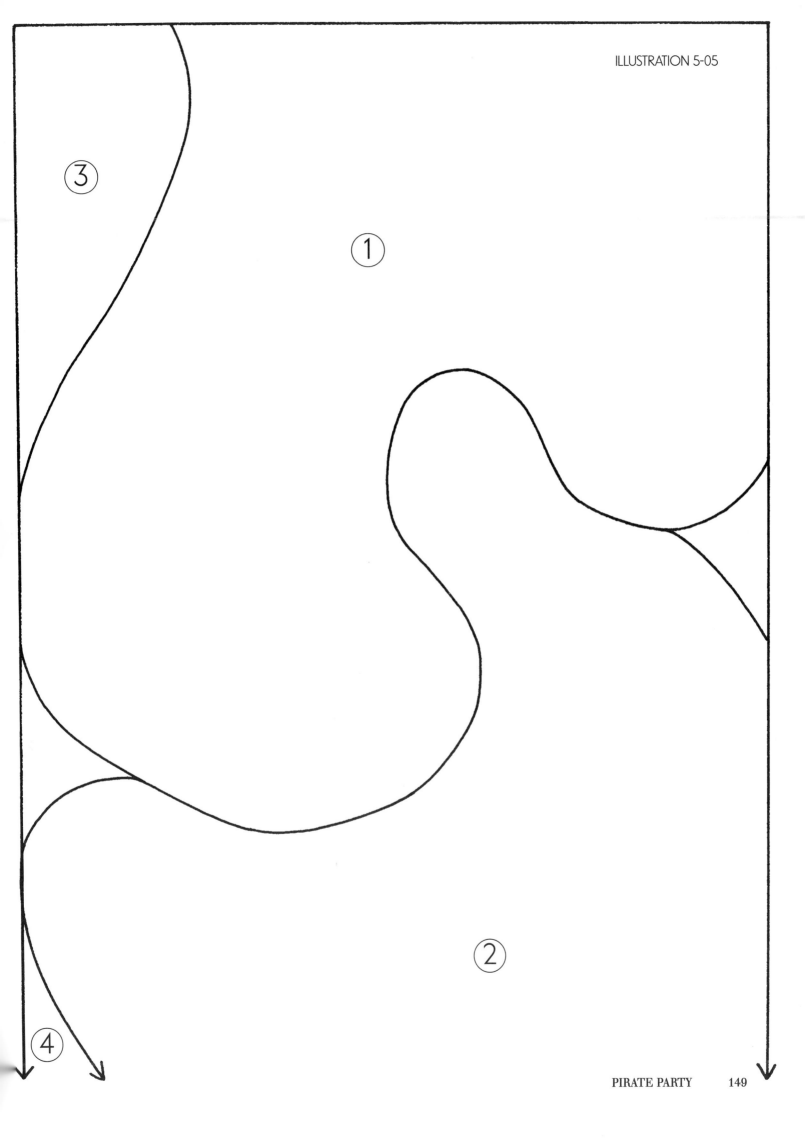

ILLUSTRATION 5-05

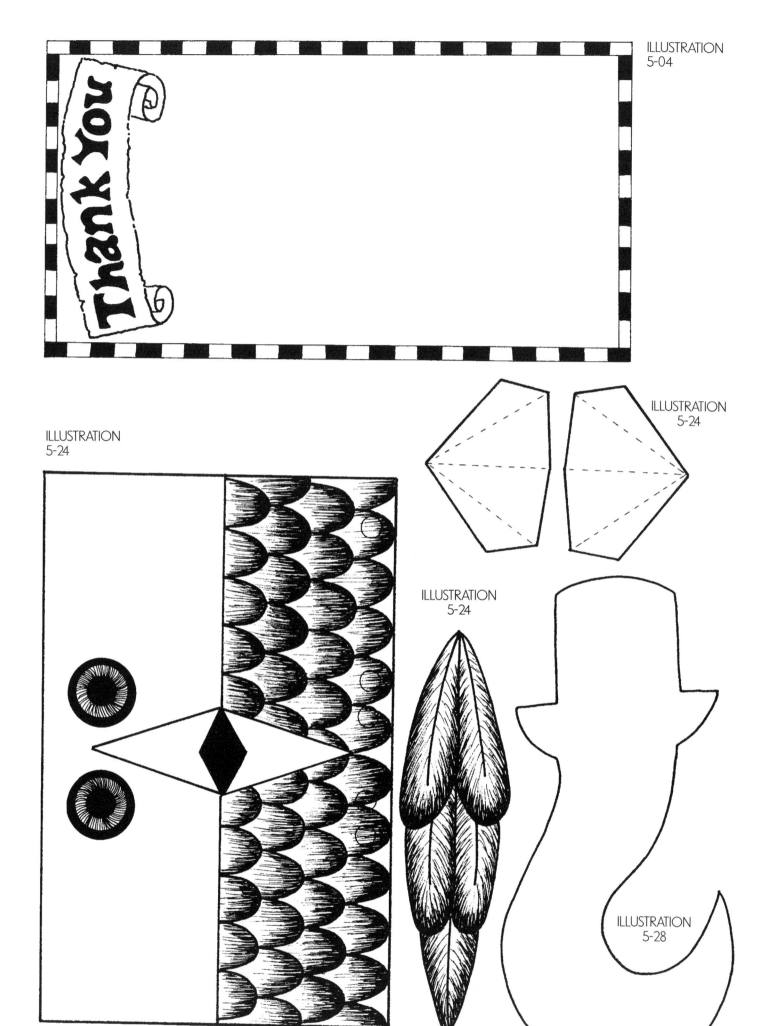

ILLUSTRATION
5-04

ILLUSTRATION
5-24

ILLUSTRATION
5-24

ILLUSTRATION
5-24

ILLUSTRATION
5-28

ILLUSTRATION
5-22

ILLUSTRATION
5-26

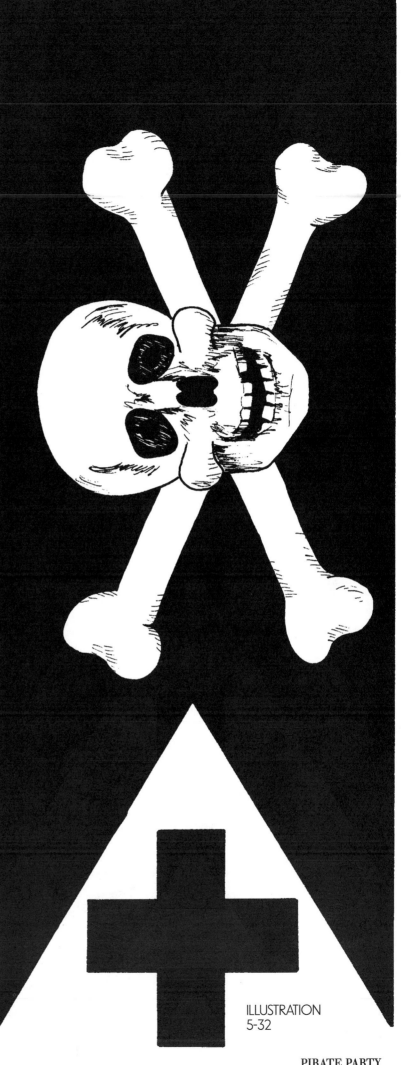

ILLUSTRATION
5-20

ILLUSTRATION
5-12

ILLUSTRATION 5-09

ILLUSTRATION
5-32

PIRATE PARTY 153

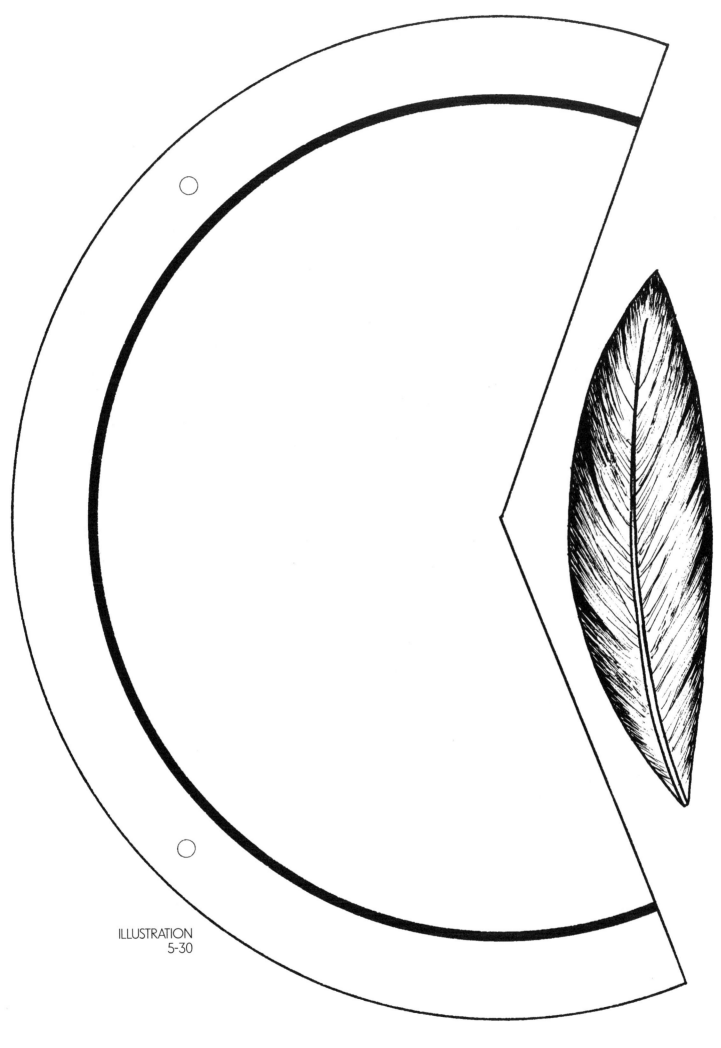

ILLUSTRATION
5-30

Dinosaur
Party

CHAPTER 6

Millions and millions of years ago, dinosaurs roamed the earth. But they have returned for a very special event. Your birthday party! Let's make them feel welcome by creating a prehistoric bash.

ILLUSTRATION 6-01

BABY DINOSAUR INVITATION

A baby dinosaur has hatched just in time to tell your friends all about your birthday celebration.

Estimated Time: 3–4 minutes each

WHAT YOU NEED:

- Illustration 6–03 "Baby Dinosaur Invitation" (page 170)
- Copier paper or copier card stock (green, purple, orange or white) ❀
- Envelopes (3 5/8" x 6 1/2")
- Scissors
- Craft knife (adult use only)
- Felt-tip pen (black)
- Crayons, markers and/or colored pencils ❀❀

❀ Card stock is preferred for this project.

❀❀ Optional

ILLUSTRATIONS 6–02

WHAT YOU DO:

1. Make one photocopy of Illustration 6–03. This is your "master copy."
   Fill out all party information with felt-tip pen on master copy (Illustration 6–02 #1).
2. Photocopy as many invitations as needed (Illustration 6–02 #2).
3. Color invitations, if desired.
4. Using craft knife, cut slit along dotted line on egg (Illustration 6–02 #3).
5. With scissors, cut out both egg and baby dinosaur (Illustration 6–02 #4).
6. Slip baby dinosaur through slit of the egg, feet first (Illustration 6–02).

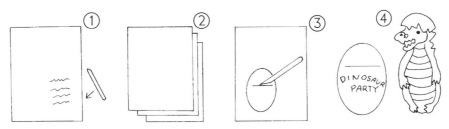

ILLUSTRATIONS 6–02 #1–4

 THE EXTRA TOUCH

- Glue "Dinosaur Stickers" (page 164) to seal envelope.

DINOSAUR THANK-YOU NOTE

The "Dinosaur Thank-You Note" (Illustration 6–04) is on the same page as the "Baby Dinosaur Invitation." When you photocopy the invitation, you will also be copying the thank-you note. Simply cut out the thank-you note, and write your personal message in the space provided.

Estimated Time: 1 minute each

MENU

Your dinosaurs will be roaring for something to eat, so treat them to some of these special treats. Choose foods from each group, and follow the recipes on the pages listed below.

DRINKS:

BRONTOSAURUS CAKE

Estimated time: 1–1 1/2 hours

Long ago, the brontosaurus was as big as ten elephants! It takes a mighty hungry crowd to eat a whole brontosaurus, but no doubt your bunch can.

INGREDIENTS:

1   "Basic Cake" recipe in Appendix A, on pages 343 and 344; or use your favorite box cake mix
2   "Buttercream Frosting" recipes in Appendix A, on page 345; or use 2 cans of your favorite canned frosting
10   Orange wedges
12   Candy corns
1   Marshmallow (cut in half)
1   Licorice whip or twist (red)
1/2 c. Candy-coated chocolates
     Green food coloring
     13" x 18" tray or foil-covered board
     Illustration 6–05 "Brontosaurus Cake Pattern" (page 171)

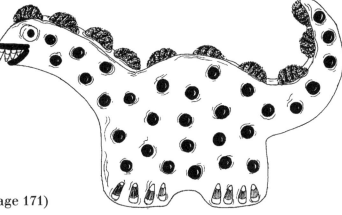

ILLUSTRATION 6-06

DIRECTIONS:

1. Prepare and bake cake in one 9" x 13" cake pan as directed in recipe or cake package.
2. Cool cake completely on wire rack.
3. Wrap in plastic wrap and freeze cake at least 45 minutes. (Freezing the cake does not affect its flavor and makes it easier to work with. It also enables you to make the cake ahead of time, to help balance your work load for the party.)
4. Trace Illustration 6–05 "Brontosaurus Cake Pattern" on wax paper. Extend lines 1" on cake pattern where arrows indicate.
5. Cut out wax paper pattern into sections and reassemble on top of cake.
6. Using long knife, cut cake into sections by following pattern (Illustration 6–06 #1).
7. Assemble sections on tray into shape of brontosaurus (Illustration 6–06 #2).
8. In a bowl, tint frosting green by adding a few drops of food coloring and mix until color is uniform.
9. Frost connecting sections of cake with green frosting.
10. Frost sides and top of entire cake with green frosting.
11. Push orange wedges into "top" of brontosaurus as shown in Illustration 6–06.

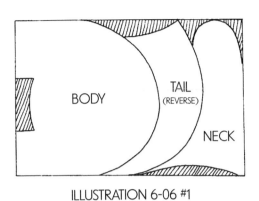

ILLUSTRATION 6-06 #1

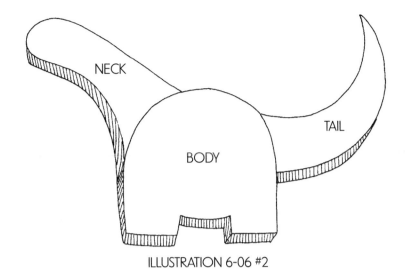

ILLUSTRATION 6-06 #2

12. Cut 2 pieces of licorice, each approximately 2" in length, and place on face to form outline of mouth or "lips."
13. Push 4 candy corns into mouth to form "teeth."
14. Place marshmallow half on face to form "eyeball."
15. Place one candy-coated chocolate into center of marshmallow "eyeball," using dab of frosting to hold in place.
16. Push 4 candy corns at base of each foot to form "claws."
17. Dot body of brontosaurus with rest of candy-coated chocolates.

PREHISTORIC CAKE

Estimated Time: 20–30 minutes

INGREDIENTS:
1	Frosted store-bought cake (round or rectangular) ❀ Dinosaur cookies or plastic toy dinosaurs (at least 1 for each child)
1 bunch	Mint leaves
13 oz.	Chocolate-covered malt balls and/or gumdrops
1 c.	Flaked coconut Food coloring (green)

❀ without decorative flowers or trim

ILLUSTRATION 6-07

DIRECTIONS:
1. Place frosted cake on a plate or serving platter.
2. Mix flaked coconut with a few drops of green food coloring in a bowl. Sprinkle tinted coconut on top of cake to make the "grass."
3. Press dinosaur cookies or plastic toy dinosaurs, standing up, into top of cake, forming groups of animals in a "prehistoric scene."
4. Use mint leaves to create "trees" and "bushes" around dinosaurs.
5. Gumdrops and malt balls can be used for "rocks" and "boulders."
6. Trim bottom of cake with gumdrops or malt balls (Illustration 6–07).

👉 THE EXTRA TOUCH
- Add "palm trees" and/or "mountains." See "Treasure Island Cake" (page 132).
- Drip red frosting on top of "mountains" to suggest erupting volcanoes.

DECORATIONS

Make your dinosaurs feel at home with a few of these easy-to-make decorations. Save money by using some of these decorations as favors in your loot bags.

PARTY STREAMERS

Estimated time: 1–2 minutes per streamer

Select one (or more) of the streamers suggested below, and follow the directions for "Party Streamers" in **CRAFT TIPS** (page 349).

- **Leaf Streamer** Pattern CT-06 (page 362)
  Use green crepé paper.
- **Flower Streamer** Pattern CT-01 (page 361)
  Use bright colored crepé paper.

 TIMESAVER

- Hang crepé paper streamers (in pre-packaged rolls) around party area.

FLYING PTERODACTYL

Estimated time: 3–4 minutes each

Hang these prehistoric pterodactyls in party area, or tie to children's wrists and watch their delight as the pterodactyls take wing.

WHAT YOU NEED:

- Illustration 6–09 "Flying Pterodactyl" (page 172)
- Copier paper or copier card stock (white or bright colors)
- Scissors
- Hole punch
- String (30" length)
- Crayons, colored pencils, and/or markers ❁

❁ Optional

ILLUSTRATION 6-08

ILLUSTRATION 6-08 #1

WHAT YOU DO:

1. Photocopy Illustration 6–09 onto copier paper or card stock.
2. Color pterodactyl, if desired.
3. Cut out pterodactyl.
4. Fold pterodactyl in half, along dotted line.
5. Punch hole on the outside of each wing, as marked on Illustration 6-09.
6. Tie string to each wing and hang in party area.

 THE EXTRA TOUCH

- Fasten pterodactyl to child's wrist as a take-home party favor by following these steps:
  1. Punch out inner holes of pterodactyl and loop 8" length elastic cord through holes (Illustration 6–08 #1).
  2. Tie two ends of cord together, adjusting length to fit child's wrist.
  3. As children raise and lower their wrist, pet pterodactyl will actually "fly."

BRONTOSAURUS STRAWS

Estimated time: 1–2 minutes each

Care to share a drink with a thirsty brontosaurus? Use Illustration 6–11 "Brontosaurus" (page 170) and follow directions for "Drinking Straws" in **CRAFT TIPS** (page 353).

BRONTOSAURUS SUCKERS

Estimated time: 1–2 minutes each

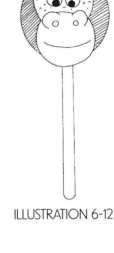

ILLUSTRATION 6-12

Make your own "Brontosaurus Suckers." Use Illustration 6–11 "Brontosaurus" (page 170) and follow directions for "Party Suckers" in **CRAFT TIPS** (page 353).

💡 MORE DECORATING IDEAS...

- Make placemats by photocopying illustration 6-24 "Triceratops Hat" (page 175) onto copier paper (white or bright colors). Provide crayons for children to color placemats, if desired.
- Make placemats by having children glue "Dinosaur Stickers" (page 164) onto 9" x 12" sheet of construction paper. Provide crayons, markers and/or colored pencils for children to color placemats, if desired.

ILLUSTRATION 6-10

- Place toy dinosaurs in center of table with some potted house plants.
- Add a model of a volcano as part of your table arrangement.
- Cut out "Dinosaur Stick Puppets" (page 164) and decorate party table, walls or make a mobile in and around party area.
- Cover party table with butcher paper and make dinosaur claw prints. Follow the directions for "Paw Print Tablecloth" in **CRAFT TIPS** (page 353).
- Make your own "Dinosaur Egg Balloons." Using one balloon for each child, and one small, plastic dinosaur per balloon, stretch balloon and then drop toy dinosaur inside (Illustration 6–13 #1).

ILLUSTRATION 6-13 # 1

ILLUSTRATION 6-13 #2

Inflate balloon and knot at end. With felt-tipped marker (black), draw "crack" lines on balloon with marker (Illustration 6–13 #2). Tie string or ribbon to balloon and hang as a decoration during party and later give to children as a favor.

- Photocopy "Brontosaurus Cake" illustration 6-01 (page 156) and tape on front door or front of party area to greet guests.

LOOT BAGS

Select one (or more) of the following loot bags and follow the directions for "Loot Bags" in **CRAFT TIPS** (page 350).

- **Sticker Bag** (page 350)
  Use illustration 6-19 "Dinosaur Stickers" (page 173).
- **Treasure Box** (page 351)
  Use illustration 6-19 "Dinosaur Stickers" (page 173).
- **Mask Bag** (page 351)
  Use illustration 6-24 "Triceratops Mask" (page 175).

LOOT BAG "LOOT"

Looking for something to put in those loot bags? Here are some creative suggestions you can make, or if you are short of time, you can buy.

LOOT YOU CAN MAKE:
- **Dinosaur Stickers** (page 164)
- **Brontosaurus Straws** (page 161)
- **Brontosaurus Suckers** (page 161)
- **Dinosaur Polaroid® Photo Frame** (page 163)
- **Dinosaur Claws** (page 165)
- **Dinosaur Eggs** (in "Dinosaur Egg Hunt" page 168)
- **Dino-Snout** (page 166)
- **Cave Man Mix** (page 333)
- **Cookie Puppets** (page 329) Use dinosaur cookie cutter.
- **Dino-Critters** (page 331)
- **Caramel Corn Boulders** (page 333)

LOOT YOU CAN BUY:
- Plastic toy dinosaurs
- Small books about dinosaurs
- Dinosaur stickers
- Dinosaur rubber stamps
- Dinosaur pencil sharpeners
- Dinosaur cookie cutters
- Inflatable dinosaurs
- Stuffed dinosaurs
- Dinosaur-shaped fruit candies
- Dinosaur graham crackers

ACTIVITIES

How about having some fun with all those dinosaurs?

Don't feel as if you have to do all of these activities—there isn't enough time at any party. Discuss with your child which ones he or she would like do and plan your party activities accordingly.

ARRIVAL ACTIVITY

As each child arrives, let him/her pick a special name, such as "Brontosaurus Barry," "Sandy Stegosaurus," "Tommy the Pterodactyl," and the like. Announce their name with a little fanfare.

PREHISTORIC CAVE

Recommended age: 2 and older

WHAT YOU NEED:
- Blankets
- Duct tape or cloth-backed masking tape
- Card table or dining table

WHAT YOU DO:
1. Cover table with blankets.
2. Secure blankets in place with tape to form opening to cave (Illustration 6–16).

THE EXTRA TOUCH
- Place potted house plants around cave to suggest prehistoric foliage.
- If you want to lengthen cave, add more tables and/or chairs.

ILLUSTRATION 6-16

⟲DINO-KID PHOTO BACKDROP

Recommended for all ages

Use Illustration 6–17 "Dino-Kid Photo Backdrop Pattern" and follow the directions for "Photo Backdrop" in **CRAFT TIPS** (page 354) to give children and their parents the best party favor they can have—a memorable "Dino-Kid Snapshot." You can take a Polaroid® photograph and hand it out at the party (see "Polaroid® Photo Frame below), or you can use a 35 mm camera and send a photo along with your thank-you note.

ILLUSTRATION 6-17

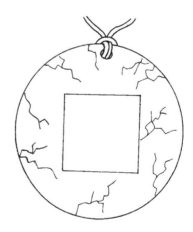

ILLUSTRATION 6-18

DINOSAUR POLAROID® PHOTO FRAME

Recommended for all ages

Hand out these wonderful memories at the party by using a Polaroid® photo and follow the directions for "Polaroid® Photo Frame" in **CRAFT TIPS** (page 357).

THE EXTRA TOUCH
- Color frame with crayons, markers and/or colored pencils.
- Decorate with dinosaur rubber stamps.
- Photocopy illustration 6-19 "Dinosaur Stickers" (page 173). Reduce to half-size, then cut out and glue on frame.
- Draw crack lines on frame to look like a dinosaur egg (Illustration 6-18).

CRAFTS

Children will have fun making these crafts as a group activity during the party or you can make these crafts yourself ahead of time and save money on party favors. Select one or two of the crafts for your party from the following list.

DINOSAUR STICKERS

Recommended age: 3 and older for gluing
5 and older for cutting and gluing

Make your own party stickers for children to use in various crafts and activities in this chapter. Use Illustration 6–19 "Dinosaur Stickers" (page 173) and follow directions for "Party Stickers" in **CRAFT TIPS** (page 352).

EDIBLE DOUGH DINOSAURS

Recommended age: 4 and older

WHAT YOU NEED:

- 1 recipe of "Edible Dough," in **RECIPES** page 331 (makes 6 servings)
- 9" paper plates
- 1 cupcake tin or 4–6 small bowls
- Dinosaur cookie cutters and rolling pin ❀
- Raisins, nuts, small candies and/or cereal

_____
❀ Optional

WHAT YOU DO:

Before the party:
1. Place raisins, nuts, small candies and/or cereal in cupcake tin or small bowls.
2. Divide "Edible Dough" into equal portions for each guest.

During the party:
3. Have children sit at a table or work area and give each child his/her own paper plate and lump of "Edible Dough."
4. Place cupcake tin or small bowls within easy reach of each child.
5. Sculpt dough into dinosaur shapes or roll out and cut out dinosaur shapes with cookie cutters.
6. Tell children to create their own dinosaur(s) with their dough, using raisins, nuts, small candies and cereal to form "eyes," "horns," "scales," "claws," "mouths," etc.
7. After children have created their dinosaurs, they can eat them!

DINOSAUR STICK PUPPETS

Recommended age: 5 and older

WHAT YOU NEED:

- Illustrations 6–22 "Dinosaur Stick Puppets" (page 174)
- Scissors (child-safe)
- Copier paper (bright colors) or copier card stock ❀
- Craft sticks or drinking straws
- Transparent tape
- Colored pencils, crayons and/or markers ❀❀

_____
❀ Card stock is preferred for this project.

❀❀ Optional

WHAT YOU DO:

Before the party:

1. Photocopy illustration 6-22 "Stick Puppets" onto copier paper or card stock.

During the party:

2. Color stick puppets, if desired.
3. Cut out stick puppets.
4. Tape stick or straw to back of puppet.

TRICERATOPS HAT OR MASK

Recommended age: 5 and older

WHAT YOU NEED:

- Illustration 6–24 "Triceratops" (page 175)
- Copier paper or copier card stock (white or bright colors) ❀
- One 14" length of elastic cord (or one 14" length of yarn)
- Scissors (child-safe)
- Craft knife (adult use only)
- Hole punch
- Markers, crayons and/or colored pencils ❀❀
- Transparent tape ❀❀

❀ Card stock is preferred for this project.

❀❀ Optional

WHAT YOU DO:

Before the party:

1. Photocopy Illustration 6–24 onto copier paper or card stock.
2. Using craft knife, cut along dotted lines on horns.
3. If using a copier paper, reinforce holes with transparent tape before punching holes.

During the party:

4. Color hat, if desired.
5. Cut out hat with scissors.
6. Bend out horns.
7. Punch holes in both sides of hat, as marked on illustration.
8. Tie one end of elastic cord through one hole in hat.
9. Thread other end of cord through other hole in hat and adjust length to fit child's head; then knot cord in place.
10. Using craft knife, carefully cut out eyes.

DINOSAUR CLAWS

Recommended age: 5 and older

WHAT YOU NEED:

- Illustration 6–26 "Dinosaur Claws" (page 176)
- Copier card stock (white, green or bright colors)
- Two 7" lengths of elastic cord (or two 7" lengths of yarn)
- Scissors (child-safe)
- Hole punch
- Transparent tape ❀

❀ Optional

WHAT YOU DO:

Before the party:

1. Photocopy Illustration 6–26 onto card stock.

During the party:

2. Cut out claws.
3. Punch holes in claws, as marked on the illustration.

4. Tie one end of elastic cord through one hole in each claw.
5. Thread other end of cord through other hole in each claw and adjust length to fit child's hand; then knot cord in place (Illustration 6-25 #1).

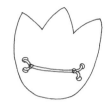

ILLUSTRATION 6-25 #1

DINO-SNOUT

Recommended age: 6 and older

WHAT YOU NEED:
- Illustration 6–28 "Dino-Snout" (page 174)
- Copier paper or copier card stock (white or green) ❀
- Scissors (child-safe)
- Stapler
- Hole punch
- One 20" length of elastic cord (or one 20" length of yarn)
- Transparent tape ❀❀
- Markers, crayons, and/or colored pencils ❀❀

❀ Card stock is preferred for this project.

❀❀ Optional

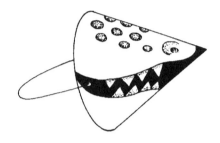

WHAT YOU DO:
Before the party:
1. Photocopy Illustration 6–28 onto copier card stock.
2. If using copier paper, reinforce holes with transparent tape before punching holes.

During the party:
3. Color snout, if desired.
4. Cut out snout (6–27 #1).
5. Bend and staple to form cone shape of snout (Illustration 6–27 #2).
6. Punch holes in snout, as marked on illustration.
7. Tie one end of elastic cord through one hole in snout.
8. Thread other end of cord through other hole in snout and adjust length to fit child's head; then knot cord in place.

6-27 #1

6-27 #2

GAMES

Select several of the games for your party from the following list. Don't feel as if you have to play all of them—there just isn't time. But you should plan a few extra games. Here are some unique games for your Dinosaur Party.

⟳ CAVEMAN BASH PIÑATA

Recommended age: 3 years and older

WHAT YOU NEED:
- 1 large paper grocery bag
- 1 full sheet of newspaper
- Long rope or cord (minimum of 18'–20')
- Scissors
- White glue
- String
- Poster paint (gray)
- Plastic foam meat tray or pie tin
- Sponge
- Prizes (wrapped candy, peanuts in a shell, small boxes of raisins, small dinosaur toys)

WHAT YOU DO:

1. Tear newspaper into pieces and crumple into small wads.
2. Crumple paper bag.
3. Open paper bag and fill with prizes and pieces of newspaper.
4. Gather top of bag together and tie string around "neck" of bag.
5. Pour poster paint into tray or pie tin.
6. Dip sponge in paint and blot pattern on boulder.
7. Tie one end of long rope around neck or top of the boulder, and loop other end over a tree limb, beam or other support.
8. Pull on rope to make piñata move up and down as children try to hit it.
9. For more suggestions and safety tips, see "Piñata Fun" in **GAMES** (page 368).

PIN THE DINOSAURS IN THE PREHISTORIC LAND

Recommended age: 3 years and older

WHAT YOU NEED:

- Illustration 6–19 "Dinosaur Stickers" (page 173)
- Copier paper or copier card stock (white)
- Scissors
- Butcher paper or poster board (green or white)
- Masking tape or double-stick tape
- Pencil
- Blindfold
- White glue or transparent tape
- Crayons, markers and/or colored pencils ❈

❈ Optional

HOW TO PLAY:

Before the party:

1. Photocopy Illustration 6–19 onto copier paper, so that there is at least one sticker per guest, plus one set of stickers to make the "game board."
2. Cut out one sticker for each child.
3. Cut out one set dinosaur stickers for the game board.
4. Glue or tape a complete set of dinosaur stickers on butcher paper or poster board and make your own prehistoric landscape.
5. Use crayons, markers and/or colored pencils to add vines, trees, ponds, volcanoes, rocks and other elements to your prehistoric landscape, if desired.
6. Tape butcher paper or poster board to a wall in the party area.

During the party:

7. Have children line up (single file), at least five feet away.
8. Place stickers in a bag and have each child pull out one sticker.
9. Write each child's name on the front of their dinosaur sticker and place a piece of double-stick tape or masking tape rolled on itself on back of dinosaur sticker
10. Tell children to look at the prehistoric scene and to find the dinosaur sticker that matches their sticker.
11. Blindfold first player in line (birthday child) and turn child 2–3 times. Then hand child his/her sticker and tell him/her to place the sticker on top of the matching dinosaur sticker on the "game board."
12. The winner is the player who gets their dinosaur sticker closest to its mate.

DINOSAUR EGG HUNT

Recommended age: 3 years and older

Young children always love treasure hunts. You may want to give children one of the loot bags listed below to help them gather their goods.

WHAT YOU NEED:
- Plastic eggs
- Small, plastic toy dinosaurs
- "Loot Bags" (page 162) One for each child

HOW TO PLAY:
1. Before the party, place one toy dinosaur in each egg. Then hide eggs throughout party area.
2. Have children search for their "eggs" and gather their goods in a loot bag.

↻ CAVE DWELLER RELAY RACE

Recommended age: 6 years and older

WHAT YOU NEED:
- 2 empty soda bottles (1 or 2 liter size)
- 2 wooden dowels (1/2" in diameter and approximately 30" in length)
- Duct tape or cloth-backed adhesive tape
- Newspaper (4–8 sheets)
- 4 brown paper lunch bags
- Wide-tipped, felt marker (black)
- String or bag of flour

HOW TO PLAY:
Before the party:
1. Make "prehistoric boulders" by crumpling newspaper and stuffing 1–2 sheets into each lunch bag.
2. Fold top of lunch bag over and tape bag closed with duct tape (Illustration 6–31 #1).
   [NOTE: Even though game calls for only 2 bags or "boulders" per team, have extra bags on hand, just in case your cave dwellers get a little carried away.]
3. Using felt-tip pen, make distinguishing marks on boulders for each team, e.g., small circles for one team and small "x's" for the other team.
4. Make the cave dweller "club" by placing one dowel in each soda bottle and taping dowel in place (Illustration 6–31 #2).
5. Set up an obstacle course in party area, using boxes, chairs, bushes, trees, etc.
6. Mark course with string or by dripping flour from bag.

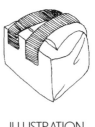

ILLUSTRATION
6-31 #1

During the party:
7. Divide children into two teams.
8. Line up both teams at start/finish line.
9. To start game, first player from each team uses the "club" to knock his/her team's "boulder" through obstacle course. (Remind children to hit only their own team's boulder.)
10. Each player keeps hitting their boulder through the entire course in order to complete his/her turn. The next player from each team then takes his/her turn through obstacle course.
11. The first team to finish the course, wins.

ILLUSTRATION
6-31 #2

MORE GAMES...

It's always a good idea to plan some extra party games. Here are some standard party games, adapted for your Dinosaur Party. Specific directions for these games are listed in **APPENDIX D: GAMES**, beginning on page 363.

↻ FEED THE DINOSAUR

Recommended age: 3 years and older

Follow the directions for "Bean Bag Toss" in **GAMES** (page 364). Use the "Dino-Kid Photo Backdrop" (page 163) as the theme backdrop.

DINOSAUR EXTINCTION

Recommended age: 5 years and older

Follow the directions for "Sardines" in **GAMES** (page 369), and use the extinction of the dinosaurs as the theme for playing the game.

DINOSAUR SCRAMBLE

Recommended age: 6 years and older

Follow the directions for "Animal Scramble" in **GAMES** (page 364), and use "Dinosaur Stickers" (page 164) to play the game.

DINOSAUR EGG RELAY RACE

Recommended age: 6 years and older

Follow the directions for "Egg Relay Race" in **GAMES** (page 366) and use plastic eggs (stuffed with toy dinosaurs) as the theme objects for the game.

DINOSAUR DIG

Recommended age: 3 years and older

Follow the directions for "Searching for Buried Treasure" in **GAMES** (page 369) and use toy dinosaurs as the theme objects for the game.

TYRANNOSAURUS TAG

Recommended age: 6 years and older

Follow the directions for "Tag" in **GAMES** (page 371), using the tyrannosaurus as it to play the game.

CATCH THE DINOSAUR BY THE TAIL

Recommended age: 5 years and older

Follow the directions for "Catch the Tail" in **GAMES** (page 365) and use a dinosaurs as the theme for the game.

DINOSAUR'S BUFF

Recommended age: 5 years and older

Follow the directions for "Blindman's Buff" in **GAMES** (page 364) and use the sounds of wild dinosaurs in playing the game.

ICE AGE TAG

Recommended age: 5 years and older

Follow the directions for "Freeze Tag" in **GAMES** (page 366). You may want to explain a little about the Ice Age and how it affected the dinosaurs to set the stage for the game.

DUCK, DUCK, PTERODACTYL!

Recommended age: 4 years and older

Follow the directions for "Duck, Duck, Goose" in **GAMES** (page 365) and use the pterodactyl (and other favorite dinosaurs) as the goose to play the game.

ILLUSTRATION
6-04

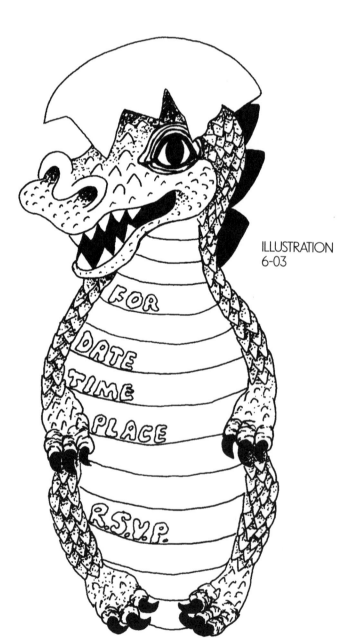

ILLUSTRATION
6-11

ILLUSTRATION
6-03

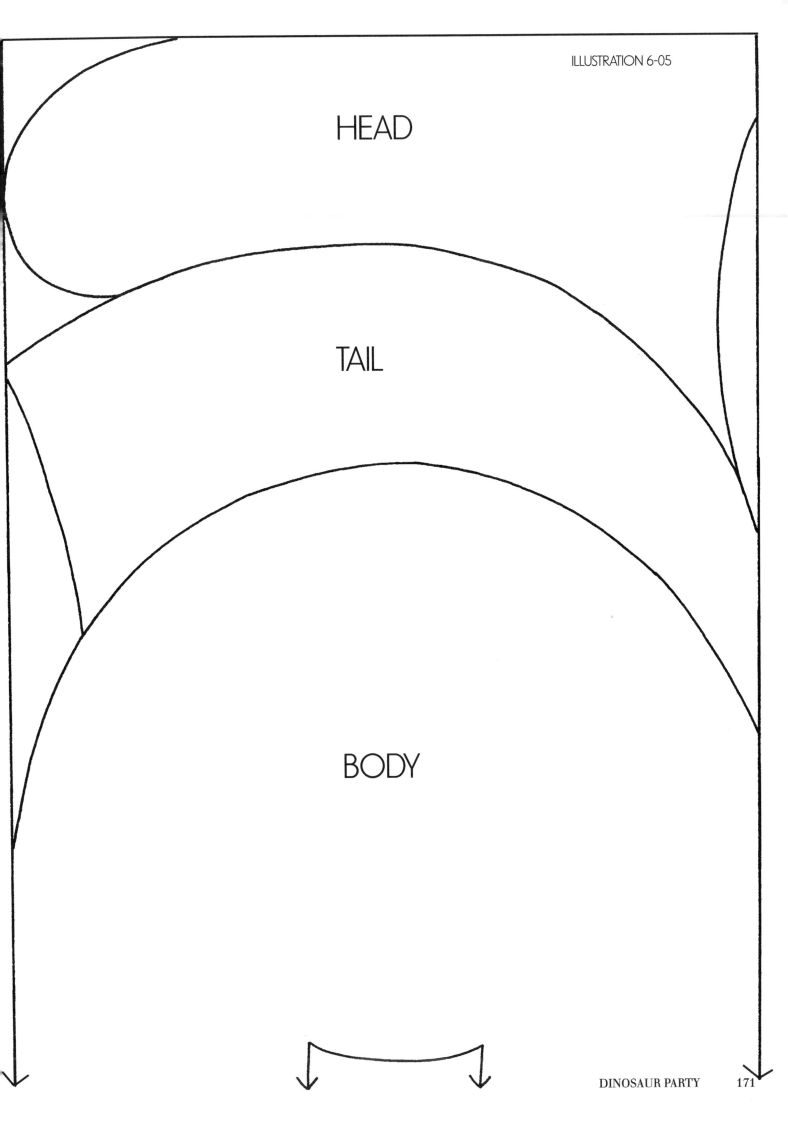

ILLUSTRATION 6-05

HEAD

TAIL

BODY

ILLUSTRATION 6-09

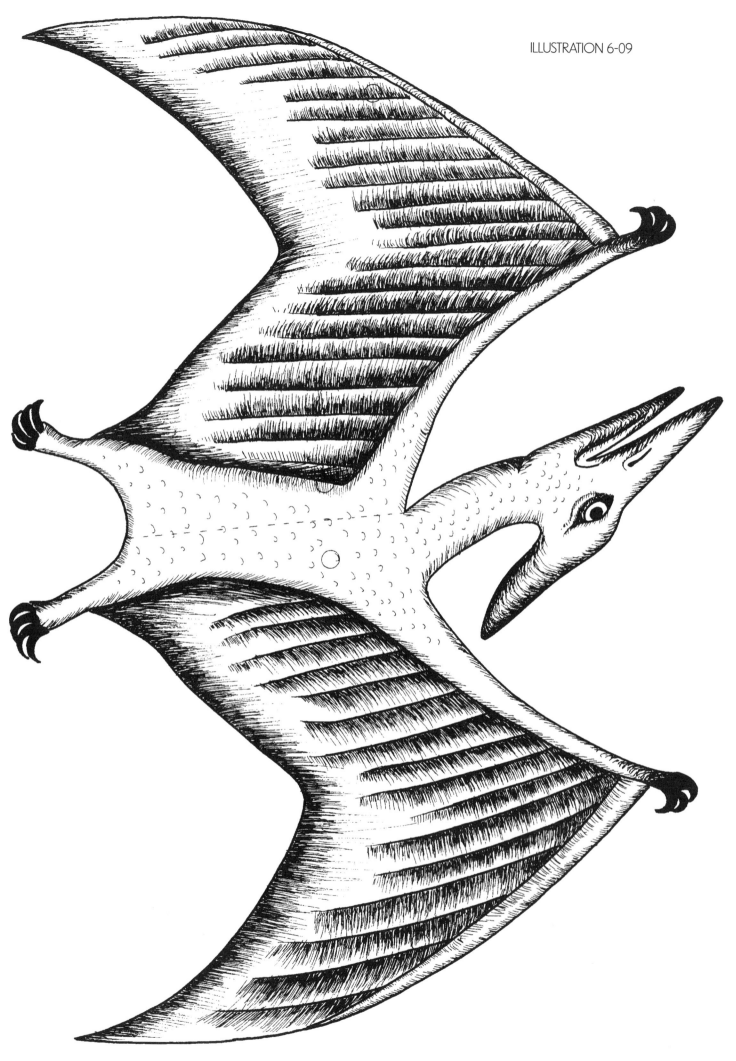

ILLUSTRATION 6-19

ILLUSTRATION 6-22

ILLUSTRATION
6-28

ILLUSTRATION 6-24

ILLUSTRATION 6-26

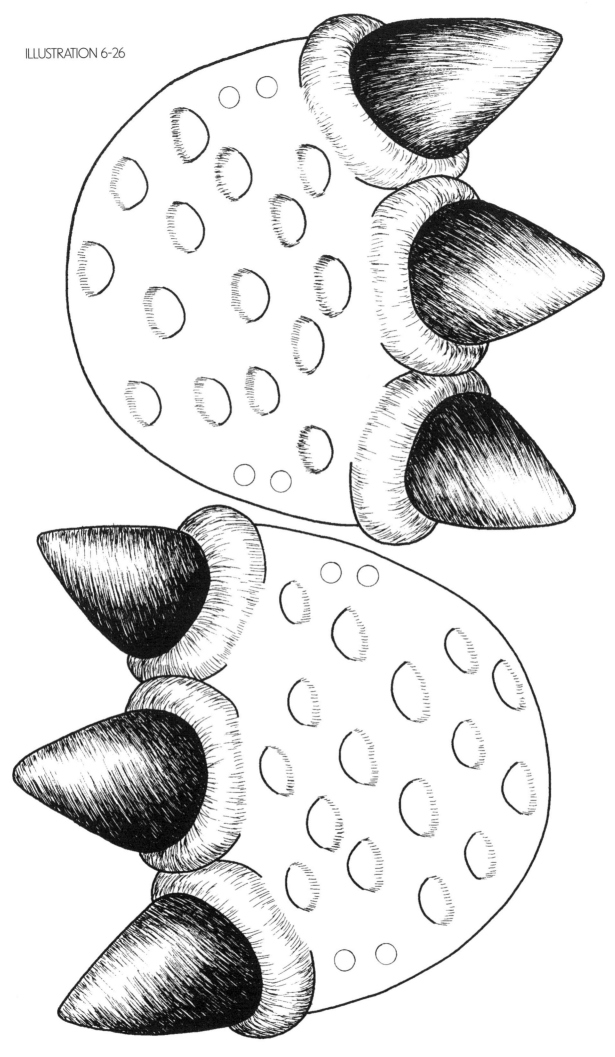

Circus Party

CHAPTER 7

Ladies and gentlemen! Boys and girls! Welcome to the "Greatest Birthday Party on Earth." The circus has come to town—just in time for your birthday! So step right this way and treat yourself to a very *special* birthday party.

ILLUSTRATION 7-01

CIRCUS INVITATION

Estimated Time: 3–4 minutes each

WHAT YOU NEED:

- Illustration 7–03 "Circus Invitation" (page 194)
- Copier paper or copier card stock (white) ❀
- Envelopes (3 5/8" x 6 1/2")
- Scissors
- Craft knife (adult use only)
- Felt-tip pen (black)
- Crayons, markers and/or colored pencils ❀❀

❀ Card stock is preferred for this project.

❀❀ Optional

WHAT YOU DO:

1. Make one photocopy of Illustration 7–03. This is your "master copy." Fill out party information with felt-tip pen on master copy (Illustration 7–02 #1).
2. Photocopy as many invitations as needed (Illustration 7–02 #2).
3. Color invitation, if desired.
4. Using craft knife, cut slit along dotted line on ball (Illustration 7–02 #3).
5. With scissors, cut out legs and clown (Illustration 7–02 #4).
6. Slip legs through slit on ball, tab side first (Illustration 7–02).

ILLUSTRATIONS 7-02

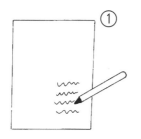

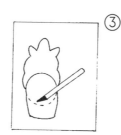
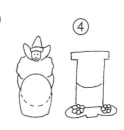

ILLUSTRATIONS 7-02 #1-4

👉 THE EXTRA TOUCH

- Glue "Clown Stickers" (page 187) to seal envelope.
- Ask children to come to party in circus costumes.

CIRCUS THANK-YOU NOTE

The "Circus Thank-You Note" (Illustration 7–04) is on the same page as the "Circus Invitation." When you photocopy the invitation, you will also be copying the thank-you note. Simply cut out the thank-you note, and write your personal message in the space provided.

Estimated Time: 1 minute each

MENU

And now, in the center ring, feast your eyes on some truly delicious delights. Choose foods from each group, and follow the recipes on the pages listed below.

DRINKS:

EATS:

CAKE AND ICE CREAM:

PINK ELEPHANT CAKE

Estimated time: 1–1 1/2 hours

INGREDIENTS:

1	"Basic Cake" recipe in Appendix A, on pages 343 and 344; or use your favorite box cake mix
2	"Buttercream Frosting" recipes in Appendix A, on page 345; or use 2 cans of your favorite canned frosting
3 c.	Flaked coconut
1	Marshmallow (cut in half)
11	Candy corns
15	Candy-coated chocolates
6	Gumdrops
1	Licorice twist (red)
	Food coloring (red)
	Food coloring (blue)
	13" x 18" tray or foil-covered board
	Illustration 7–05 "Elephant Cake Pattern" (page 195)

ILLUSTRATION 7-06

DIRECTIONS:

1. Prepare and bake cake in one 9" x 13" cake pan as directed in recipe or cake package.
2. Cool cake completely on wire rack.
3. Wrap in plastic wrap and freeze cake at least 45 minutes. (Freezing the cake does not affect its flavor and makes it easier to work with. It also enables you to make the cake ahead of time to help balance your work load for the party.)
4. Trace Illustration 7–05 "Elephant Cake Pattern" on wax paper. Extend lines 1" on cake pattern as indicated by arrows.

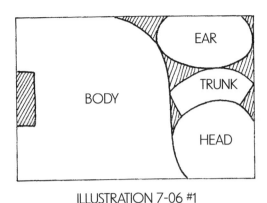

ILLUSTRATION 7-06 #1

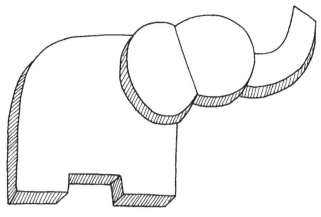

ILLUSTRATION 7-06 #2

5. Cut out wax paper pattern into sections and reassemble on top of cake.
6. Using long knife, cut cake into sections, according to pattern (Illustration 7–06 #1).
7. Assemble sections on a tray into shape of elephant (Illustration 7–06 #2).
8. Tint 1 cup plain frosting blue by mixing with a few drops of blue food coloring. Tint remaining frosting pink by adding a few drops of red food coloring. Mix until color is uniform.
9. Frost connecting sections of cake with pink frosting.
10. Spread blue frosting on top of elephant's head to form a "hat" and on the back to make a "saddle blanket" (Illustration 7–06).
11. Frost remaining sides and top of elephant with pink frosting.
12. Place coconut in bowl and tint pink by adding a few drops of red food coloring and mix until color is uniform.
13. Sprinkle pink coconut on pink areas of cake.
14. Cut 1 piece of licorice, approximately 4" in length, and push into elephant's rear to form "tail." Clip end of licorice to fray the tail.
15. Cut 1 piece of licorice, approximately 2" in length, and push into elephant's hat to form "tassel." Clip end of licorice to fray the tassel.
16. Push 1 candy corn into mouth to form "tusk."
17. Place remaining candy corns along edge of blanket and hat (Illustration 7–06).
18. Place one marshmallow half on face to form "eyeball."
19. Push one candy-coated chocolate into center of "eyeball," using dab of frosting to hold in place.
20. Push 3 gumdrops into each foot to form "toe nails."
21. Use candy-coated chocolates to decorate blanket and hat (Illustration 7–06).

CLOWN–FACE CAKE

Estimated Time: 20–30 minutes

INGREDIENTS:

1	White-frosted, store-bought cake (round) ❊
1 pkg.	Licorice twists (red)
1 1/2 c.	Gumdrops
2	Chocolate chips

❊ without decorative flowers or trim

DIRECTIONS:

1. Place frosted cake on plate or serving platter.
2. Cut licorice twists into sections, approximately 3"–5" in length.
3. Push licorice twist pieces into side of cake, forming zig-zag pattern around cake (Illustration 7–07).
4. Push 1 gumdrop into center of each pattern (Illustration 7–07).

ILLUSTRATION 7-07

5. Arrange gumdrops around top of cake to form "hair."
6. Place 1 red gumdrop in middle of cake to form "nose."
7. Use 2 chocolate chips to form "eyes."
8. Cut one 4" piece of licorice to form "mouth."
9. Cut four 1" pieces of licorice to form "eyebrows" and corners of "mouth."

DECORATIONS

Your clowns can have fun with a few of these easy-to-make decorations. Save money by using some of these decorations as favors in your loot bags.

PARTY STREAMERS

Estimated time: 1–2 minutes per streamer

Select one (or more) of the streamers suggested below, and follow the directions for "Party Streamers" in **CRAFT TIPS** (page 349).

- **Star Streamer** Pattern CT-03 (page 360)
  Use bright colors of crepé paper.
- **Triangle Streamer** Pattern CT-05 (page 361)
  Use bright colors of crepé paper.
- **Doll Streamer** Pattern CT-02 (page 359)
  Use bright colors of crepé paper.

 TIMESAVER
- Hang crepé paper streamers (in pre-packaged rolls) around party area.

FLYING TRAPEZE

Estimated time: 4–5 minutes each

This project can be completed ahead of time, or during the party as a craft activity.

WHAT YOU NEED:
- Illustration 7–09 "Flying Trapeze" (page 196)
- Copier paper or copier card stock (white or bright colors)
- Scissors
- Transparent tape
- Plastic drinking straw
- String or yarn (approximately 24" in length)
- Crayons, markers and/or colored pencils ❀
- White glue, glitter, sequins and/or feathers ❀

❀ Optional

WHAT YOU DO:
1. Photocopy Illustration 7–09 onto copier paper or card stock.
2. Color illustration, if desired.
3. Cut out illustration.
4. Decorate acrobats by gluing on glitter, feathers, and sequins, if desired.
5. Tape hands (or feet) of acrobats to straw.
6. Tie string to both ends of the straw and hang in party area.

SILLY CLOWN STRAWS

Estimated time: 1–2 minutes each

Watch the giggles as children share a drink with a silly clown. (Illustration 7-10) Use Illustration 7–11 "Silly Clown" (page 194) and follow directions for "Drinking Straws" in **CRAFT TIPS** (page 353).

CLOWN SUCKERS

Estimated time: 1–2 minutes each

Make your own "Clown Suckers." (Illustration 7-12) Use Illustration 7–11 "Silly Clown" (page 194) and follow directions for "Party Suckers" in **CRAFT TIPS** (page 353).

ILLUSTRATION 7-10

ILLUSTRATION 7-12

MORE DECORATING IDEAS...

- Hang brightly-colored balloons around party area.
- Set up a camping tent and decorate with balloons and streamers to make your own "Big Top" or stage area for "Side Shows."
- Using alternating red and white streamers, twist streamers to make a spiral pattern. Tie or tape streamers from the corners and sides of ceiling to the center of ceiling.
- Decorate party area with stuffed animals, animal posters or circus posters.
- Sprinkle confetti on top of party table.
- Cover party table with brightly-colored wrapping paper.
- Make placemats by photocopying illustration 7-26 "Clown Mask"(page 198) onto copier paper (white or bright colors). Provide crayons for children to color placemats, if desired.
- Make placemats by having children glue "Clown Stickers"(page 187) onto 9" x 12" sheet of construction paper. Provide crayons, markers and/or colored pencils for children to color placemats, if desired.
- Decorate party area with "Clown Balloons" (page 187).
- Photocopy "Pink Elephant Cake" Illustration 7-01 (page 178) and tape to front door or front of party area to greet guests.

LOOT BAGS

Select one (or more) of the following loot bags and follow the directions for "Loot Bags" in **CRAFT TIPS** (page 350).

- **Magic Bag** (page 351)
- **Mask Bag** (page 351)
  Use illustration 7-26 "Clown Mask" on page 198.
- **Sticker Bag** (page 350)
  Use illustration 7-18 "Clown Stickers" on page 196.
- **Treasure Box** (page 351)
  Use illustration 7-18 "Clown Stickers" on page 196.

LOOT BAG "LOOT"

Looking for something to put in those loot bags? Here are some creative suggestions you can make, or if you are short of time, you can buy.

LOOT YOU CAN MAKE:

- **Clown Stickers** (page 187)
- **Safari Stickers** (page 87)
- **Magic Stickers** (page 232)
- **Silly Clown Straws** (page 183)
- **Clown Suckers** (page 183)
- **Circus Polaroid® Photo Frame** (page 186)
- **Animal Snouts** (page 89)
- **Pop-Up Clown** (page 187)
- **Clown Nose** (in "Clown Costume" page 189)
- **Crunchy Circus Critters** (page 331)
- **Cookie Puppets** (page 329) Use animal cookie cutters.
- **Honey Bee Kazoo** (page 32)
- **Crunchy Caramel Corn** (page 333)

LOOT YOU CAN BUY:

- Plastic toy animals
- Small books about the circus, circus performers or circus animals
- Clown or circus animal stickers
- Clown or circus animal rubber stamps
- Clown or circus animal cookie cutters
- Clown hat
- Clown nose
- Clown face paint
- "Gags" or novelty items
- Novelty whistles, top hats and/or bow ties
- Toy musical instruments
- Note pads, pencils with clown or circus animal themes
- Animal crackers
- Roasted peanuts (in the shell)
- Crackerjacks®

ACTIVITIES

Are you ready to start "The Greatest Show on Earth?"

Don't feel as if you have to do all of these activities—there isn't enough time at any party. Discuss with your child which ones he or she would like do and plan your party activities accordingly.

ARRIVAL ACTIVITY

As each child arrives, let him/her pick a special name, such as "Ring Master Roger," "Carol the Clown," "Acrobat Annie," "Tony the Trapeze Artist," and the like. Announce each name with a little fanfare. Hand out tickets (purchased in rolls from stationery or party stores) as children enter the party or at a "Ticket Booth" (see below).

↻ACTIVITY BOOTH

Estimated time: 1 hour to make the activity booth

WHAT YOU NEED:

- 1 card table or cardboard box
- 2 "Newspaper Rolls" ❀
- Duct tape or cloth-backed adhesive tape
- Transparent tape
- Wrapping paper (bright colors)
- Butcher paper
- Wide-tipped, felt marker (black)
- Crepé paper streamers (bright colors) ❀❀
- Balloons ❀❀

❀ See "Newspaper rolls" in **CRAFT TIPS** (page 355)

❀❀ Optional

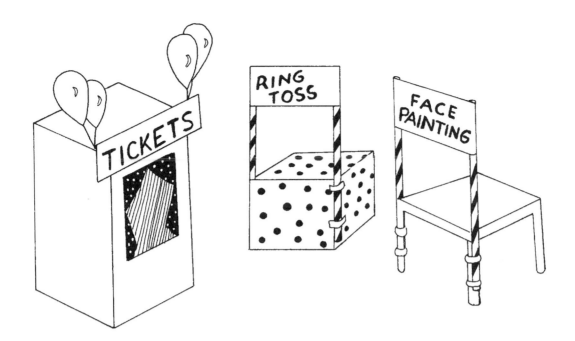

WHAT YOU DO:

1. Cover tabletop or cardboard box with wrapping paper or butcher paper. Tape paper in place.
2. Cover newspaper rolls with crepé paper and use transparent tape to keep crepé paper in place.
3. Use duct tape or cloth-backed tape to secure newspaper roll to table legs or sides of box.
4. To make a banner, cut 12"–18" wide strips of butcher paper (4"–5" longer than width of booth).
5. With marker, write name of activity booth on paper. Roll each end of banner around cardboard tube or newspaper rolls and then tape in place. (See list of "Suggested Activity Booths" below.)

 THE EXTRA TOUCH

- Decorate butcher paper using poster paint and animal or star-shaped sponges.
- Use streamers and/or balloons to add more color to your booth.
- Use a refrigerator box for a ticket booth or puppet theatre. See **CRAFT TIPS** (page 355) for tips on cutting "Cardboard Play Structures" in **CRAFT TIPS** (page 355) for additional suggestions.

💡 MORE IDEAS...

- Pass out food from "Vendor Trays," made from empty cardboard soda boxes (flats) and rope or sturdy ribbon used as shoulder straps.

SUGGESTED ACTIVITY BOOTHS

- Ticket Booth (above)
- Photos (page 186)
- Art and Crafts (page 186–190)
- Clown Bean Bag Toss (page 192)
- Circus Squirt Ball (page 192)
- Food Booth (page 180)
- Face Painting (below)
- Circus Ring Toss (page 190)
- Peanut Toss (page 190)
- Puppet Show (page 56)

CLOWN FACE PAINTING
(Non-Toxic Make-Up)

Recommended age: 3 and older

Use Illustration 7–18 "Clown Stickers" (page 196) as examples and follow the directions for "Face Painting Make-Up" in **CRAFT TIPS** (page 354).

 THE EXTRA TOUCH

- See "Animal Face Painting" (page 87) for additional face make-up ideas.

CLOWN PHOTO BACKDROP

Recommended for all ages

Use Illustration 7–19 "Clown Photo Backdrop Pattern" and follow the directions for "Photo Backdrop" in **CRAFT TIPS** (page 354) to give children and their parents the best party favor they can have—a memorable "Circus Snapshot."

You can take a Polaroid® photograph and hand it out at the party (see "Polaroid® Photo Frame below), or you can use a 35 mm camera and send a photo along with your thank-you note.

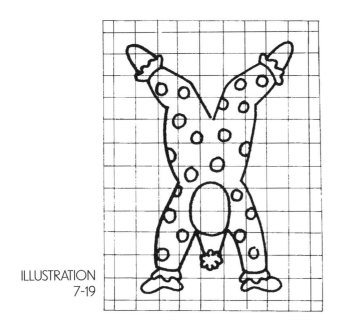

ILLUSTRATION 7-19

ILLUSTRATION 7-20

CIRCUS POLAROID® PHOTO FRAME

Recommended for all ages

Hand out these wonderful memories at the party by using a Polaroid® photo and follow the directions for "Polaroid® Photo Frame" in **CRAFT TIPS** (page 357).

☞ THE EXTRA TOUCH

- Color frames with crayons, markers and/or colored pencils.
- Glue on gummed stars, or glue and glitter (Illustration 7-20).
- Photocopy (Illustration 7-18) "Clown Stickers" (Page 196) and reduce to half size then glue to frame.

CIRCUS SHOWS

Have family and friends volunteer to perform a trick or stunt they have mastered and would enjoy sharing with children. Include a ring master to introduce these acts by "stage names," such as "Dorothy the Magnificent" or "Jolly Molly." (See "Magic Tricks," pages 229–232, for suggestions.)

CLOWN PARADE

After children have put on their clown make-up and clown costumes, have them parade around the party area. Music and noisemakers will add to the fun. See "Honey Bee Kazoo" (page 32), "Spoons" (page 115), "Wacky Harp" (page 210) or "Indian Drum" (page 116).

CRAFTS

Children will have fun making these crafts as a group activity during the party or you can make these crafts yourself ahead of time and save money on party favors. Select one or two of the crafts for your party from the following list.

CLOWN STICKERS

Recommended age: 3 and older for gluing
5 and older for cutting and gluing

Make your own party stickers for children to use in various crafts and activities in this chapter. Use Illustration 7–18 "Clown Stickers" (page 196) and follow directions for "Party Stickers" in **CRAFT TIPS** (page 352).

You could also use Illustration 9–26 "Magic Stickers" (page 241) or Illustration 3–21 "Safari Stickers" (page 101), and follow directions for "Party Stickers" in **CRAFT TIPS** (page 352).

CLOWN BALLOON

Recommended age: 5 and older

WHAT YOU NEED:
- 9" balloon (white)
- 9" paper plate
- Felt markers (black and red)
- Scissors
- White glue
- Construction paper (red)
- Yarn scraps
- String
- Sharp pencil

ILLUSTRATION
7-21

WHAT YOU DO:
Before the party:
1. Inflate balloon and tie at end.
2. Punch hole in center of plate with pencil point.
3. Pull end of balloon through hole in plate (Illustration 7–21 #1).

During the party:
4. Draw a silly clown face on balloon with markers (Illustration 7-21).
5. Cut "nose" from red construction paper and glue to balloon.
6. To make "hair," cut scraps of yarn or fringe construction paper and glue to balloon.

ILLUSTRATION
7-21 #1

👉 THE EXTRA TOUCH
- Add a collar to the clown using the "Clown Costume" (page 189); or add a "Clown Hat" (page 188).

POP-UP CLOWN

Recommended age: 5 and older

WHAT YOU NEED:
- 1 sock (toddler or preschool size)
- Paper cup (8 oz.)
- 1 drinking straw
- 4 cotton balls
- Rubberband
- Felt scraps (bright colors)
- Yarn (orange or red)
- 2 fake eyes
- Pom poms (approximately 1/2" in diameter)
- White or tacky glue
- Scissors
- Sharp pencil

ILLUSTRATION
7-22

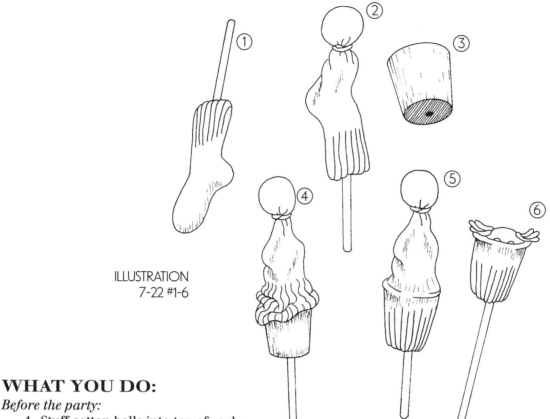

ILLUSTRATION
7-22 #1-6

WHAT YOU DO:

Before the party:

1. Stuff cotton balls into toe of sock.
2. Insert straw into toe of sock (Illustration 7–22 #1).
3. Tightly wind rubberband around toe of sock, securing straw in place (Illustration 7–22 #2).
4. With pencil, poke hole in bottom of cup at its center (Illustration 7–22 #3).
5. Push end of straw through hole in cup (Illustration 7–22 #4).
6. Slide sock over cup, and glue in place (Illustration 7–22 #5).

During the party:

7. Tie a bow around "neck" of clown with pieces of yarn (approximately 8" in length).
8. Glue on fake eyes and glue pieces of yarn for "hair."
9. Glue on pom poms for "nose" and clown's outfit.
10. Use felt scraps to make "hat," "collar," "mouth" and other details (Illustration 7–22).
11. Push and pull on straw to make puppet pop in and out (Illustration 7–22 #6).

CLOWN HAT

Recommended age: 5 and older

WHAT YOU NEED:

- Illustration 7–24 "Clown Hat" (page 197)
- Copier paper or copier card stock (white or bright colors) ❀
- One 20" length of elastic cord (or one 20" length of yarn)
- Scissors (child-safe)
- Hole punch
- Stapler
- Transparent tape
- Crayons, markers and/or colored pencils ❀❀

❀ Card stock works better for this project.

❀❀ Optional

WHAT YOU DO:

Before the party:

1. Photocopy Illustration 7–24 "Clown Hat" onto copier paper or card stock.
2. If using copier paper, reinforce holes with transparent tape before punching holes.

During the party:
3. Color hat, if desired.
4. Cut out hat.
5. Bring two ends of hat together and staple into cone shape (Illustration 7–23 #1).
6. Punch two holes in hat, as marked on illustration.
7. Tie one end of elastic cord through one hole in hat.
8. Thread other end of cord through other hole in hat and adjust length to fit child's head; then knot cord in place.

ILLUSTRATION
7-23 #1

CLOWN MASK

Recommended age: 5 and older

WHAT YOU NEED:
- Illustration 7–26 "Clown Mask" (page 198)
- Copier paper or copier card stock (white or bright colors) ✿
- One 14" length of elastic cord (or one 14" length of yarn)
- Scissors (child-safe)
- Craft knife (adult use only)
- Hole punch or sharp pencil
- Markers, crayons and/or colored pencils ✿✿
- Transparent tape ✿✿

✿ Card stock is preferred for this project.

✿✿ Optional

WHAT YOU DO:

Before the party:
1. Photocopy Illustration 7–26 onto copier paper or card stock.
2. Cut out two eye holes with craft knife.
3. If using a copier paper, reinforce holes with transparent tape before punching holes.

During the party:
4. Color mask, if desired.
5. Cut out mask.
6. Punch a hole in both sides of mask, as marked on illustration.
7. Tie one end of elastic cord through one hole in mask.
8. Thread other end of cord through other hole in mask and adjust length to fit child's head; then knot cord in place.

CLOWN COSTUME

Recommended age: 6 and older

WHAT YOU NEED:
- Illustration 7–28 "Clown Costume" (page 199)
- Copier paper or copier card stock (white or bright colors) ✿
- Scissors
- Hole punch
- One 20" length of elastic cord (or one 20" length of yarn)
- Two 12" lengths of yarn (or two 12" lengths of 1/4" ribbon)
- Transparent tape ✿✿
- Crayons, markers and/or colored pencils ✿✿

✿ Card stock is preferred for this project.

✿✿ Optional

WHAT YOU DO:

Before the party:
1. Photocopy Illustration 7–28.
2. If using a copier paper, reinforce holes with transparent tape before punching holes.

During the party:
3. Color collar and nose, if desired.
4. Cut out around collar and nose.
5. Punch holes in collar and nose, as marked on illustration.
6. Tie one end of elastic cord through one hole in nose.
7. Thread other end of cord through other hole in nose and adjust length to fit child's head; then knot cord in place.
8. Tie a 12" piece of yarn or ribbon through each hole in collar.
9. Adjust yarn ribbon to fit child's neck and tie in a bow in back.

GAMES

Select several of the games for your party from the following list. Don't feel as if you have to play all of them—there just isn't time. But you should plan for a few extra games. Here are some unique games for your Circus Party.

↻ CIRCUS RING TOSS

Recommended age: 4 years and older

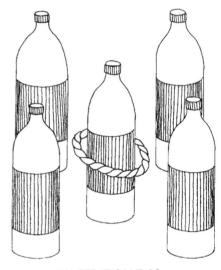

WHAT YOU NEED:
- 1 card table
- 5 soda bottles (2-liter) ❧
- 7 feet of heavy rope (1/4"–1/2" in diameter)
- Duct tape
- Scissors

❧ Use full soda bottles or fill empty bottles with sand or water.

HOW TO PLAY:
Before the party:
1. Cut rope into 5 pieces, each 15" in length.
2. To make rings, bring ends of each piece of rope together to form a circle.
3. With duct tape, tape ends together (Illustration 7–29 #1).
4. Set bottles on card table, approximately 6" apart (Illustration 7–29).
5. Have birthday child toss rings on bottles to establish a comfortable "playing distance" for your child's age group.

ILLUSTRATION 7-29

During the party:
6. Have children form a single line, with birthday child first.
7. Each player takes a turn (5 tosses) to see how many bottles he/she can ring.

ILLUSTRATION 7-29 #1

PEANUT TOSS

Recommended age: 4 years and older

WHAT YOU NEED:
- 6 "Clown Hats" (page 188)
- Duct tape
- 1 bowl of peanuts (in the shell)

HOW TO PLAY:
Before the party:
1. Tape clown hats to a wall, approximately 6" apart .
2. Have birthday child toss peanuts into hats to establish a comfortable "playing distance" for your child's age group.

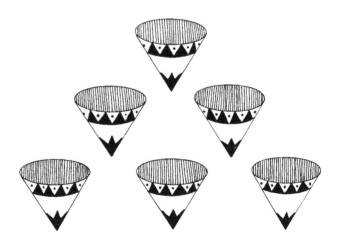

3. To play, have children form a single line, with birthday child first.
4. Each player takes 6 peanuts from the bowl and tries to toss them into the hats.

PIN THE NOSE ON THE CLOWN

Recommended age: 3 years and older

WHAT YOU NEED:
- Illustration 7–26 "Clown Mask" (page 198)
- Copier paper
- Construction paper (red)
- Duct tape (at least 2" wide)
- Masking tape or double-stick tape
- Scissors (adult use)
- Pencil
- Blindfold

HOW TO PLAY:
Before the party:
1. Make one photocopy of illustration 7-26 "Clown Mask."
2. Trace one clown nose for each child onto construction paper and cut out noses.

During the party:
3. Tape "Clown Mask" onto a wall in the game area and have children line up (single file), at least five feet away.
4. Write each child's name on front of clown nose and place a piece of masking tape rolled on itself (or double-stick tape) on the back of the nose.
5. Blindfold the first player in line (birthday child first) and turn child 2–3 times. Then hand child his/her clown nose and tell him/her to place the nose on top of the nose of the clown.

RINGMASTER

Recommended age: 2–5 years of age

Here is a twist on the traditional game of "Follow the Leader."

HOW TO PLAY:
1. Have children form a circle with birthday child in center.
2. Tell children that this is a game of "Follow the Leader," but a very special kind of leader, a ring leader, as in the circus ringmaster.
3. Ringmaster then names an animal or circus performer and everyone walks around the circle sounding and acting like the ringmaster's choice. (For example: ponies that trot and whinny; lions and tigers that growl; trumpeting elephants that swing their trunks; strong men/women lifting barbells; trapeze artists that fly through the air or walk on a tightrope; clowns "clowning around.")
4. Continue game until everyone has had a turn as ringmaster.

TIGHTROPE WALKER

Recommend age: 3 years and older

WHAT YOU NEED:
- One piece of rope (at least 12' in length)
- Book ❀

❀ Optional

HOW TO PLAY:
During the party:
1. Stretch rope on the ground and tell children that rope is a "tightrope," and that they must walk from one end to the other, and back again, without "falling."

2. Have birthday child start game by standing at one end of "tightrope" and have other children line up around "tightrope"—at least 3 feet away.
3. Tell children to act like lions and tigers, growling at the tightrope walker. They can't touch, but they can try to scare him/her into falling off the "tightrope."
4. Let everyone have a chance to walk the "tightrope."
5. To increase the challenge, and fun for older groups, try this variation:
   Ages 7 and older: Balance a book on their heads.

MORE GAMES...

It's always a good idea to plan some extra party games. Here are some standard party games, adapted for your Circus Party. Specific directions for these games are listed in **APPENDIX D: GAMES**, beginning on page 363.

↻CLOWN BEAN BAG TOSS

Recommended age: 3 years and older

Follow the directions for "Bean Bag Toss" in **GAMES** (page 364). Use "Circus Clown Photo Backdrop" (page 186) as theme backdrop.

CIRCUS TRAMPOLINE

Recommended age: 2–5 years of age

Follow the direction for "Trampoline" in **GAMES** (page 371), and use circus animal or toy clown as the theme object in the game.

↻CIRCUS SQUIRT BALL

Recommended age: 4 years and older

Follow the directions for "Squirt Ball" in **GAMES** (page 370).

CLOWN RELAY RACE

Recommended age: 6 years and older

Follow the directions for "Quick Change Relay Race" in **GAMES** (page 368) and use brightly-colored, oversized clothing to play the game.

DROP THE PEANUT IN THE BOTTLE

Recommended age: 4 years and older

Follow the directions for "Drop the Clothespin in the Bottle" in **GAMES** (page 365), and use peanuts to play the game.

RINGMASTER RED LIGHT, GREEN LIGHT

Recommended age: 5 years and older

Follow the directions for "Red Light, Green Light" in **GAMES** (page 369), using a "Circus Ringmaster" to lead the game.

THANK YOU

ILLUSTRATION
7-04

ILLUSTRATION 7-11

FOR
TIME
DATE
PLACE
R.S.V.P.

CIRCUS
★
PARTY

ILLUSTRATION 7-03

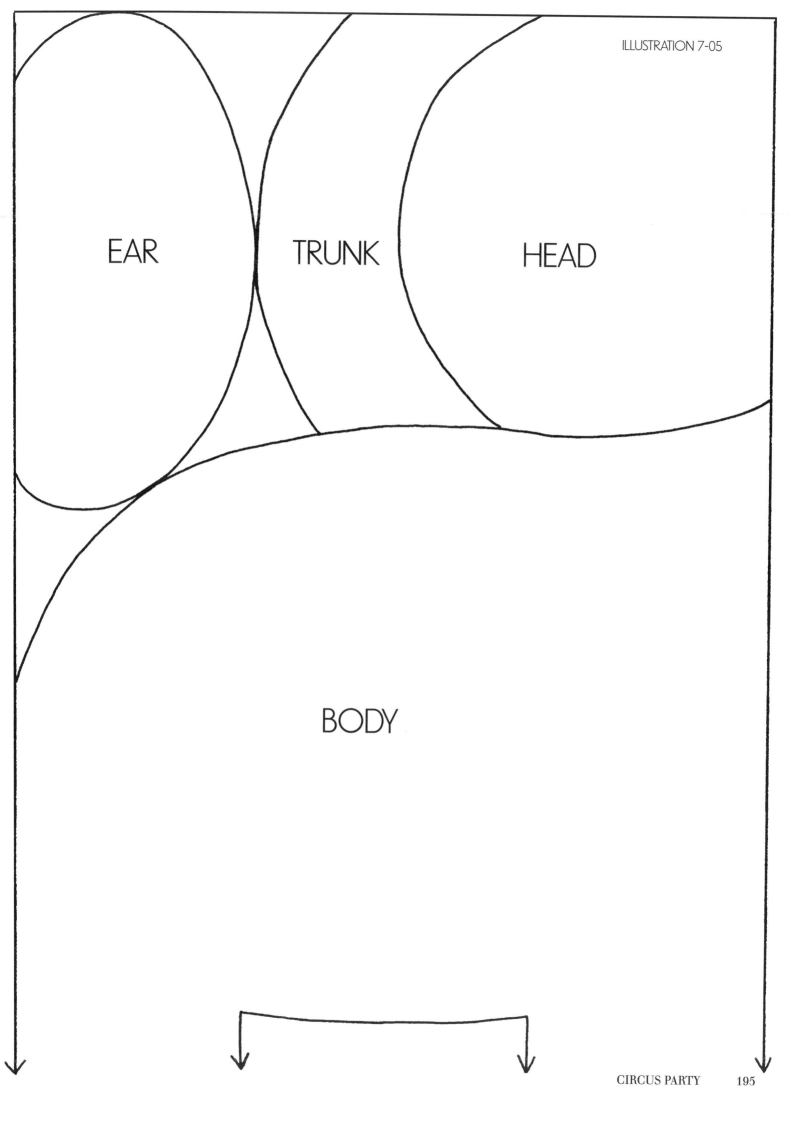

ILLUSTRATION 7-05

EAR

TRUNK

HEAD

BODY

ILLUSTRATION 7-09

ILLUSTRATION 7-18

ILLUSTRATION
7-24

ILLUSTRATION 7-26

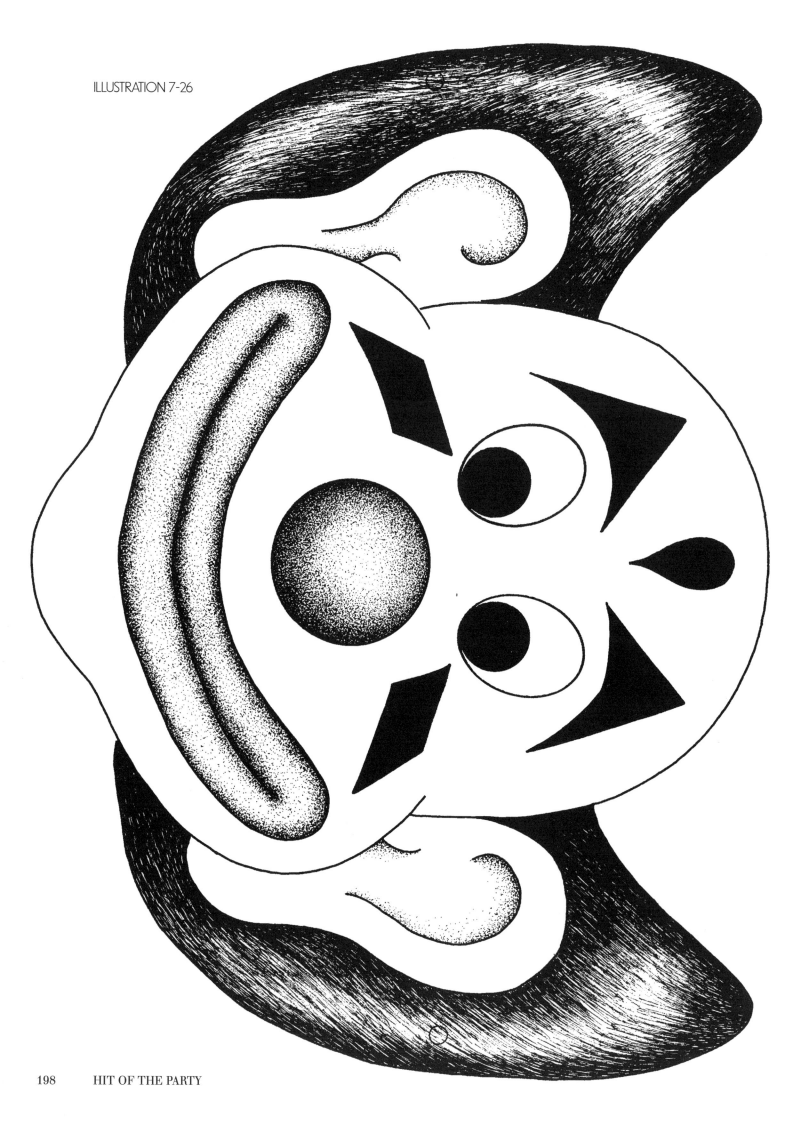

ILLUSTRATION 7-28

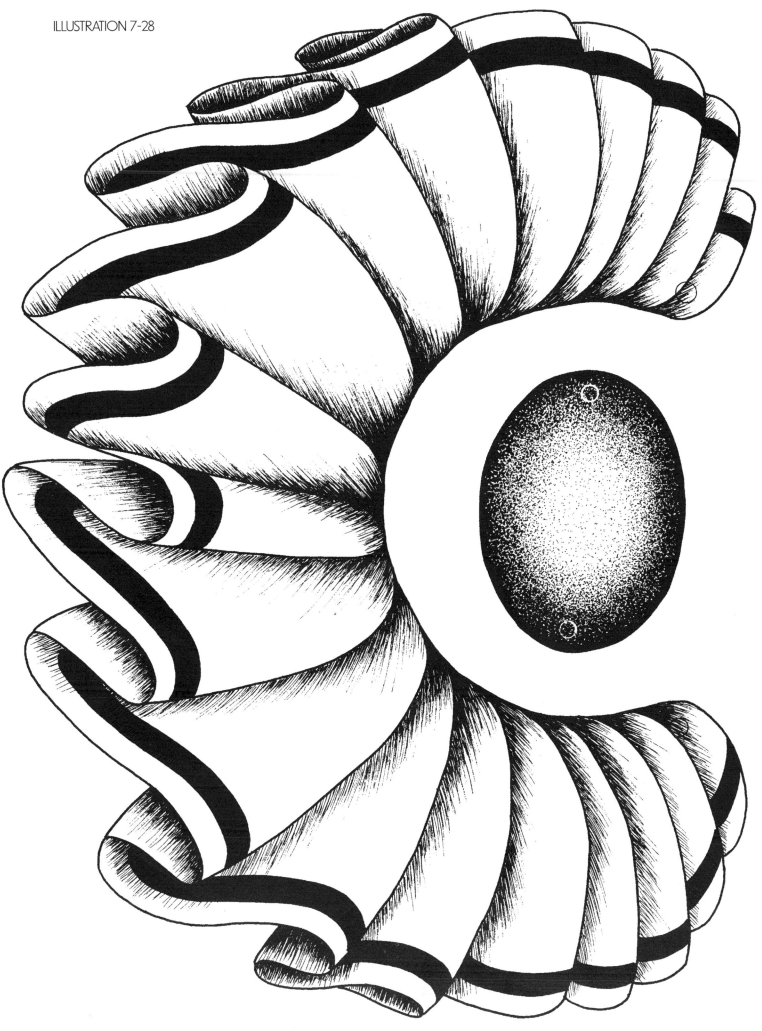

Backward Party

Up or down. In or out. Forward or BACKWARD! Finally, a chance to do *everything* BACKWARD, and there's nothing "wrong" with doing things BACKWARD in this party. For instance, you can say "Good-bye" when first greeting your guests and say "Hello" when they leave! Just about anything goes! So, have a "!YADHTRIB YPPAH."

ILLUSTRATION 8-01

BACKWARD INVITATION

Estimated Time: 4–5 minutes each

WHAT YOU NEED:

- Illustration 8–03 "Backward Invitation" (page 216)
- Copier paper or copier card stock (white or bright colors)
- Envelopes (3 5/8" x 6 1/2")
- Pencil
- Scissors
- White glue or transparent tape
- Felt-tip pen (black)
- Crayons, markers and/or colored pencils ❁

❁ Optional

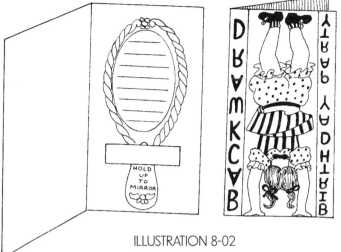

ILLUSTRATION 8-02

WHAT YOU DO:

1. Make one photocopy of Illustration 8–03. This is your "master copy." Fill out party information on "mirror" BACKWARD with felt-tip pen on master copy (Illustration 8–02 #1).
   (You may want to write out information in pencil first and check it in a mirror.)
2. Photocopy as many invitations as needed (Illustration 8–02 #2).

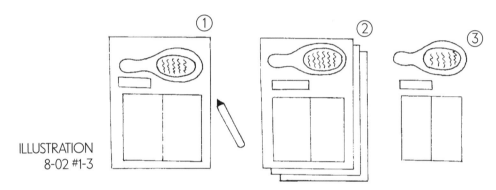

ILLUSTRATION 8-02 #1-3

3. Color invitation, if desired.
4. With scissors, cut out card, mirror and mirror holder (Illustration 8–02 #3).
5. Fold invitation in half and decide if you want the "girl" or the "boy" on the front (Illustration 8–02).
6. Open invitation and lay mirror on right side.
7. Glue or tape mirror holder in place (Illustration 8–02).

 THE EXTRA TOUCH

- Glue "Backward Stickers" (page 210) to seal envelope.
- Ask your guests to wear their clothes backward and inside out to the party.

BACKWARD THANK-YOU NOTE

Photocopy the "Backward Thank-You Note" (Illustration 8–04 on page 217) onto copier paper (white or bright colors). Simply cut out the thank-you note, and write your personal message in the space provided.

Estimated Time: 1 minute each

MENU

Reverse the order of the meal and serve the cake first! (Kids will *really* like that!) Put your placemats on the floor and have kids eat *under* the table. Choose foods from each group, and follow the recipes on the pages listed below.

UPSIDE-DOWN KID CAKE

Estimated time: 1–1 1/2 hours

INGREDIENTS:

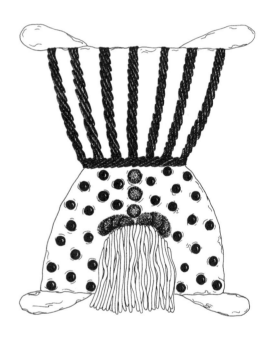

1	"Basic Cake" recipe in Appendix A, on pages 343 and 344; or use your favorite box cake mix
2	"Buttercream Frosting" recipes in Appendix A, on page 345; or use 2 cans of your favorite canned frosting
4	Licorice whips
8	Licorice twists (red or black)
2	Wedge-shaped jelled candies
1/2 c.	Chocolate chips
3	Gumdrops
	Food coloring (red)
	Food coloring (favorite colors)
	13" x 18" tray or foil-covered board
	Illustration 8–05 "Upside Down Kid Cake Pattern" (page 218)

DIRECTIONS:

1. Prepare and bake cake in one 9" x 13" cake pan as directed in recipe or cake package.
2. Cool cake completely on wire rack.
3. Wrap in plastic wrap and freeze cake at least 45 minutes. (Freezing the cake does not affect its flavor and makes it easier to work with. It also enables you to make the cake ahead of time, to help balance your work load for the party.)
4. Trace Illustration 8–05 "Upside-Down Kid Cake Pattern" on wax paper. Extend lines 1" on cake pattern where arrows indicate.
   [NOTE: Make a "V" in pattern, as indicated with dotted lines, for a boy.]
5. Cut out wax paper pattern into sections and reassemble on top of cake.
6. Using long knife, cut cake into sections by following pattern (Illustration 8–06 #1).
7. Assemble sections of cake on tray into shape of "Upside-Down Kid" (Illustration 8–06 #2).
8. In a bowl, tint 1/2 cup frosting pink by adding a few drops of red food coloring and mix until color is uniform.
9. Frost connecting sections of "hands" and "feet" with pink frosting.

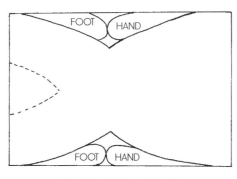

ILLUSTRATION 8-06 #1

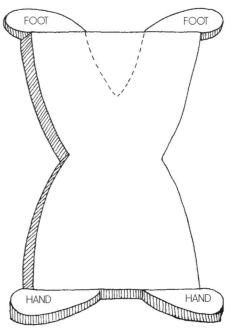

10. Frost tops and sides of "hands" and "feet" with pink frosting.
11. In another bowl, tint remaining frosting your favorite color by adding a few drops of food coloring and mix until color is uniform.
12. Frost remaining sections of cake with favorite color of frosting.
13. Cut licorice whips into 3"–4" pieces to make hair.
14. Use chocolate chips to make polka-dots on shirt or blouse and licorice twists to make stripes on pants or skirt.
15. Use gumdrops for "buttons" and use jelled wedges for the collar.

ILLUSTRATION 8-06 #2

 BACKWARD CAKE

Estimated time: 20–30 minutes

INGREDIENTS:

1	Frosted store-bought cake (round or rectangular)
1	Tube gel frosting (green)
30–40	Candy-coated chocolates
10–15	Candy corns
15–20	Gumdrops
12–20	Animal-shaped cookies

DIRECTIONS:

1. Press cookies into side and center of cake, UPSIDE DOWN.
2. Suggest grass by decorating bottom edge of cake with green gel frosting.
3. Decorate with candy corns, gumdrops and candy-coated chocolates.

ILLUSTRATION 8-07

THE EXTRA TOUCH

- Make your cake even more fun by baking your own "boy" and "girl" cookies for the top and sides on your cake. See "Cookie Dough" in **RECIPES** (page 330) or use store-bought, refrigerated cookie dough and cut out with "boy" or "girl" cookie cutters (Illustration 8-07).

DECORATIONS

Your guests won't know whether they are coming or going with a few of these easy-to-make decorations. Save money by using some of these decorations as favors in your loot bags.

PARTY STREAMERS

Estimated time: 1–2 minutes per streamer

Use the streamer suggested below, and follow the directions for "Party Streamers" in **CRAFT TIPS** (page 349).

- **Doll Streamer** Pattern CT-02 (page 359)
  Use bright colors of crepé paper and hang upside down.

* Hang crepé paper streamers (in pre-packaged rolls) around party area.

BACKWARD STRAWS

Estimated time: 1–2 minutes each

Make your own "Backward Straws" (Illustration 8-08) and watch children giggle as they sip those delicious drinks. Use Illustration 8–09 "Backward Face" (page 217) and follow directions for "Drinking Straws" in **CRAFT TIPS** (page 353).

BACKWARD SUCKERS

Estimated time: 1–2 minutes each

Make your own "Backward Suckers." (Illustration 8-10) Use Illustration 8–09 "Backward Face" (page 217) and follow directions for "Birthday Party Suckers" in **CRAFT TIPS** (page 353).

ILLUSTRATION 8-08

ILLUSTRATION 8-10

💡 MORE DECORATING IDEAS...

* Make BACKWARD signs and hang in party area. Here are some suggestions:

  YADHTRIB YPPAH POTS
  OG RETNE
  RETNE TON OD YAW ENO
  NOITUAC DLEIY

* Write children's names BACKWARD on sheets of construction paper and use as placemats.
* Hang up out-of-season holiday decorations, like Christmas or Halloween decorations for child's birthday party.
* Hang pictures in the house UPSIDE DOWN or BACKWARD.
* Draw upside-down faces on balloons and hang in party area.
* Make placemats by photocopying illustration 8-24 "Backward Mask"(page 220) or Illustration 8-22 Funny Features (page 219) onto copier paper (white or bright colors). Provide crayons for children to color placemats, if desired.
* Make placemats by having children glue "Backward Stickers"(page 210) onto 9" x 12" sheet of construction paper. Provide crayons, markers and colored pencils for children to color placemats.
* Photocopy "Upside-Down Kid Cake" illustration 8-01 (page 202) and tape to front door or front of party area to greet guests.

LOOT BAGS

Select one (or more) of the following loot bags and follow the directions for "Loot Bags" in **CRAFT TIPS** (page 350).

* **Sticker Bag** (page 350)
  Use illustration 8-19 "Backward Stickers" on page 217.
* **Treasure Box** (page 351)
  Use illustration 8-19 "Backward Stickers" on page 217 or "Funny Features" on page 219.
* **Mask Bag** (page 351)
  Use illustration 8-24 "Backward Mask" on page 220.

LOOT BAG "LOOT"

Looking for something to put in those loot bags? Here are some creative suggestions you can make, or if you are short of time, you can buy.

LOOT YOU CAN MAKE:

- **Backward Stickers** (See page 210)
- **Backward Straws** (See page 206)
- **Backward Suckers** (See page 206)
- **Backward Polaroid® Photo Frame** (page 208)
- **Backward Cap** (See page 212)
- **Backward Shirt** (See page 211)
- **Wacky Harp** (See page 210)
- **Cookie Puppets** (See page 329) Place cookie upside down on stick.
- **Nuts and Bolts** (See page 333)

LOOT YOU CAN BUY:

- Small mirrors
- Small books about silly or nonsensical rhymes
- Rubber stamps (which you can then turn UPSIDE DOWN)
- "Gags" or novelty items
- Favors from other holidays
- Silly magic tricks

ACTIVITIES

Party the start to ready you are? (or "Are you ready to start the party?")

Don't feel as if you have to do all of these activities—there isn't enough time at any party. Discuss with your child which ones he or she would like to do and plan your party activities accordingly.

ARRIVAL ACTIVITY

As each child arrives, announce your guest's first name last, and last name first. Then, write guest's names BACKWARD on a self-sticking name tag (available at most stationery stores) and stick on shirt or blouse.

BACKWARD OBSTACLE COURSE

Recommended for all ages

Children will enjoy climbing through, jumping over, sliding down, peering into, and crawling under this obstacle course—especially when you tell them they have to do everything BACKWARD! Each obstacle course will be different, depending on how you put it together, how large your party area is, and what items you have available.

WHAT YOU NEED:

- Recycled appliance box(es) large enough for children to crawl through
- Chairs (sturdy enough for children to climb on)
- Cushions
- Old tires
- Outdoor playground equipment (if available)
- Wooden shelving boards (1/2" by 10" or 12" wide, at least 6' in length)

WHAT YOU DO:

1. Using a little imagination, and whatever materials you have around your house, you can create a BACKWARD and UPSIDE-DOWN world for children to climb over, under and through.
2. Courses can be made for indoors or outdoors and can be as large or small, simple or complex as you have the time and space to make it.

 **THE EXTRA TOUCH**

- Add "Backward Signs" (page 206) to obstacle course.

⟲ BACKWARD PHOTO BACKDROP

Recommended for all ages

Use Illustration 8–15 "Backward Photo Backdrop Pattern" and follow the directions for "Photo Backdrop" in **CRAFT TIPS** (page 354) to give children and their parents the best party favor they can have—a memorable "Backward Snapshot."

You can take a Polaroid® photograph and hand it out at the party (see "Polaroid® Photo Frame below), or you can use a 35 mm camera and send a photo along with your thank-you note.

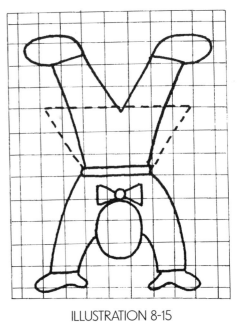

ILLUSTRATION 8-15

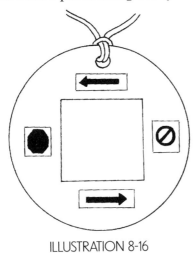

ILLUSTRATION 8-16

BACKWARD POLAROID® PHOTO FRAME

Recommended for all ages

Hand out these wonderful memories at the party by using a Polaroid® photo and follow the directions for "Polaroid® Photo Frame" in **CRAFT TIPS** (page 357).

 **THE EXTRA TOUCH**

- Color with crayons, markers and/or colored pencils.
- Glue on "Backward Stickers" (page 210).
- Mount photo in "Backward Polaroid® Photo Frame" UPSIDE DOWN.

BACKWARD MURAL

Recommended age: 6 and older

WHAT YOU NEED:

- Butcher paper
- Masking tape
- Crayons

WHAT YOU DO:

1. Lay large sheet of butcher paper on floor or on flat, outside surface (sidewalk or driveway) and tape in place.
2. Tell children to paint a silly, upside-down, BACKWARD mural—with their opposite hand or to take off their shoes and draw with their toes (Illustration 8-17).
3. When completed, use tape to hang up in party area as a mural.

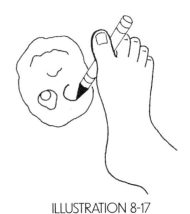

ILLUSTRATION 8-17

VARIATION

- As an alternative to a mural, use individual sheets of drawing paper or construction paper and tape on floor or flat outside surface.

 ## WRONG-WAY CARS

Recommended age: 5 and older

WHAT YOU NEED:

- Cardboard box (approximately 16" x 20" x 24")
- Lightweight rope
- Scissors
- One sheet 22" x 28" lightweight poster board (any color)
- White glue
- Poster paints and brushes; crayons and/or markers ✿

✿ Optional

WHAT YOU DO:

Before the party:

1. Cut out opening in bottom of box, approximately 14" wide and 16" long (Illustration 8–18 #1).
2. Punch holes in corners of bottom (Illustration 8–18 #1).
3. Cut off any top flaps to box.
4. Make 2 shoulder straps for driver by tying a knot in one end of each rope, threading rope through both holes on one side, and tying a knot in other end of each rope. Adjust length to fit child's shoulders (Illustration 8–18 #2).
5. To make "wheels," cut out four 10" circles from poster board and glue on sides of car.

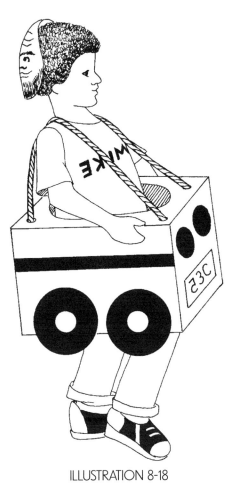

ILLUSTRATION 8-18

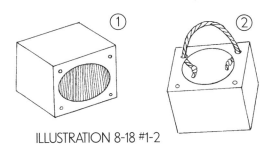

ILLUSTRATION 8-18 #1-2

 ## THE EXTRA TOUCH

1. Use poster paints, crayons and/or markers to add color and details, such as lights, grill, doors, and/or BACKWARD license plates, etc., if desired (Illustration 8-18).
2. Stage a race and have children "drive" their cars BACKWARD; or set up an obstacle course and have children drive through course, BACKWARD!

BACKWARD PARADE

Recommended age: 5 and older

WHAT YOU DO:

1. Have children wear clothes inside out and BACKWARD, or have guests put on costumes BACKWARD, such as the "Backward Mask" (page 211), the "Backward Shirt" (page 211), or the "Backward Cap" (page 212).
2. Line children up and have them face—and march—backward. (Be sure to clear all obstacles in their path.)
3. If possible, give children a musical instrument to play, like a "Wacky Harp" (page 210) or a "Honey Bee Kazoo" (page 32).

CRAFTS

Children will have fun making these crafts as a group activity during the party or you can make these crafts yourself ahead of time and save money on party favors. Select one or two of the crafts for your party from the following list.

BACKWARD STICKERS

Recommended age: 3 and older for gluing
5 and older for cutting and gluing

Make your own party stickers for children to use in various crafts and activities in this chapter. Use Illustration 8–19 "Backward Stickers" (page 217) and follow directions for "Party Stickers" in **CRAFT TIPS** (page 352).

WACKY HARP

Recommended age: 6 and older

WHAT YOU NEED:
- Plastic or metal lids from jars (larger is better)
- Rubberbands (various sizes)
- Construction paper (bright colors)
- Scissors (child-safe)
- White glue
- Duct tape or cloth-backed tape

WHAT YOU DO:
1. Cut a circle out of construction paper to fit inside each lid.
2. Glue circle inside lid (Illustration 8–20 #1).
3. Stretch rubberbands over lid (at least four per lid) and tape in place on back side. (Illustration 8–20 #2).
4. Pluck rubberbands to play harp.

ILLUSTRATION 8-20

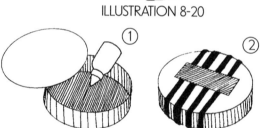

ILLUSTRATION 8-20 #1-2

FUNNY FACE

Recommended age: 6 years and older

WHAT YOU NEED:
- 9" paper plate
- Illustration 8–22 "Funny Features" (page 219)
- Copier paper (white)
- Scissors (child-safe)
- Hole punch
- White glue
- Yarn
- Crayons, markers and/or colored pencils ✿

_____
✿ Optional

WHAT YOU DO:
Before the party:
1. Photocopy Illustration 8–22 onto copier paper.
During the party:
2. Color "Funny Face," if desired.
3. Cut out different facial features from "Funny Features."
4. Combine features from different faces and create a strange, unusual, silly, upside-down and/or BACKWARD face. Then glue features in place on paper plate (Illustration 8-21).
5. Cut yarn into strands to form hair, and glue in place.

ILLUSTRATION 8-21

BACKWARD MASK

Recommended age: 5 and older

WHAT YOU NEED:

- Illustration 8–24 "Backward Mask" (page 220)
- Copier paper or copier card stock (white or bright colors) ❀
- One 14" length of elastic cord (or one 14" length of yarn)
- Scissors (child-safe)
- Hole punch or sharp pencil
- Crayons, markers and/or colored pencils ❀❀
- Transparent tape ❀❀

_____

❀ Card stock is preferred for this project.

❀❀ Optional

ILLUSTRATION 8-23

WHAT YOU DO:

Before the party:

1. Photocopy Illustration 8–24 onto copier paper or card stock.
2. If using copier paper, reinforce holes with transparent tape before punching holes.

During the party:

3. Color masks, if desired.
4. Cut out mask.
5. Punch two holes in mask, as marked on illustration.
6. Tie one end of elastic cord through one hole in mask.
7. Thread other end of cord through other hole in mask and adjust length to fit child's head; then knot cord in place (Illustration 8-23).
8. Wear mask on BACK of head.

BACKWARD SHIRT

Recommended age: 5 years and older

WHAT YOU NEED:

- T-shirts (white or solid colors, one for each child)
- Fabric paint (and brushes)
- Fabric puff paints
- Cardboard
- Newspaper

WHAT YOU DO:

Before the party:

1. Wash T-shirts and tumble dry.
2. Cut a sheet of cardboard to fit inside each shirt.

During the party:

3. Cover large work area (like the party table) with newspaper.
4. Give each child a shirt with cardboard or newspaper inside.
5. Set out puff paints, fabric paints (and brushes) in work area, and have children paint their own designs on shirt.
6. Working on the front or BACK or front of the shirt, children can write their own name BACKWARD; create a silly picture or statement, UPSIDE DOWN and/or BACKWARD, of course (Illustration 8-25).
7. Carefully collect shirts and let fabric paint dry, away from party activities. (Tell parents to run shirts in dryer one cycle, at a medium temperature after paint has completely dried to set paint.)

ILLUSTRATION 8-25

☞ THE EXTRA TOUCH

- Purchase some "iron on" decals, and iron on the designs UPSIDE DOWN or SIDEWAYS.

BACKWARD CAP

Recommended age: 6 and older

WHAT YOU NEED:

- Solid-colored baseball caps, painter's caps or other fabric hats (one for each child)
- Fabric paint (and brushes)
- Fabric puff paints
- Newspaper
- Sequins, feathers, fabric scraps, yarn, pom poms, fake eyes, buttons, pipe cleaners, felt scraps, etc.
- Muffin tin or small bowls
- White or tacky glue

ILLUSTRATION 8-26

WHAT YOU DO:

During the party:

1. Cover large work area (like party table) with newspaper.
2. Give each child their own hat.
3. Set out puff paints, fabric paints (and brushes) in work area, as well as glue, sequins, feathers, fabric scraps, yarn, pom poms, etc. (in muffin tray) and have children decorate their hats.
4. Children can write their own names (BACKWARD); draw a (BACKWARD) portrait of themselves; or create silly or unusual pictures (UPSIDE DOWN and/or BACKWARD, of course).
5. Glue on sequins, feathers, fabric scraps, yarn, pom poms, etc., as desired (Illustration 8-26).
6. Carefully collect hats and let dry away from party activity.

GAMES

Select several of the games for your party from the following list. Don't feel as if you have to play all of them—there just isn't time. But you should plan for a few extra games. Here are some unique games for your Backward Party.

↻ BACKWARD BEAN BAG TOSS

Recommended age: 5 years and older

Here's a chance to use up all those one-of-kind (unpaired) socks, as well as any outgrown baby socks—and have fun at the same time!

WHAT YOU NEED:

- One 5-gallon bucket or box
- Dry beans (at least 1 pound)
- Children's socks (8–12 individual socks)

WHAT YOU DO:

1. Fill each sock half-full with beans, and tie knot at end of sock (Illustration 8–27 #1).
2. Depending on their age, children stand at a challenging distance from bucket or box, *WITH THEIR BACK TO THE TARGET*, and toss bean bags over their shoulder and into the bucket or box.

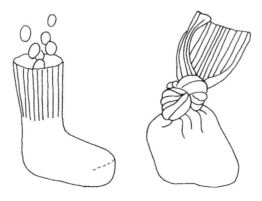

ILLUSTRATION 8-27 #1

BACKWARD RELAY RACE

Recommended age: 6 years and older

HOW TO PLAY:

1. Divide children into two relay teams.
2. Mark a start/finish line for the relay race, and a turn-around point, (like a tree or a chair) which should be between 15'–20' from the start/finish line.
3. Explain to children that each player must run BACKWARD, as fast as he/she can, to the turn-around point and back.
4. The first team to have all players complete the race, wins.

CRAWLING-BACKWARD RELAY RACE

Recommended age: 6 years and older

HOW TO PLAY:

1. Divide the children into two relay teams.
2. Each team stands (single file), at arm's length with legs spread apart, and both teams facing the same direction.
3. The first person in each line gets down on hands and knees and crawls BACKWARD through the legs of all of the players on his/her team (Illustration 8-29).
4. When completing the crawl, first player stands up and assumes the original position.
5. The first team to have all players complete the crawl, wins.

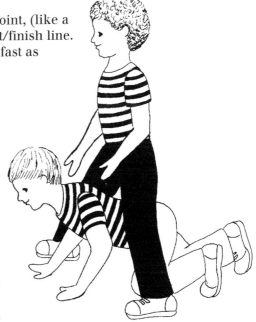

ILLUSTRATION 8-29

ILLUSTRATION 8-30

BACKWARD-BALL RELAY RACE

Recommended age: 6 years and older

WHAT YOU NEED:

- 2 rubber balls (approximately 12" in diameter)

HOW TO PLAY:

1. Divide children into two relay teams.
2. Each team stands single file, at arm's length with both teams facing the same direction.
3. Have all players sit down in place.
4. The first person in each line gets a ball and passes it BACKWARD, OVER their head to the player behind them (Illustration 8-30).
5. When the last player gets the ball, he/she runs to the front of the line and continues passing the ball.
6. The first team to have the leader return to the front of the line, wins.

VARIATIONS
- Start the game with the LAST person in line and have children pass the ball toward the front of the line.
- Play game with children standing, feet spread apart, and pass the ball through their legs.

BACKWARD-EGG RELAY RACE

Recommended age: 7 years and older

WHAT YOU NEED:
- 2 spoons
- 2 boiled eggs or plastic eggs

HOW TO PLAY:
1. Divide children into two relay teams, and give each team a spoon and an egg.
2. Mark a start/finish line for the relay race, and a turn-around point (like a tree or a chair), which should be between 15–20' from the starting line.
3. Explain to children that each player must place the egg on the spoon, and walk BACKWARD, as fast as he/she can, to the turn-around point and back, balancing the egg on the spoon. The first team to have all players complete the race, wins.
4. Make sure children understand that they cannot hold the egg while they walk. If the egg falls, they must stop, place the egg back on the spoon, and continue the race. Anyone caught holding the egg will have to start his/her turn all over.

BACKWARD PULLING RACE

Recommended age: 8 years and older

HOW TO PLAY:
1. Divide the children into two relay teams.
2. Each team stands single file, at arm's length, with both teams facing the same direction.
3. The first player of each team reaches his/her left hand back between his/her legs and grasps the right hand of the player just behind him/her.
4. Each team member grasps the player behind him/her until entire line is linked.
5. The last player lies flat on his/her back, still holding on the hand in front of him/her.

6. As soon as the last player is flat, the leader shouts, "Go!" and the entire line takes small steps BACKWARD, until each player is lying down.
7. As soon as all players are lying down, the last player gets up and pulls the entire line upright.
8. The first team to be upright, and standing in place, wins.

MORE GAMES...

It's always a good idea to plan some extra party games. Here are some standard party games, adapted for your Backward Party. Specific directions for these games are listed in **APPENDIX D: GAMES**, beginning on page 363.

BACKWARD HIDE-AND-SEEK

Recommended age: 5 years and older

Follow the directions for "Sardines" in **GAMES** (page 369).

GREEN LIGHT, RED LIGHT

Recommended age: 5 years and older

Follow the directions for "Red Light, Green Light" in **GAMES** (page 369), and start from the finish line and walk BACKWARD.

GOOSE, DUCK, DUCK

Recommended age: 4 years and older

Follow the directions for "Duck, Duck, Goose" in **GAMES** (page 365), and walk BACKWARD.

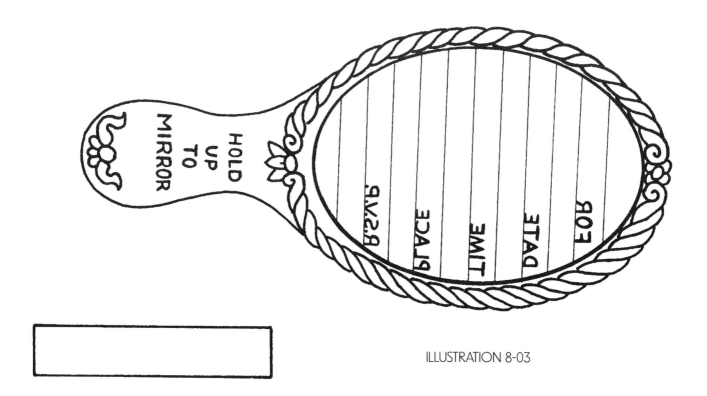

ILLUSTRATION 8-03

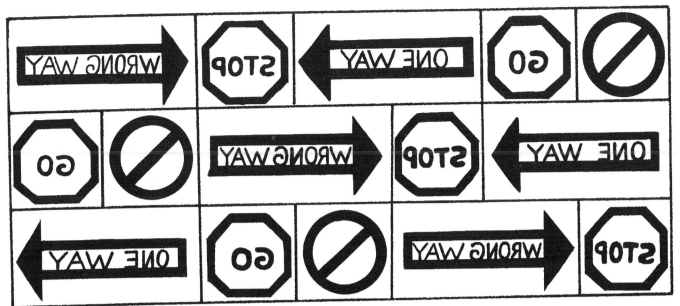

ILLUSTRATION 8-19

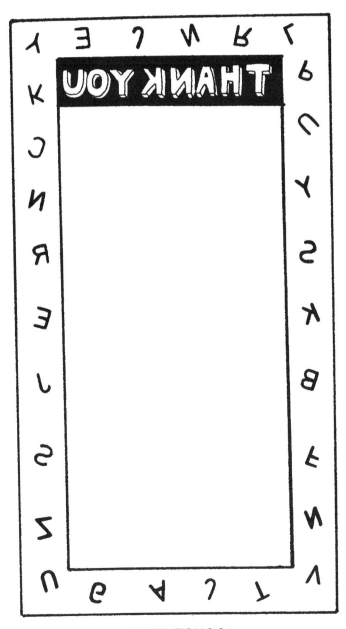

ILLUSTRATION 8-04

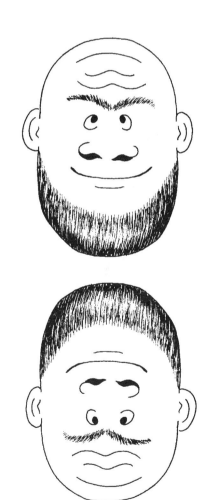

ILLUSTRATION 8-09

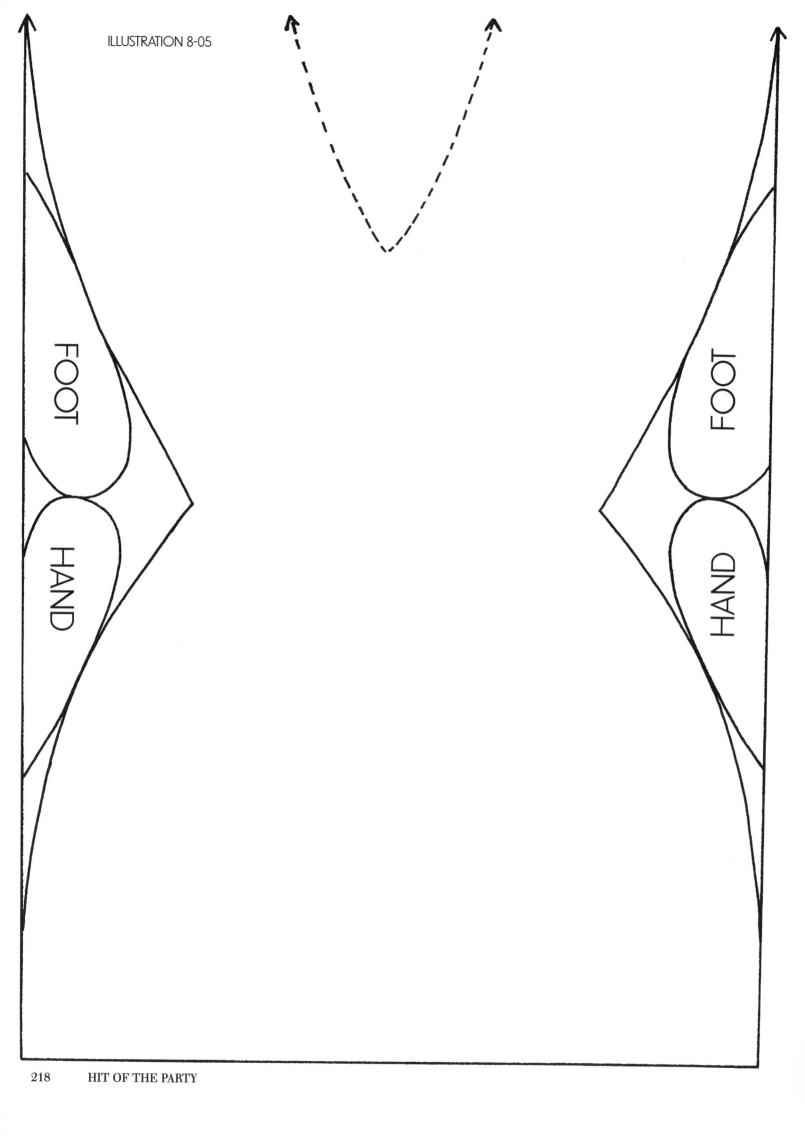

ILLUSTRATION 8-05

FOOT

HAND

FOOT

HAND

ILLUSTRATION
8-22

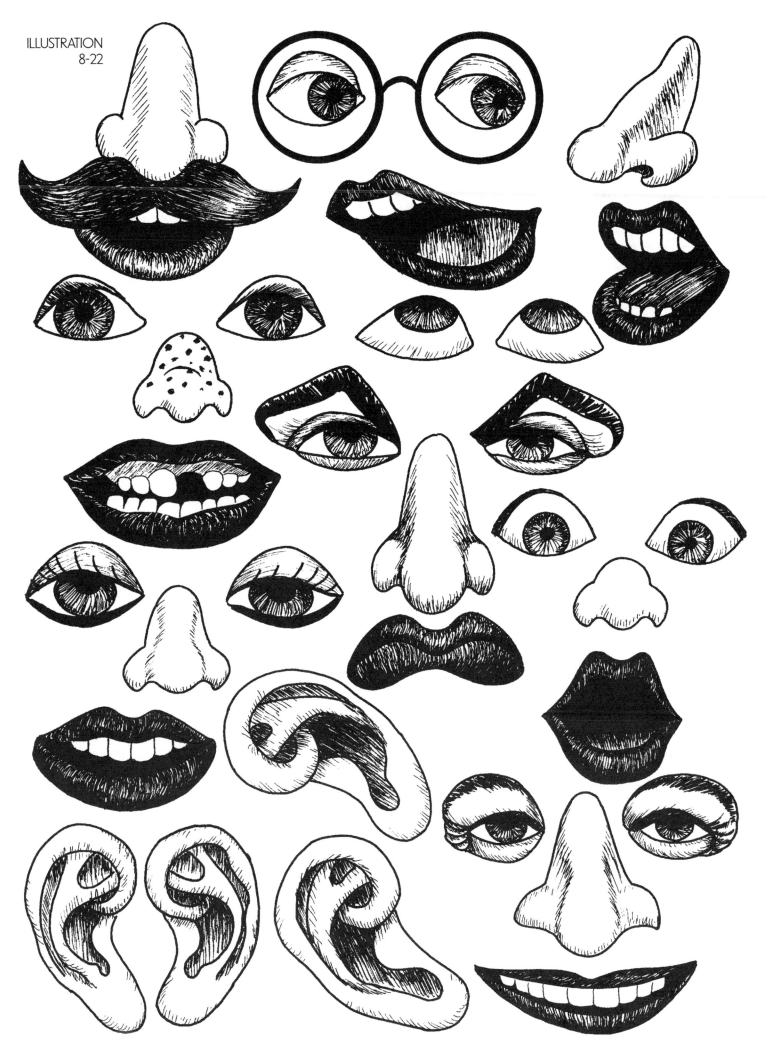

ILLUSTRATION 8-24

Magic Party

CHAPTER 9

Wizards and magicians are conjuring up a magic spell to turn this day into the most amazing birthday party ever! So, wave your magic wand. Your wishes are about to come true.

ILLUSTRATION 9-01

RABBIT-IN-THE-HAT INVITATION

Estimated Time: 3–4 minutes each

Abracadabra! Pull this rabbit from the hat and your guests will suddenly appear at your party.

ILLUSTRATION 9-02

WHAT YOU NEED:

- Illustration 9–03 "Rabbit-in-the-Hat Invitation" (page 238)
- Copier paper or copier card stock (white or bright colors) ❀
- Envelopes (3 5/8" x 6 1/2")
- Scissors
- Craft knife (adult use only)
- Felt-tip pen (black)

❀ Card stock is preferred for this project.

WHAT YOU DO:

1. Make one photocopy of Illustration 9–03. This is your "master copy." Fill out all party information with felt-tip pen on master copy (Illustration 9–02 #1).
2. Photocopy as many invitations as needed (Illustration 9–02 #2).
3. Using craft knife, cut slit along dotted line on hat (Illustration 9–02 #3).
4. With scissors, cut out both hat and rabbit (Illustration 9–02 #4).
5. Slip rabbit through slit of hat, feet first (Illustration 9–02).

ILLUSTRATION 9-02 #1-4

 THE EXTRA TOUCH

- Glue "Magic Stickers" (page 232) to seal envelope.
- Glue glitter to invitation.

MAGIC THANK-YOU NOTE

The "Magic Thank-You Note" (Illustration 9–04) is on the same page as the "Rabbit-in-the-Hat Invitation." When you photocopy the invitation, you will also be copying the thank-you note. Simply cut out the thank-you note, and write your personal message in the space provided.

Estimated Time: 1 minute each

MENU

It won't take any magic to make these scrumptious yummies disappear. Choose foods from each group, and follow the recipes on the pages listed below.

DRINKS:

RABBIT-IN-THE-HAT CAKE

Estimated time: 1–1 1/2 hours

INGREDIENTS:

1   "Basic Cake" recipe in Appendix A, on pages 343 and 344; or use your favorite box cake mix

1   "Buttercream Frosting" recipe in Appendix A, on page 345; or use 1 can of your favorite canned frosting

1   "Chocolate Frosting" recipe in Appendix A, on page 345; or use 1 can of your favorite canned frosting

2 c. Flaked coconut

1   Jelly bean (pink)

2   Jelly beans (red)

1   Marshmallow (cut in half)

1   Marshmallow (cut in quarters)

1   Licorice whip or twist (red)

    Red food coloring

    13" x 18" tray or foil-covered board

    Illustration 9–05 "Rabbit-in-the-Hat Cake Pattern" (page 239)

ILLUSTRATION 9-06

DIRECTIONS:

1. Prepare and bake cake in one 9" x 13" cake pan as directed in recipe or cake package.
2. Cool cake completely on wire rack.
3. Wrap in plastic wrap and freeze cake at least 45 minutes. (Freezing the cake does not affect its flavor and makes it easier to work with. It also enables you to make the cake ahead of time, to help balance your work load for the party.)
4. Trace Illustration 9–05 "Rabbit-in-the-Hat Cake Pattern" on wax paper. Extend lines 1" on cake pattern where arrows indicate.
5. Cut out wax paper pattern into sections and reassemble on top of cake.
6. Using long knife, cut cake into sections by following pattern (Illustration 9–06 #1).
7. Assemble sections on tray into shape of rabbit-in-the-hat (Illustration 9–06 #2).
8. Frost connecting sections of cake with white frosting.
9. Frost sides and top of hat sections of cake with chocolate frosting.
10. Place 1/4 cup buttercream frosting in a bowl and add a few drops of red food coloring to tint frosting pink. Mix until color is uniform.
11. Spread pink frosting inside "ears" (Illustration 9–06).
12. Frost sides and top of rabbit sections with white frosting.
13. Sprinkle coconut evenly over white sections of rabbit's "head," gently pressing coconut into cake.
14. Place marshmallow halves on face to form "eyeballs" (Illustration 9–06).

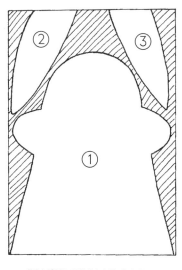

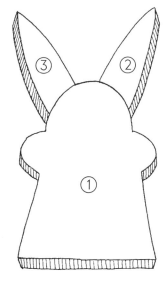

ILLUSTRATION 9-06 #1   ILLUSTRATION 9-06 #2

15. Place one red jelly bean into center of each marshmallow "eyeball," using dab of pink frosting to hold in place.
16. Push pink jelly bean into face to form "nose."
17. Cut sections of licorice and place on face to form "mouth" and "whiskers."
18. Place two quarter-slices of marshmallow in "mouth" for "teeth."

 **MAGIC CAKE**

Estimated time: 20–30 minutes

INGREDIENTS:

1	Frosted store-bought cake (round or rectangular)
12	Drinking straws (at least one for each guest)
12	Large gumdrops (at least one for each guest)
30–40	Small gumdrops
30–40	Candy corns
	Candy sprinkles (bright colors)

DIRECTIONS:

1. Push one end of straw into bottom of large gumdrop.
2. Place other end of straw into top of cake.
3. Shake candy sprinkles on top and sides of cake.
4. Decorate top edge of cake with small gumdrops.
5. Make stars around side of cake by placing 5 candy corns around a small gumdrop.

DECORATIONS

Create some magic at home with a few of these easy-to-make decorations. Save money by using some of these decorations as favors in your loot bags.

PARTY STREAMERS

Estimated time: 1–2 minutes per streamer

Select one (or more) of the streamers suggested below, and follow the directions for "Party Streamers" in **CRAFT TIPS** (page 349).

- **Star Streamer** Pattern CT-03 (page 360)
  Use bright colors of crepé paper.
- **Triangle Streamer** Pattern CT-05 (page 361)
  Use bright colors of crepé paper.

TIMESAVER

- Hang crepé paper streamers (in pre-packaged rolls) around party area.

STARS AND THE MOON

Estimated time: 5–7 minutes

WHAT YOU NEED:

- Illustration 9–09 "Stars and the Moon" (page 240)
- Copier paper or copier card stock (white or yellow) ✿
- Scissors
- Hole punch or sharp pencil
- Lightweight string or thread

_____

✿ Card stock is preferred for this project.

ILLUSTRATION 9-08

WHAT YOU DO:

1. Photocopy Illustration 9–09 "Stars and the Moon" onto copier paper or card stock.
2. Cut out around stars and moons.
3. Punch holes in stars and moons.
4. Cut 6 strings, in whatever lengths desired.
5. Tie one end of each string through the hole in each star and moon.
6. Hang stars and moon from trees, ceilings, windows, patio covers or on long strings or streamers that stretch across party area.

 THE EXTRA TOUCH

- Using a glue stick, add glitter and some sparkle to your "Stars and Moon."

RABBIT STRAWS

Estimated time: 1–2 minutes each

Care to share a drink with a silly rabbit? (Illustration 9-10) Use Illustration 9–11 "Magic Rabbit Straws" (page 238) and follow directions for "Drinking Straws" in **CRAFT TIPS** (page 353).

RABBIT SUCKERS

Estimated time: 1–2 minutes each

Make your own "Rabbit Suckers." (Illustration 9-12) Use Illustration 9–11 "Magic Rabbit" (page 238) and follow directions for "Party Suckers" in **CRAFT TIPS** (page 353).

💡 MORE DECORATING IDEAS...

- Make placemats by having children glue "Magic Stickers"(page 232) onto 9" x 12" sheet of construction paper. Provide crayons, markers and/or colored pencils for children to color placemats, if desired.

ILLUSTRATION 9-10

ILLUSTRATION 9-12

- Place stuffed rabbits in hats on party table and/or around party area.
- Tie scarves together and hang as "banners" across room.
- Make a mobile out of playing cards by taping string to cards.
- Scatter playing cards on party table and around party area.
- Throw confetti on party table.
- Make your own "Magic Balloons." Using one balloon for each child, and one small, plastic toy per balloon, stretch balloon and then drop toy inside. Inflate balloon and knot at end. Decorate balloons with gummed stars, ribbon, glue and glitter. Tie string or ribbon to balloon and hang as a decoration during party and later give to children as a favor (Illustration 9-13 #1–2).

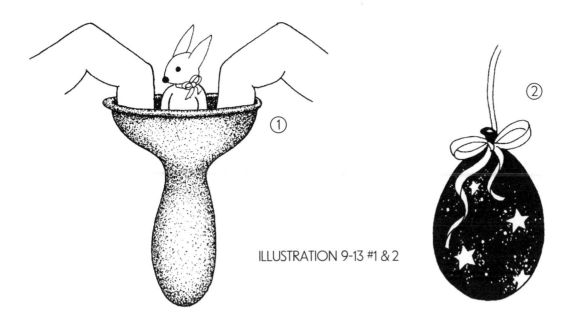

ILLUSTRATION 9-13 #1 & 2

- Photocopy "Rabbit-in-the-Hat Cake" illustration 9-01 (page 222) and tape to front door or front of party area to greet guests.

LOOT BAGS

Select one (or more) of the following loot bags and follow the directions for "Loot Bags" in **CRAFT TIPS** (page 350).

- **Magic Bag** (page 351)
- **Hat Bag** (page 351)
  Use illustration 9-30 "Magician's Hat" on page 242.
- **Treasure Box** (page 351)
  Use illustration 9-26 "Magic Stickers" on page 241.
- **Sticker Bag** (page 350)
  Use illustration 9-26 "Magic Stickers" on page 241.

LOOT BAG "LOOT"

Looking for something to put in those loot bags? Here are some creative suggestions you can make, or if you are short of time, you can buy.

LOOT YOU CAN MAKE:

- **Magic Stickers** (page 232)
- **Rabbit Straws** (page 226)
- **Rabbit Suckers** (page 226)
- **Magic Polaroid® Photo Frame** (page 229)
- **Magic Wand** (in "Magician's Costume" page 234)
- **Magic Wheels** (page 232)
- **Magician's Cape** (page 235)
- **Pop-Up Rabbit** (page 233)
- **Cookie Wands** (page 329)

LOOT YOU CAN BUY:

- Magic tricks/novelty toys
- Playing cards
- Small books with magic tricks
- Top hat
- Magic wand
- Kaleidoscopes

ACTIVITIES

How about making some of your own magic?

Don't feel as if you have to do all of these activities—there isn't enough time at any party. Discuss with your child which ones he or she would like to do and plan your party activities accordingly.

ARRIVAL ACTIVITY

As each child arrives, let him/her pick a special name, as in "Mark the Amazing Magician," "Sammy the Swami," "Beth the Magic Bunny," and the like. Announce their name with a little fanfare.

 MAGIC MAZE

Recommended age: 2 and older

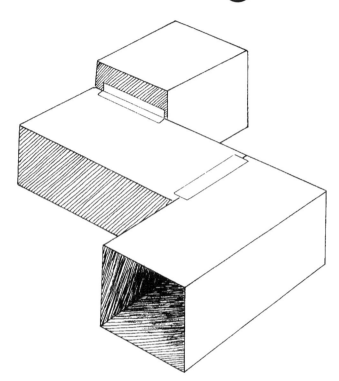

WHAT YOU NEED:

- Cardboard boxes (various sizes)
- Craft knife (adult use only)
- Duct tape or cloth-backed masking tape

WHAT YOU DO:

1. Assemble boxes in maze pattern.
2. Cut opening in connecting sides of boxes big enough for children to crawl through.
3. Tape ends together to secure in place.

RABBIT-IN-THE-HAT PHOTO BACKDROP

Recommended for all ages

Use Illustration 9–16 "Rabbit-in-the-Hat Photo Backdrop Pattern" and follow the directions for "Photo Backdrop" in **CRAFT TIPS** (page 354) to give children and their parents the best party favor they can have—a memorable "Magic Snapshot."

You can take a Polaroid® photograph and hand it out at the party (see "Polaroid® Photo Frame below), or you can use a 35 mm camera and a photo along with your thank-you note.

ILLUSTRATION
9-16

MAGIC POLAROID® PHOTO FRAME

Recommended for all ages

Hand out these wonderful memories at the party by using a Polaroid® photo and follow the directions for "Polaroid® Photo Frame" in **CRAFT TIPS** (page 357).

 THE EXTRA TOUCH

- Color frame with crayons, markers and/or colored pencils.
- Glue "Magic Stickers" (page 232) to "Photo Frame."
- Glue glitter and gummed stars to "Photo Frame" (Illustration 9-17).

MAGIC SHOW

Recommended for all ages

ILLUSTRATION 9-17

WHAT YOU NEED:
- Magic tricks (See following sections.)
- Rope
- Full-size sheet
- Card table
- Tablecloth
- Clothespins or safety pins

WHAT YOU DO:
Before the party:
1. Practice the magic tricks described below so you will be comfortable performing them in front of a group.
2. Stretch rope across party area and hang a sheet up as a curtain. Use pins to secure in place (Illustration 9-18).
3. Set card table in front of curtain and cover with tablecloth.
4. Have all props and magic tricks ready under table.

ILLUSTRATION 9-18

 THE EXTRA TOUCH

- Decorate Magic Show with "Stars and the Moon" (page 226) and "Star Streamers" (page 225).

MAGIC TRICKS

PENNY TRICK

WHAT YOU NEED:
- Hat ❀
- Pennies (6)

❀ Top hat if you can get one.

WHAT YOU DO:
1. Pick 6 pennies (each with a different date) and place them in a hat.
2. Have a volunteer pick a penny and pass it around to everyone. Then put the penny back in the hat.
3. Shake pennies around and, looking away from the hat, pick out the penny that was passed around.

THE TRICK IS:
You can tell which penny was passed around because it will be the warmest.

BALLOON TRICK

WHAT YOU NEED:
- Light-colored balloon (yellow)
- Dark-colored balloon (blue)
- Straight pin

WHAT YOU DO:
Before the party:
1. Insert yellow balloon inside blue balloon (Illustration 9–20 #1).
2. Inflate both balloons at the same time, but inflate the blue balloon slightly more, so there is a small amount of air space between the two.

During the party:
3. Hold pin so that it is concealed under tip of your finger.
4. Tell audience that with a few "magic words," you will turn the blue balloon into a yellow balloon.

THE TRICK IS:
With pin, prick the outer balloon to pop it, careful not to pop the inner balloon (Illustration 9-20 #2).

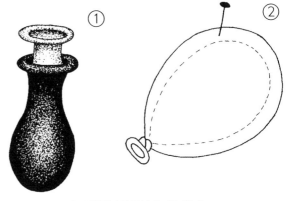

ILLUSTRATION 9-20 #1-2

CUP TRICK

WHAT YOU NEED:
- Cup
- Apple

WHAT YOU DO:
1. Tell your audience that you can "push an apple through the handle of a cup."

THE TRICK IS:
Put your finger through the handle and push the apple (Illustration 9-21).

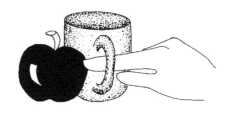

ILLUSTRATION 9-21

DISAPPEARING PENCIL

WHAT YOU NEED:
- Pencil
- Handkerchief
- Shirt with long sleeves

WHAT YOU DO:
Before the party:
1. Put on long-sleeved shirt.
2. Hold pencil upright in hand (Illustration 9–22 #1).
3. Cover pencil with handkerchief (Illustration 9–22 #2).
4. Remove handkerchief and reveal that the pencil has disappeared!

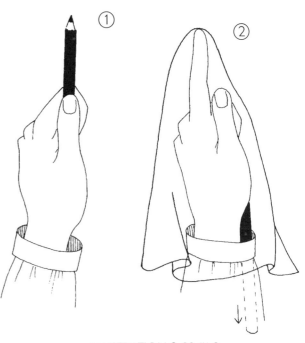

ILLUSTRATION 9-22 #1-2

THE TRICK IS:

After you cover the pencil with the handkerchief, replace it with your finger; before you remove the handkerchief, let pencil slip down your sleeve.

PALM READING

WHAT YOU NEED:

- Red marker (water based, not permanent)

WHAT YOU DO:

1. Hide marker in one hand.
2. Ask your audience if anyone wants to have his or her palm read.
3. Pick a volunteer and tell him to give you his palm.
4. As he extends a hand, make a red "X" on palm with marker.

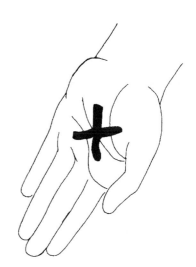

MAGIC BAG

WHAT YOU NEED:

- Coat with side pockets
- 2 paper (lunch) bags
- 1 handful of confetti
- Scissors
- White glue
- 2 sheets facial tissues (white)
- Straight pin

WHAT YOU DO:

Before the party:

1. Make a few small holes with pin in one of the bags (Illustration 9–24 #1).
2. Put confetti in bottom of the bag with the pinholes (Illustration 9–24 #2).
3. Cut 1/2" off top of second bag (Illustration 9–24 #3).
4. Insert second bag into first bag, making all sides fit flush (Illustration 9–24#4).
5. Glue top edges of inside bag to outside bag (Illustration 9–24 #5).

During the party:

6. Hold up bag and tell your audience that you are holding an ordinary bag.

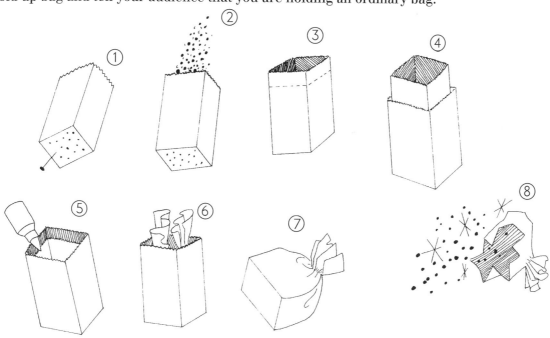

ILLUSTRATIONS 9-24 #1–8

7. Open bag, and in plain view, drop both tissues inside (Illustration 9–24 #6).
8. Blow up bag and pop (Illustration 9–24 #7).
9. When you pop the bag, confetti will explode and the tissues will "disappear" (Illustration 9–24 #8).

THE SECRET IS:

When you pop the bag, the confetti distracts your audience, and it will look like the tissue exploded into tiny pieces. During that moment, quickly crumple up the bag (with the tissues inside) and slip into a side pocket of your coat.

A MESSAGE FROM BEYOND

WHAT YOU NEED:
- Small fish bowl or round vase
- Votive candle
- Plain, white paper
- Lemon juice
- Small paint brush

WHAT YOU DO:

Before the party:
1. Dip paint brush in lemon juice and write a "message from beyond" on a piece of white paper.

During the party:
2. Place a votive candle inside glass fish bowl or round vase.
3. Light candle and hold paper over top of bowl (Illustration 9–25).
4. Watch your message mysteriously appear!
   [Suggested messages: "I am coming to get you!" "Help! Get me out of here!"]

ILLUSTRATION 9-25

CRAFTS

Children will have fun making these crafts as a group activity during the party or you can make these crafts yourself ahead of time and save money on party favors. Select one or two of the crafts for your party from the following list.

MAGIC STICKERS

Recommended age: 3 and older for gluing
5 and older for cutting and gluing

Make your own party stickers for children to use in various crafts and activities in this chapter. Use Illustration 9–26 "Magic Stickers" (page 241) and follow directions for "Party Stickers" in **CRAFT TIPS** (page 352).

You could also make "Space Stickers" for the Magic Party. Use Illustration 12–19 "Space Stickers" (page 307), and follow directions for "Party Stickers" in **CRAFT TIPS** (page 352).

MAGIC WHEELS

Recommended age: 6 and older

WHAT YOU NEED:
- Illustration 9–27 "Magic Wheels" (page 241)
- Copier paper (white)
- One sheet lightweight poster board or cardboard (any color)
- Scissors
- White glue
- Yarn or string (approximately 24" in length)
- Sharp pencil

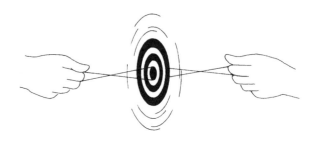

ILLUSTRATION 9-28

WHAT YOU DO:

Before the party:
    1. Photocopy Illustration 9–27 onto copier paper.

During the party:
    2. Cut out magic wheel with scissors.
    3. Trace wheel on poster board or cardboard. Then cut out traced cardboard circle.
    4. Glue a copy of each wheel to each side of poster board or cardboard wheel (Illustration 9-28 #1).
    5. Punch two holes through middle of wheel, where marked on illustration.
    6. Poke string through holes and tie tight knot (Illustration 9–28) forming large loop.
    7. Slide cardboard circle into center of loop (Illustration 9–28).
    8. Hold onto ends of loop and rotate circle several times to wind it up.
    9. Pull outward (towards ends of loop) to start wheel spinning (Illustration 9–28).
   10. When you pull again, you will reverse the spin.

ILLUSTRATION
9-28 #1

 THE EXTRA TOUCH

* Use markers or colored pencils to color wheel and watch the different patterns as the wheel spins.

POP-UP RABBIT

Recommended age: 5 and older

WHAT YOU NEED:

* One white sock (toddler or preschool size)
* One paper or plastic drinking cup
* One drinking straw
* Four cotton balls
* One rubberband (small)
* Felt scraps (pink)
* Yarn (pink or black)
* Two fake eyes
* White or tacky glue
* Scissors
* Sharp pencil

WHAT YOU DO:

Before the party:
    1. Stuff cotton balls into toe of sock.

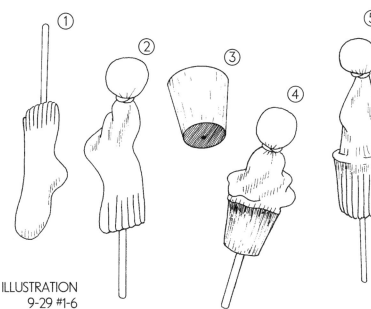
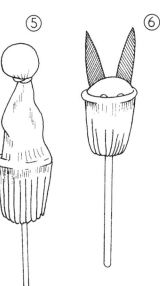

ILLUSTRATION
9-29 #1-6

2. Insert straw into toe of sock (Illustration 9–29 #1).
3. Tightly wind rubberband around toe of sock, securing straw in place (Illustration 9–29 #2).
4. Punch a hole in bottom of cup with pencil point (Illustration 9–29 #3).
5. Push end of straw through cup (Illustration 9–29 #4).
6. Slide sock over cup, and glue in place (Illustration 9–29 #5).
7. Cut out felt "ears" (2 for each puppet) and felt "nose" (one for each puppet).

During the party:

8. Tie yarn into a bow around "neck" of rabbit (approximately 8" in length).
9. Glue on fake eyes, felt "ears," and felt "nose."
10. Glue on pieces of yarn for "whiskers."
11. When glue is dry, push and pull puppet on stick to make rabbit move up and down (Illustration 9–29 #6).

MAGICIAN'S COSTUME

Recommended age: 5 and older

WHAT YOU NEED:

- Illustration 9–30 "Magician's Costume" (page 242)
- Copier paper or copier card stock (white) ✿
- One 14" length of elastic cord or one 14" length of yarn (for hat)
- Scissors (child-safe)
- Craft knife (adult use only)
- Hole punch or sharp pencil
- Drinking straw (for wand)
- Transparent tape
- Glue, glitter and sequins ✿✿
- Crayons, markers, colored pencils ✿✿

_____

✿ Card stock is preferred for this project.

✿✿ Optional

WHAT YOU DO:

Before the party:

1. Photocopy Illustration 9–30 "Magician's Costume" onto copier paper or card stock.
2. Using the craft knife, make slits on hat, as indicated in illustration. (If using copier paper, instead of card stock, you will have to reinforce holes with transparent tape before punching holes).

During the party:

3. Color hat and/or star, if desired.
4. Cut out hat, wand and star.
5. Insert band through slits on hat (Illustration 9–30 #1).

ILLUSTRATION 9-30 #1

ILLUSTRATION 9-30 #2

6. Punch a hole in ends of headband, as marked on illustration.
7. Tie one end of elastic cord through one hole in headband.
8. Thread other end of cord through other hole in headband and adjust length to fit child's head; then knot cord in place.
9. Tape a straw to the back of each star (Illustration 9–30 #2).
10. Decorate front of hat and star with glue, glitter and/or sequins, if desired.

MAGICIAN'S CAPE

Recommended age: 5 and older

WHAT YOU NEED:
- One 30-gallon plastic trashbag (black)
- Scissors
- One 36" length of 1/4" ribbon (black)
- Duct tape

WHAT YOU DO:
1. Cut trashbag along side and bottom to make two large rectangles (Illustration 9–32 #1).
2. Lay ribbon across top of bag, approximately 1/2" from edge. (Illustration 9–32 #2).
3. Fold top of bag over ribbon, forming a 1/2" casing for ribbon and tape slot in place (Illustration 9–32 #3).
4. Gather cape at the top (Illustration 9–32).
5. Tie cape around child's neck.
6. If cape is too long, trim with scissors.

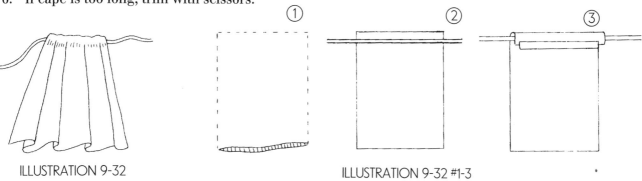

ILLUSTRATION 9-32

ILLUSTRATION 9-32 #1-3

GAMES

Select several of the games for your party from the following list. Don't feel as if you have to play all of them—there just isn't time. But you should plan for a few extra games. Here are some unique games for your Magic Party.

MAGICIAN'S CARD TOSS

Recommended age: 5 years and older

WHAT YOU NEED:
- 2 decks of playing cards (each deck with a different pattern or color on back)
- Top hat or basket

HOW TO PLAY:
1. Divide children into two teams.
2. Have children sit on opposite sides of a circle and place hat or basket in the center of the circle.
3. Give each team its own deck and divide cards equally among team members.
4. Rotating clockwise, children take turns tossing cards into hat or basket.
5. Team with most cards in hat or basket wins.

ILLUSTRATION 9-33

DISAPPEARING ROOM

Recommended age: 6 years and older

WHAT YOU NEED:
- Items to serve as obstacles in an obstacles course, such as chairs, tables, ladder(s), cardboard boxes
- Blindfold

HOW TO PLAY:
1. Create an obstacle course in party area for children to walk through, step over and/or crawl under.
2. Bring children to the course and tell them that they are to go through the course, one at a time, blindfolded. (Give children a few minutes to walk through the course to become familiar with the location of the different obstacles.)
3. Take children to another area, where they cannot see or hear anything going on in the obstacle course.
4. Quickly remove all obstacles from the "obstacle course."
5. Now the fun begins! Blindfold the first player (birthday child) and take him/her to the start of the "obstacle course." Tell player to start the course, and as he/she plays, "caution" him/her about the different "obstacles." (Try not to laugh out loud or you might give away the game.)
6. Once the child has figured out the game, take the blindfold off, and bring out the next "victim."
7. Each player who completes the course can then watch the others play the game.

ESCAPE ARTIST GAME

Recommended age: 7 years and older

WHAT YOU NEED:
- 2 ropes (heavy), each approximately 10' in length

HOW TO PLAY:
1. Divide children into two teams, lined up single file.
2. Give each team one rope.
3. At start of game, first person in line ties a knot in the rope. He/she then passes the rope to the next player on the team, who ties a knot in the rope. The game continues until every player has tied a knot in his/her team's rope.
4. Teams then exchange ropes.
5. The race begins as the first player of each team unties a knot on the rope. The rope is passed on to the next player, who unties another knot in the rope.
6. The first team to untie all of the knots on its rope, wins.

INVISIBLE SCARF

Recommended age: 4 years and older

WHAT YOU NEED:
- Scarf

HOW TO PLAY:

1. Have children sit in a circle. Select one child to be the "magician" (birthday child first).
2. The magician walks around the outside of the circle, carrying the scarf in one hand. When magician wants someone to be "It," magician drops the scarf behind that child.
3. As soon as "It" realizes the scarf is behind him/her, "It" gets up and chases the magician around the circle. Magician races back to "It's" spot in the circle.
4. If the magician gets there first, "It" becomes the next magician. If "It" outruns the magician, magician remains playing the magician, and the game continues.

MORE GAMES...

It's always a good idea to plan some extra party games. Here are some standard party games, adapted for your Magic Party. Specific directions for these games are listed in **APPENDIX D: GAMES**, beginning on page 363.

↻ RABBIT-IN-THE-HAT BEAN BAG TOSS

Recommended age: 5 years and older

Follow the directions for "Bean Bag Toss" in **GAMES** (page 364). Use the "Rabbit-in-the-Hat Photo Backdrop" (page 228) as the theme backdrop.

WHO HAS THE PENNY?

Recommended age: 5 years or older

Follow the directions for "Who Has it?" in **GAMES** (page 371). Use a shiny penny as the theme toy in playing this game.

QUICK CHANGE ARTIST RELAY RACE

Recommended age: 6 years and older

Follow the directions for "Quick Change Relay Race" in **GAMES** (page 368).

THE VANISHING ACT

Recommended age: 5 years and older

This game is "hide-and-seek" in reverse. Follow the directions for "Sardines" in **GAMES** (page 369).

MAGIC CARPET RIDE

Recommended age: 6 years and older

Follow the directions for "Stepping Stones" in **GAMES** (page 370). Throughout the race, children's feet must never touch the ground as they walk on their "magic carpet."

MAGIC TAG

Recommended age: 6 years and older

Follow the directions for "Freeze Tag" in **GAMES** (page 366), and use a "Magic Wand" from the magician's costume (page 234) to play the game.

MAGIC MEMORY GAME

Recommended age: 8 years and older

Follow the directions for "Memory Game" in **GAMES** (page 367), and use common household objects to play the game.

ILLUSTRATION
9-04

ILLUSTRATION
9-11

THANK YOU

Magic Party

FOR

DATE

TIME

PLACE

R.S.V.P.

ILLUSTRATION 9-03

ILLUSTRATION 9-05

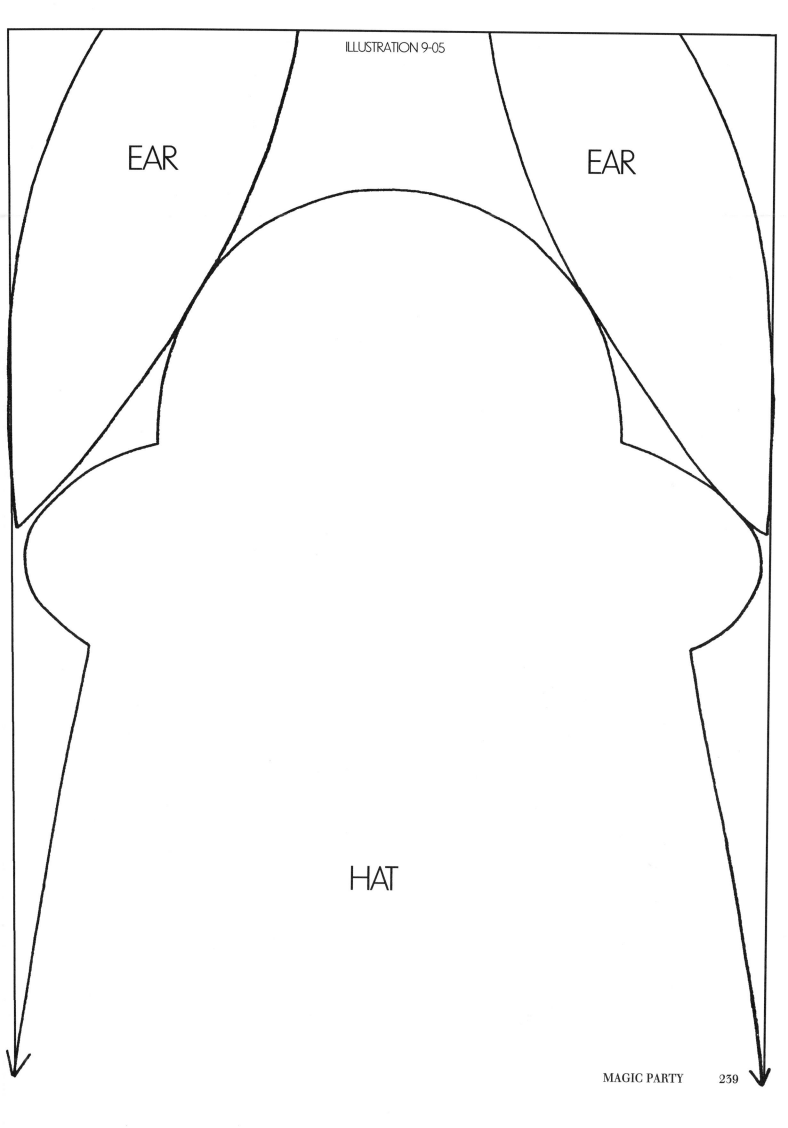

EAR

EAR

HAT

ILLUSTRATION 9-09

HIT OF THE PARTY

ILLUSTRATION 9-26

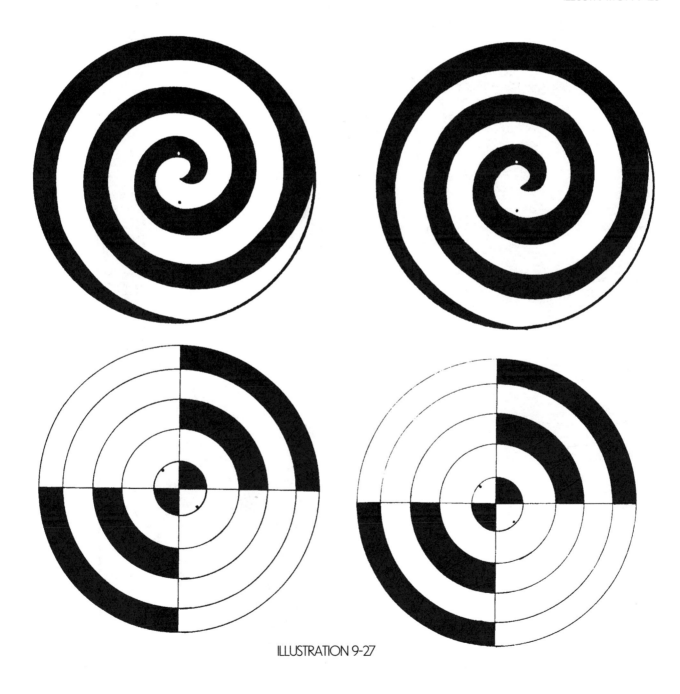

ILLUSTRATION 9-27

ILLUSTRATION 9-30

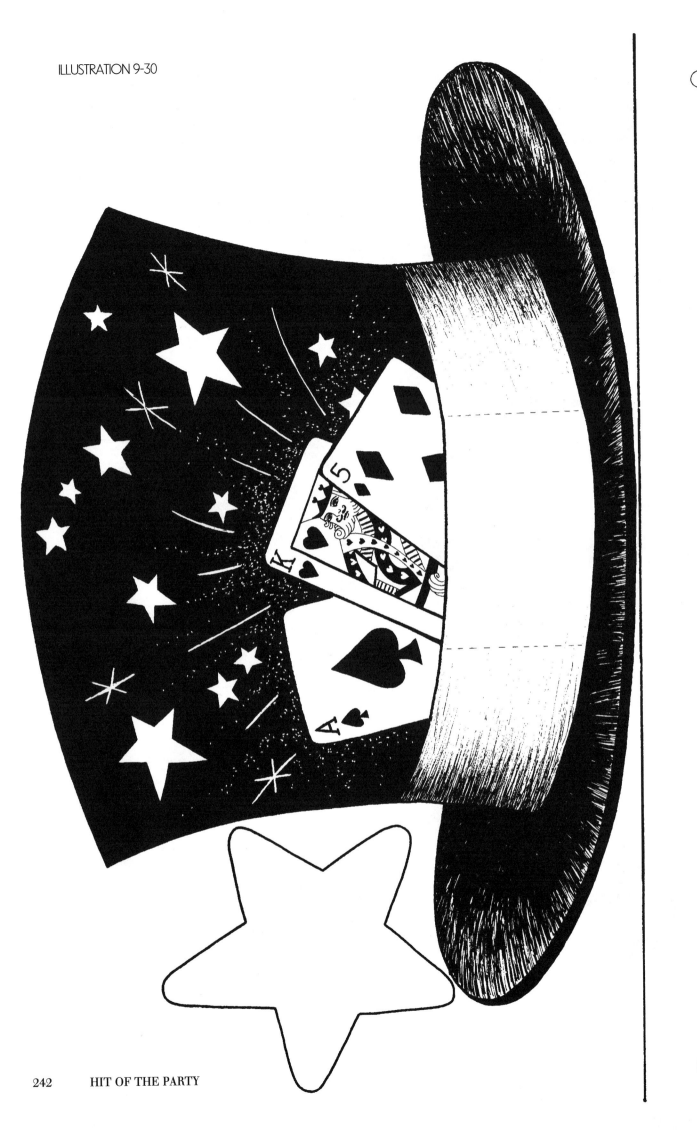

HIT OF THE PARTY

Dress-Up Tea Party

CHAPTER 10

This is an elegant party for young ladies! Come join the fun and dress in all your fancy finery. You are one year older today, and very grown up!

ILLUSTRATION 10-01

DRESS UP TEA PARTY

TEAPOT INVITATION

Estimated Time: 3–4 minutes each

Let this darling teapot invite your guests to your special day. Guests will delight in pulling out the RSVP and finding that it is a tea bag!

WHAT YOU NEED:

- Illustration 10–03 "Teapot Invitation" (page 258)
- Copier paper (white or pink) or copier card stock ✿
- 5" thread and straight pin
- Envelopes (3 5/8" x 6 1/2")
- Scissors
- White glue
- Craft knife (adult use only)
- Felt-tip pen (black)
- Crayons, markers and/or colored pencils ✿✿

ILLUSTRATION 10-02

———

✿ Card stock is preferred for this project.

✿✿ Optional

WHAT YOU DO:

1. Make one photocopy of Illustration 10–03. This is your "master copy." Fill out all party information with felt-tip pen on master copy (Illustration 10–02 #1).
2. Photocopy as many invitations as needed (Illustration 10–02 #2).
3. Color invitations, if desired.
4. Using craft knife, cut slit along dotted line on teapot (Illustration 10–02 #3).
5. With scissors, cut out tab, tea bag, teapot and heart (Illustration 10–02 #4).
6. Punch hole where indicated on tab and tea bag with straight pin (Illustration 10–02 #5).
7. Tie thread on tea bag and tab (Illustration 10–02 #6).
8. Slip tea bag through slit of the teapot (Illustration 10–02).
9. Cut out heart and glue on back of envelope to seal.

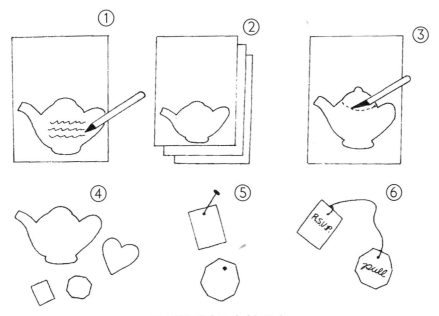

ILLUSTRATION 10-02 #1-6

👉 THE EXTRA TOUCH

- Ask children to come dressed in their mother's clothes.

DRESS-UP THANK-YOU NOTE

The "Dress-up Tea Party Thank-You Note" (Illustration 10–04) is on the same page as the "Teapot Invitation." When you photocopy the invitation, you will also be copying the thank-you note. Simply cut out the thank-you note, and write your personal message in the space provided.

Estimated time: 1 minute each

MENU

Those lovely, little ladies will delight in tasting the treats on your table. Choose foods from each group, and follow the recipes on the pages listed below.

DRINKS:

EATS:

CAKE AND ICE CREAM:

TEAPOT CAKE

Estimated time: 1–1 1/2 hours

INGREDIENTS:

ILLUSTRATION 10-06

1	"Basic Cake" recipe in Appendix A on pages 343 and 344; or use your favorite box cake mix
2	"Buttercream Frosting" recipes in Appendix A on page 345; or two cans of your favorite canned frosting
1	Tube gel frosting (green)
1/2 c.	Heart-shaped candies or other small candies
4	Gumdrops (pink)
	Red food coloring
	Wax paper
	Toothpicks
	13" x 18" tray or foil-covered board
	Illustration 10–05 "Teapot Cake Pattern" (page 259)

DIRECTIONS:

1. Prepare and bake cake in two 8" round cake pans as directed in recipe or cake package.
2. Cool cake completely on wire rack.

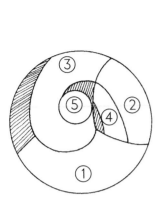

ILLUSTRATION 10-06 #1

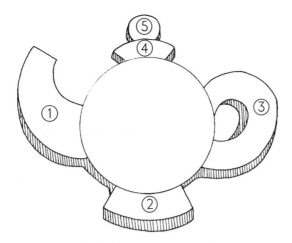

ILLUSTRATION 10-06 #2

ILLUSTRATION 10-06 #3

3. Wrap in plastic wrap and freeze cake at least 45 minutes. (Freezing the cake does not affect its flavor and makes it easier to work with. It also enables you to make the cake ahead of time, to help balance your work load for the party.)
4. Trace Illustration 10–05 "Teapot Cake Pattern," on wax paper. Cut out wax paper pattern into sections and reassemble on top of one cake round.
5. Using long knife, cut cake into sections by following pattern (Illustration 10–06 #1).
6. Assemble sections on a tray into shape of a teapot (Illustration 10–06 #2).
7. Tint buttercream frosting pink by adding a few drops of red food coloring and mix until color is uniform.
8. Frost connecting sections of cake with pink frosting.
9. Frost top and sides of cake with pink frosting.
10. Cut gumdrops into three slices each (Illustration 10–06 #3).
11. Arrange slices in a flower pattern in center of teapot (Illustration 10–06).
12. Draw a zig-zag line around top edges of cake with green gel frosting (Illustration 10–06).
13. Decorate with candy hearts of other small candies.

DOLL CAKE

Estimated Time: 20–30 minutes

Here's a quick way to decorate a store bought cake—and one your guests will find utterly charming.

INGREDIENTS:

1	Frosted store-bought cake (round)
1	Doll (either half-doll or doll 7 1/2" in height) ❀
8	Gumdrops (pink)
8 1/2 oz.	Heart-shaped candies or other small candies

❀ available at craft and hobby stores

DIRECTIONS:

1. Place frosted cake on a plate or serving platter.
2. Insert half-doll into center of cake or cut out hole in center of cake or insert 7 1/2" doll in hole.
3. Cut 8 gumdrops into 3 slices each, yielding a total of 24 slices.
4. Stick gumdrop slices in rows across doll's chest to form bodice.
5. Arrange a row of slices around "waist."
6. Trim tops and bottom edges of cake with gumdrops, heart or other small candies (Illustration 10–07).

ILLUSTRATION 10-07

DECORATIONS

It doesn't take much to create an elegant setting for your young ladies. You can use decorations as craft activities at your party. Or, save money by giving some of these decorations out as favors in your loot bags.

PARTY STREAMERS

Estimated time: 1–2 minutes per streamer

Select one (or more) of the streamers suggested below, and follow the directions for "Party Streamers" in **CRAFT TIPS** (page 349).

- **Flower Streamer** Pattern CT-01 (page 361)
  Use bright colors of crepé paper.
- **Doll Streamer** Pattern CT-02 (page 359)
  Use pink crepé paper and the "girl" pattern.

 TIMESAVER

- Hang crepé paper streamers (in pre-packaged rolls) around party area.

PLACE-CARD DOLL

Estimated time: 2–3 minutes each

WHAT YOU NEED:
- Illustration 10–09 "Place-Card Doll" (page 260)
- Copier paper or copier card stock (white or pink)
- Scissors
- Stapler
- Crayons and/or markers ❊

❊ Optional

This project can be completed ahead of time, or during the party as a craft activity.

ILLUSTRATION 10-08

ILLUSTRATION 10-08 #1

WHAT YOU DO:
1. Photocopy Illustration 10–09 onto copier paper or card stock.
2. Write out name of each guest on front of "apron" (Illustration 10-08).
3. Color dolls, if desired.
4. Cut out doll along outer lines.
5. Bring ends of doll together and staple into cone shape (Illustration 10–08 #1).

☞ **THE EXTRA TOUCH**

- Glue sequins, feathers, lace, ribbon and/or paper flowers to doll

THE FLOWER STRAWS

Estimated time: 1–2 minutes each

Make your own "Flower Straws" (Illustration 10-10) and watch children giggle as they sip those delicious drinks. Use Illustration 10–11 "The Flower Straw" (page 258) and follow directions for "Drinking Straws" in **CRAFT TIPS** (page 353).

ILLUSTRATION 10-10

 **FLOWER SUCKERS**

Estimated time: 1–2 minutes each

Make your own "Flower Suckers." (Illustration 10-12) Use Illustration 10–11 "Flower Straw" (page 258) and follow directions for "Party Suckers" in **CRAFT TIPS** (page 353).

💡 MORE DECORATING IDEAS...

- Use a lace tablecloth to cover party table.
- Set out pink plastic tablecloth and white doily placemats.
- Cover table with butcher paper and make "Heart Prints" with heart-shaped sponge and tempera paint.
- Make placemats by photocopying illustration 10-21 "Dress-Up Costume" (page 261) onto copier paper (white or bright colors). Provide crayons for children to color placemats, if desired.
- Make placemats by having children glue "Flower Stickers"(page 252) onto 9" x 12" sheet of construction paper. Provide crayons, markers and/or colored pencils for children to color placemats, if desired.
- Decorate party area with dolls and teddy bears.
- Buy flowering plants in inexpensive pony packs. Pot each one in a paper cup, with guest's name written on outside, and use as place-setting. Then give away as a party favor.
- Tape "Flower Stickers" (page 252) to pipe cleaners or straws and place in small vases or small cups of soil (Illustration 10-13).
- Arrange fresh flowers in a short vase and place on party table.
- Photocopy "Teapot Cake" illustration 10-01 (page 244) and tape to front door or front of party area.

ILLUSTRATION 10-12

ILLUSTRATION 10-13

LOOT BAGS

Select one (or more) of the following loot bags and follow the directions for "Loot Bags" in **CRAFT TIPS** (page 350).

- **Picnic Basket** (page 350)
- **Sticker Bag** (page 350)
  Use illustration 10-19 "Flower Sticker (page 260.)
- **Treasure Box** (page 351)
  Use illustration 10-19 "Flower Stickers" (page 260.)
- **Hat Bag** (page 351)
  Use illustration 10-21 "Dress-up Hat" (page 261.)

LOOT BAG "LOOT"

Looking for something to put in those loot bags? Here are some creative suggestions you can make, or if you are short of time, you can buy.

LOOT YOU CAN MAKE:

- **Flower Stickers** (page 252)
- **Flower Straws** (page 248)
- **Flower Suckers** (page 249)
- **Dress-Up Polaroid® Photo Frame** (page 251)
- **Paper Doll and Clothes** (page 253)
- **Candy Necklace** (page 253)
- **Yarn Doll** (page 253)
- **Dress-up Jewelry** (in "Dress-up Costume" page 252)
- **Flower Cookie Pops** (page 329)
- **Cookie Puppets** (page 329)

LOOT YOU CAN BUY:

- Costume jewelry
- Hair bows
- Small dolls
- Coin purses
- Address books
- Tiara
- Comb and brush
- Child make-up sets
- Flower seeds
- Heart-shaped candies wrapped in tissue paper and tied with a ribbon.

ACTIVITIES

Your little ladies will be anxious to get started, so let the fun begin!

Don't feel as if you have to do all of these activities—there isn't enough time at any party. Discuss with your child which ones he or she would like to do and plan your party activities accordingly.

ARRIVAL ACTIVITY

Have a trunk or box of "dress-up" clothes waiting by the door, old hats, scarves, shawls, shoes (no high heels!), dresses, gloves, etc. As each guest arrives, let her pick her own dress-up wardrobe and put it on. (Keep a large mirror nearby.)

Once a wardrobe has been selected, introduce guests with a special name, as in "Lady Linda," "The Elegant Miss Emma," "Divine Diane," and the like. Announce their name with a little fanfare.

 ## THE EXTRA TOUCH

- Have child make-up and nail polish for guests to put on as one of their first activities. Have several hand mirrors available so children can see their handiwork.

 PLAY HOUSE

Recommended for all ages

With a recycled appliance box, and a little imagination, you can create an activity center where children can play while the other guests arrive.

WHAT YOU NEED:

- Large cardboard box (refrigerator/large appliance)
- Scissors
- Craft knife (adult use only)
- Ruler
- Pencil
- Duct tape or cloth-backed masking tape
- Fabric or towel (large enough to cover any windows)
- Crayons, markers and/or poster paints ❀

❀ Optional

WHAT YOU DO:

1. Draw door and windows where you want them.
2. Using craft knife, cut out door and windows. *[NOTE: See "Cardboard Play Structures" in **CRAFT TIPS** (page 355) for suggestions on safe and easy ways to cut cardboard and making hinged doors/windows.]*
3. Make a "[Birthday Child's Name] Play House" sign out of any leftover cardboard.
4. Take a piece of fabric or towel, slightly larger than the window, and tape to inside of the window, as a curtain.
5. Paint or draw decorative trim or flowers on the outside of the house; paint or draw furniture on the walls of the inside of the house.

FLOWER PHOTO BACKDROP

Recommended for all ages

Use Illustration 10–17 "Flower Photo Backdrop Pattern" and follow the directions for "Photo Backdrop" in **CRAFT TIPS** (page 354) to give children and their parents the best party favor they can have—a memorable "Dress-Up Tea Party Snapshot."

You can take a Polaroid® photograph and hand it out at the party (see "Polaroid® Photo Frame below), or you can use a 35 mm camera and send a photo along with your thank-you note.

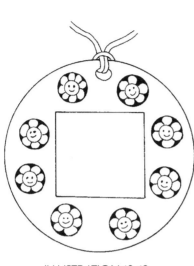

ILLUSTRATION 10-18

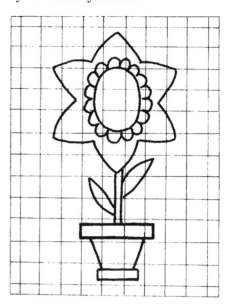

ILLUSTRATION 10-17

DRESS–UP POLAROID® PHOTO FRAME

Recommended for all ages

Hand out these wonderful memories at the party by using a Polaroid® photo and follow the directions for "Polaroid® Photo Frame" in **CRAFT TIPS** (page 357).

THE EXTRA TOUCH

- Glue "Flower Stickers" (page 252) on frame (Illustration 10-18).

FASHION SHOW

Recommended for ages 6 and older

WHAT YOU NEED:
- Box or trunk of "dress-up" clothes, including hats, costume jewelry, shoes (no heels) and other finery
- "Dress-Up Costume" (page 252)
- "Candy Necklace" (page 253)

WHAT YOU DO:
1. Mark off a "runway" approximately 10'-15'.
2. Put on some music, and have your young ladies put on their own fashion show.
3. Have fun describing the outfits as the young models stroll down the runway.

CRAFTS

Children will have fun making these crafts as a group activity during the party or you can make these crafts yourself ahead of time and save money on party favors. Select one or two of the crafts for your party from the following list. Don't feel as if you have to all of them—there just isn't time.

FLOWER STICKERS

Recommended age: 3 and older for gluing
5 and older for cutting and gluing

Make your own party stickers for children to use in various crafts and activities in this chapter. Use Illustration 10–19 "Flower Stickers" (page 260) and follow directions for "Party Stickers" in **CRAFT TIPS** (page 352).

You could also make "Teddy Bear Picnic Stickers" for the Dress-Up Tea Party. Use Illustration 1–29 "Teddy Bear Picnic Stickers" (page 44), and follow directions for "Party Stickers" in **CRAFT TIPS** (page 352).

DRESS-UP COSTUME

Recommended age: 5 and older

WHAT YOU NEED:

- Illustration 10–21 "Dress-Up Costume" (page 261)
- Copier paper (pink or white) or copier card stock ❀
- One 14" length of elastic cord or one 14" length of yarn (for hat)
- One 18" length of yarn or one 18" length of 1/4" ribbon (for necklace)
- Rubberbands
- Scissors (child-safe)
- Craft knife (adult use only)
- Hole punch
- Crayons, markers and/or colored pencils ❀❀
- Transparent tape ❀❀

❀ Card stock is preferred for this project.

❀❀ Optional

WHAT YOU DO:

Before the party:

1. Photocopy Illustration 10–21 "Dress-up Costume" onto copier paper or card stock.
2. Using the craft knife, make slit on hat, as indicated by dotted lines. (If using copier paper, instead of card stock, you will have to reinforce holes with transparent tape before punching holes).

During the party:

3. Color hat and jewelry, if desired.
4. Cut out hat, hatband and jewelry.
5. Punch a hole in ends of hatband and jewelry, as marked on illustration.
6. Slip band through slits in hat (Illustration 10–20 #1).
7. Tie one end of elastic cord through one hole in headband.
8. Thread other end of cord through other hole in headband and adjust length to fit child's head; then knot cord in place.
9. To make necklace, thread yarn or ribbon through heart and tie around child's neck.
10. To wear earrings, tie rubberband through hole; then slip rubberband over ear (Illustration 10–20 #2).

    [NOTE: On the same page as the "Dress-Up Costume" is a pair of lips. The lips are used in the game, "Pin the Kiss on the Birthday Girl." However, you may want to use the lips to make name tags and pin the lips on the guests.]

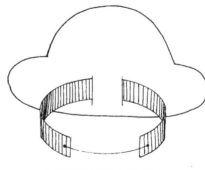

ILLUSTRATION 10-20 #1

ILLUSTRATION
10-20 #2

 THE EXTRA TOUCH

- Dress-up the "Dress-up Hat" by gluing on feathers, sequins, lace trim, glitter and/or "Flower Stickers" (above).
- Add beads to necklace. See "Indian Bead Necklace" (page 117).

CANDY NECKLACE

Recommended age: 5 and older

WHAT YOU NEED:
- Yarn or string (36" lengths for each necklace)
- Hollow licorice sticks (cut into 1/2"–3/4" pieces)
- "O-shaped" candies and cereals
- Cupcake pans, muffin tins or small bowls

WHAT YOU DO:
Before the party:
1. Fill cupcake pans, muffin tins or small bowls with candies and cereals.

During the party:
2. Place containers of candy and cereal on party table.
3. Give each child a length of string or yarn and have children string their own necklaces.

 THE EXTRA TOUCH
- Use licorice whips instead of yarn or string and the entire necklace is edible.
- Have children make bracelets to match their new necklaces.

PAPER DOLL AND CLOTHES

Recommended age: 5 or older

WHAT YOU NEED:
- Illustration 10–24 "Paper Doll and Clothes" (page 262)
- Copier paper or copier card stock (pink or white)
- Scissors (child-safe)
- Crayons or colored pencils ❀

❀ Optional

WHAT YOU DO:
Before the party:
1. Photocopy Illustration 10–24 onto copier paper.

During the party:
2. Color paper dolls and clothes, if desired.
3. Cut out dolls with scissors.

 THE EXTRA TOUCH
- Roll up a photocopy of paper doll and clothes and tie with a ribbon. Then place in loot bag. Include crayons, markers and/or colored pencils and child-safe scissors.

YARN DOLL

Recommended age: 7 and older

WHAT YOU NEED:
- One 4 oz. skein of 4-ply yarn (pink) will make 9 dolls
- 6 feet of 4-ply yarn (red) per doll
- Cardboard (8 1/2" x 11") or thin book (8 1/2" x 11") per doll
- One cotton ball per doll
- Two fake, wiggly eyes per doll
- White or tacky glue

WHAT YOU DO:
1. Wrap pink yarn around length of board or book, 36 times (Illustration 10–25 #1).
2. Trim end of yarn even with board or book (Illustration 10–25 #1).
3. Cut a 6" strand of pink yarn and slip it under all strands of yarn at one end of board (Illustration 10–25 #1).

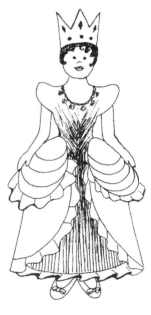

ILLUSTRATION 10-25

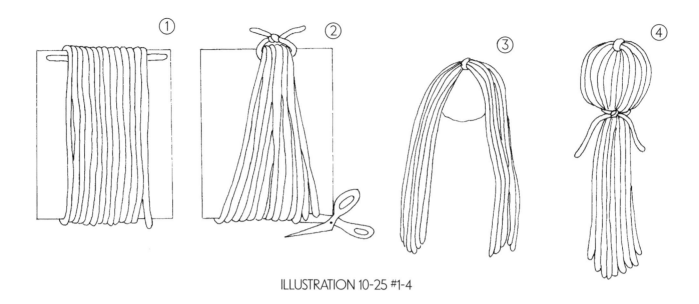

ILLUSTRATION 10-25 #1-4

4. Pull all strands together by tying a tight knot with pink piece of yarn (Illustration 10–25 #2).
5. Using scissors, cut through all yarn at the other end (Illustration 10–25 #2).
6. Place knotted yarn bundle over a cotton ball (Illustration 10–25 #3).
7. Arrange yarn strands so cotton ball is covered (Illustration 10–25 #4).
8. Tie a 12" piece of pink yarn around neck in a tight knot (Illustration 10–25 #4).
9. Using 9 strands of yarn at a time, braid 2 arms (Illustration 10–25 #5).
10. Tie a 3" strand of pink yarn around each "wrist" and knot in place (Illustration 10–25 #5).
11. Tie a 12" strand of red yarn around "waist" in a tight knot and then tie yarn into a bow (Illustration 10–25 #5).
12. Glue fake eyes on "face."
13. Glue a 1/2" piece of red yarn to form "mouth."
14. Using one 6" strand of red yarn, tie all nine of the 6" strands of red yarn to the knot on top of the head to form "hair" (Illustration 10–25).

ILLUSTRATION 10-25 #5

 THE EXTRA TOUCH

• Make accessories for doll from felt scraps, buttons, sequins, and/or feathers.

GAMES

Select several of the games for your party from the following list. Don't feel as if you have to play all of them, but you should plan for a few extra games. Here are some unique games for your Dress-Up Tea Party.

PIN THE KISS ON THE BIRTHDAY GIRL

Recommended age: 3 years and older

WHAT YOU NEED:

- Large sheet of butcher paper
- Illustration 10–27 "Kissing Lips" (page 261) ❀
- Copier paper or copier card stock (white or pink)
- Masking tape or double-stick tape
- Pencil
- Blindfold
- Scissors
- Crayons or poster paints

HOW TO PLAY:

Before the party:

1. Photocopy Illustration 10–27 "Kissing Lips" onto copier paper or copier card stock, and cut out one pair of lips for each guest.
2. Make a body-tracing of birthday child on butcher paper. Cut out tracing and have birthday child draw or paint on clothing, facial and body features, including a tracing of "kissing lips" where mouth is.

During the party:

3. Hang birthday child's body-tracing on flat wall or garage door.
4. Write each guest's name on front of "Kissing Lips" and place a piece of double-stick tape (or masking tape rolled onto itself) on back of lips.
5. Blindfold first in line (birthday child first) and spin child 2–3 times. Then hand child her "Kissing Lips" and tell her to place lips on birthday child's "mouth."

TIME FOR A COMMERCIAL!

Recommended for ages 7 years and older

WHAT YOU NEED:

- Ordinary household products, like mouthwash, shampoo, cereal, pet food, etc.

HOW TO PLAY:

1. Give each child a different product or divide group into teams and give each team one product.
2. Have each child or team take turns presenting a (60 second) commercial.

↻RELAY CROQUET

Recommended age: 6 years and older

WHAT YOU NEED:

- Two broom handles or two dowels (1/2" diameter and 30" in length)
- Two 2-liter empty soda bottles
- Duct tape
- Two tennis balls or small rubber balls
- Matched sets of empty oatmeal boxes, juice and/or coffee cans (at least six sets)
- Sand
- String or bag of flour

HOW TO PLAY:

Before the party:

1. To make croquet "mallets" (one for each team), slide empty 2-liter bottle over one end of dowel (or broom handle) and let stick rest at bottom of bottle.

2. Use duct tape to secure the bottle in place (Illustration 10–28 #1).
3. To make croquet "wickets," pour sand into matched sets of empty oatmeal boxes, juice and/or coffee cans. To use "wickets," place two boxes or cans of each set 4–6" apart, and hit the ball between them.
4. Lay out croquet course in party area.
5. Mark course with string or by dropping flour from bag.

During the party:
6. Divide children into two teams.
7. The first member of each team starts the game by hitting the ball through the course.
8. The first team to have all players complete the course, wins.

ILLUSTRATION 10-28 #1

WHO AM I?

Recommended age: 7 years and older

WHAT YOU NEED:
- Index cards (3" x 5")
- Safety pins
- Pen or pencil

HOW TO PLAY:
1. Write out names of various professionals, such as: doctor, teacher, scientist, lawyer, judge, airline pilot, actress, dancer, singer, artist, politician, fire fighter, policewoman, etc.
2. Pin one card on the back of each child without letting that child know what he/she is.
3. Each child tries to find out who or what he/she is by asking everyone else "yes" or "no" questions. (For example: "Do I help people who are sick?" "Do I wear a badge?" "Do I work with children?" "Do I entertain people?")
4. The game is played until everyone guesses who or what they are.

NECKLACE RELAY RACE

Recommended age: 6 years and older

WHAT YOU NEED:
- 2 bowls
- 16 oz. large tube-shaped pasta
- 2 shoe laces (24"–30" in length)

HOW TO PLAY:
Before the party:
1. Place an equal number of pasta "beads" in each bowl or basket.
2. Tie one bead on the end of each shoe lace to keep other beads from slipping off.

During the party:
3. Divide children into two relay teams.
4. Mark a start/finish line for relay race and place bowls 15'–20' from start/finish line.
5. Give first player of each team a shoelace.
6. Explain to children that each team has its own bowl of "beads." The first player from each team starts the game by racing to the bowl and threading one "bead" on the shoelace.
7. That player then races back to the start/finish line and hands over the necklace to the next player in line.
8. The next player rushes to the bowl and threads a second bead on the shoelace; then races back to the start/finish line, and hands shoelaces to the next player in line.
9. The first team to complete the necklace, wins.

MORE GAMES...

It's always a good idea to plan some extra party games. Here are some standard party games, adapted for your Dress-up Tea Party. Specific directions for these games are listed in **APPENDIX D: GAMES**, beginning on page 363.

⟳TEA PARTY TOSS

Recommended age: 3 years and older

Follow the directions for "Bean Bag Toss" in **GAMES** (page 364). Use "Flower Photo Backdrop" (page 351) as the theme backdrop.

CRY, CRY BABY

Recommended age: 4 years and older

Follow the directions for "Duck, Duck Goose" in **GAMES** (page 365), and select one child to be the "mommy" (birthday child first) and have mommy walk around the outside of the circle, tapping each child on the head or shoulder lightly, saying, "Cry." When mommy wants someone to be be "It," mommy taps that child and says, "Baby."

DRESS-UP RELAY RACE

Recommended age: 6 years and older

Follow the directions for "Quick Change Relay Race" in **GAMES** (page 368), and use "dress-up" clothes for the young ladies to wear.

TEA TIME MUSICAL CHAIRS

Recommended age: 6 years and older

Follow the directions for "Fun Time Musical Chairs" in **GAMES** (page 366), and select "sophisticated" music.

DRESS-UP MEMORY GAME

Recommended age: 8 years or older

Follow the directions for "Memory Game" in **GAMES** (page 367), and include costume jewelry, make-up items, toiletries and other dress-up items.

DROP THE BEADS IN THE BOTTLE

Recommended age: 4 years and older

Follow the directions for "Drop the Clothespins in the Bottle" in **GAMES** (page 365), and use beads (plastic or wooden) to play the game.

TEA PARTY EGG RELAY RACE

Recommended age: 6 years and older

Follow the directions for "Egg Relay Race" in **GAMES** (page 366).

TEA TIME STEPPING STONES

Recommended age: 6 years and older

Follow the directions for "Stepping Stones" in **GAMES** (page 370).

ILLUSTRATION
10-04

Thank You

ILLUSTRATION
10-11

pull

Dress up Tea Party
for
Birthday
Date
Time
Place

r.s.v.p.

ILLUSTRATION
10-03

ILLUSTRATION 10-05

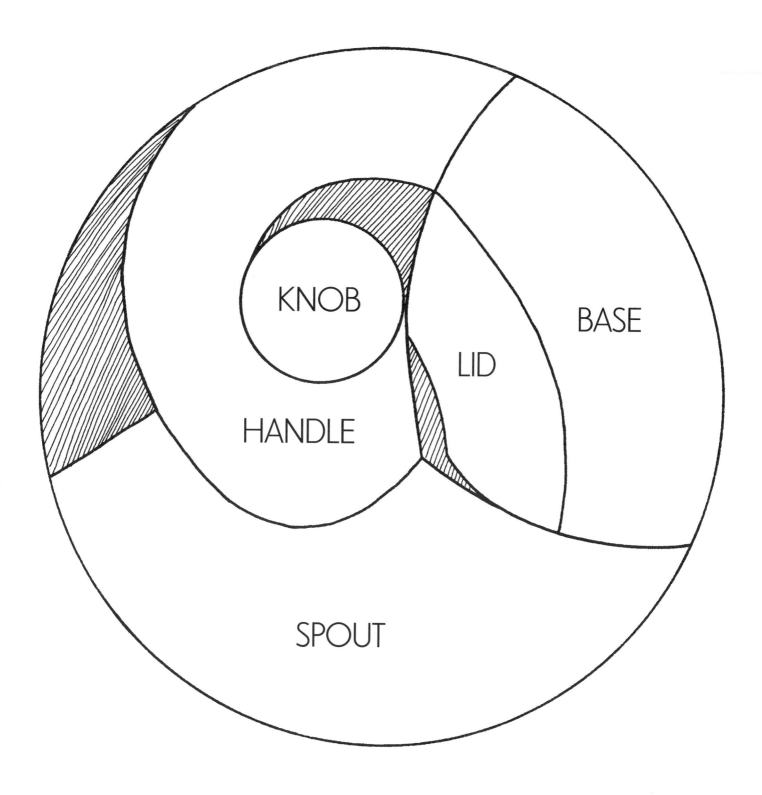

ILLUSTRATION
10-19

ILLUSTRATION
10-09

ILLUSTRATION
10-21

ILLUSTRATION
10-27

ILLUSTRATION 10-24

Under the Sea Party

CHAPTER 11

Under the waves, where fishies swim and play, sea creatures are gathering together for a wondrous event...your birthday party! So, dive in and join the fun.

ILLUSTRATION 11-01

SHARK INVITATION

Estimated Time: 2–3 minutes each

WHAT YOU NEED:

- Illustration 11–03 "Shark Invitation" (page 280)
- Copier paper (white or blue)
- Envelopes (3 5/8" x 6 1/2")
- Scissors
- Felt-tip pen (black)
- Crayons, colored pencils, markers, and/or watercolors ❀

❀ Optional

ILLUSTRATION 11-02

WHAT YOU DO:

1. Make one photocopy of Illustration 11–03. This is your "master copy." Fill out all of party information with felt-tip pen on master copy (Illustration 11–02 #1).
2. Photocopy as many invitations as needed (Illustration 11–02 #2).
3. Color invitations, if desired.
4. Cut out invitations along outer lines (Illustration 11–02 #3).
5. Fold invitation in half, lengthwise, with design on outside (Illustration 11–02 #4).
6. With scissors, cut along dotted line (Illustration 11–02 #5).
7. Fold back flaps, making sharp creases, to form two triangles (Illustration 11–02 #6).
8. Fold flaps back to original position and open invitation (Illustration 11–02 #7).
9. Fold invitation so design is on the inside (Illustration 11–02 #8).
10. Holding paper so it looks like a tent, put finger on top triangle and push down. Then, pinch two folded edges of top triangle so that triangle is pushed through to other side of paper (Illustration 11–02 #9).
11. Perform same step for bottom triangle as in top triangle.
12. Fold invitation in half, widthwise, with design on outside (Illustration 11–02 #10).
13. Open and close invitation (Illustration 11-02) and see shark flash its teeth!

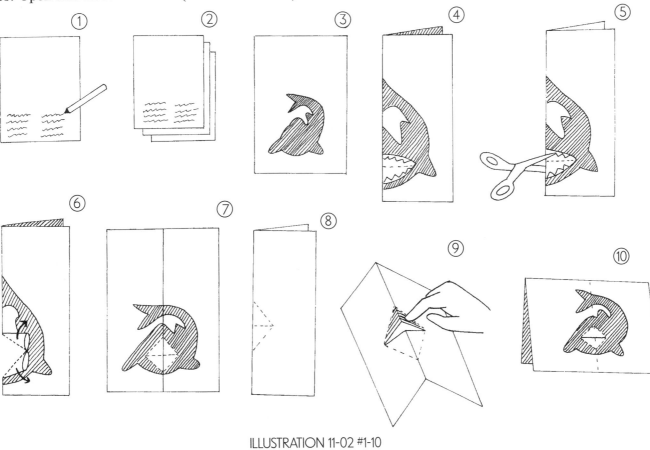

ILLUSTRATION 11-02 #1-10

- Glue "Under-the-Sea Stickers" (page 272) to seal envelope.

SHARK THANK-YOU NOTE

The "Shark Thank-You Note" (Illustration 11–04) is on page 281. Photocopy and cut out the thank-you note, then write your personal message in the space provided.
Estimated time: 10–15 minutes

MENU

Dive in for a few of these deep-sea delights. Choose foods from each group, and follow the recipes on the pages listed below.

DRINKS:

EATS:

Gummi Fish/Gummi Worms
Fish-Shaped Crackers

CAKE AND ICE CREAM:

SWIMMING FISH CAKE

Estimated time: 1–1 1/2 hours

INGREDIENTS:

1	"Basic Cake" recipe in Appendix A, on pages 343 and 344; or use your favorite box cake mix
2	"Buttercream Frosting" recipes in Appendix A, on page 345; or use 2 cans of your favorite canned frosting
1 c.	Candy corns
1	Marshmallow (cut in half)
1 c.	Gummi worms
1	Chocolate cookie 1 1/2"–2"
2	Wedge jelled candies (orange)
1	Chocolate chip
	Food coloring (yellow)
	Food coloring (red)
	Wax paper
	13" x 18" tray or foil-covered board
	Illustration 11–05 "Swimming Fish Cake Pattern" (page 282)

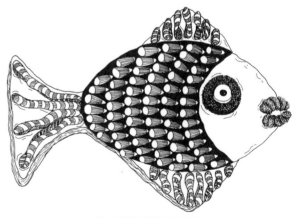

ILLUSTRATION 11-06

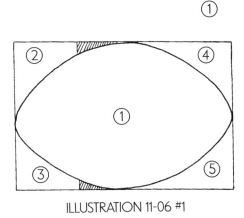

ILLUSTRATION 11-06 #1

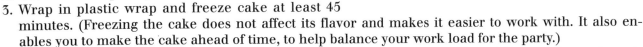

ILLUSTRATION 11-06 #2

DIRECTIONS:

1. Prepare and bake cake in one 9" x 13" cake pan as directed in recipe or cake package.
2. Cool cake completely on wire rack.
3. Wrap in plastic wrap and freeze cake at least 45 minutes. (Freezing the cake does not affect its flavor and makes it easier to work with. It also enables you to make the cake ahead of time, to help balance your work load for the party.)
4. Trace Illustration 11–05 "Swimming Fish Cake Pattern" on wax paper. Extend lines 1/2" on cake pattern where arrows indicate.
5. Cut out wax paper pattern into sections and reassemble on top of cake.
6. With long knife, cut cake into sections (Illustration 11–06 #1).
7. Assemble sections on tray into shape of a fish (Illustration 11–06 #2).
8. Tint one cup frosting orange with equal amounts of red and yellow food coloring.
9. Tint remaining frosting yellow.
10. Frost connecting sections of cake with yellow frosting.
11. Frost body top of fish orange, where indicated by shaded areas of illustration (Illustration 11–06 #2).
12. Frost sides and remaining sections of cake yellow.
13. Place chocolate cookie on face to form the "eye."
14. Place a marshmallow half on cookie to form an "eyeball."
15. Dip chocolate chip in frosting and place on "eyeball" to form "pupil."
16. Cut gummi worms to fit on "fins" (Illustration 11–06).
17. Place candy corns in rows across orange section of cake to make "scales."
18. Push 2 jelled wedges on face to form "lips."

⏰ MERMAID CAKE

Estimated Time: 20–30 minutes

INGREDIENTS:

1	Frosted store-bought cake (round)
1	Doll (either half-doll or doll 7 1/2" in height) ❀
8	Gumdrops (green)
1/2 c.	Gummi fish
3	Gummi worms
	Candy sprinkles (blue)

❀ Available at craft and hobby stores

ILLUSTRATION
11-07

DIRECTIONS:

1. Place frosted cake on a plate or serving platter.
2. Sprinkle top and sides of cake with blue sprinkles.
3. Insert half-doll into center of cake or cut out hole in center of cake and place 7 1/2" doll in hole.
4. Cut 8 gumdrops into 3 slices each, yielding a total of 24 slices.
5. Stick 2 gumdrop slices to doll's chest to form "top."
6. Overlap remaining gumdrop slices to form lower body of mermaid.
7. Use two gummi worms to form top of tail and cut one gummi worm in half to form bottom of tail.
8. Decorate top and sides of cake with gummi fish (Illustration 11-07).

SHARK CAKE

- Turn your "Mermaid Cake" into a "Shark Cake" by substituting toy shark as centerpiece. You will not need gumdrops or gummi worms for "Shark Cake," but you may want to add more gummi fish around toy shark. (Illustration 11-08)

DECORATIONS

Make your sea creatures feel at home with a few of these easy-to-make decorations. Save money by using some of these decorations as favors in your loot bags.

ILLUSTRATION 11-08

PARTY STREAMERS

Estimated time: 1–2 minutes each

Select one (or more) of the streamers suggested below, and follow the directions for "Party Streamers" in **CRAFT TIPS** (page 349).

- **Wave Streamer** Pattern CT-04 (page 359)
  Use blue crepé paper and twist when hanging up to look like rolling waves.
- **Leaf Streamer** Pattern CT-06 (page 362)
  Use green crepé paper and twist when hanging up to look like seaweed.

TIMESAVER

- Hang crepé paper streamers (in pre-packaged rolls) around party area.

TROPICAL FISH

Estimated time: 1–2 minutes each

WHAT YOU NEED:

- Illustration 11–10 "Tropical Fish" (page 283)
- Copier paper or copier card stock (white or bright colors) ✿
- String
- Scissors
- Sharp pencil or hole punch

———————
✿ Card stock is preferred for this project.

ILLUSTRATION 11-09

WHAT YOU DO:

1. Photocopy Illustration 11–10 onto copier paper or card stock.
2. Cut out fish illustration.
3. Punch small hole in fish, as indicated in illustration.
4. Tie string to fish and hang in party area (Illustration 11-09).

STARFISH STRAWS

Estimated time: 1–2 minutes each

Care to share a drink with a thirsty starfish? (Illustration 11-11) Use Illustration 11–12 "Starfish" (page 283) and follow directions for "Drinking Straws" in **CRAFT TIPS** (page 353).

STARFISH SUCKERS

Estimated time: 1–2 minutes each

Make your own "Starfish Suckers." (Illustration 11-11) Use Illustration 11–12 "Starfish" (page 283) and follow directions for "Theme Party Suckers" in **CRAFT TIPS** (page 353).

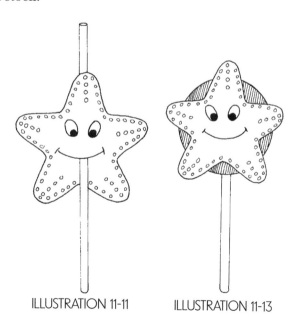

ILLUSTRATION 11-11   ILLUSTRATION 11-13

♀ MORE DECORATING IDEAS...

- Hang blue and/or white balloons in party area.
- Cover table with blue plastic tablecloth, blue plastic tarp.
- Decorate center of table with sea shells.
- Photocopy Illustration 11–10 "Tropical Fish" (page 283) onto copier paper. Cut out fish and arrange on tablecloth.
- Make placemats by having children glue "Under-the-Sea Stickers" (page 272) onto 9" x 12" sheet of construction paper. Provide crayons, markers and/or colored pencils for children to color placemats, if desired.
- Place gold fish bowl (with gold fish) in center of party table.
- Replace white light bulbs with blue light bulbs.
- Make an octopus balloon by taping 8 pink streamers to a pink balloon and draw eyes with black marker. Hang in party area (Illustration 11-14).
- Make a jellyfish by taping white streamers to a white balloon and hang in party area.
- Photocopy "Swimming Fish Cake" illustration 11-01 (page 264) and tape to front door or front of party area to greet guests.

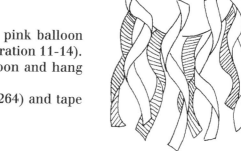

LOOT BAGS

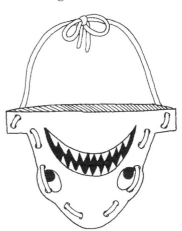

ILLUSTRATION 11-14

Select one (or more) of the following loot bags and follow the directions for "Loot Bags" in **CRAFT TIPS**.

- **Sticker Bag** (page 350)
  Use illustration 11-22 "Under-the-Sea Stickers" on page 281.
- **Treasure Box** (page 351)
  Use illustration 11-22 "Under-the-Sea Stickers" on page 281.
- **Hat Bag** (page 351)
  Use illustration 11-27 "Shark Hat" on page 284.
- Purchase plastic sand bucket and use as a loot bag.

LOOT BAG "LOOT"

Looking for something to put in those loot bags? Here are some creative suggestions you can make, or if you are short of time, you can buy.

LOOT YOU CAN MAKE:
- **Under-the-Sea Stickers** (page 272)
- **Starfish Straws** (page 268)
- **Starfish Suckers** (page 268)
- **Under-the-Sea Polaroid® Photo Frame** (page 271)
- **Mermaid Doll** (page 273)
- **Shell Necklace** (in "Mermaid Costume" page 275)
- **Biting Shark Puppet** (page 272)
- **Cookie Wands** (page 329)
- **Star Fish Critters** (page 331)

LOOT YOU CAN BUY:
- Gummi fish or gummi worms (or both)
- Wind-up fish toys
- Sand bucket and shovel
- Mermaid or fish stickers
- Rubber stamps of mermaids or fishes
- Stuffed or plastic mermaid/fish toys
- Sea shells or shell necklaces (available in most craft stores)
- Fish-shaped fruit candies

- Toy boats
- Mermaid/fish-theme bubble bath
- Live goldfish in a plastic bag ❀

_____

❀ Check with pet store for proper instructions to package and care for goldfish.

ACTIVITIES

How about having some fun with all those sea creatures?

Don't feel as if you have to do all of these activities—there isn't enough time at any party. Discuss with your child which ones he or she would like to do and plan your party activities accordingly.

ARRIVAL ACTIVITY

As each child arrives, let him/her pick a special name, as in "Mary the Mermaid," "Steven the Shark," "Octopus Oscar," and the like. Announce each name with a little fanfare.

 SUBMARINE

Recommended for all ages

WHAT YOU NEED:

- Large cardboard box (refrigerator/large appliance)
- Plastic wrap (blue, if available)
- Scissors
- Craft knife (adult use only)
- Ruler or yardstick
- Large bowl
- Pencil
- Duct tape or cloth-backed masking tape
- 2 "saltine" cracker boxes

WHAT YOU DO:

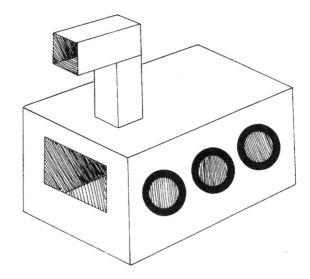

1. Draw porthole(s) and front viewing station.
2. Using craft knife, cut out viewing station and porthole(s). (For suggestions in cutting cardboard, see "Cardboard Play Structures" in **CRAFT TIPS** page 355.)
3. Line inside of portholes with plastic wrap and tape in place.
4. Tape cracker boxes to top of cardboard box to make a "periscope."

THE EXTRA TOUCH

- Use crayons, markers and/or poster paints and paint or draw outlines of portholes or sea creatures on outside of submarine.
- Photocopy Illustration 11–22 "Under-the-Sea Stickers" (page 281) onto brightly-colored copier paper. Cut out stickers and glue to outside of plastic wrap (in portholes) so that fish can be seen when looking through portholes from inside submarine.

 UNDER-THE-SEA PHOTO BACKDROP

Recommended for all ages

Use Illustration 11–18 #1 "Biting Shark Photo Backdrop Pattern" or Illustration 11–18 #2 "Mermaid Photo Backdrop Pattern" and follow the directions for "Photo Backdrop" in **CRAFT TIPS** (page 354) to give children and their parents the best party favor they can have—a memorable "Under-the-Sea Snapshot."

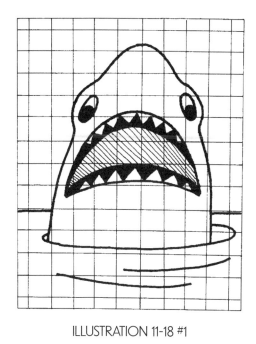

ILLUSTRATION 11-18 #1

ILLUSTRATION 11-18 #2

You can take a Polaroid® photograph and hand it out at the party (see "Polaroid® Photo Frame below), or you can use a 35 mm camera and send a photo along with your thank-you note.

 THE EXTRA TOUCH
- Glue "Tropical Fish" (page 268) onto "Photo Backdrop."

UNDER-THE-SEA POLAROID® PHOTO FRAME

Recommended for all ages

Hand out these wonderful memories at the party by using a Polaroid® photo and follow the directions for "Polaroid® Photo Frame" in **CRAFT TIPS** (page 357).

 THE EXTRA TOUCH
- Glue "Under-the-Sea Stickers" (page 272) onto frame (Illustration 11-19).
- Glue on glitter and sequins.

ILLUSTRATION 11-19

BLOWING BUBBLES

Recommended age: 4 and older

WHAT YOU NEED:
- Bucket or tub of water
- Liquid dish washing detergent (Dawn® or Joy® detergent work best.)
- Pipe cleaners (1 for each guest) ❀

❀ Use the thinner string, not the chenille stem.

WHAT YOU DO:
1. Add detergent to water.
2. Make a loop at the end of each pipe cleaner and twist to secure in place.
3. Have children dip wand in soapy water and blow bubbles "under the sea."

ILLUSTRATION 11-20

CATCH A FISH

Recommended age: 3 and older

WHAT YOU NEED:
- Wading pool or wash tub (filled with water)
- Goldfish or guppies (one per child)
- Small fish net
- Clear plastic bags
- Rubberbands

WHAT YOU DO:
1. Place fish in water and have each child take a turn catching a fish with net.
2. Put fish in bag with water. Blow air in bag and tie at top with a rubberband (Illustration 11-21).
3. Do this activity just before children go home.
   [Note: Check with pet store for proper method to prepare water and package fish.]

ILLUSTRATION 11-21

CRAFTS

Children will have fun making these crafts as a group activity during the party or you can make these crafts yourself ahead of time and save money on party favors. Select one or two of the crafts for your party from the following list.

UNDER-THE-SEA STICKERS

Recommended age: 3 and older for gluing
5 and older for cutting and gluing

Make your own party stickers for children to use in various crafts and activities in this chapter. Use Illustration 11–22 "Under-the-Sea Stickers" (page 281) and follow directions for "Party Stickers" in **CRAFT TIPS** (page 352).

BITING SHARK PUPPETS

Recommended age: 6 and older

WHAT YOU NEED:
- Envelope—legal size (1 for each guest)
- Scissors (child-safe)
- Markers (black)
- Transparent tape
- Crayons, markers and/or colored pencils ❀

❀ Optional

WHAT YOU DO:
Before the party:
1. Seal envelopes.

During the party:
2. Cut 1/2" from one end of envelope to make opening for child's hand (Illustration 11–23 #1).

ILLUSTRATION 11-23

ILLUSTRATION 11-23 #1-3

3. Cut a triangular notch (approximately 3" wide) on opposite end of envelope to form a "mouth" (Illustration 11–23 #2).
4. To make "fin," tape triangular notch to the top of envelope (Illustration 11–23 #3).
5. With marker, draw features of shark's face (Illustration 11-23).
6. Color sharks, if desired.
7. Have child place hand into puppet and move fingers apart to make mouth open and close.

MERMAID DOLL

Recommended age: 7 and older

WHAT YOU NEED:

- One 4 oz. skein of 4-ply yarn (green) will make 9 dolls
- 8 feet of 4-ply yarn (red) per doll
- Cardboard (8 1/2" x 11") or thin book (8 1/2" x 11") per doll
- One cotton ball per doll
- Two fake, wiggly eyes per doll
- White or tacky glue

WHAT YOU DO:

1. Wrap green yarn around length of board or book, 36 times (Illustration 11–24 #1).
2. Trim end of yarn even with board or book (Illustration 11–24 #1).
3. Cut a 6" strand of green yarn and slip it under all strands of yarn at one end of board (Illustration 11–24 #1).
4. Pull all strands together by tying a tight knot with green piece of yarn (Illustration 11–24 #2).
5. Using scissors, cut through all yarn at the other end (Illustration 11–24 #2).
6. Place knotted yarn bundle over a cotton ball (Illustration 11–24 #3).
7. Arrange yarn strands so cotton ball is covered (Illustration 11–24 #4).
8. Tie a 12" piece of green yarn around "neck" in a tight knot (Illustration 11–24 #4).
9. Using 9 strands of yarn at a time, braid 2 "arms" (Illustration 11–24 #5).
10. Tie a 3" strand of green yarn around each "wrist" and knot in place.

ILLUSTRATION 11-24

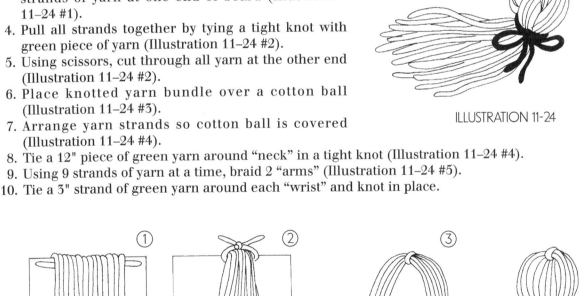

ILLUSTRATION 11-24 #1-4

11. Tie a 12" piece of red yarn around "waist" in a tight knot and then tie yarn into a bow (Illustration 11–24 #5).
12. Braid remaining yarn into a "tail" (Illustration 11–24 #5).
13. Tie a 12" strand of red yarn approximately 2–3" from bottom of tail into a knot, and then tie into a bow (Illustration 11–24).
14. Glue fake eyes on face.
15. Glue a 1/2" piece of red yarn to form "mouth."
16. Using one 6" strand of red yarn, tie nine of the 6" strands of red yarn to the knot on top of the head to form "hair" (Illustration 11–24).

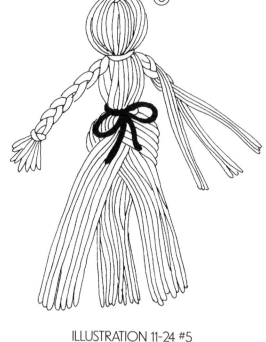

ILLUSTRATION 11-24 #5

AQUARIUM COLLAGE

Recommended age: 3 and older

WHAT YOU NEED:
- "Under-the-Sea Stickers" (page 272)
- Two 9" paper plates
- Scissors
- Scissors (child-safe)
- White glue
- Plastic wrap (clear or blue)
- Shell macaroni
- Small pebbles and/or dried beans
- Scraps of yarn (blue, green or brown)
- Hole punch
- Crayons, markers and/or colored pencils ❀

❀ Optional

WHAT YOU DO:
Before the party:
1. Cut out one 6" circle from center of one plate (Illustration 11–25 #1).
2. Glue a 7" x 7" piece of plastic wrap (clear or blue) over inside of hole on the cut plate (Illustration 11–25 #2).

During the party:
3. Color stickers, if desired.
4. Using "Under-the-Sea Stickers," pebbles, pinto beans, shell macaroni and yarn, have each child create their own underwater scene on a paper plate.
5. Glue cut plate (with plastic "window") onto the plate with the collage (Illustration 11–25 #3).
6. To hang, punch hole through both plates at top and tie on a 12" piece of yarn (Illustration 11–25).

ILLUSTRATION 11-25

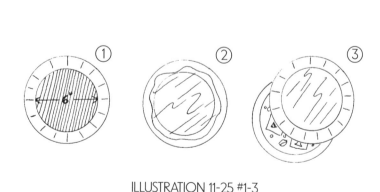

ILLUSTRATION 11-25 #1-3

SHARK COSTUME

Recommended age: 5 and older

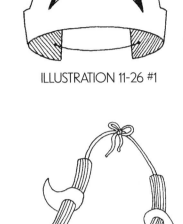

ILLUSTRATION 11-26 #1

WHAT YOU NEED:

- Illustration 11–27 "Shark Costume" (page 284)
- Copier paper or copier card stock (white or bright colors) ✼
- One 14" length of elastic cord (or one 14" length of yarn)
- One 36" length of yarn
- Scissors (child-safe)
- Hole punch
- Crayons, markers and/or colored pencils≠
- Transparent tape ✼✼

———————
✼ Card stock works better for this project.

✼✼ Optional

WHAT YOU DO:

Before the party:

1. Photocopy Illustration 11–27 "Shark Costume" onto copier paper or card stock.
2. If using copier paper, reinforce holes with transparent tape.

During the party:

3. Color hat, if desired.
4. Cut out hat and teeth.
5. Punch a hole in each end of hat and teeth, as marked on illustration.
6. Tie one end of elastic cord through one hole in headband.
7. Thread other end of cord through other hole in headband and adjust length to fit child's head; then knot cord in place.
8. Thread yarn through teeth and tie at the end to make necklace.

ILLUSTRATION 11-26 #2

 THE EXTRA TOUCH

- Make several different versions of a shark-tooth necklace. (See "Indian Bead Necklace," page 117, for directions.)
- Alternate teeth and beads in stringing necklace (Illustration 11-26 #2).
- Add blue and green hollow pasta to your necklace.

MERMAID COSTUME

Recommended age: 7 and older

WHAT YOU NEED:

- Illustration 11–29 "Mermaid Costume" (page 285)
- Copier paper or copier card stock (green, white or other bright colors) ✼
- One 14" length of elastic cord or one 14" length of yarn (for hat)
- One 36" length of yarn or one 36" length of 1/4" ribbon (for necklace)
- Scissors (child-safe)
- Hole punch or sharp pencil
- Crayons, markers and/or colored pencils ✼✼
- Glue and glitter ✼✼
- Transparent tape ✼✼

———————
✼ Card stock works better for this project.

✼✼ Optional

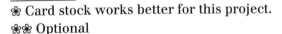

ILLUSTRATION 11-28

WHAT YOU DO:

Before the party:

1. Photocopy Illustration 11–29 onto copier paper or card stock.
2. If using copier paper, reinforce holes with transparent tape before punching holes.

During the party:

3. Color illustrations, if desired.
4. Cut out hat and shell.
5. Cut out along solid lines of hair as marked on illustration.
6. Punch holes as marked on hat and shell.
7. Accordion-fold hair (Illustration 11–28 #1).
8. Fold hair over band of hat along dotted line (Illustration 11–28 #2).
9. Decorate hat and shell with glue and glitter, if desired.
10. Tie one end of elastic cord through one hole in headband.
11. Thread other end of cord through other hole in headband and adjust length to fit child's head; then knot cord in place.
12. Thread yarn or ribbon through hole in shell and tie around child's neck.

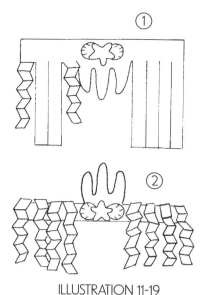

ILLUSTRATION 11-19

 THE EXTRA TOUCH

- Make several different versions of a mermaid necklace. (See "Indian Bead Necklace" page 117, for directions.)
- Add blue and green hollow pasta to your necklace.

GAMES

Select several of the games for your party from the following list. Don't feel as if you have to play all of them—there just isn't time. But you should plan for a few extra games. Here are some unique games for your Under-the-Sea Party.

MAGNET FISHING FUN

Recommended age: 2 years and older

WHAT YOU NEED:

- Illustration 11–10 "Tropical Fish" (page 283)
- Copier paper or copier card stock (bright colors) ✿
- Scissors
- Paper clips
- String (one 3'–4' length for each fishing pole)
- Strong magnet (one for each fishing pole)
- Empty wrapping paper tube (one for each fishing pole)
- Large box, washtub or wading pool
- Sharp pencil or hole punch

✿ Card stock is preferred for this project.

HOW TO PLAY:

Before the party:

1. Photocopy fish onto copier paper or card stock.
2. Cut out fish.
3. Punch a hole in fish (near mouth) and thread paper clips through hole.

ILLUSTRATION 11-30

4. Place fish in box, wash tub or wading pool.
5. Tie a string to cardboard tube and tie or tape other end of string to magnet.
6. Have children take turns fishing.

☞ THE EXTRA TOUCH
- Instead of paper fish, use party favors or gifts to give your guests when they catch their "fish."

SCHOOL OF FISH

Recommended age: 7 years and older

This is an excellent game to teach group cooperation and to focus everyone's efforts on one goal.

HOW TO PLAY:
1. Mark a start line and a finish line, opposite of one another in party area, at least 15'-20' apart (Illustration 11–31 #1).
2. Choose one child (birthday child first) to be the "shark," who starts the game standing behind the finish line.
3. Remaining children play a "school of fish" and line up behind the start line (single file), holding each other's waists.
4. At signal, school of fish tries to cross the finish line while shark tries to tag the last "fish" in line. The school of fish can sway or spiral to protect last "fish" in line (Illustration 11–31 #2).
5. If the shark tags the last "fish," he/she continues playing the shark.
   If the school of fish crosses the finish line without getting caught, the "head" of the school becomes the next shark, and the shark becomes the next "tail."

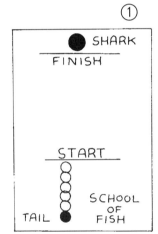
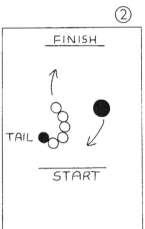

ILLUSTRATION
11-31 #1-2

CRAB-WALK RELAY

Recommended age: 6 years or older

HOW TO PLAY:
1. Divide children into two relay teams.
2. Mark a start/finish line for the relay race, and a turn-around point (like a tree or a chair), which should be between 15'-20' from the start/finish line.
3. Explain to children that each player must run the race on "all fours" (hands and feet), walking like a crab as fast as he/she can, to the turn-around point and back.
4. The first team to have all players complete the race, wins.

SEA HUNT

Recommended age: 3 years and older

Young children always love treasure hunts. You may want to give children one of the loot bags listed below to help them gather their goods.

WHAT YOU NEED:
- Small, plastic toy sea creatures or wrapped treats
- Loot Bags (Page 269) Have one for each child.

HOW TO PLAY:

1. At some point in the party, have someone move children out of view and hide toys and/or treats throughout game area.
2. Have children search for their "treasures" and gather their goods in a loot bag.

PIN THE FISH IN THE SEA

Recommended age: 3 years and older

WHAT YOU NEED:

- Illustration 11–22 "Under-the-Sea Stickers" (page 281)
- Copier paper or copier card stock (white)
- Scissors
- Butcher paper or poster board (blue or white)
- Masking tape or double-stick tape
- Pencil
- Blindfold
- White glue or transparent tape
- Crayons, markers and/or colored pencils ✿

✿ Optional

HOW TO PLAY:

Before the party:

1. Photocopy Illustration 11–22 onto copier paper so that there is at least one sticker per guest, plus one set of stickers to make the "game board."
2. Cut out one sticker for each child.
3. Cut out one set of "Under-the-Sea Stickers" for the game board.
4. Glue or tape one set of "Under-the-Sea Stickers" on butcher paper or poster board and make your own underwater "seascape."
5. Use crayons, markers and/or colored pencils to add sea weed, rocks and other elements to your sea scape, if desired.
6. Tape game board to wall in party area.

During the party:

7. Have children line up (single file), at least five feet away.
8. Place stickers in a bag and have each child pull out one sticker.
9. Write each child's name on the front of their sticker and place a piece of double-stick tape or masking tape rolled onto itself on back of sticker.
10. Tell children to look at the game board and to find the sticker that matches their sticker.
11. Blindfold first player in line (birthday child) and turn child 2–3 times. Then hand child his/her sticker and tell him/her to place the sticker on top of the matching sticker on the game board.
12. See who can get their "Under-the-Sea" sticker closest to its mate.

MORE GAMES...

It's always a good idea to plan some extra party games. Here are some standard party games, adapted for your Under-the-Sea Party. Specific directions for these games are listed in **APPENDIX D: GAMES**, beginning on page 363.

↻ FEED THE SHARK

Recommended age: 3 years and older

Follow the directions for "Bean Bag Toss" in **GAMES** (page 364). Use "Shark Photo Backdrop" (page 271) as the theme backdrop. Turn bean bags into a fish by drawing "eyes" and a "mouth" on each bag with permanent black marker.

UNDER-THE-SEA MUSICAL CHAIRS

Recommended age: 6 years and older

Follow the directions for "Fun Time Musical Chairs" in **GAMES** (page 366), and select music with "sea" themes or a soundtrack of "water sounds."

UNDER-THE-SEA SARDINES

Recommended age: 5 years and older

Follow the directions for "Sardines" in **GAMES** (page 369).

UNDER-THE-SEA SCRAMBLE

Recommended age: 6 years and older

Follow the directions for "Animal Scramble" in **GAMES** (page 364). Use "Under-the-Sea Stickers" (page 272) to play the game.

CATCH THE SHARK BY THE TAIL

Recommended age: 5 years and older

Follow the directions for "Catch the Tail" in **GAMES** (page 365) and use a "shark" as the theme animal.

SAVE THE MERMAID/MERMAN FROM THE SHARK

Recommended age: 5 years and older

Follow the directions for "Save the Prince/Princess from the Dragon" in **GAMES** (page 369), and use a "shark" as the theme animal.

BITE, BITE, SHARK!

Recommended age: 4 years and older

Follow the directions for "Duck, Duck, Goose" in **GAMES** (page 365) and have one child be a fish and walk around the outside of circle tapping each child on the shoulder lightly saying, "bite." When fish wants someone to be "It," fish taps that child and says, "shark."

SCHOOL OF FISH

Recommended age: 5 years and older

Follow the directions for "Blob" in **GAMES** (page 365).

FLYING FISH

Recommended age: 2–5 years of age

Follow the directions for "Trampoline" in **GAMES** (page 371) and use a stuffed fish as the theme object in the game.

ILLUSTRATION 11-03

ILLUSTRATION 11-04

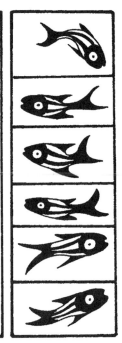

ILLUSTRATION 11-22

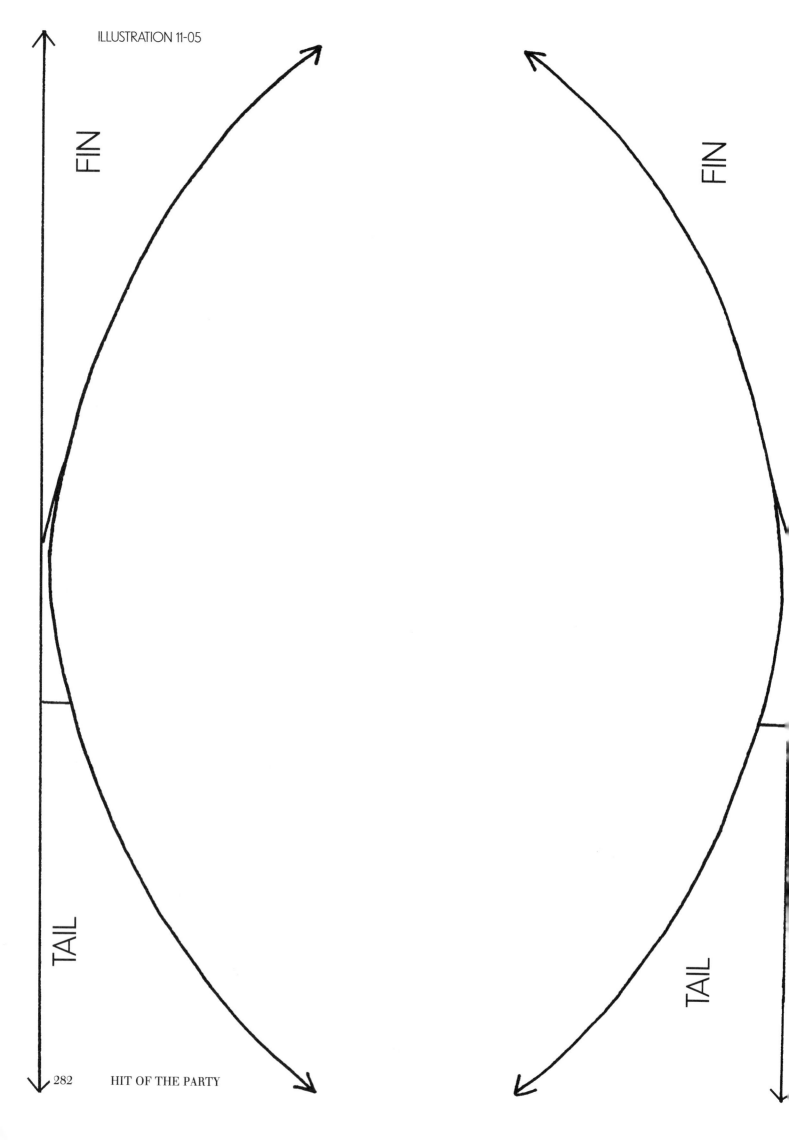

ILLUSTRATION 11-05

FIN

FIN

TAIL

TAIL

HIT OF THE PARTY

ILLUSTRATION 11-10

ILLUSTRATION 11-12

284   HIT OF THE PARTY

ILLUSTRATION 11-27

ILLUSTRATION 11-29

Journey Into Space Party

CHAPTER 12

Blast off into outer space on a journey to far-away galaxies. Your rocket ship awaits—for a birthday party that is out of this world!

ILLUSTRATION 12-01

BLAST-OFF INVITATION

Estimated Time: 3–4 minutes each

WHAT YOU NEED:

- Illustration 12–03 "Blast-Off Invitation" (page 304)
- Copier paper or copier card stock (yellow or white) ❀
- Envelopes (3 5/8" x 6 1/2")
- Scissors
- Craft knife (adult use only)
- Felt-tip pen (black)
- Crayons, markers and/or colored pencils ❀❀

❀ Card stock is preferred for this project.

❀❀ Optional

WHAT YOU DO:

1. Make one photocopy of Illustration 12–03. This is your "master copy." Fill out party information with felt-tip pen on master copy (Illustration 12–02 #1).
2. Photocopy as many invitations as needed (Illustration 12–02 #2).
3. Color invitation, if desired.
4. Using craft knife, cut slit along dotted line on earth (Illustration 12–02 #3).
5. With scissors, cut out rocket ship and card (Illustration 12–02 #4).
6. Slip rocket ship through slit of earth, tab side first (Illustration 12–02).

ILLUSTRATION 12-02

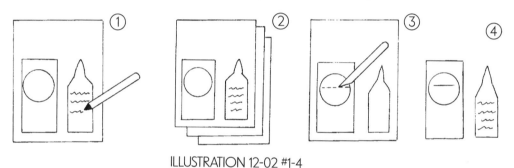

ILLUSTRATION 12-02 #1-4

 **THE EXTRA TOUCH**

- Glue "Space Stickers" (page 296) to seal envelope.

SPACE THANK-YOU NOTE

The "Space Thank-You Note" (Illustration 12–04) is on the same page as the "Blast-Off Invitation." When you photocopy the invitation, you will also be copying the thank-you note. Simply cut out the thank-you note, and write your personal message in the space provided.

Estimated Time: 1 minute each

MENU

Create a menu that is out of this world! Choose foods from each group, and follow the recipes on the pages listed below.

DRINKS:

Blast-Off Punch ....Page 314
Star Cooler ....Page 314

EATS:

Little Dipper ....Page 315
Cheese Wands ....Page 317

CAKE AND ICE CREAM:

FLYING SAUCER CAKE

Estimated time: 1–1 1/2 hours

INGREDIENTS:

1	"Basic Cake" recipe in Appendix A, on pages 343 and 344; or use your favorite box cake mix
2	"Buttercream Frosting" recipes in Appendix A, on page 345; or use 2 cans of your favorite canned frosting
2	Cookies (2"–3" in diameter)
2	Marshmallows (cut in half)
4	Lifesavers® (red)
4	Chocolate chips
14	Gumdrops
1	Licorice whip (red)
3	Licorice twists (red)
	Food coloring (yellow, blue and green)
	Wax paper
	13" x 18" tray or foil-covered board
	Illustration 12–05 "Flying Saucer Cake Pattern" (page 305)

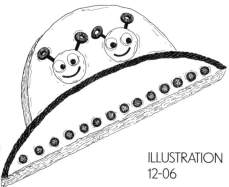

ILLUSTRATION
12-06

DIRECTIONS:

1. Prepare and bake cake in one 9" x 13" cake pan as directed in recipe or cake package.
2. Cool cake completely on wire rack.
3. Wrap in plastic wrap and freeze cake at least 45 minutes. (Freezing the cake does not affect its flavor and makes it easier to work with. It also enables you to make the cake ahead of time, to help balance your work load for the party.)
4. Trace Illustration 12–05 "Flying Saucer Cake Pattern" on wax paper. Extend lines 1/2" on cake pattern where indicated.
5. Cut out wax paper pattern into sections and reassemble on top of cake.
6. Using long knife, cut cake into sections, according to pattern (Illustration 12–06 #1).
7. Assemble sections on a tray into shape of flying saucer (Illustration 12–06 #2).
8. Tint 1/4 cup frosting green by adding a few drops of food coloring and mixing until color is uniform.
9. Tint half of the remaining frosting yellow and tint the other half of remaining frosting blue.
10. Frost connecting sections of cake with blue frosting.
11. Spread blue frosting on base of flying saucer.
12. Frost top of flying saucer with yellow frosting.
13. To make Martian "heads," frost top of cookies green.
14. Place green cookies on yellow portion of cake (Illustration 12–06).
15. To make Martian "eyeballs," place 2 marshmallow halves on each head.
16. Place one chocolate chip in the center of each "eyeball," using dab of frosting to hold in place.

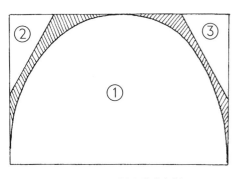

ILLUSTRATION 12-06 #1

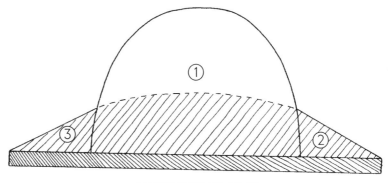

ILLUSTRATION 12-06 #2

17. Cut licorice whip into small pieces to make Martian "antennae" and "mouths."
18. Place one Lifesaver® at the end of each "antenna."
19. Trim flying saucer with red licorice twists (Illustration 12–06).
20. Place row of gumdrops along bottom of flying saucer for "landing lights."

⏰ROCKET SHIP CAKE

Estimated time: 20–30 minutes

INGREDIENTS:

1	Frosted store-bought cake (rectangular) ❀
1-2 c.	Gumdrops
4	Lifesavers® (red)
1 pkg.	Licorice twists (red)
6	Candy corns
16	Jelly beans or gumdrops (red)
	Candy Sprinkles (blue)

❀ without decorative flowers or trim

DIRECTIONS:

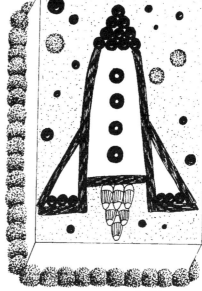

ILLUSTRATION 12-07

1. Place frosted cake on plate or serving platter.
2. Use licorice twists to make an outline of a rocket ship.
3. Place 10 red jelly beans or gumdrops on nose of ship.
4. Use 6 red jelly beans or gumdrops for landing lights on bottom of wings.
5. Place 4 red Lifesavers® down center of rocket for windows.
6. Arrange candy corns below ship to make rocket exhaust.
7. Scatter blue sprinkles around rocket to suggest space.
8. Place several gumdrops or other round candies around ship to suggest planets and stars.
9. Trim bottom of cake with gumdrops (Illustration 12-07).

DECORATIONS

Create a world of your own with a few of these easy-to-make decorations. Save money by using some of these decorations as favors in your loot bags.

PARTY STREAMERS

Estimated time: 1–2 minutes each

Follow the directions for "Party Streamers" in **CRAFT TIPS** (page 349).

- **Star Streamer** Pattern CT-03 (page 360)
  Use yellow, red and/or blue crepé paper.

 **TIMESAVER**
- Hang crepé paper streamers (in pre-packaged rolls) around party area.

ROCKET AND STARS

Estimated time: 5–7 minutes

WHAT YOU NEED:
- Illustration 12–08 "Rocket and Stars" (page 306)
- Copier paper or copier card stock (white or bright colors) ❀
- Scissors
- Hole punch or sharp pencil
- Lightweight string or thread

❀ Card stock is preferred for this project.

WHAT YOU DO:
1. Photocopy Illustration 12–08 "Rockets and Stars" onto copier paper or card stock.
2. Cut out around stars and rockets.
3. Punch holes in each star and rocket (Hang ship from nose or wing).
4. Cut 6 strings, one for each set of stars and rocket, in whatever lengths desired.
5. Tie one end of each string through holes in each star and rocket.
6. Hang rocket and stars from trees, ceilings, windows, patio covers or on long strings or streamers that stretch across room or yard.

 THE EXTRA TOUCH
- Using a glue stick and glitter, add some sparkle to your "Rocket and Stars."

MARTIAN STRAWS

Estimated time: 1–2 minutes each

Watch the giggles as children share a drink with a silly Martian. (Illustration 12-09) Use Illustration 12–10 "Martian" (page 308) and follow directions for "Drinking Straws" in **CRAFT TIPS** (page 353).

MARTIAN SUCKERS

Estimated time: 1–2 minutes each

Make your own "Martian Suckers." (Illustration 12-11) Use Illustration 12–10 "Martian" (page 308) and follow directions for "Party Suckers" in **CRAFT TIPS** (page 353).

ILLUSTRATION 12-09

💡 **MORE DECORATING IDEAS...**

ILLUSTRATION 12-11

- Cover party table with crinkled aluminum foil.
- Cover table with black trashbags and scatter with confetti and paper stars.
- Decorate party table with "Moon Rocks" (rocks painted gold or silver or covered with aluminum foil).
- Hang "The Stars and the Moon" (page 226) in party area.
- Make placemats by photocopying illustration 12-26 "Space Helmet"(page 309), illustration 12-28 "Martian Hat" (page 310) or Illustration 12-08 "Rocket Ship and Stars" (page 306) onto copier paper (white or bright colors). Provide crayons for children to color placemats, if desired.

- Make placemats by having children glue "Space Stickers"(page 296) onto 9" x 12" sheet of construction paper. Provide crayons, markers and/or colored pencils for children to color placemats, if desired.
- Hang up Christmas lights (for an evening or inside party) to suggest stars.
- Draw lines on balloons with colored markers to look like moons and planets. Hang balloons in party area (Illustration 12-12).
- Draw Martian faces on green balloons.
- Use a globe as a centerpiece for the party table.
- Replace white light bulbs with blue light bulbs.
- Hang up space posters.
- Make "Robot Piñata" (page 295) and hang in party area.
- Photocopy "Flying Saucer Cake" Illustration 12-01 (page 288) and tape to front door or front of party area to greet guests.

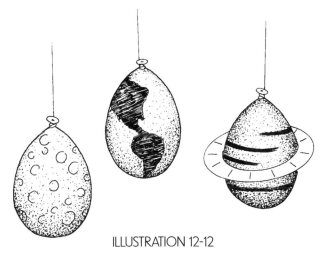

ILLUSTRATION 12-12

LOOT BAGS

Select one (or more) of the following loot bags and follow the directions for "Loot Bags" in **CRAFT TIPS** (page 350).

- **Magic Bag** (page 351)
- **Sticker Bag** (page 350)
  Use Illustration 12-19 "Space Stickers" on page 307.
- **Mask Bag** (page 351)
  Use Illustration 12-26 "Space Helmet" on page 309.
- **Treasure Box** (page 351)
  Use Illustration 12-19 "Space Stickers" on page 307.

LOOT BAG "LOOT"

Looking for something to put in those loot bags? Here are some creative suggestions you can make, or if you are short of time, you can buy.

LOOT YOU CAN MAKE:
- **Space Stickers** (page 296)
- **Martian Straws** (page 292)
- **Martian Suckers** (page 292)
- **Space Polaroid® Photo Frame** (page 295)
- **Space Shuttle** (page 297)
- **Moon Rocks from Moon Rock Hunt** (page 299)
- **Telescope** (page 297)
- **Cookie Wands** (page 329)
- **Space Mix** (page 333)
- **Asteroids** (page 333)

LOOT YOU CAN BUY:
- Space-theme comic books
- Toy spaceships
- Glow-in-the-dark space stickers
- Space-theme rubber stamps
- Freeze-dried ("astronaut") food
- NASA educational/collectible products (cards/stamps/stickers)

- Flashlight
- Novelty light "sticks"
- Astrological charts ("star maps")
- Kaleidoscope
- Small world globes
- Gummed stars

ACTIVITIES

Are you ready to blast-off?

Don't feel as if you have to do all of these activities—there isn't enough time at any party. Discuss with your child which ones he or she would like to do and plan your party activities accordingly.

ARRIVAL ACTIVITY

As each child arrives, let him/her pick a special name, as in "Arnold the Astronaut," "Mary the Martian," "Captain Chris," and the like. Announce each name with a little fanfare.

↻ SPACESHIP

Recommended for all ages

With a recycled appliance box, and a little imagination, you can create an activity center with many uses. For instance, children can play in the "Spaceship" while other guests arrive. After the party, your child will enjoy many adventures in the "Spaceship."

WHAT YOU NEED:
- Large cardboard box (refrigerator/large appliance)
- Scissors
- Craft knife (adult use only)
- Stapler
- Ruler
- Pencil
- Large bowl
- Duct tape (silver-backed)
- Aluminum foil
- One 22" x 28" sheet of lightweight poster board (red)

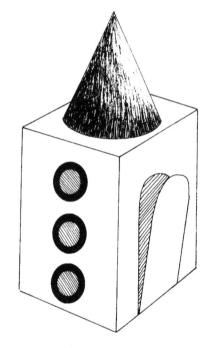

WHAT YOU DO:
1. Using top of a large bowl, trace circles on side of box for spaceship "portholes."
2. Mark "door" toward bottom of spaceship for astronauts to enter.
3. Cut out portholes and door using craft knife. (For suggestions in cutting cardboard, see "Cardboard Play Structures" in **CRAFT TIPS** page 355.)
4. Cover ship with aluminum foil and tape foil in place.
5. To make the "nose," draw a semicircle on poster board and cut out with scissors (Illustration 12-15 #1).
6. Pull corners of semicircle together to form a cone and staple in place (Illustration 12-15 #1).
7. Tape cone to top of box.

ILLUSTRATION 12-15

ILLUSTRATION 12-15 #1

FLYING SAUCER PHOTO BACKDROP

Recommended for all ages

Use Illustration 12–16 "Flying Saucer Photo Backdrop Pattern" and follow the directions for "Photo Backdrop" in **CRAFT TIPS** (page 354) to give children and their parents the best party favor they can have—a memorable "Flying Saucer Snapshot."

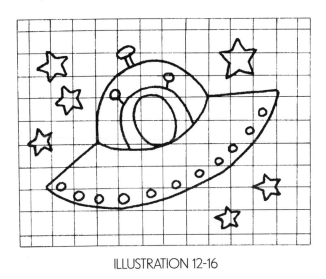

ILLUSTRATION 12-16

ILLUSTRATION 12-17

You can take a Polaroid® photograph and hand it out at the party (see "Polaroid® Photo Frame below), or you can use a 35 mm camera and send a photo along with your thank-you note.

☞ THE EXTRA TOUCH

- Glue "Rocket and Stars" (page 292) on backdrop.

SPACE POLAROID® PHOTO FRAME

Recommended for all ages

Hand out these wonderful memories at the party by using a Polaroid® photo and follow the directions for "Polaroid® Photo Frame" in **CRAFT TIPS** (page 357).

☞ THE EXTRA TOUCH

- Glue on "Space Stickers" (page 296), gummed stars and/or glitter (Illustration 12-17).

↻ ROBOT PIÑATA

Estimated time: 30–45 minutes

WHAT YOU NEED:

- Cardboard boxes (various sizes)
- Cardboard (paper towel or toilet paper) tubes
- Empty cans (soup or soda pop cans)
- Paper cups
- Styrofoam pieces
- Aluminum foil or silver spray paint
- Metal nuts and washers
- Bottle caps and lids
- Sequins
- "Space Stickers" (page 296)
- White glue
- Duct tape (silver-backed)
- Pipe cleaners
- Rope or cord (minimum of 18'–20')
- Prizes (wrapped candy, peanuts in a shell, small boxes of raisins, small toys)
- "Loot Bags" (see page 293)

ILLUSTRATION 12-18

WHAT YOU DO:

1. Fill robot's body with prizes before assembly.
2. Before assembling robot, cut 2 holes in back and thread rope through holes (Illustration 12-18 #1).
3. Tie rope in a knot to secure in place.
4. Glue or tape boxes, tubes, styrofoam pieces and cans into the shape of a robot.
5. Cover "robot" with aluminum foil or spray with silver paint.
6. Glue on nuts, washers, caps, lids, sequins, pipe cleaners and space stickers to add details (Illustration 12-18).
7. Suspend robot with rope over a tree limb, beam or other support.
8. Give each child a loot bag to collect his/her prizes.
9. Pull on rope to make piñata move up and down as children try to hit it.
10. See "Piñata Fun" in **GAMES** (page 368) for safety suggestions.

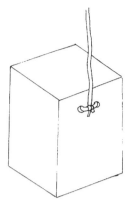

ILLUSTRATION 12-18 #1

CRAFTS

Children will have fun making these crafts as a group activity during the party or you can make these crafts yourself ahead of time and save money on party favors. Select one or two of the crafts for your party from the following list.

SPACE STICKERS

Recommended age: 3 and older for gluing
5 and older for cutting and gluing

Make your own party stickers for children to use in various crafts and activities in this chapter. Use Illustration 12–19 "Space Stickers" (page 307) and follow directions for "Party Stickers" in **CRAFT TIPS** (page 352).

You could also make "Magic Stickers" for the Space Party. Use Illustration 9–26 "Magic Stickers" (page 241), and follow directions for "Party Stickers" in **CRAFT TIPS** (page 352).

FLYING SAUCER

Recommended age: 5 and older

WHAT YOU NEED:

- "Space Stickers" (above)
- 9" paper plates
- 8 oz. paper cups or 6 1/2" paper salad bowls
- Aluminum foil
- Bendable straws
- Metal nuts and washers
- String
- Sharp pencil
- Markers and/or poster paints
- Sequins, bottle caps, buttons
- Gummed stars
- White glue
- Transparent tape

WHAT YOU DO:

1. Punch a small hole in bottom of cup or bowl.
2. Thread string through hole and tie a knot in string.
3. Glue bowl or cup to bottom of plate (Illustration 12–20 and 12–21).

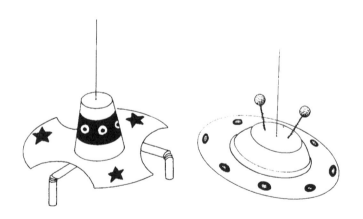

ILLUSTRATION 12-20   ILLUSTRATION 12-21

4. Tape bendable straws around bottom of plate to form "landing gear" (Illustration 12–20).
5. Cut notches in plate between landing gear to add interest to design (Illustration 12–20).
6. To decorate, glue on sequins, bottle caps, buttons, space stickers, metal nuts and washers; paint or use markers to draw patterns; or cover completely with aluminum foil.
7. Hang spaceships in party area and have children take their spacecraft home after the party.

 TELESCOPE

Recommended age: 3 and older

WHAT YOU NEED:

- One cardboard tube (paper towel or wrapping paper tube)
- One 5" x 5" piece of colored plastic wrap ❀
- Rubberband

❀ Use a different color for each telescope

ILLUSTRATION 12-22

WHAT YOU DO:

1. Wrap plastic wrap over one end of cardboard tube.
2. Secure in place with rubberband.
3. If using different colors of plastic wrap, have children trade off using telescopes and notice how their world changes.

THE EXTRA TOUCH

- Glue colored paper around telescope.
- Glue "Space Stickers" (page 296) or gummed stars on telescope (Illustration 12-22).

SPACE SHUTTLE

Recommended age: 5 or older

WHAT YOU NEED:

- Illustration 12–24 "Space Shuttle" (page 308)
- Copier paper (white or bright colors)
- Scissors (child-safe)
- Crayons, markers and/or colored pencils
- Transparent tape

ILLUSTRATION 12-23

WHAT YOU DO:

Before the party:
1. Photocopy Illustration 12–24 "Space Shuttle" onto copier paper.

During the party:
2. Color spaceship, if desired.
3. Cut out around outer lines of square.
4. Fold toward the back of ship, along dotted lines (Illustration 12–23 #1–4).
5. Fold toward the front, along dotted line (Illustration 12–23 #5).
6. Spread wings (Illustration 12–23 #6).
7. Place a piece of tape on top of spaceship near the nose (Illustration 12–23).
8. Hold spaceship near back and throw upward to launch.

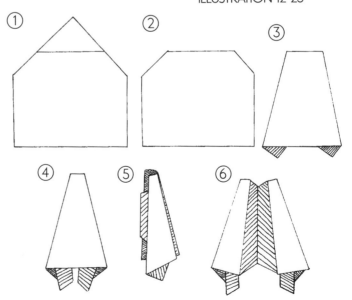

ILLUSTRATION 12-23 #1-6

ASTRONAUT HELMET

Recommended age: 5 or older

WHAT YOU NEED:

- Illustration 12–26 "Astronaut Helmet" (page 309)
- Copier paper or copier card stock (white) ✿
- One 14" length of elastic cord (or one 14" length of yarn)
- Scissors (child-safe)
- Hole punch
- Crayons, markers and/or colored pencils ✿✿
- Transparent tape ✿✿

―――――――――
✿ Card stock is preferred for this project.

✿✿ Optional

ILLUSTRATION 12-25

WHAT YOU DO:

Before the party:
1. Photocopy Illustration 12–26 "Astronaut Helmet" onto copier paper or card stock.
2. If using copier paper, reinforce holes with transparent tape before punching holes.

During the party:
3. Color helmet, if desired.
4. Cut out helmet.
5. Cut out face mask.
6. Punch holes in helmet, as marked on illustration.
7. Tie one end of elastic cord through one hole in helmet.
8. Thread other end of cord through other hole in helmet and adjust length to fit child's head; then knot cord in place (Illustration 12-25).

MARTIAN HAT

Recommended age: 5 and older

WHAT YOU NEED:

- Illustration 12–28 "Martian Hat" (page 310)
- Copier paper or copier card stock (white or green) ✿
- One 14" length of elastic cord (or one 14" length of yarn)
- Scissors (child-safe)
- Hole punch
- Crayons, markers and/or colored pencils ✿✿
- Transparent tape ✿✿

―――――――――
✿ Card stock is preferred for this project.

✿✿ Optional

WHAT YOU DO:

Before the party:
1. Photocopy Illustration 12–28 "Martian Hat" onto copier paper or card stock.
2. If using copier paper, reinforce holes with transparent tape before punching holes.

During the party:
3. Color hat, if desired.
4. Cut out hat.
5. Punch a hole in ends of tabs, as marked on illustration.
6. Tie one end of elastic cord through one hole in headband.
7. Thread other end of cord through other hole in headband and adjust length to fit child's head; then knot cord in place (Illustration 12-27).

ILLUSTRATION 12-27

 SPACE SUIT

Recommended age: 7 and older

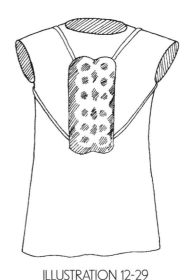

ILLUSTRATION 12-29

WHAT YOU NEED:

- One 30-gallon trashbag (steel-colored or white)
- One egg carton
- One sheet of aluminum foil (12" x 24")
- Pencil
- Two 20" lengths of 1/4" elastic cord (or two 20" lengths of yarn)
- White glue
- Sequins, bottle caps, nuts, washers and "Space Stickers" (page 296) ❀

❀ Optional

WHAT YOU DO:

Before the party:

1. Cut arm and neck holes in trashbag (Illustration 12–29 #1).

During the party:

2. To make "jet pack," start by punching 8 holes in top of egg carton (Illustration 12–29 #2).
3. Tie elastic cords through holes in egg carton to form the "straps" and adjust length to fit child's shoulders; then knot cord in place (Illustration 12–29 #2).
4. Wrap bottom and sides of egg carton with aluminum foil by gently pressing foil around cups and indentations (Illustration 12–29 #3).
5. Glue edges of foil to carton to secure in place.
6. Decorate jet pack and space suit with sequins, bottle caps, nuts, washers and space stickers, if desired.
7. Have child put trashbag suit on first and then slip on jet pack.

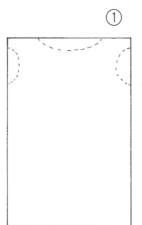  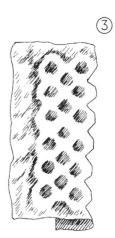

ILLUSTRATION 12-29 #1-3

GAMES

Select several of the games for your party from the following list. Don't feel as if you have to play all of them—there just isn't time. But you should plan for a few extra games. Here are some unique games for your Space Party.

MOON ROCK HUNT

Recommended age: 3 years and older

WHAT YOU NEED:

- Loot Bags (page 293) one for each child
- Candies or small favors
- Aluminum foil

HOW TO PLAY:

1. Wrap loot in aluminum foil to make your own "Moon Rocks."
2. Hide "Moon Rocks" throughout party area.
3. Have each child search for "Moon Rocks" and gather goods in a loot bag.

FLYING SAUCER RING TOSS

Recommended age: 5 years and older

WHAT YOU NEED:
- 1 card table
- 5 paper plates (9")
- 5 or more soda bottles (2-liter) ❀
- Scissors
- Aluminum foil
- 6" x 6" sheets of construction paper (bright colors)
- White glue or transparent tape
- Wide-tipped, felt marker (black)

❀ Use full soda bottles or fill empty bottles with sand or water.

ILLUSTRATION 12-30

WHAT YOU DO:
Before the party:
1. To make your "flying saucers," start by cutting out a 6" circle in center of paper plates (Illustration 12–30 #1).
2. Then cover each "saucer" with aluminum foil, gluing down edges (Illustration 12–30 #2).
3. With marker, write the name of planets on construction paper. *[NOTE: If you use 10 bottles, one for the sun and nine for the planets, you can recreate our own solar system.]*
4. Glue construction paper labels to bottles.
5. Set bottles on card table, approximately 6" apart (Illustration 12–30).

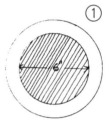

ILLUSTRATION 12-30 #1-2

HOW TO PLAY:
1. Have children form a single line, with birthday child first.
2. Each player takes a turn (5 tosses) to see how many "flying saucers" he/she can land on the planets.

SPACE BEANIE WALK

Recommended age: 6 years and older

WHAT YOU NEED:
- 2 paper plates (9")
- 2 paper bowls (6 1/2")
- 2 ping pong balls
- Scissors
- White glue
- Hole punch
- Two 20" lengths of elastic cord (or two 20" lengths of yarn)

WHAT YOU DO:
1. To make "Space Beanie," turn paper bowls upside down, and glue one paper plate on top of each bowl, top side up (Illustration 12–31 #1).
2. Punch a hole on opposite sides of bowl (Illustration 12–31 #2).
3. Tie one end of elastic cord through one hole in beanie.
4. Thread other end of cord through other hole in beanie and adjust length to fit child's head; then knot cord in place.

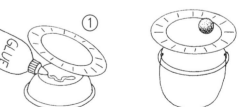

ILLUSTRATION 12-31 #1-2

HOW TO PLAY:

1. Divide children into two relay teams.
2. Mark start/finish line for the relay race, and a turn-around point, (like a tree or a chair), which should be between 15–20' from the start/finish line.
3. Give the first player in each team a "Space Beanie" and show children how to put it on.
4. Then place a ping pong ball on top of the beanie and tell children that in this race, they must walk as fast as they can to the turn-around point and back, balancing the ball on top of their "Space Beanie."
5. Any player who drops the ball during the race must stop, replace the ball, and then continue the race.
6. Upon completing the course, the first player tags the next player in line, gives him/her the beanie, and the race continues.
7. The first team to have all players complete the race, wins.

SPACE RACE

Recommend age: 6 years and older

WHAT YOU NEED:

- Nine chairs
- Nine sheets 9" x 12" (or larger) of construction paper (bright colors)
- Transparent tape

HOW TO PLAY:

Before the party:

1. Write out the name of each planet on construction paper, in order from the sun:
   Mercury, Venus, Earth, Mars, Jupiter, Saturn, Uranus, Neptune and Pluto
2. Stagger chairs in a zig-zag pattern in party area and tape names of each planet on back of each chair (Illustration 12-32).
3. Divide children into two relay teams.
4. First child on each team must run a zig-zag pattern through chairs, holding his/her ankle and hopping on one foot throughout the race.
5. After first child hops to the last chair, he/she comes back and tags the next player in line, who takes his/her turn.
6. The first team to have all players complete the race, wins.

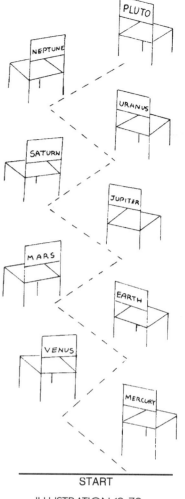

ILLUSTRATION 12-32

MOON RACE

Recommended age: 5 years and older

WHAT YOU NEED:

- Two chairs
- Four 9" paper plates
- Scissors
- Stapler
- Transparent tape
- String
- Wide-tipped, felt marker (any dark color)

WHAT YOU DO:

Before the party:

1. Cut out a quarter wedge from 2 paper plates (Illustration 12–33 #1).
2. Make 2 cones (one from each plate) by sliding cut edges over one another and staple in place (Illustration 12–33 #2).
3. Cut 2 lengths of string (approximately 10' in length) and thread one end of each string through each of the cones.
4. Place 2 chairs approximately 9 feet apart and tie both ends of each string to chairs (Illustration 12–33 #3).
5. Write out the names, "Moon" and "Earth" on remaining 2 paper plates and tape each sign to one of the chairs.

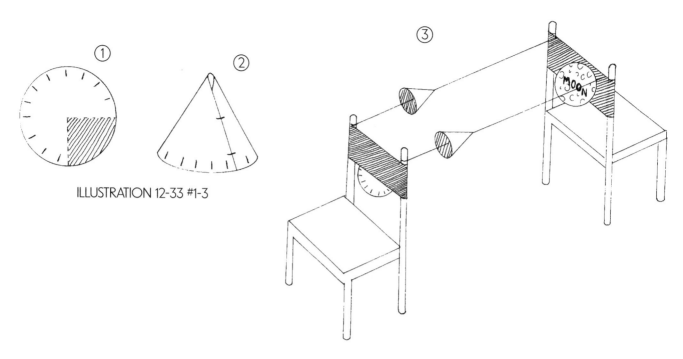

ILLUSTRATION 12-33 #1-3

HOW TO PLAY:

1. Make sure the string is taught between the "Earth" and "Moon," and pull both cones ("rocket ships") to the "Earth."
2. Divide children into two relay teams, and have each team line up behind each "rocket ship."
3. First child on each team must blow the rocket ship from the "Earth" to the "Moon."
4. Once reaching the moon, the player pulls the rocket ship back to "Earth," tags the next player, and the game continues.
5. The first team to have all players complete the race, wins.

MORE GAMES...

It's always a good idea to plan some extra party games. Here are some standard party games, adapted for your Space Party. Specific directions for these games are listed in **APPENDIX D: GAMES**, beginning on page 363.

↻ SPACE TOSS

Recommended age: 3 years and older

Follow the directions for "Bean Bag Toss" in **GAMES** (page 364). Use the "Flying Saucer Photo Backdrop" (page 296) as the theme backdrop.

THE ALIEN BLOB

Recommended age: 5 years and older

Follow the directions for "Blob" in **GAMES** (page 365).

PHASER TAG

Recommended age: 5 years and older

Follow the directions for "Freeze Tag" in **GAMES** (page 366).

LASER BALL

Recommended age: 4 years and older

Follow the directions for "Squirt Ball" in **GAMES** (page 370).

MUSICAL PLANETS

Recommended age: 5 years and older

Follow the directions for "Fun Time Musical Chairs" in **GAMES** (page 366), using space-theme music to play the game. (You might want to name each of the chairs with different planet names.)

SPACEMAN'S BUFF

Recommended age: 5 years and older

Follow the directions for "Blindman's Buff" in **GAMES** (page 364). Have children make different robot-beeping noises to play the game.

MOON WALK

Recommended age: 6 years and older

Follow the directions for "Stepping Stones" in **GAMES** (page 370).

MOON ROCK RACE

Recommended age: 6 years and older

Follow the directions for "Egg Relay Race" in **GAMES** (page 366), using "Moon Rocks" (rocks painted with gold or silver or covered with aluminum foil) instead of eggs in the race.

ILLUSTRATION 12-04

FOR

TIME

DATE

PLACE

R.S.V.P.

ILLUSTRATION 12-03

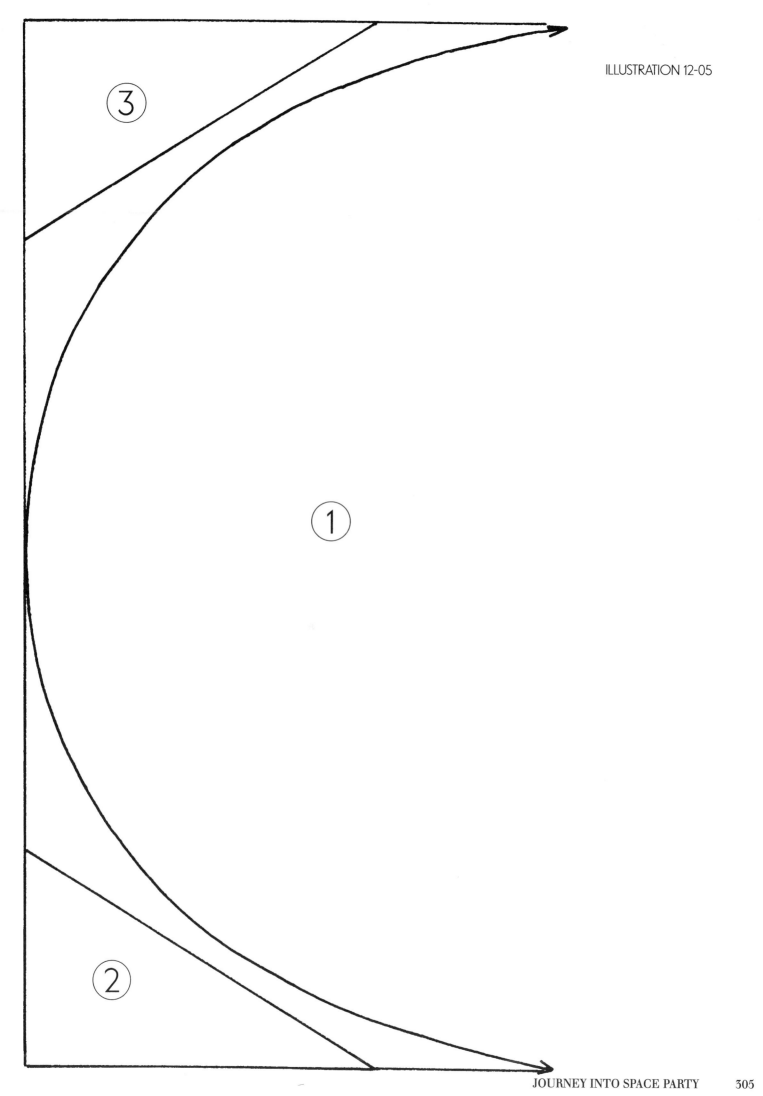

ILLUSTRATION 12-05

ILLUSTRATION 12-08

ILLUSTRATION 12-19

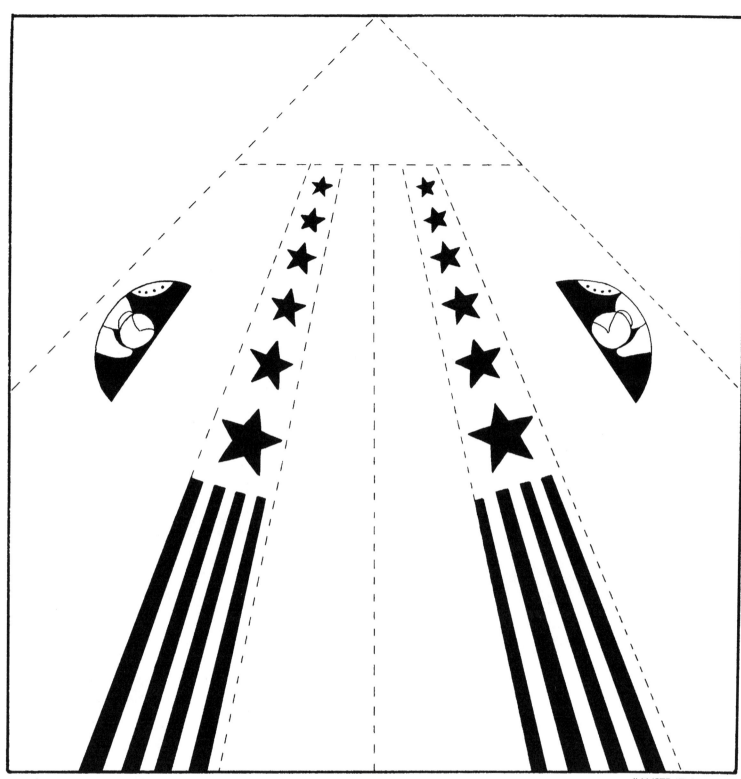

ILLUSTRATION 12-24

ILLUSTRATION 12-10

ILLUSTRATION
12-26

ILLUSTRATION 12-28

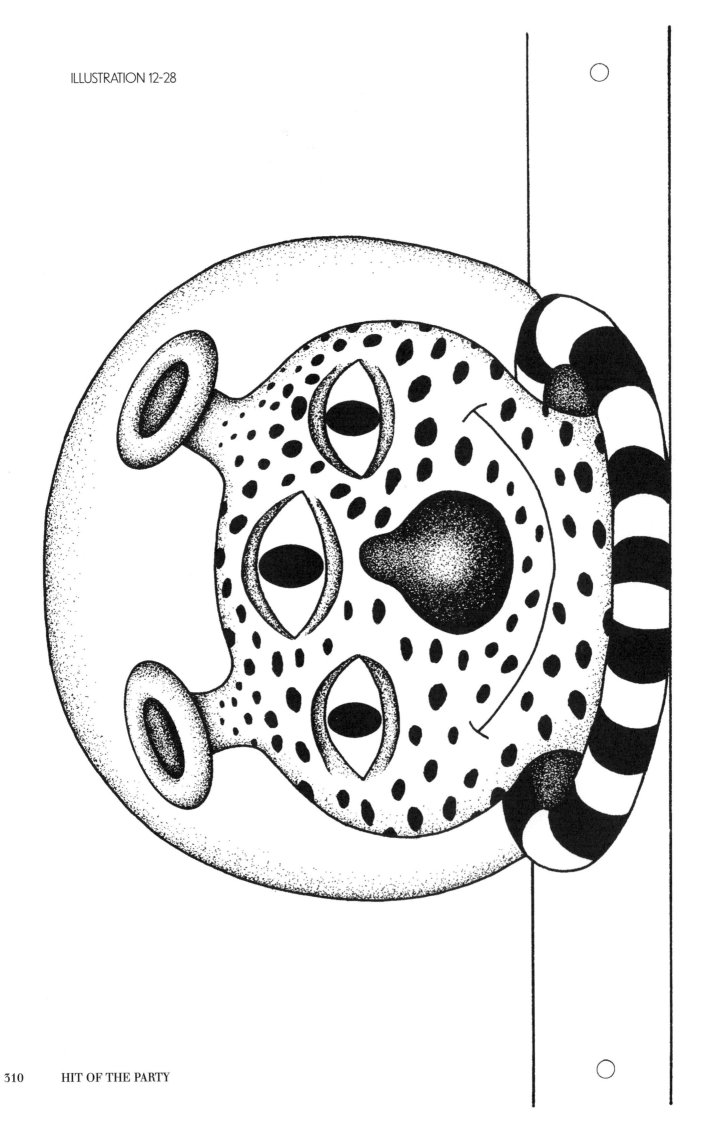

Recipes

Here are some real kid-pleasing recipes that are as much fun to make as they are to eat. Try some and see for yourself.

A HEALTHY SUGGESTION...

Parties are special occasions, where tasty treats are part of the celebration. This doesn't mean, however, that the foods you serve have to be unhealthy for you or your guests. You can make recipes healthier by choosing products that are low in fat, low in cholesterol and low in salt. Even mayonnaise, yogurt, cream cheese, ice cream, hot dogs, and chips are available in healthier choices.

PUNCH

Kids can get very thirsty running around and having fun. Each of these recipes is both easy and delicious—and will quench everyone's thirst.

HONEY BEE PUNCH
BIG SPLASH PUNCH
TEA TIME HONEY PUNCH
(Makes 24 4-ounce servings)

INGREDIENTS:
1	10 oz. pkg. frozen strawberries (partially thawed)
1/2 c.	honey
2	12 oz. cans frozen lemonade concentrate
2	32 oz. bottles of club soda (chilled)

DIRECTIONS:
1. Puree strawberries in blender.
2. In a storage container, combine strawberry puree, honey and lemonade concentrate.
3. Refrigerate until ready to serve.
4. Just before serving, add club soda and ice.

BERRY BEARY PUNCH
BERRY FAIRY PUNCH
CLOWN COOLER
PINK LADY PUNCH
(Makes 24 4-ounce servings)

INGREDIENTS:
1	10 oz. pkg. frozen strawberries (partially thawed)
1	10 oz. pkg. frozen raspberries (partially thawed)
1	12 oz. can frozen lime juice concentrate
1	32 oz. bottle of ginger ale (chilled)
1	32 oz. bottle of club soda (chilled)
1 pt.	vanilla ice cream or "Fruit Ice Ring" (See "The Extra Touch" next page.)
1/4 c.	grenadine syrup ❀

❀ Optional

DIRECTIONS:
1. Puree strawberries and raspberries in blender.
2. In a storage container, combine puree, lime juice, and grenadine syrup.
3. Refrigerate until ready to serve.
4. Just before serving, pour chilled mixture into a punch bowl. Add ginger ale, club soda and scoops of vanilla ice cream or "Fruit Ice Ring." (See "The Extra Touch next page.)

FRUIT ICE RING

At least one day before the party, make a "Fruit Ice Ring" for the punch to add a festive touch, and to keep the drink cool. Here's how:

1. Use whole strawberries, fresh or frozen; or sliced citrus fruits (oranges, lemons and limes).
2. Lay fruits at the bottom of a ring mold or bundt pan.
3. Add 1" of water and place in freezer until frozen.
4. Fill the ring mold or bundt pan 3/4 full with water and freeze.
5. When ready to serve, run warm water over mold or pan for 10–15 seconds to release ice ring.

JUNGLE JUICE
CRAZY MIXED-UP PUNCH

(Makes 30 4-ounce servings)

INGREDIENTS:

1   10 oz. pkg. frozen strawberries (partially thawed)
1   12 oz. can frozen orange juice concentrate
1   12 oz. can frozen lime juice concentrate
1   20 oz. can crushed pineapple
1   32 oz. bottle of lemon lime soda (chilled)
1   32 oz. bottle of club soda (chilled)
2   trays ice cubes or 1 "Fruit Ice Ring" (See "The Extra Touch"above)

DIRECTIONS:

1. Puree strawberries and crushed pineapple in blender.
2. In a storage container, combine puree, frozen orange juice concentrate, and lime juice concentrate.
3. Refrigerate until ready to serve.
4. Just before serving, pour chilled mixture into a punch bowl. Add club soda, lemon lime soda and ice cubes or "Fruit Ice Ring" (above).

MERLIN'S MAGIC PUNCH
ROUNDUP PUNCH

(Makes 24 4-ounce servings)

INGREDIENTS:

2   12 oz. frozen apple juice concentrate
1   32 oz. bottle of ginger ale
1   32 oz. bottle of club soda
1/4 c.   honey
1/2 tsp. ground nutmeg
1/2 tsp. ground ginger
2   trays ice cubes

DIRECTIONS:

1. In a small saucepan, heat 1 cup of apple juice concentrate, honey, nutmeg and ginger.
2. Bring to boil for 1 minute.
3. In a storage container, combine heated mixture and remaining apple juice concentrate.
4. Refrigerate until ready to serve.
5. Just before serving, pour chilled mixture into a punch bowl. Add ginger ale, club soda and ice cubes.

THE EXTRA TOUCH

COLORED ICE CUBES

Add colored ice cubes for a simple but dramatic effect. Here's how:

Add grenadine or food coloring to the water before pouring into ice cube trays. Place in freezer at least one day before the party.

BLAST-OFF PUNCH
SWAMP COOLER
UNDER-THE-SEA SLUSH
(Makes 26 4-ounce servings)

INGREDIENTS:
1   12 oz. can frozen lemonade
1   12 oz. can frozen limeade
1   32 oz. bottle of club soda
1   32 oz. bottle of lemon lime soda
    green food coloring (few drops)
1 pt. lime sherbet or 2 trays of ice cubes

DIRECTIONS:
1. Combine lemonade, limeade, club soda, lemon lime soda and green food coloring in a punch bowl.
2. Drop scoops of lime sherbet or ice cubes into punch.
3. Serve immediately.

 ## THE EXTRA TOUCH

ICE AGE DINOSAUR CUBES

"Ice Age Dinosaur Cubes" will bring a chilling thrill to your guests. Place one dinosaur-shaped fruit candy in each compartment of your ice cube trays before you fill with water. Place in freezer at least one day before the party.

YO HO PIRATE PUNCH
SILVER SALOON SODA
(Makes 24 4-ounce servings)

INGREDIENTS:
1   64 oz. bottle root beer
1   32 oz bottle ginger ale
1 qt. vanilla ice cream

DIRECTIONS:
1. Combine root beer and ginger ale in a punch bowl.
2. Drop scoops of ice cream into punch.
3. Serve immediately.

MERMAID'S DELIGHT
STAR COOLER
DISAPPEARING PUNCH
(Makes 26 4-ounce servings)

INGREDIENTS:
1 12 oz. can frozen lemonade concentrate
1 12 oz. can frozen apple juice concentrate
1 32 oz. bottle lemon lime soda
1 32 oz. bottle club soda
1 pt. vanilla ice cream or 2 trays ice cubes
  blue food coloring

DIRECTIONS:
1. Combine apple juice, lemon lime soda, club soda and at least 30 drops of blue food coloring in a punch bowl.

2. Drop scoops of ice cream or ice cubes into punch.
3. Serve immediately.

☞ **THE EXTRA TOUCH**

FISHIE CUBES

- "Fishie Cubes" will bring giggles to your guests. Place one fish-shaped fruit candy in each compartment of your ice cube tray before you fill with water. Place in freezer at least one day before the party.

SEVEN-DOWN

INGREDIENTS:

1 can of 7 Up® soda per child ❀

DIRECTIONS:

1. Make a hole in the bottom of soda can with a hammer and a clean awl or screwdriver.
2. Serve soda cans upside down.

❀ You may want to keep a few more cans on hand. However, don't puncture the extra cans until requested.

DIPS

Tired of the usual dips and chips? Try one of these kid-pleasing recipes, and watch it disappear before your very eyes. Careful, your adult guests won't be able to keep their chips out of these dips either.

AVOCADO DIP
DODGE CITY DIP
DINO DIP
LITTLE DIPPER DIP
(Serves 12)

INGREDIENTS:

2	ripe avocados
4 Tbs.	yogurt or mayonnaise
8 oz.	cream cheese (softened)
1/2 tsp.	garlic salt
	juice from 1/2 of a small lemon
1/4 c.	toasted chopped almonds

DIRECTIONS:

1. Mash avocados and then add remaining ingredients.
2. Mix ingredients until well blended.
3. Cover and refrigerate until ready to serve.
4. Serve with tortilla chips or raw vegetables.

ALLAH PEANUT BUTTER DIP
WRONG-WAY DIP
ELEPHANT DUNK DIP
(Serves 12)

INGREDIENTS:
4 Tbs. peanut butter (smooth or chunky)
4 Tbs. mayonnaise or yogurt
8 oz.   cream cheese (softened)
2 Tbs. honey
4 Tbs. chopped peanuts

DIRECTIONS:
1. Mix ingredients until well blended.
2. Cover and refrigerate until ready to serve.
3. Serve with crackers, fruit or raw vegetables.

TUNA DIP
WALK-THE-PLANK DIP
(Serves 12)

INGREDIENTS:
1   6 1/2 oz. can of white tuna (well drained)
4 Tbs. yogurt or mayonnaise
8 oz.   cream cheese (softened)
1 tsp. prepared mustard
2 Tbs. black olives (finely chopped) ❀

❀ Optional

DIRECTIONS:
1. Mix ingredients until well blended.
2. Cover and refrigerate until ready to serve.
3. Serve with tortilla chips, crackers or raw vegetables.

HONEY-ORANGE DIP
(Serves 12)

INGREDIENTS:
2 Tbs.   yogurt or mayonnaise
8 oz.   cream cheese (softened)
2 Tbs.   honey
2 Tbs.   frozen orange juice concentrate
1/2 tsp. vanilla extract

DIRECTIONS:
1. Mix ingredients until well blended.
2. Cover and refrigerate until ready to serve.
3. Serve with fresh fruit.

SNACKS

These tasty and nutritious snacks are quick and easy to make. Imagine how much fun kids will have waving a "Cheese Wand" or chomping into a "Funny-Face Cracker."

CHEESE WANDS
CHEESE SWORDS
(Makes 12 servings)

INGREDIENTS:
- 12   slices American cheese (individually wrapped) for "Cheese Wands"
- 6   slices American cheese (individually wrapped) for "Cheese Swords"
- 12   bread sticks
- 2 oz. cream cheese (softened)

DIRECTIONS FOR "CHEESE WANDS":
1. Using a star-shaped cookie cutter, cut out a star from each slice of cheese.
2. Secure a star on the end of each bread stick with a dab of cream cheese.

DIRECTIONS FOR "CHEESE SWORDS":
1. Cut each slice of cheese diagonally, forming 2 triangles.
2. Secure each triangle on the end of each bread stick with a dab of cream cheese.

FAIRY FINGERS
(Makes 12 servings)

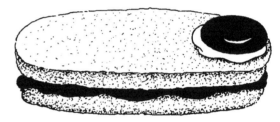

INGREDIENTS:
- 1   pkg. ladyfingers (12 per pkg.)
- 12   red or pink jelly beans
- 4 oz.   cream cheese (softened)
- 1/4 c.   favorite jam

DIRECTIONS:
1. Split each ladyfinger in half, lengthwise.
2. Spread cream cheese on one side of ladyfinger, and jam on the other.
3. Press 2 halves together.
4. Secure a jelly bean on one end with a dab of cream cheese to form a "finger nail."

CLOWN SMILES
CHESHIRE CAT SMILES
MAGIC SMILES
FUNNY FROWNS
(Makes 24 servings)

INGREDIENTS:
- 3   medium red apples
- 1/2 c.   peanut butter
- 1   8 oz. package miniature marshmallows
  juice of 1/2 lemon or orange

DIRECTIONS:
1. Core apples and slice each one into 16 sections.
2. Squeeze orange or lemon juice over apple slices to help keep them from turning brown.
3. Spread peanut butter on 1 side of each apple slice.
4. Place 4–5 marshmallows on 1 apple slice.
5. Top with a second apple slice, and press down gently.
6. Clown smiles should be made on the day of the party.

FRUIT KABOBS
FRUIT CUPS
(Makes 24 servings)

INGREDIENTS:

24   wooden skewers
1 pt. strawberries (cut in half)
1 lb. grapes
1 lb. cheese chunks (any type)
1   16 oz. can pineapple chunks
1   small melon (scooped into balls or cut into chunks)
     juice of 1 medium orange

DIRECTIONS:

1. Skewer alternating fruits/cheeses on wooden skewers.
2. Place skewers flat in plastic container or glass baking dish.
3. Squeeze orange juice over skewers.
4. Cover and refrigerate until time to serve.

Variation: Fruits and cheeses can be served in cups as well.

MARBLEIZED EGGS
BRONTOSAURUS EGGS
CRACKED-UP EGGS
(Makes 12 servings)

INGREDIENTS:

12   hard-boiled eggs
     food coloring

DIRECTIONS:

1. Tap hard-boiled eggs to form fine cracks over entire surface, but DO NOT remove the shells.
2. Place eggs in a container and completely cover eggs with cold water.
3. Add a few drops of food coloring and swish the water gently or rock the container until the color is uniform.
4. Cover and let stand in refrigerator overnight.
5. Remove eggs from liquid and discard liquid.
6. Peel eggs and store refrigerated in covered container until ready to serve. (Eggs can also be individually wrapped in plastic wrap.)

DEVILED EGGS
(Makes 12 servings)

INGREDIENTS:

6   hard-boiled eggs
1 tsp. prepared mustard
2 Tbs. mayonnaise

DIRECTIONS:

1. Peel each egg and cut in half, lengthwise.
2. Scoop out yolks and mash in a bowl.
3. Add mustard and mayonnaise, and mix together until smooth.
4. Scoop yolk mixture into each egg white half.

EGG BOATS

(Makes 12 servings)

INGREDIENTS:

12 "Deviled Eggs"
3   slices American cheese (individually wrapped)
12 toothpicks

DIRECTIONS:

1. Cut each slice of cheese into 4 triangles, or "sails," by making 2 diagonal lines from opposite corners, as shown in Illustration A–08 #1.
2. Insert a toothpick into the sail, forming the "mast."
3. Push the bottom tip of the mast into the boat.
4. Cover and refrigerate until ready to serve.

ILLUSTRATION A-08 #1

EGG FISHIES

(Makes 12 servings)

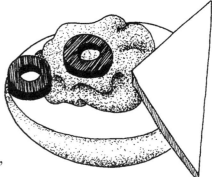

INGREDIENTS:

12 "Deviled Eggs"
2   slices American cheese (individually wrapped)
24 olive slices

DIRECTIONS:

1. Cut each slice of cheese into 8 triangles or "tails" as shown in Illustration A–09 #1.
2. Place each tail at the "end" of the egg.
3. Push 1 slice of olive toward the front of the egg to form the "eye" and 1 slice of olive at the front tip of the egg to create the "mouth."
4. Cover and refrigerate until ready to serve.

EGG WIZARDS
EGG CLOWNS

(Makes 12 servings)

INGREDIENTS:

12 "Deviled Eggs"
2   slices American cheese (individually wrapped)
1   grated carrot
24 raisins
12 candied cherries
1   2 oz. jar of pimentos

DIRECTIONS:

1. Cut each slice of cheese into 8 triangles, or "hats," as shown in Illustration A-09 #1.
2. Place each hat at the "top" of the egg.
3. Push grated carrots into the mixture, just under the hat, forming the clown's "hair."
4. Place 2 raisins below the hair to create the "eyes."
5. Set 1 cherry in the middle of the mixture to form the "nose."
6. Push 1 slice of pimento under the nose to mark the "mouth."
7. Cover and refrigerate until ready to serve.

ILLUSTRATION A-09 #1

EGG CATS
(Makes 12 servings)

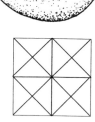

INGREDIENTS:

- 12   "Deviled Eggs"
- 2   slices American cheese (individually wrapped)
- 24   raisins
- 12   grapes
- 1   2 oz. jar of pimentos

DIRECTIONS:

1. Cut each slice of cheese into 16 triangles, or "ears," as shown in Illustration A-11 #1.
2. Place 2 ears at the "top" of the egg.
3. Place 2 raisins on the face to create the "eyes."
4. Set 1 grape in the middle of the mixture to form the "nose."
5. Push 1 slice of pimento under the nose to mark the "mouth."
6. Cover and refrigerate until ready to serve.

ILLUSTRATION A-11 #1

PEACH SALADS
PEAR SALADS
(Makes 12 servings)

INGREDIENTS:

- 12   peach or pear halves (canned)
- 8 oz.   cream cheese (softened)
- 2 Tbs.   honey
- 2 Tbs.   orange juice concentrate
- 1/2 tsp.   vanilla extract
- 12   cup cake liners

DIRECTIONS:

1. Fruit halves should be drained and patted dry with paper towels.
2. Place fruit halves in cup cake liners.
3. Mix cream cheese, honey, orange juice concentrate and vanilla extract in a bowl until well blended.
4. Spread cream cheese mixture evenly across the top of each fruit half.

PEACH BLOSSOMS
(Makes 12 servings)

INGREDIENTS:

- 12   "Peach Salads"
- 1 pt.   sliced strawberries
- 12   grapes or blueberries

DIRECTIONS:

1. Arrange strawberry slices around the edge of the peach half to form "flower petals."
2. Push a grape or blueberry into the middle of mixture to form the center of the flower.
3. Cover and refrigerate until ready to serve.

CLOWN PEARS
PEAR MAGICIANS
SILLY-FACE PEARS
PIRATE PEARS
COWPOKE PEARS
(Makes 12 servings)

INGREDIENTS:

12	"Pear Salads"
2	carrots (grated)
4	strawberries (sliced)
12	candied cherries
1	licorice whip (cut into 12 pieces, 1" long)
24	raisins

DIRECTIONS:

1. Put 1 strawberry slice toward the "top" of the pear to form the "hat."
2. Push grated carrots into the mixture, just under the hat, forming the "hair."
3. Place 2 raisins below the hair to create the "eyes."
4. Set 1 cherry in the middle of the mixture to form the "nose."
5. Push 1 piece of licorice under the nose to mark the "mouth."
6. Cover and refrigerate until ready to serve.

LION-FACE PEACHES
(Makes 12 servings)

INGREDIENTS:

12	"Peach Salads"
3	carrots (grated)
12	grapes
1	licorice whip (cut into 24 pieces, 1/2" long)
24	raisins

DIRECTIONS:

1. Push grated carrots around the outer edge of the peach to form the mane.
2. Place 2 raisins toward the top of the mixture to create the "eyes."
3. Set 1 grape in the middle of the mixture to form the "nose."
4. Push 2 pieces of licorice under nose in an inverted "V," to mark "mouth."
5. Cover and refrigerate until ready to serve.

PEAR FISHIES
(Makes 12 servings)

INGREDIENTS:

12	"Pear Salads"
12	blueberries
1	licorice whip
1 c.	sliced almonds
1 16 oz.	can mandarin oranges (slices)

DIRECTIONS:

1. Place 2 orange slices on one end of peach to form a tail.
2. Set 1 blueberry in the middle of other end to form the "eye."
3. Place a small piece of licorice whip on the "head" to make the "lips."
4. Arrange almond slices in rows along "top" of peach to form the "scales."

STEGOSAURUS PEARS
(Makes 12 servings)

INGREDIENTS:

- 12   "Pear Salads"
- 12   raisins
- 12   green grapes (cut in half)
- 2   20 oz. cans pineapple chunks (well drained)

DIRECTIONS:

1. Place 2 grape halves at the bottom of pear to make the feet.
2. Arrange pineapple chunks in rows along "top" of pear to form the "scales."
3. Set 1 raisin in the middle of head to form the "eye."

ROCKET SHIPS
(Makes 12 servings)

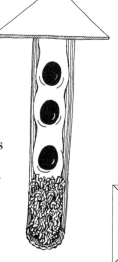

INGREDIENTS:

- 12   celery stalks
- 3   slices American cheese (individually wrapped)
- 4 oz. cream cheese (softened)
- 36   blueberries or raisins
- 1   grated carrot

DIRECTIONS:

1. Fill celery stalks with cream cheese.
2. Cut each slice of cheese into 4 triangles by making 2 diagonal lines from opposite corners, as shown in Illustration A-08 #1.
3. Place 1 slice of cheese as the space capsule at the top of each celery stalk.
4. Place 3 blueberries (or raisins) down the center of the celery stalk, forming the "windows" of the spaceship.
5. Push grated carrots into the bottom of the stalk, forming the rocket exhaust.
6. Cover and refrigerate until ready to serve.

ILLUSTRATION A-08 #1

FUNNY-FACE CRACKERS
MARTIAN-FACE CRACKERS
(Makes 24 servings)

INGREDIENTS:

- 24   crackers or mini-rice cakes
- 2/3 c. peanut butter (smooth or crunchy style) or cream cheese
- 1/2 c. raisins
         nuts, dried fruits, and cereals ✿

___

✿ Optional

DIRECTIONS:

1. Spread peanut butter on crackers.
2. Arrange raisins on crackers to make a "Funny Face," "Martian Face" or any design you want.

DINOSAUR SMACKERS
ANIMAL SMACKERS
TEDDY BEAR SMACKERS
(Makes 24 servings)

INGREDIENTS:
24   "Dinosaur Graham Crackers," "Teddy Bear Graham
         Crackers" or "Animal Crackers"
2/3 c.   peanut butter (smooth or crunchy style) or cream cheese

DIRECTIONS:
1. Spread peanut butter or cream cheese on 12 crackers.
2. Top with the other 12 crackers to make "smackers."

SANDWICH FILLINGS AND SPREADS

What faster, easier way to fill those tummies than with these easy, nutritious and fun-to-eat sandwich fillings and spreads. It is a good idea to offer two or more choices of sandwich fillings, since children's tastes differ so much.

EGG SALAD
(Makes 8 servings)

INGREDIENTS:
8   hard-boiled eggs (finely chopped)
4 oz.   softened cream cheese
1/8 c.   mayonnaise
1 c.   shredded American or cheddar cheese
1 tsp.   prepared mustard
1 Tbs.   chopped pickled relish

DIRECTIONS:
1. Mix cream cheese, mayonnaise and mustard together until smooth.
2. Stir in chopped eggs, cheese and relish until evenly mixed.

TUNA SALAD
(Makes 8 sandwiches)

INGREDIENTS:
2   6 1/2 oz. cans of tuna, well drained.
4 oz.   softened cream cheese
1/8 c.   mayonnaise
1 c.   shredded American or cheddar cheese
1 tsp.   prepared mustard
1/4 c.   chopped black olives ❀

❀ Optional

DIRECTIONS:
1. Mix cream cheese, mayonnaise and mustard together until smooth.
2. Stir in tuna, cheese and black olives until evenly mixed.

CHICKEN SALAD
(Makes 8 sandwiches)

INGREDIENTS:
- 2   6 1/2 oz. cans of chicken, well drained.
- 4 oz.   softened cream cheese
- 1/8 c.   mayonnaise
- 1 c.   shredded jack or Swiss cheese
- 1 tsp.   prepared mustard
- 1/4 c.   toasted chopped almonds

DIRECTIONS:
1. Mix cream cheese, mayonnaise and mustard together until smooth.
2. Stir in chicken, cheese and almonds until evenly mixed.

HAM SALAD
(Makes 8 sandwiches)

INGREDIENTS:
- 12 oz.   cooked ham (finely chopped)
- 4 oz.   softened cream cheese
- 1/8 c.   mayonnaise
- 1 c.   shredded American or cheddar cheese
- 1 tsp.   prepared mustard
- 1 Tbs.   honey
- 1/2 c.   crushed pineapple (well drained)

DIRECTIONS:
1. Mix cream cheese, mayonnaise, honey and mustard together until smooth.
2. Stir in ham, cheese and pineapple until evenly mixed.

PEANUT BUTTER

Try some variations on an old standby: peanut butter and jelly. Add one of the following ingredients instead of the jelly:

- Sliced bananas
- Honey
- Chopped apples
- Soft cream cheese
- Chocolate chips
- Chopped nuts
- Chopped raisins
- Coconut
- Chopped celery
- Grated carrots

SANDWICH SHAPES

Sandwiches are probably the easiest food to serve for lunch at your party. Sliced meats and cheeses are always popular, but you can take any sandwich and turn it into something new and exciting just by varying its shape. Use any type of cookie cutter, such as:

- Stars
- Hearts
- Animals
- Dinosaurs

Make sandwiches ahead of time, cover and store until serving. What could be easier!

OPEN-FACED COOKIE CUTTER SANDWICHES

DIRECTIONS:
1. Chill bread first for ease of cutting.
2. Cut out bread shapes with cookie cutter.
3. Spread butter (or cream cheese) on bread.
4. Cut out same shapes from slices of meat or cheese.
5. Place meat or cheese on bread.

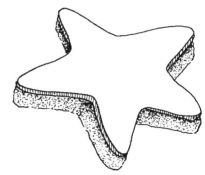

6. Top with sandwich toppings to accent the shape of the bread. (When using sliced meat or cheese, use toppings that will not roll off.)
   [NOTE: Sandwich spreads may be used instead of meat or cheese. When using sandwich spreads, it is not necessary to first spread butter or cream cheese on bread.}

TOPPINGS

- Black olives (sliced or chopped)
- Pimentos (sliced)
- Pickles (sliced)
- Raisins
- Coconut
- Berries

- Carrots (sliced or grated)
- Tomatoes (sliced)
- Cucumbers (sliced)
- Nuts
- Candied cherries
- Grapes

CLOSED COOKIE CUTTER SANDWICHES

DIRECTIONS:

1. Chill bread first for ease of cutting.
2. Cut out bread shapes with cookie cutter.
3. Spread butter (or cream cheese) on bread.
4. Cut out same shapes from slices of meat or cheese.
5. Place meat or cheese on bread.
6. Top with another slice of bread.
   [NOTE: Sandwich spreads may be used instead of meat or cheese. When using sandwich spreads, it is not necessary to first spread butter or cream cheese on bread.}

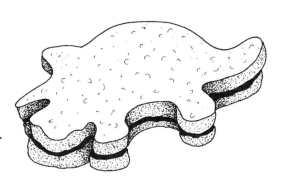

YUMMY CHEESE BISCUITS
(Makes 12–16 servings)

INGREDIENTS:

2 1/4 c.	buttermilk biscuit mix
1/2 c.	milk
1 c.	shredded jack or cheddar cheese
1	egg

DIRECTIONS:

1. Stir biscuit mix, milk, cheese and egg together in a large bowl until ingredients are just combined.
2. On a lightly-floured surface, roll out dough into a 10" circle about 1/4" thick.
3. Cut out dough with 3"–4" cookie cutters. (Biscuits may be cut into any desired shape.)
4. Bake at 425° for 8–10 minutes or until golden brown.
5. Cool on wire racks.
6. Biscuits may be served as is, or split and filled. (See "Biscuit Sandwich," below.)

☞ **THE EXTRA TOUCH**
- Color biscuits by adding a few drops of food coloring to milk.

BISCUIT SANDWICHES

DIRECTIONS:

1. Make "Yummy Cheese Biscuits" (above) using your favorite cookie cutter.
2. Chill biscuits in refrigerator 15–20 minutes or until cold.
3. Gently split in half with knife and fill with favorite sandwich spread.
4. Wrap each sandwich individually in plastic wrap.
5. Refrigerate until ready to serve.

CHECKERBOARD SANDWICHES

DIRECTIONS:
1. Make an equal number of sandwiches out of both dark and light breads.
2. Trim off crusts.
3. Cut into same size squares.
4. Place squares on serving tray, alternating dark and light "sandwiches."
5. Cover and refrigerate until serving time.

SAILBOAT SANDWICHES
PIRATE SHIP SANDWICHES

DIRECTIONS:
1. Cut small rolls in half.
2. Hollow out some of the bread in center of each half and fill with sandwich filling.
3. Cut a square slice of cheese diagonally, forming 2 triangular "sails."
4. Insert a toothpick into the sail, forming the "mast."
5. Push the bottom tip of the mast into the sandwich.

TELESCOPE SANDWICHES
SPYGLASS SANDWICHES
RINGS-OF-SATURN SANDWICHES

DIRECTIONS:
1. Trim crusts from bread slices.
2. Flatten each slice lightly with rolling pin.
3. Spread about 2 Tbs. of your favorite sandwich filling on each slice of bread.
4. Tightly roll bread slices (like a jelly roll) to form a "telescope" or "spyglass."
5. Wrap each sandwich individually in plastic wrap.
6. Refrigerate until ready to serve.

TO MAKE "RINGS-OF-SATURN SANDWICHES":
1. Slice chilled sandwiches into 1" thick pieces.

BACKWARD SANDWICHES

1. Trim the crusts off 2 slices of bread.
2. Spread butter (or cream cheese) on 1 slice of bread.
3. Top with other slice of bread.
4. Cut the sandwich into 5 strips, lengthwise.
5. Using 2 slices of thinly-sliced pressed meat per sandwich, overlap 1 slice of meat with the other.
6. Then put 1 sandwich strip on the edge of the slices of meat, and roll up the sandwich strip inside the meat, as shown in Illustration A-28 #1-2.
7. Continue rolling up remaining strips of sandwiches inside slices of meat.
8. Cover and refrigerate until ready to serve.

ILLUSTRATION
A-28 #1-2

HOT FOODS

Serving hot foods at a party can be much easier than you think. All the foods in this section can be prepared ahead of time and baked just before or during the party.

Try some of these delicious new twists on some old favorites. You can keep foods hot by covering them with foil and storing in warm place until you are ready to serve them.

[NOTE: Foods which contain meats or dairy products should not be left out more than 2 hours.]

HOT DOG WAGON WHEELS
CAPTAIN'S WHEELS
(Makes 12 servings)

INGREDIENTS:

6	English muffins
6	hot dogs
1	16 oz. can baked beans
2 c.	shredded cheddar or American cheese

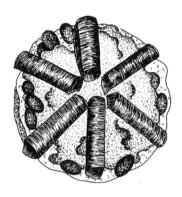

DIRECTIONS:

1. Split English muffins in half and arrange on a cookie sheet.
2. Spread beans on top of muffins.
3. Sprinkle cheese on top of beans.
4. Cut hot dogs in thirds. Then cut each third lengthwise into 4 strips as shown in Illustration A–31.
5. Arrange 6 hot dog strips in a wheel pattern on top of each muffin.
6. Bake at 375° for 10–12 minutes or until cheese has melted.

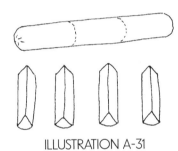

HIDDEN TREASURES
(Makes 8 servings)

ILLUSTRATION A-31

INGREDIENTS:

1/2 c.	baked beans
6	hot dogs (chopped)
1	28 oz. pkg. refrigerated crescent rolls
1 c.	shredded cheddar cheese

DIRECTIONS:

1. Mix together beans, hot dogs and cheese in a large bowl.
2. Unroll 2 dough triangles and pinch perforations together to seal, forming a rectangle.
3. Press each rectangle into a muffin cup.
   [HINT: for more even baking, place dough in the outer cups of the muffin tin.]
4. Place about 1/3 cup of filling mixture in the center of each dough rectangle.
5. Fold 4 corners of dough over the filling, one at a time, and seal by pinching perforations together.
6. Bake at 375° for 18–20 minutes or until dough is golden brown.
7. Remove from pans and cool slightly on a wire rack.

HAPPY-FACE PIZZAS
FLYING-PIZZA SAUCERS
SILLY-FACE PIZZAS
(Makes 12 servings)

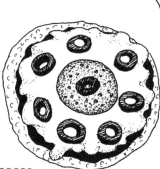

INGREDIENTS:
6	English muffins
2 c.	shredded American or cheddar cheese
16 oz.	jar pizza sauce

Suggested Toppings:
4 oz.	pkg. sliced pepperoni
1	4 oz. can sliced olives
1/4 c.	sliced mushrooms

DIRECTIONS:
1. Split muffins in half and arrange on cookie sheet.
2. Spread sauce on muffins and top with shredded cheese.
3. Arrange toppings to create a "happy face," a "silly-face" or a "flying saucer."
4. Bake at 375° for 5–10 minutes or until cheese melts.

DRUMSTICKS
PTERODACTYL WINGS
BUFFALO WINGS
JUNGLE DRUMSTICKS
(Makes 28 servings)

INGREDIENTS:
2 lbs.	chicken drumettes or wings
1/2 c.	soda crackers (approximately 14 crackers)
1/2 c.	seasoned bread crumbs
1/4 c.	grated Parmesan cheese
1/2 c.	milk

DIRECTIONS:
1. Place soda crackers in a plastic bag and roll with a rolling pin to crush into small pieces.
2. Mix crushed crackers, seasoned bread crumbs and Parmesan cheese in a bowl.
3. Dip chicken in milk and roll in crumb mixture.
4. Lay chicken in single layer on a 9" x 13" baking pan.
5. Bake at 350° for 30–40 minutes or until fork-tender and crust is golden color.

CRAZY DOGS
BLAST-OFF DOGS
(Makes 8 servings)

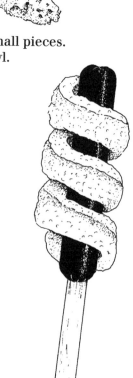

INGREDIENTS:
8	hot dogs
8	craft sticks or wooden skewers
1	cans refrigerator dough bread sticks

DIRECTIONS:
1. Push a craft stick halfway into each hot dog.
2. Wrap a dough strip around each hot dog, forming a spiral pattern, and place on a cookie sheet.
3. Bake at 425° for 10–15 minutes or until golden brown.
4. Cool on wire racks.

BEAR CLAWS
TIGER CLAWS
DRAGON CLAWS
TYRANNOSAURUS CLAWS
FLYING SAUCER BISCUITS
BISCUIT FLOWERS
(Makes 20 servings)

INGREDIENTS:

2 cans	refrigerated biscuit dough
1 tsp.	cinnamon
1/4 c.	sugar
1/3 c.	peanuts

DIRECTIONS:
1. Mix cinnamon and sugar together in a bowl.
2. Pat each biscuit into a 3" circle.
3. With a knife, make five cuts in a circle to form toes.
4. Press one side of biscuit into sugar and cinnamon.
5. Place claws on cookie sheet, sugar side up.
6. Push a peanut into each toe.
7. Bake according to package directions.

TO MAKE "DRAGON CLAWS" AND "TYRANNOSAURUS CLAWS":
1. Substitute green candy sprinkles for the cinnamon and sugar.

TO MAKE "FLYING SAUCER BISCUITS":
1. Make six cuts in biscuit and substitute "red hots" for the peanuts.

TO MAKE "BISCUIT FLOWERS":
1. Make six cuts in biscuits.
2. Press your thumb into the center and fill indentations with a candied or maraschino cherry, or 1/2 teaspoon of jam.

TREATS

Children of all ages look forward to treats—and these scrumptious foods will delight the eyes and mouths of your special guests.

COOKIE POPS
COOKIE PUPPETS
COOKIE WANDS
FLOWER COOKIE POPS
SHERIFF'S COOKIE BADGES
(Makes 12–16 servings)

You may want to turn this treat into a party activity by having children decorate their own cookies. To make it easier for kids, place toppings in a muffin tin, put frosting in bowls and provide plastic knives for spreading. Then be prepared for lots of fun!

TO MAKE THE COOKIE DOUGH

INGREDIENTS:
1/2 c.   butter (at room temperature)
3/4 c.   sugar
1   egg
1 Tbs.   milk
1 tsp.   vanilla extract
2 c.   all-purpose flour
1/4 tsp.   salt
1 tsp.   baking powder
12–16   craft sticks
1   recipe "Cookie Icing" (page 345)
           small candies, raisins, nuts, coconuts, candied cherries, licorice whips, miniature marshmal-
           lows, chocolate chips

TIMESAVER
- Instead of making "Cookie Icing," use canned frosting.

DIRECTIONS:
1. Cream together butter and sugar until fluffy.
2. Beat in egg, milk and vanilla extract with butter mixture.
3. Mix dry ingredients in separate bowl.
4. Stir dry ingredients into creamed butter mixture.
5. Cover and refrigerate for at least 2 hours.

TO MAKE "COOKIE POPS"
1. Shape dough into 1 1/4" balls.
2. Insert a craft stick halfway into the center of each ball.
3. Place on ungreased cookie sheet.
4. Grease the bottom of a drinking glass.
5. Dip bottom of glass in a bowl of sugar, coating with a layer of sugar.
6. Flatten ball with bottom of glass.
7. Space cookie pops 2" apart on ungreased cookie sheet.
8. Bake at 375° for 12–18 minutes or until the edges begin to brown slightly.
9. Cool 1 minute on cookie sheet, then remove to wire rack.
10. Cool completely before decorating.
11. Spread with "Cookie Icing" and decorate with assorted candies.
12. Store in airtight container.

TO MAKE "COOKIE PUPPETS"
1. Roll out dough 3/8" thick.
2. Cut out shapes with cookie cutters.
3. Place cookies on ungreased cookie sheet 2" apart and carefully insert a craft stick halfway into the center of each cookie.
4. Bake at 375° for 12–18 minutes or until the edges begin to brown slightly.
5. Cool 1 minute on cookie sheet, then remove to wire rack.
6. Cool completely before decorating.
7. Spread with "Cookie Icing" and decorate with assorted candies.
8. Store in an airtight container.

TO MAKE "COOKIE WANDS"
* Follow the directions for making "Cookie Puppets," but use a star-shaped cookie cutter.

TO MAKE "FLOWER COOKIE POPS"

* Follow the directions for making
  "Cookie Pops," and place candy corns
  around the edges to form the petals.

TO MAKE "SHERIFF'S COOKIE BADGES"

* Follow the directions for making "Cookie Wands,"
  (omitting the craft stick), and place a red hot candy
  on each point of the star.

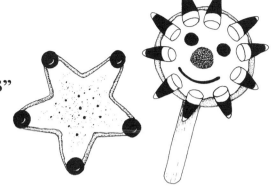

 THE EXTRA TOUCH

• Wrap in colored plastic wrap and tie with ribbon to make a great take-home treat.

CRUNCHY CRITTERS
BEARY CRUNCHY CRITTERS
DINO CRITTERS
CRUNCHY CIRCUS CRITTERS
STARFISH CRITTERS

(Makes 12–16 servings)

INGREDIENTS:

1/2 c.	sugar
3/4 c.	light corn syrup
3/4 c.	peanut butter (smooth or crunchy)
6 c.	puffed rice cereal

DIRECTIONS:

1. Heat syrup and sugar mixture in a heavy, 2 qt. saucepan over medium heat, stirring constantly, until mixture begins to boil.
2. At point of boil, remove from heat, and stir in peanut butter, until mixture is melted.
3. Place cereal in a large bowl.
4. Pour peanut butter mixture over cereal and mix until cereal is uniformly coated.
5. Using the back of a buttered spoon, or a piece of wax paper, press mixture in ungreased 9" x 13" baking pan.
6. Cool completely.
7. Cut into shapes with cookie cutter(s). [HINT: To make cutting easier, you may want to place a pot holder between the cookie cutter and your hand.]

 THE EXTRA TOUCH

Wrap in colored plastic wrap and tie with a ribbon for a great take-home treat.

EDIBLE DOUGH

(Makes 48 servings)

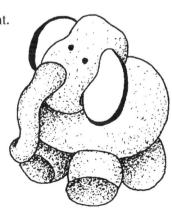

You may want to turn this treat into a party activity by having the children make their own shapes and/or characters. To make it easier for kids, place toppings in a muffin tin. Then just watch the fun begin!

INGREDIENTS:

1/2 c.   honey
1/2 c.   peanut butter
1 c.   instant evaporated powdered milk
1 c.   quick cooking oat cereal
1 tsp.   vanilla extract
          cocoa powder ❀
          almond slices ❀
          chocolate chips ❀
          raisins ❀
          dried fruits ❀
          nuts ❀
          candies ❀
          marshmallows ❀

❀ Optional toppings to create your own characters

DIRECTIONS:

1. Mix peanut butter and honey in a bowl.
2. Add evaporated milk, oats and vanilla extract and mix together.
3. Cover cookie sheet with wax paper.
4. Shape dough into whatever form you want.
5. When you have finished shaping the dough, decorate with any of the toppings listed above.
6. Place on cookie sheet.
7. Cover and chill for 30 minutes or until ready to serve.

HONEY BEE TREATS
(Makes 48 servings)

INGREDIENTS:

1 recipe   "Edible Dough"
1/2 c.   almond slices
          cocoa powder

DIRECTIONS:

1. Cover cookie sheet with wax paper.
2. Using a teaspoon, make oval shaped ball to form the body of the "bee," and place "bee" on cookie sheet.
3. Dip a toothpick in cocoa powder and gently press toothpick across body of the "bee" to make "stripes."
4. Push an almond slice into each side of "bee" to create "wings."
5. Cover and chill for 30 minutes or until ready to serve.

FUNNY BUNNIES
(Makes 48 servings)

INGREDIENTS:

1 recipe   "Edible Dough"
1/2 c.   almond slices
1/2 c.   chocolate chips
          cocoa powder

DIRECTIONS:

1. Cover cookie sheet with wax paper.
2. Using a teaspoon, make oval shaped ball to form the body of the "bunny," and place "bunny" on cookie sheet.

3. Push an almond slice into each side of "bunny's" head to create "ears."
4. Press 1 chocolate chip in the center of "bunny's" head to make the "nose."
5. Dip a toothpick in cocoa powder and gently poke 2 holes into the "bunny's" head to form the "eyes."
6. Dip a toothpick in cocoa powder and gently press an inverted "V" below the nose to create the "mouth."
7. Cover and chill for 30 minutes or until ready to serve.

TRAIL MIX
CAVEMAN MIX
SPACE MIX
PICNIC MIX
NUTS AND BOLTS
(Makes 12 1/4 cup servings)

INGREDIENTS:

1 pkg.	mixed, dried fruit bits (six ounces)
3/4 c.	peanuts
1/2 c.	flaked coconut
3/4 c.	miniature marshmallows

DIRECTIONS:
1. In a mixing bowl, combine fruit, nuts, coconut and marshmallows.
2. Place in an airtight container and store in a cool and dry area.

VARIATION
• Add dry cereal, granola, mixed nuts, chocolate chips, carob chips or raisins.

CRUNCHY CARAMEL CORN
GOLDEN NUGGETS
ASTEROIDS
CARAMEL CORN BOULDERS
(Makes 3 1/2 quarts or 14 1 cup servings)

INGREDIENTS:

3/4 c.	unpopped popcorn
2 c.	brown sugar (packed)
1 c.	butter
1/2 c.	corn syrup (light)
1 tsp.	salt
1 tsp.	baking soda
1–2 c.	peanuts ❀

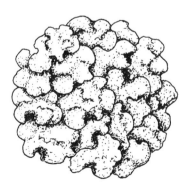

———
❀ Optional

DIRECTIONS:
1. Pop popcorn and remove any unpopped kernels.
2. Place warm popcorn in a large metal bowl and keep warm in oven at 200°.
3. Put butter, corn syrup and salt in a large sauce pan.
4. Bring butter mixture to boil. Stir continuously for five minutes.
5. Remove mixture from heat and add baking soda. (Candy will foam.)
6. Stir mixture well as it cools and stir in peanuts.
7. Pour mixture over popcorn and mix until evenly coated.

8. Spread coated popcorn on two greased cookie sheets.
9. Bake at 200° for one hour, stirring occasionally.
10. Cool corn completely.
11. Break into clusters.
12. Place in airtight containers and store in a cool and dry area.

TO MAKE "ASTEROIDS" OR "BOULDERS":

1. Instead of spreading coated mixture on cookie sheet (Step #8 above), shape coated popcorn into balls by using two buttered spoons.
2. Bake at 200° for approximately one hour.
3. Place popcorn balls on wax paper to cool.

WIGGLIES
(Makes 12–18 servings)

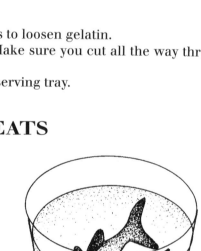

INGREDIENTS:

2   6 oz. packages of flavored gelatin
1 1/2 c.   water
1 c.   lemon-lime soda
1   8 oz. cup of yogurt (fruit flavored)

DIRECTIONS:

1. Stir boiling water into gelatin.
2. Let gelatin dissolve completely.
3. Mix soda and yogurt together in a separate bowl until smooth.
4. Add yogurt and soda mixture to gelatin.
5. Pour mixture into a 13" x 19" glass or metal pan.
6. Chill 3 hours or until gelatin sets.
7. To cut wigglies, dip bottom of pan in warm water for 15 seconds to loosen gelatin.
8. With cookie cutter or a knife, cut gelatin into desired shape. (Make sure you cut all the way through the layer.)
9. Carefully lift "Wigglies" out of pan (with spatula) and place on serving tray.

UNDER-THE-SEA TREATS
(Makes 12 servings)

INGREDIENTS:

5   envelopes unflavored gelatin
1/4 c.   honey or 1/2 cup sugar
1 c.   apple juice (cold)
4 c.   apple juice (heated to boiling)
16   drops blue food coloring (approximately)
1 pkg.   gummi fish
12   clear plastic drinking cups

DIRECTIONS:

1. Pour cold juice into a bowl.
2. Mix in blue food coloring.
3. Sprinkle gelatin over cold juice and let stand for 1 minute.
4. Bring 4 cups apple juice to a boil and add honey or sugar.
5. Add gelatin mixture to boiling juice and stir until completely dissolved.
6. Pour into plastic cups.
7. Chill 1 1/2 hours or until partially set.
8. Mix in gummi fish and chill 1 1/2 hours or until completely set.

ICE CREAMS

Just about everyone loves ice cream, especially children! Yet dishing out ice cream at a birthday party can be difficult, what with children screaming and ice cream melting. There's got to be a better way.

There is. Prepare individual servings ahead of time! This will make serving during the party much easier, and ice cream can be stored up to 1 week ahead of time in your freezer. Also, individual servings determine how much each child will get, which reduces the "they're-getting-more-than-me" anxiety.

Follow the directions in this section, and watch how a few, simple additions to a scoop of ice cream can create a fun and tasty treat.

TOY ICE CREAMS
(Makes 12 servings)

INGREDIENTS:

3 pints	ice cream (any flavor)
12	paper cupcake liners
2 c.	flaked coconut ❀
	green food coloring ❀
	plastic figures, such as horses, dinosaurs, circus animals, jungle animals, cowboys and Indians

❀ Optional

DIRECTIONS:

1. Place coconut in a bowl and tint green by adding a few drops of food coloring and mixing until color is uniform.
2. Place cupcake liner in cake pan or on a small tray.
3. Scoop out 12 ice cream balls, placing each in its own cupcake liner.
4. Sprinkle ice cream with green coconut.
5. Push a toy into top of each ice cream scoop.
6. Cover pan and keep frozen until ready to serve.

TO MAKE "TREASURE ISLAND ICE CREAMS":

1. Follow directions for "Toy Ice Cream," substituting "Pirate Flag Sticker" (page 139) glued to a toothpick.
2. Make an "X" out of black licorice and set on top of ice cream scoop.

UPSIDE-DOWN ICE CREAM CONES
(Makes 12 servings)

INGREDIENTS:

3 pints	ice cream (any flavor)
12	sugar cones
12	paper cupcake liners
1	small jar chocolate sauce

DIRECTIONS:

1. Place cupcake liners in cake pan or on a small tray.
2. Put 1–2 tablespoons chocolate sauce in each cupcake liner.
3. Scoop out 12 ice cream balls, placing each in its own cupcake liner.
4. Push inverted sugar cone into the top of each ice cream ball.
5. Cover pan and keep frozen until serving.

TEDDY BEAR ICE CREAMS
(Makes 12 servings)

INGREDIENTS:

3 pints	ice cream (any flavor)
12	paper cupcake liners
12	vanilla wafers (cut in half)
36	chocolate chips
1	tube red gel frosting

DIRECTIONS:

1. Place paper cupcake liners in cake pan or on a small tray.
2. Scoop out 12 ice cream balls, placing each ball in its own cupcake liner.
3. Place ice cream in freezer for 20 minutes or until firm.
4. Working with 2 or 3 ice cream balls at one time, push cookie halves into the sides of each ice cream ball to form the ears.
5. Push 2 chocolate chips into the front of the ball to form the eyes and 1 chip into the middle of the ball to make the nose.
6. Pipe the mouth on with red gel frosting.
7. Return ice cream balls to freezer as you finish decorating the remaining ice cream balls.
8. Cover pan and keep frozen until ready to serve.

MONKEY ICE CREAMS
(Makes 12 servings)

INGREDIENTS:

3 pints	chocolate ice cream
12	paper cupcake liners
12	vanilla wafers (whole)
12	vanilla wafers (cut in half)
24	chocolate chips
1	tube red gel frosting or regular frosting (tinted red)

DIRECTIONS:

1. Place paper cupcake liners in cake pan or on a small tray.
2. Scoop out 12 ice cream balls, placing each ball in its own cupcake liner.
3. Place ice cream in the freezer for 20 minutes or until firm.
4. Working with 2 or 3 ice cream balls at one time, push a cookie into the center of each ice cream ball to form the muzzle and two cookie halves into the sides to form the ears.
5. Push 2 chocolate chips into the front of the ball to form the eyes.
6. Draw the mouth on with red gel or red frosting.
7. Return ice cream balls to freezer as you finish decorating the remaining balls.
8. Cover pan and keep frozen until ready to serve.

FISHIE ICE CREAMS
(Makes 12 servings)

INGREDIENTS:

3 pints	orange sherbet
12	paper cupcake liners
12	miniature marshmallows (cut in half)
18	orange wedge gel candies (sliced in half lengthwise)
6	melted chocolate chips
1	toothpick
2	red licorice whips

DIRECTIONS:

1. Place paper cupcake liners in cake pan or on a small tray.
2. Scoop out 12 sherbet balls, placing each ball in its own cupcake liner.
3. Place ice cream in the freezer for 20 minutes or until firm.
4. Working with 2 or 3 sherbet balls at one time, push 2 orange wedge slices into the end of each ball to form a tail.
5. Push 1 orange wedge slice on the top of each ball to form the dorsal or top fin.
6. Push 1 miniature marshmallow half into both sides of the front of the ball to form the eyes.
7. Using the toothpick, dot the centers of the eyes with the melted chocolate.
8. To make the mouth, press bits of licorice whips into sherbet.
9. Return sherbet balls to freezer as you finish decorating remaining balls.
10. Cover pan and keep frozen until ready to serve.

BRONTOSAURUS ICE CREAMS
DRAGON ICE CREAMS
ALIEN ICE CREAMS
(Makes 12 servings)

INGREDIENTS:

3 pints	green-colored ice cream (mint, pistachio, or lime sherbet)
12	paper cupcake liners
12	miniature marshmallows (cut in half)
36	candy corns
24	chocolate chips
6	melted chocolate chips
1	toothpick
2	red licorice whips

DIRECTIONS:

1. Place cupcake liners in cake pan or on a small tray.
2. Scoop out 12 ice cream (or sherbet) balls, placing each ball in its own cupcake liner.
3. Place ice cream (or sherbet) in the freezer for 20 minutes or until firm.
4. Working with 2 or 3 ice cream (or sherbet) balls at one time, push 3 candy corns, along the top of each ball to form a row of "scales."
5. Push 1 miniature marshmallow half into both sides of the front of each ball to form the "eyes."
6. Using the toothpick, dot the centers of the eyes with the melted chocolate.
7. To make the mouth, you can press bits of licorice whips into the ice cream (or sherbet) to create the "mouth."
8. Push 2 chocolate chips into the front of each ball to form the "nostrils."
9. Return ice cream (or sherbet) balls to freezer as you finish decorating the remaining balls.
10. Cover pan and keep frozen until ready to serve.

FLYING SAUCER ICE CREAMS
(Makes 12 servings)

INGREDIENTS:

3 pints	ice cream (any flavor)
12	sugar cookies (approximately 3" in diameter)
1	13 ounce bag of jelly beans
12	2" pieces of licorice twists
12	LifeSaver® candies

DIRECTIONS:

1. Place cookies in cake pan or on a small tray.
2. Scoop out 12 ice cream balls, placing each ball in the center of a cookie.

3. Place ice cream (or sherbet) in the freezer for 20 minutes or until firm.
4. Cut the tips off of each licorice twist, at a 45° angle, and insert pointed end into a LifeSaver® candy, forming an "antenna" for the flying saucer.
5. Working with 2 or 3 ice cream balls at one time, push the antenna into the center of each ball so that each LifeSaver® candy "transmitter" rests above the surface, as shown in the illustration.
6. Push 6 jelly beans around the circumference of each ball, forming a ring of "landing lights" around the flying saucer.
7. Return ice cream balls to freezer as you finish decorating the remaining balls.
8. Cover pan and keep frozen until ready to serve.

FAIRY HAT ICE CREAMS
WIZARD HAT ICE CREAMS
(Makes 12 servings)

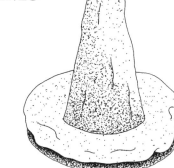

INGREDIENTS:

1 qt.	ice cream (any flavor)
12	sugar cones
12	sugar cookies (approximately 3" in diameter)
3	recipes "Cookie Icing" (See page 345)
	food coloring
	colored sprinkles

DIRECTIONS:
1. Working with 2 or 3 cones at a time, gently pack each cone with ice cream, leveling the top of every cone.
2. Lay each cone on its side in a cake pan or on a small tray.
3. As you finish cones, place them in the freezer for 20 minutes or until firm.
4. Mix frosting in a bowl with a few drops of food coloring, using birthday child's favorite color.
5. Frost the tops of each cookie and set aside.
6. Working with 2 or 3 ice cream cones at one time, place cone in the center of a cookie.
7. Lightly frost each cone.
8. Shake colored sprinkles ("fairy dust") on the frosted cone and cookie.
9. Return fairy hats to freezer as you finish decorating remaining cones.
10. Cover pan and keep frozen until ready to serve.

TEEPEE ICE CREAMS
(Makes 12 servings)

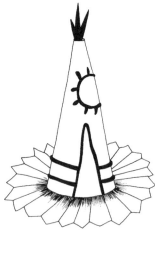

INGREDIENTS:

1 qt.	ice cream (any flavor)
12	sugar cones
12	paper cupcake liners (flattened)
2	recipes "Cookie Icing" (See page 345)
1	tube chocolate gel frosting
36	toothpicks

DIRECTIONS:
1. Carefully cut off 1/4" of the tip of each cone.
2. Working with 2 or 3 cones at a time, gently pack each cone with ice cream, leveling the top of every cone.
3. Lay each cone on its side, placing in a cake pan or on a small tray.
4. As you finish cones, place them in the freezer for 20 minutes or until firm.
5. Working with 2 or 3 ice cream cones at one time, place the top of each cone in the center of a flattened paper cupcake liner.
6. Lightly frost cones. As you complete each cone, place frosted cones in freezer until frosting has hardened.
7. Working on 1 cone at a time, pipe chocolate icing on frosted surface, creating geometric designs. (See illustration for sample designs.)

8. Insert toothpicks into the tip, signifying the center poles of the teepee.
9. Return teepees to freezer as you finish decorating remaining cones.
10. Cover pan and keep frozen until ready to serve.

CLOWN ICE CREAM CONES
(Makes 12 servings)

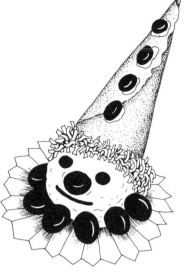

INGREDIENTS:

3 pints	ice cream (any flavor)
12	paper cupcake liners
12	sugar cones
24	chocolate chips
12	red gumdrops or red candied cherries
1 1/2 c.	flaked coconut
	red food coloring
1	13 oz. bag jelly beans or gumdrops
2	red licorice whips
1/4 c.	buttercream frosting
48	candy-coated chocolates

DIRECTIONS:

1. Place paper cupcake liners in cake pan or on a small tray.
2. Scoop out 12 ice cream balls, placing each ball in its own cupcake liner.
3. Press an ice cream cone on the top of each ball at an angle, to form the clown's "hat."
4. Place ice cream in the freezer for 20 minutes or until firm.
5. Mix coconut with a few drops of red food coloring in a bowl.
6. Working with 2 or 3 ice cream balls at one time, press flaked coconut around the top of the head to form the clown's "hair."
7. Press jelly beans or gumdrops around the base to create the "collar."
8. Push a candied cherry or gumdrop in center of face to form the "nose."
9. Push 2 chocolate chips into the front of the ball to form the "eyes."
10. Press bits of licorice whips into the ice cream to create the "mouth."
11. Dip 4 candy-coated chocolates into frosting and press onto "hat."
12. Return ice cream balls to freezer as you finish decorating the remaining balls.
13. Cover pan and keep frozen until ready to serve.

FLOWER POT ICE CREAMS
(Makes 12 servings)

INGREDIENTS:

1 qt.	chocolate ice cream
12	flat-bottom ice cream cones
12	chocolate cream-filled cookies (crushed)
12	gummi worms
12	craft sticks
12	"Flower Stickers" (See page 252)
	white glue
	scissors

DIRECTIONS:

1. Glue one "flower sticker" to each craft stick.
2. Working with 2 or 3 cones at a time, gently pack each cone with ice cream, leveling the top of every cone.
3. As you finish cones, place them upright in a cake pan or on a small tray.
4. Sprinkle crushed cookie on top of ice cream.
5. Insert craft stick into the center of ice cream.
6. Press a gummi worm into each ice cream.
7. Return flower pots to freezer as you finish decorating remaining cones.
8. Cover pan and keep frozen until ready to serve.

TREASURE CHEST ICE CREAMS
SUNKEN TREASURE ICE CREAMS
MAGIC BOX ICE CREAMS
(Makes 12 servings)

INGREDIENTS:

3 pints	ice cream (any flavor)
12	paper cupcake liners
60	square-shaped cookies (approximately 1 1/2" x 1 1/2")
1 lb.	assorted small candies (gumdrops, candy-coated chocolates, chocolate coins)

DIRECTIONS:

1. Place paper cupcake liners in cake pan or on a small tray.
2. Scoop out 12 ice cream balls, placing each ball in its own cupcake liner.
3. Place ice cream in the freezer for 20 minutes or until firm.
4. Working with 2 or 3 ice cream balls at one time, place 4 cookies around each ball, forming a box or "treasure chest."
5. Press 1 cookie into the top of the back edge, forming an open "lid" for the chest.
6. Press in small candies over the top of chest to create the "jewels," "doubloons," and other assorted treasures.
7. Return treasure chests to freezer as you finish decorating remaining ice cream balls.
8. Keep frozen until ready to serve.

Cake Tips

The birthday cake is the highlight of the party. Here are some mouth-watering cake recipes, and helpful hints to make your cakes a success.

BAKING TIPS

1. Preheat oven.
2. Prepare all types of baking pans by first greasing and then lightly flouring before adding cake batter.
3. If you have trouble with your cake sticking to the baking pan, line the bottom of each pan with wax paper.
4. When pouring the batter into the pans, divide equally between pans and tap the sides to release any air bubbles.
5. While cake is baking, do not open the oven door for the first 20–25 minutes.
6. Check cake after the shortest baking time given. There are three signs that a cake is done:
   a) Note whether cake has begun to pull away from the sides of baking pan.
   b) Insert a wooden toothpick into center of cake. Toothpick should come out clean.
   c) Lightly touch cake in center. If done, cake will be firm to the touch and spring back.
7. To remove cake from baking pan(s):
   a) Allow cake to cool in pan for about 10 minutes.
   b) Run a knife along edges to loosen sides of cake.
   c) Place a wire rack over top of pan and invert rack and pan together.
   d) Remove pan and wax paper.
   e) Take a slightly dampened cloth towel and cover cakes until completely cooled.

CUTTING AND ASSEMBLING CAKE DESIGNS

1. Freeze cake for easy handling:
   a) Cool cake completely.
   b) Wrap in plastic wrap.
   c) Place wrapped cake back into baking pan to protect it.
   d) Freeze at least 45 minutes. (Cake may be stored for up to 2 months in freezer if placed in airtight freezer bag.)
2. Trace cake pattern onto wax paper. Cut out each piece of wax paper pattern with scissors. Assemble pattern on top of cake. Cut out cake sections by cutting along wax paper pattern.
3. Assembling cake on a serving tray is like putting a simple puzzle together:
   a) You will need a tray or platter large enough for the cake. If you do not have one, cover a board or cookie sheet with foil.
   b) Position each section on the serving tray as specified by the design.
   c) Place frosting between the connecting sections, using the frosting to hold the pieces together.
   d) Press the sections together to form the final shape.

FROSTING CAKES

1. To prevent crumbs from getting in the frosting:
   a) Gently brush entire cake with pastry brush after assembly.
   b) Frost the cake with a "base coat" before starting the final frosting. To make a base coat, set aside approximately 1/2 c. of frosting and place in bowl. Thin with small amount of milk (approximately 3–4 Tbs.) to make it spread smoothly and evenly.
   c) Apply base coat of frosting, using a spatula and making broad strokes.
   d) Let base coat dry for 10–15 minutes.
2. Add an even layer of buttercream frosting:
   a) Start by placing a mound of frosting on top of the cake.
   b) Spread frosting outward with a spatula.
   c) Try not to touch the surface of the cake with the spatula or else crumbs will begin to appear in your frosting.
   d) Frost the sides of the cake by working from the top down.
3. If your design calls for a smooth finish:
   a) Allow buttercream frosting to set for 10–15 minutes.
   b) Dip a spatula in warm water and smooth with long strokes.
   c) Wipe frosting off spatula to keep working surface smooth and even.

DECORATING THE CAKE

1. Just about anything is fair game for decorating a cake. Just place the desired decoration into the frosting and *vóila*, you have yourself a masterpiece! Here are a few suggestions for what you can use to decorate your cakes:

- Dried fruits
- Nuts
- Raisins
- Frosted ice cream cones
- Cookies
- Licorice sticks/twists/bits
- Fresh fruit
- Marshmallows
- Assorted small candies
- Colored sprinkles
- Graham crackers
- Gummi worms
- Flaked coconut (plain or colored)
- Fresh flowers

2. Using a pastry bag can help give your cakes a special touch.
   a) There are a number of pastry bag products on the market, all of which offer a wide range of decorative tips.
   b) You can also make your own pastry bag. Start with a plastic sandwich bag (with recloseable top). Cut off one corner and insert a decorating tip in its place. Fill plastic bag half-full with frosting and seal bag. Squeeze frosting through the tip. Hold bag between your thumb and forefinger and apply steady pressure to push the frosting through the tip.

DECORATING CUPCAKES

Cupcakes are easy to make and easy to serve, especially if you have the party away from home, such as a park or a class party at school. Generally, the techniques used in decorating ice creams can be applied to decorating cupcakes. (See "Ice Creams" in **APPENDIX A: RECIPES**, pages 335–340.)

The following is a list of "Ice Creams" that work particularly well as cupcake decorating ideas.

- Toy Ice Creams (page 335)
- Teddy Bear Ice Creams (page 336)
- Monkey Ice Creams (page 336)
- Treasure Chest Ice Creams (page 340)
- Treasure Island Ice Creams (page 335)
- Flower Pot Ice Creams (page 339)

CAKE RECIPES

YUMMY YELLOW CAKE
(Makes 12–16 servings)

INGREDIENTS:

2 3/4 c. all-purpose flour
1 tsp.   salt
3 tsp.   baking powder
1/2 c.   unsalted butter (softened)
1 3/4 c. sugar
1 tsp.   vanilla
3   eggs
1 1/4 c. milk

DIRECTIONS:

1. Preheat oven to 375°.
2. Grease and lightly flour baking pans.
3. Combine flour, salt and baking powder in a bowl.
4. In a separate bowl, beat butter about 30 seconds. Add sugar and vanilla. Beat until well-combined.
5. Add eggs to butter mixture, one at a time, beating mixture after each egg.
6. Add dry ingredients and milk alternately to butter mixture, beating after each addition.
7. Pour into pans.
8. Bake at 375° for about 25–35 minutes for two 8" rounds; 35–45 minutes for 9" x 13" baking pan.
9. Cool 10 minutes before removing from pan.
10. Remove to cooling rack.

CHOCK-LICKITY CHOCOLATE
(Makes 12–16 servings)

INGREDIENTS:

2 c.	all-purpose flour
3/4 c.	unsweetened cocoa
1/2 tsp.	salt
1/4 tsp.	baking powder
1 3/4 tsp.	baking soda
1 c.+3 Tbs.	unsalted butter (softened)
2 c.	sugar
1 tsp.	vanilla
3	eggs
1 1/4 c.	water

DIRECTIONS:

1. Preheat oven to 350°.
2. Grease and lightly flour baking pans.
3. Combine flour, cocoa powder, salt, baking soda and baking powder in a bowl.
4. In a separate bowl, beat butter about 30 seconds. Add sugar and vanilla. Beat until well combined.
5. Add eggs to butter mixture, one at a time, beating mixture after each egg.
6. Add dry ingredients and milk alternately to butter mixture, beating after each addition.
7. Pour into pans.
8. Bake at 350° for about 25–35 minutes for two 8" rounds; 35–45 minutes for 9" x 13" baking pan.
9. Cool 10 minutes before removing from pan.
10. Remove to cooling rack.

LEMONADE LAKE CAKE
(Makes 12–16 servings)

INGREDIENTS:

1	8 oz. box white cake mix
8 oz.	sour cream
6 oz.	frozen lemonade concentrate
3 oz.	cream cheese (room temperature)
3	eggs

DIRECTIONS:

1. Preheat oven to 350°.
2. Grease and lightly flour baking pans and line with wax paper.
3. Combine all ingredients in a large mixing bowl and beat 4 minutes or until well-blended.
4. Pour into pans.
5. Bake at 350° for about 30–40 minutes for two 8" rounds; 45–60 minutes for 9" x 13" baking pan.
6. Cool 10 minutes before removing from pan.
7. Remove to cooling rack.

VARIATION:

Use the above recipe to make the cake any flavor by substituting your favorite frozen juice concentrate, except grape.

FROSTING RECIPES
BUTTERCREAM FROSTING
(Makes 3 cups)

INGREDIENTS:

1/2 c.	vegetable shortening
1/2 c.	unsalted butter (softened)
1/4 c.	milk
1 tsp.	vanilla
1 lb.	powdered sugar

DIRECTIONS:

1. Cream butter until light and fluffy.
2. Add milk and vanilla and blend until well-mixed.
3. Gradually add powdered sugar and beat until smooth.

CHOCOLATE BUTTERCREAM FROSTING
(Makes 3 cups)

INGREDIENTS:

1 c.	unsalted butter (softened)
1/8 c.	milk
1 tsp.	vanilla
5	1 oz. squares unsweetened chocolate (melted and slightly cooled)
1 lb.	powdered sugar

DIRECTIONS:

1. Cream butter until light and fluffy.
2. Beat in chocolate until well-blended.
3. Add milk and vanilla and blend until well-mixed.
4. Gradually add powdered sugar and beat until smooth.

COOKIE ICING
(Makes 1/2 cup)

This icing dries to a shiny, hard finish and is especially good for making outlines and filling in designs. When icing is dry, cookies can be stacked without sticking together.

INGREDIENTS:

1 c.	powdered sugar
2 tsp.	milk
2 tsp.	corn syrup

DIRECTIONS:

1. Stir sugar and milk in a bowl until thoroughly mixed.
2. Add corn syrup and mix until well-blended.

VARIATION:

To use icing for filling in areas, thin by adding small amount of corn syrup.

Craft Tips

APPENDIX C

Add a special touch to your party with these unique crafts. All projects are easy to make, with step-by-step instructions, as well as time-saving tips.

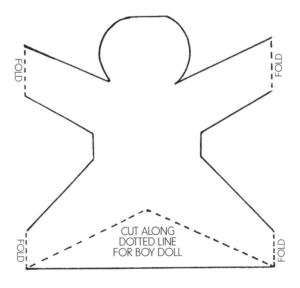

FOLD

FOLD

FOLD

FOLD

CUT ALONG
DOTTED LINE
FOR BOY DOLL

TOOLS AND MATERIALS

Most of the tools and materials used in making the projects in this book are common, everyday items. Occasionally, certain tools are required that can be dangerous. These tools should only be used by adults and they are marked "adult use only" whenever listed. All projects should be supervised by adults.

COMMONLY USED TOOLS:

Ruler
Yardstick
Paper hole punch
Stapler
Scissors (adult use only)
Scissors (safety-covered blades or "child-safe")
Craft knife (adult use only)
Balloon pump (an inexpensive plastic pump will save you both time and effort)

COMMONLY USED MATERIALS:

White glue
Tacky glue
Pencils
Crayons
Construction paper
Copier paper (16#–20#)
Paper plates
Paper bowls
Paper cups
Elastic cord
Feathers
Balloons
Crepé paper
Pasta (hollow-tube and shell)
Glitter
Ribbons

Transparent tape
Duct tape
Markers
Paint
Poster board
Copier card stock (90#–110#)
Foamcore
Pipe cleaners
Craft sticks
Wooden dowels
Yarn
String/rope
Plastic "eyes"
Envelopes (letter and legal sizes)
Sequins

COMMONLY USED RECYCLED MATERIALS:

Newspapers
Cardboard boxes
Plastic fruit baskets
Socks
Foil
Egg cartons

Cardboard tubes
Appliance boxes ❀
Soda bottles
Buttons
Paper and plastic cups

❀ To find a large appliance box, it is a good idea to start your search several weeks before the party. Call appliance, department, furniture or toy stores. Before using the box, make sure all loose staples and tacks have been removed, or covered with duct or cloth-backed tape.

BEFORE STARTING YOUR CRAFT PROJECT

Anytime you start any project from this book, it is a good idea to review both the text and the diagrams to make sure you understand the directions. Here is a simple guideline to help you organize your work.

1. Read over the list of "What you need."
2. Gather all tools and materials.
3. Read over all of the steps and illustrations in "What you do."
4. Protect your work area with newspaper.
5. Protect your clothes and childrens' clothes with an apron or an old shirt.
6. When doing projects with younger children, it is a good idea to premeasure and/or precut materials. This will not only free up your time at the party, it will help make the project run smoother.

7. Lay out enough materials and tools so children will not have to take turns or reach over one another while working. Place small decorative items in muffin tins, egg cartons and/or small plastic containers.
8. When using glue and glitter, mix the two together and apply with a craft stick.

PHOTOCOPY HINTS

One of the unique features of this book is that every chapter contains theme illustrations—an invitation, a thank-you note, decorations, favors and costumes—which you can have for your party by simply photocopying the illustrations. Here are a few suggestions:

1. Photocopy machines are available virtually everywhere. Shop around to find the best quality at the lowest price.
   - Specialized copy centers generally offer good quality machines, a wide variety of copier papers, and very competitive prices.
   - Libraries, banks, post offices and many local merchants often have self-service copier machines for public use.
   - Print shops may offer copier services and/or provide a self-service copy machine.
2. Before you make your photocopies, you should:
   - Make a list of all the pages you wish to copy and mark them with a bookmark or a paper clip for easy reference. (See page 8 for "Birthday Party Shopping Guide.")
   - Decide how many copies you want of each page.
   - Determine the weight of paper you will use for each project.
   - Select the color of your paper for each project.
   - Photocopy the same color and weight of paper at the same time. This will reduce the number of times the machine needs to be reloaded.
3. When selecting your paper, keep in mind that:
   - Copier paper (16#–20#) is relatively inexpensive, but also fairly lightweight.
   - Copier card stock (90#–110#) is heavier and more durable. It also costs more and is generally only available in certain copy centers or print shops.
   - Colored paper comes in most colors, and several weights.
   - If you plan to hand-color the photocopied image, you may want to use white paper or a very light-colored paper.
4. Some of the costumes in this book call for using copier card stock for strength and durability. If you cannot get copier card stock, you can still photocopy the design on regular copier paper, as long as you reinforce the holes with transparent tape before you punch the hole. This will keep the elastic cord or ribbon from ripping the paper.

CRAFT PROJECTS
PARTY STREAMERS

Estimated time: 5–7 minutes each

Use these directions to make the party streamers as referenced in each of the chapters.

WHAT YOU NEED:
- Selected "Streamer Pattern" (pages 359–362)
- Copier paper (white)
- Crepé paper in 20" x 7'6" folded bundle (bright colors)
- Scissors
- Pencil
- Ruler or yardstick
- Transparent tape ❀

❀ Optional

WHAT YOU DO:

1. Photocopy selected "Streamer Pattern" onto copier paper.
2. Cut out photocopied pattern and place directly on top of folded bundle.
3. Trace pattern on crepé paper.
4. Cut out design, except along "fold lines."
5. You can increase overall length of your decoration by taping two or more streamers together.

LOOT BAGS

Use these directions to make the loot bags as referenced in each of the chapters.

↻ PICNIC BASKET

Estimated time: 2–3 minutes each

WHAT YOU NEED:
- Plastic fruit basket
- Pipe cleaner
- 1/4"–1/2" wide ribbon, approximately 30" long

WHAT YOU DO:
1. Attach pipe cleaner to basket by wrapping each end through sides of basket.
2. Weave ribbon through basket, and tie in a bow.

STICKER BAG

Estimated time: 2–3 minutes each

You can make this project ahead of time, or have children make this as a craft activity during the party.

WHAT YOU NEED:
- "Theme Party Sticker Illustration" (located in each chapter)
- Copier paper (white or bright colors)
- Paper lunch bag
- One 9"x 12" (or larger) sheet heavy construction paper or lightweight poster board (white)
- Scissors
- White glue
- Stapler
- Crayons, markers and/or colored pencils ❀

❀ Optional

WHAT YOU DO:
1. Photocopy "Theme Party Sticker Illustration" onto copier paper.
2. Color stickers, if desired.
3. Cut out stickers.
4. To make handle, cut construction paper into 1 1/2" x 12" strips.
5. To attach handle, staple each end of construction paper strip to each side of paper bag.
6. Glue "Theme Party Stickers" to outside of paper bag.

MAGIC BAG

Estimated time: 1–2 minutes each

WHAT YOU NEED:

- Folded tissue paper in 18" x 27" sheets (bright colors)
- Gummed stars ✿
- Gift wrapping ribbon

_____

✿ Optional

WHAT YOU DO:

1. Place loot in the middle of two overlapping sheets of tissue paper.
2. Wrap tissue paper around loot and gather toward top.
3. Tie ribbon in a bow around top.
4. Glue gummed stars around outside as decoration.

 THE EXTRA TOUCH

- Metallic garlands with stars can add a sparkling touch. Just twist a piece of garland around the top of each loot bag.

HAT OR MASK BAG

Estimated time: 3–4 minutes each

WHAT YOU NEED:

- "Theme Hat or Mask Illustration" (located in each chapter)
- Copier paper or copier card stock (white or bright colors) ✿
- Scissors
- Hole punch
- Yarn or ribbon (approximately 50" in length)
- Crayons, markers and/or colored pencils ✿✿

_____

✿ Card stock is preferred for this project.

✿✿ Optional

WHAT YOU DO:

1. For each loot bag, make 2 photocopies of "Theme Illustration" onto copier paper or card stock .
2. Cut out both illustrations. (To save time, cut 2–4 sheets at the same time.)
3. Place illustrations back-to-back, and punch holes along perimeter of paired illustrations, leaving top section unpunched.
4. Cut a piece of yarn or ribbon, 24" in length, and thread through alternating holes.
   [NOTE: Leave enough yarn or ribbon over top of bag to form a "handle."]
5. Tie ends of yarn or ribbon together.

↻ TREASURE BOX

Estimated time: 2–3 minutes each

This loot "bag" is made from recycled "baby wipes"
boxes. You may want to make this project ahead of time, or use this
as a craft activity during the party.

WHAT YOU NEED:

- "Baby wipes" boxes (one per "Treasure Box")
- "Theme Party Sticker Illustration" (located in each chapter)
- Copier paper (white or bright colors)
- White glue or glue sticks
- Crayons, markers and/or colored pencils ✿

_____

✿ Optional

WHAT YOU DO:

1. Remove labels from each of the "baby wipes" boxes by either: 1) slowly pulling off the label; or 2) soaking the box in hot water and pulling off the label.
2. Photocopy "Theme Party Sticker Illustration" onto copier paper.
3. Color stickers, if desired.
4. Cut out stickers.
5. Glue stickers to outside of box.

 THE EXTRA TOUCH

- Glue glitter, sequins, beads, macaroni or fake jewels to box.

PARTY STICKERS

Use these directions to make the theme party stickers as referenced in each of the chapters.

Estimated time: 1–2 minutes per page

Recommended age: 3 years and older for gluing
5 years and older for cutting and gluing

WHAT YOU NEED:

- "Theme Party Sticker Illustration" (located in each chapter)
- Copier paper (white or brightly-colored)
- Scissors ✿
- Glue stick

✿ Use child-safe scissors if children will be cutting their own stickers.

WHAT YOU DO:

Before the party:
1. Photocopy "Theme Party Sticker Illustration" onto copier paper.
2. Cut out stickers. (To save time, you can cut 2–4 sheets at the same time.)

During the party:
3. Give children glue sticks.
4. Use stickers to personalize and decorate backs of envelopes, drinking cups, loot bags and/or photo frames for the various crafts and activities in each chapter.

SELF-STICKING STICKERS

Estimated time: 15 minutes to make 12 pages of stickers

You can make your own self-sticking stickers by following these simple directions.

WHAT YOU NEED:

- "Theme Party Sticker Illustration" (located in each chapter)
- Copier paper
- 1/2 cup of white glue
- 1/4 cup of vinegar
- Wide paintbrush
- Plastic wrap or wax paper
- Scissors
- Moist sponge

WHAT YOU DO:

1. Photocopy "Theme Party Stickers" onto copier paper.
2. Cover work surface with plastic wrap or wax paper.

3. Mix white glue and vinegar in a bowl.
4. Paint glue mixture on back of photocopied "Theme Party Stickers" and let dry.
5. Apply second coat of glue mixture and let dry.
6. Using scissors, cut out each "Theme Party Sticker" to make individual stickers. (To save time, cut 2–4 sheets at the same time.)
7. To use, moisten each sticker with sponge (as you would a postage stamp).

DRINKING STRAWS

Estimated time: 1–2 minutes per straw

Use these directions to make the drinking straws as referenced in each chapters.
* "Theme Illustration" (located in each chapter)
* Copier paper or copier card stock (white or bright colors)
* Scissors
* Craft knife (adult use only)
* Plastic drinking straws
* Colored pencils, crayons and/or markers ✿

———
✿ Optional

WHAT YOU DO:
1. Photocopy "Theme Illustration" onto copier paper or copier card stock.
2. With scissors, cut along outer lines of illustration.
3. Use craft knife to cut slit along dotted line (or "mouth") of illustration.
4. Color illustration, if desired, with colored pencils, crayons and/or markers.
5. Slip straw through slits.

PARTY SUCKERS

Estimated time: 1–2 minutes per sucker

Use these directions to make the party suckers as suggested in the chapters.

WHAT YOU NEED:
* Flat or disc-style suckers
* "Theme Illustration" (located in each chapter)
* Scissors
* Copier paper or copier card stock (white or bright colors)
* White glue or transparent tape

WHAT YOU DO:
1. Photocopy "Theme Illustration" onto copier paper or card stock.
2. Cut along outer lines of illustration.
3. Glue or tape illustration to one side of sucker.

PAW PRINT TABLECLOTH

Estimated time: 10–15 minutes

WHAT YOU NEED:
* Butcher paper (at least 36" wide and long enough to cover the party table)
* Masking tape
* Tempera paints (brown or bright colors)
* Paper towels
* Plastic foam meat tray or small plate

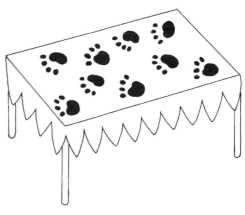

WHAT YOU DO:

1. On the day before the party, cover party table with butcher paper, folding and taping edges to underside of table.
2. Fold a paper towel so that it fits into meat tray or dish. Dampen towel.
3. Pour a small amount of paint on top of paper towel—just enough to cover surface (Illustration CT–17 #1).
4. Make a fist with each hand, placing thumb flat against the index finger (Illustration CT–17 #2).
5. Press both fists into paint, one at a time (Illustration CT–17 #3).
6. Alternate hands and press fists across tablecloth, giving the impression of an animal walking.
7. Make several sets of tracks to suggest different kinds of animals!

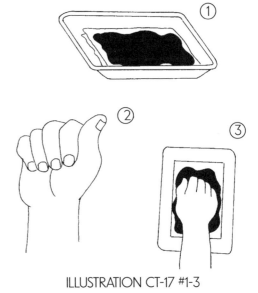

ILLUSTRATION CT-17 #1-3

 THE EXTRA TOUCH

- Experiment with different "footprints" by using different parts of your hand and fingers.

FACE PAINTING MAKE-UP (Non-Toxic)

Recommended age: 3 and older

WHAT YOU NEED:

- "Theme Make-Up Designs" (page 87, 114 and 196)
- Black eyebrow pencil (hypo-allergenic/non-toxic)
- Small paint brushes, make-up brushes, or cotton swabs
- Muffin tin
- 1 tsp. cold cream ❊
- 1 tsp. corn starch ❊
- 1/2 tsp. water ❊
- A few drops of food coloring ❊

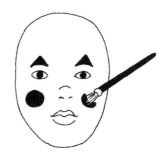

❊ For each color of make-up

WHAT YOU DO:

1. Use muffin tin as a "palette" to make each color in a separate cup.
2. Mix cold cream, corn starch, water and food coloring together to make desired colors.
3. Use black eyebrow pencil to outline "Theme Make-up Designs."
4. Paint in colors.

PHOTO BACKDROP

Estimated time: 30 minutes

WHAT YOU NEED:

- "Theme Photo Backdrop" (located in each chapter)
- 1 piece of flat cardboard or foamcore board (32" x 40")
- 1 cardboard box (approximately 12" x 12" x 16")
- Pencil
- T-square or yardstick
- Craft knife (adult use only)
- Duct tape or cloth-backed adhesive tape
- Poster paints (and brushes), markers and/or crayons
- Wide-tipped paintbrush (2"–3" tip)

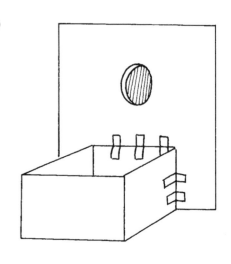

WHAT YOU DO:

1. In each chapter, a theme backdrop pattern is drawn on a grid. Each square on the grid represents 3". On your sheet of cardboard or foamcore board, draw a grid with 3" squares. Then enlarge design by matching each square on the pattern to each 3" square on your backdrop.
2. With a craft knife, cut out an oval-shaped hole for child's head to fit in the backdrop. (Test size of hole on your child.)
3. Paint in design with poster paints.
4. Lay backdrop on a flat surface and let paint dry completely.
5. Tape cardboard box to the back of the backdrop.
6. To take your snapshots, have children stand in the box, one at a time, and put their head through the hole.
7. Be ready to take a picture, as precious moments happen in split-seconds.

CARDBOARD PLAY STRUCTURES

TO CUT THICK CARDBOARD:

1. Score the line to be cut with knife or scissors.
2. Dampen along scored line with a small brush and water.
3. While cardboard is still moist, use your scissors or craft knife to make the cut.

TO MAKE A HINGED DOOR OR SHUTTERS FOR WINDOWS:

1. Draw door and windows where you want them.
2. To make a door or a shutter hinge from one side, leave "hinged" side uncut, and score the cardboard from the inside of the house. This will make the door or shutter swing outward.

NEWSPAPER ROLLS

Newspaper rolls use recycled materials in a fun way. You can use newspaper rolls as posts for "Activity Booths," as poles for flags and banners, and as child-safe jousting sticks.

WHAT YOU NEED:

- Newspaper sheets (full)
- Transparent tape
- Broom stick or dowel (3/4"–1" in diameter)

WHAT YOU DO:

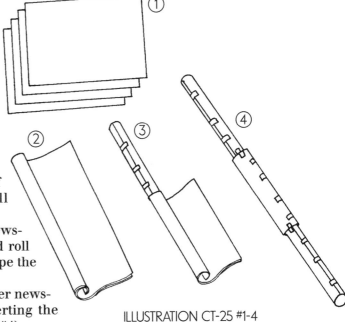

1. Lay out four full sheets of newspaper and stack neatly (Illustration CT–25 #1).
2. Starting at one of the narrow ends, roll newspapers into a tight tube. You may want to roll the newspapers around a broomstick or dowel (Illustration CT-25 #2).
3. To keep the tube from unrolling, tape 2–3 pieces of transparent tape around the outside of the roll (Illustration CT–25 #3).
4. To make the tube longer, roll four more sheets of newspaper around the first tube, overlapping the second roll about halfway up the length of the first roll. Then tape the two rolls together (Illustration CT-25 #3).
5. You can make the tube even longer by rolling another newspaper tube—narrower than the second—and inserting the third tube *inside* the second tube (Illustration CT-25 #4).
6. Tape the second tube to the third tube.
7. By continuing to connect newspaper tubes together, you can make the structure any length you want.

ILLUSTRATION CT-25 #1-4

SAVING THE MEMORIES

PHOTOGRAPHS

Taking photographs of your child's birthday party is a wonderful way to preserve the memories of this very special day. However, you need to be prepared—so you won't be disappointed. Here's a checklist to help you take better pictures:

1. **BATTERIES.** Test the batteries in your camera and flash unit ahead of time. Keep a spare supply just in case.
2. **FILM.** Buy film ahead of time. Keep both indoor and outdoor film on hand, just in case your plans change, or you want to take pictures both inside and outside.
3. **CANDID CAMERA.** Try to photograph each of your guests in candid, fun shots—not staged or "frozen" stances.
4. **COMPOSITION.** Simple, close-up shots generally work best.
5. **BACKGROUNDS.** Avoid jumbled or distracting backgrounds in the picture. Try to establish a background that is even-patterned, and avoid objects growing out of your subjects' heads.
6. **LIGHTING.** Generally, the best light for taking photographs is an even light. Bright sunlight directly on the subjects tends to bleach out highlights, leaving black shadows under the eyes and often causes subjects to squint. Backlighting, or lighting coming from behind the subject, causes the front of the subjects to go dark. (You may want to use a flash, even outdoors, to add "punch" to your photographs.)
7. **DON'T BE LEFT OUT!** It is difficult to be the photographer and run the party at the same time. Ask a (qualified) friend to take pictures. However, if you don't have anyone who can be the photographer, at some point in the party, ask someone to take a "birthday family" photograph so you will be sure to have at least some special memories of the day together.
8. **A SPECIAL "THANK YOU."** Purchase 2-for-1 prints from the party, which are generally no more expensive than single prints. Give one of the paired prints away with your thank-you note to each guest as a special remembrance of the party.
9. Don't forget to take a photograph of the cake and party area *before* the guests arrive.

VIDEOTAPES

Much of the same advice for taking photographs of your child's birthday party applies to making videotapes. The main difference, however, is that you are working with movement and sound as added dimensions. Here are a few suggestions for making birthday party videotapes more memorable:

1. **POWER UP!** Make sure your camera batteries are fully-charged. It's a good idea to recharge batteries the night before the party, and if possible, have an extra charged battery ready.
2. **NEW TAPES.** Have several unused videotapes on hand to use during the party. Nothing is worse than running out of tape, or having your precious moments destroyed by glitches in older tapes.
3. **ZOOM!** Take advantage of all of the lens features that the camera has to offer. By "zooming in," you get close-ups without getting in the way. By "zooming out," you can get a wider angle to show "the big picture." Using both close-ups and wider angles will add more variety to the videotape and show more of how the day really looked.
4. **TILT.** You can add a different look "tilting" the camera up and down. By squatting or sitting as you shoot, you can make the children look bigger than life—and add more life to the video. On the other hand, standing tall (on a chair or ladder) and angling the camera down, can offer an interesting perspective.
5. **PANNING.** To "pan" the camera means to make sweeping horizontal moves with the camera. Pan with the action as the children are racing or moving about. Panning across the entire party scene can also give your viewers a panoramic view of the party area.
6. **SOUND.** The video camera offers a wonderful chance to hear what people are saying as well as all the fun "noise" at the party.

7. **INTERVIEWS.** Try to spend some time talking with children and adult guests about the party, between and/or during activities. Of course, you don't want to get in the way of the party fun, but having these candid comments on tape can add to the memories of the day. And don't forget to interview the birthday child!

BIRTHDAY PARTY SCRAP BOOK

After the party, you will have memories of a wonderful day. Keep those precious memories together in a book you and your child will always cherish.

WHAT YOU NEED:

- 3-ring binder
- 3-hole punched see-thru plastic pages
- 8 1/2" x 11" sheets of construction paper
- Glue stick
- Scissors
- Birthday party photographs, birthday cards, invitations
- Pieces of wrapping paper, ribbon, stickers and other party decorations
- Glue and glitter

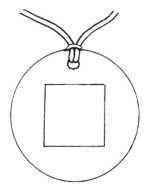

WHAT YOU DO:

1. On each sheet of construction paper, make a collage using your photographs and other mementos from the party. (For best results, try to keep the collage relatively flat.)
2. Decorate your collage with bits of ribbon, stickers or glitter.
3. Slip the collages into 3-hole punched, see-through plastic pages.
4. Store the plastic pages in a 3-ring binder. Each year, you can add more collages to a growing "Birthday Party Scrap Book."

 THE EXTRA TOUCH

- An excellent way to preserve your collage is to have each sheet laminated. Contact local printers or a laminating service. (To store in 3-ring notebook, have laminator punch 3-holes on one side of each page.)

POLAROID® PHOTO FRAME

Use these directions to make the Polaroid® Photo Frame as referenced in the chapters.

WHAT YOU NEED:

- Polaroid® camera and film (1–2 frames for each child)
- Illustration CT–23 "Photo Frame" (page 358)
- Copier card stock, poster board or heavy construction paper (bright colors)
- Craft knife and metal ruler (adult use only)
- Scissors
- Paper hole punch
- Transparent tape
- String or yarn (approximately 24" in length)

WHAT YOU DO:

1. Photocopy Illustration CT–23 "Photo Frame" onto card stock or trace pattern onto poster board or heavy construction paper.
2. Cut along outer edge of each frame with scissors.
3. Using craft knife and ruler, cut out inner square of each frame. This is the slot for the photograph.
4. Punch a hole in the frame, as marked on illustration.
5. Tie yarn or string through hole.
6. Tape photograph to the back of frame.

- Children can decorate frames as a craft project with the "Theme Party Stickers" (located in each chapter).
- Use crayons, markers and/or colored pencils to decorate frames.
- Glue on glitter, sequins, pasta, buttons, string, yarn and other decorative items.

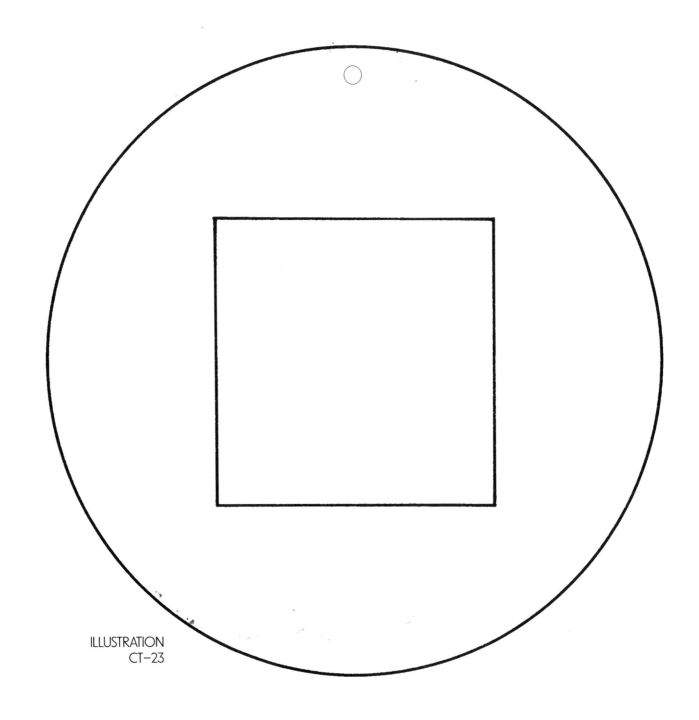

ILLUSTRATION
CT–23

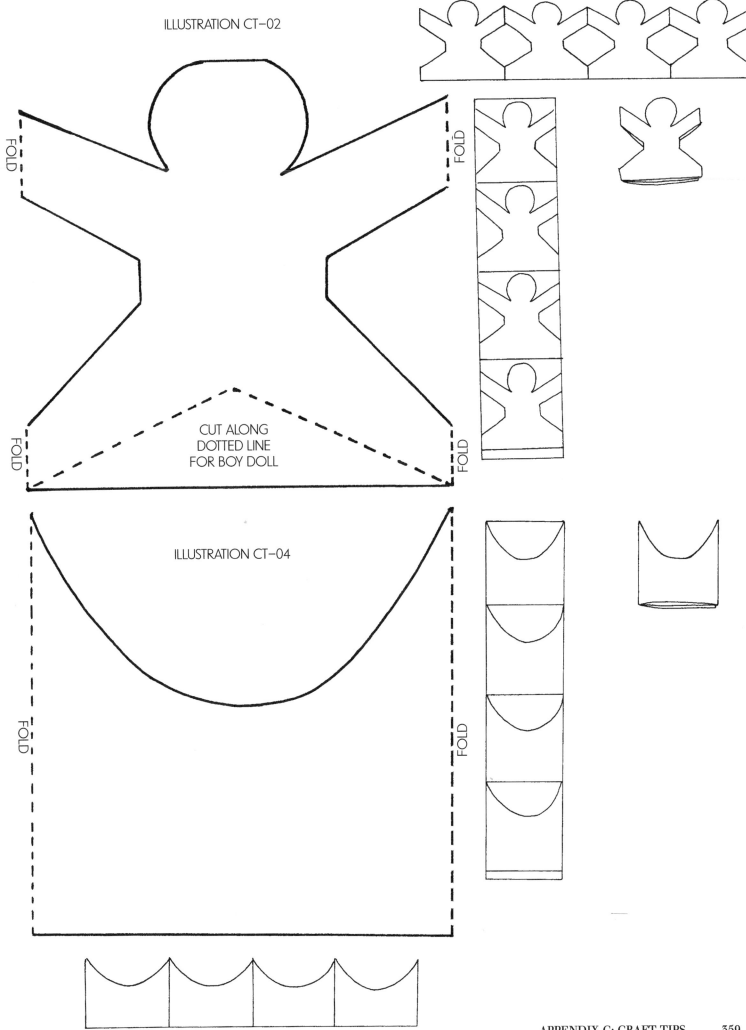

ILLUSTRATION CT–02

FOLD

FOLD

FOLD

CUT ALONG
DOTTED LINE
FOR BOY DOLL

FOLD

ILLUSTRATION CT–04

FOLD

FOLD

ILLUSTRATION CT–03

ILLUSTRATION CT–07

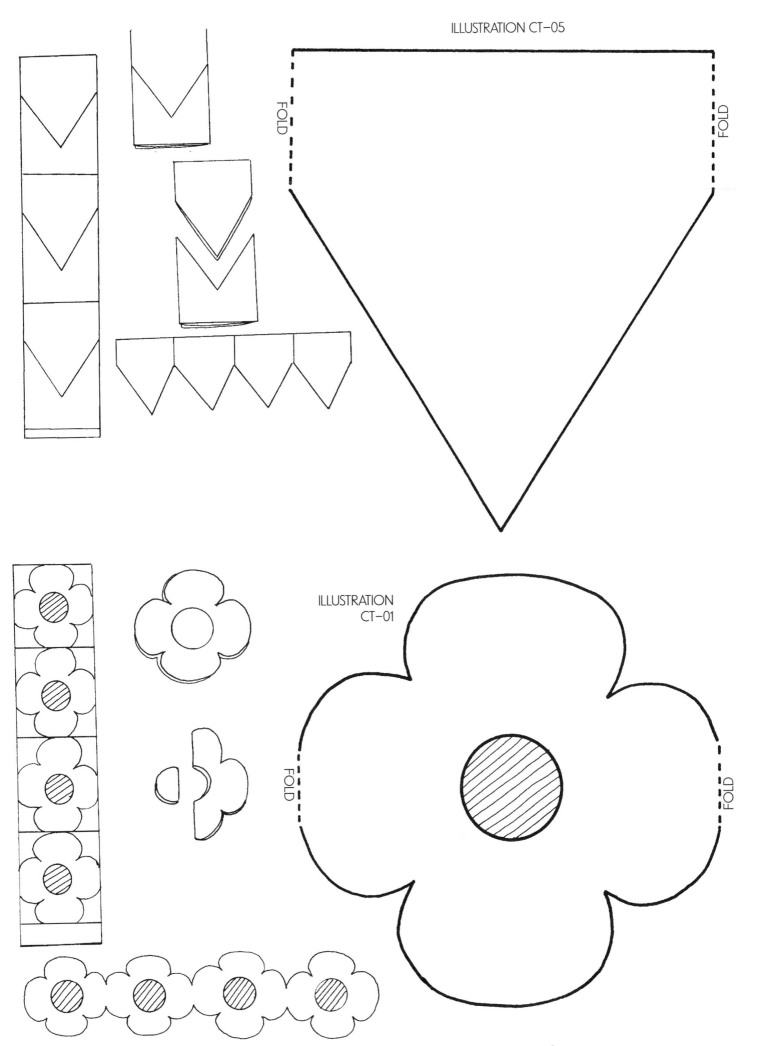

ILLUSTRATION CT-05

FOLD

FOLD

ILLUSTRATION
CT-01

FOLD

FOLD

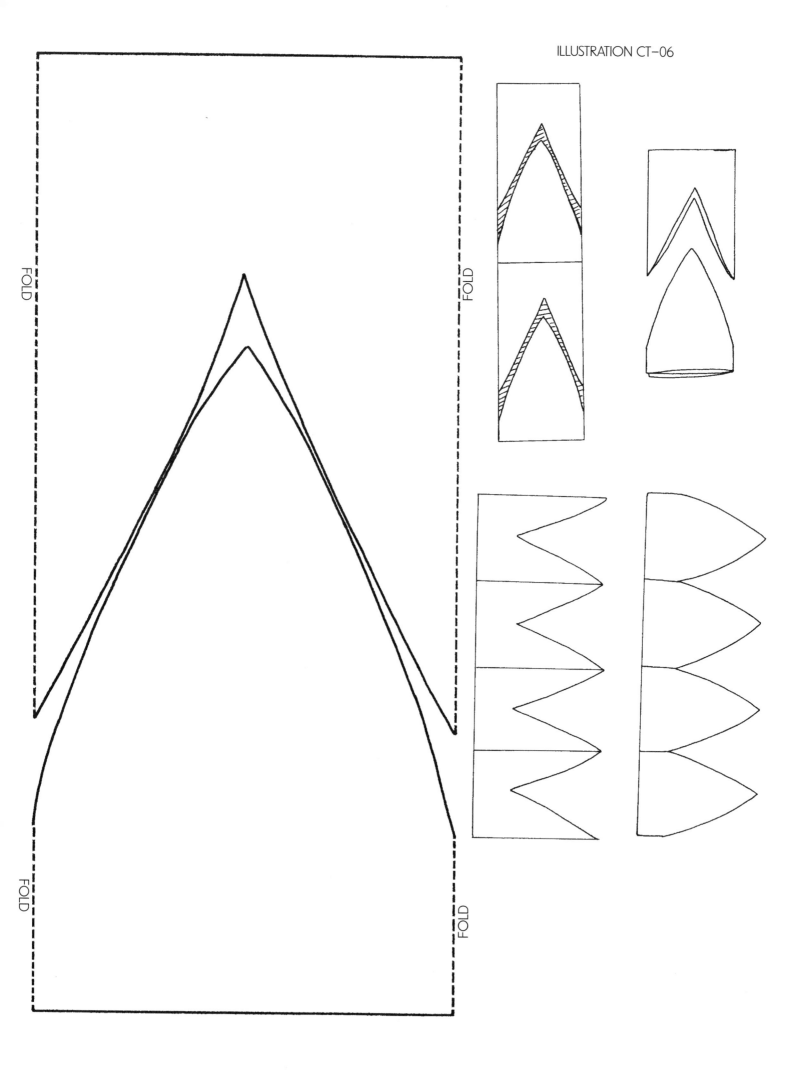

FOLD

FOLD

FOLD

FOLD

Games

Games are where the action is—they are the life of the party. So add some life to your party with a few of these old favorites especially adapted to your theme birthday party.

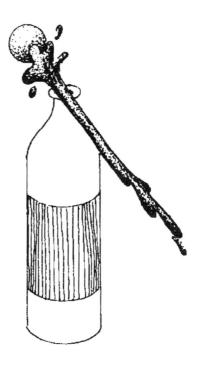

ANIMAL SCRAMBLE

Recommended age: 6 years and older

WHAT YOU NEED:
- Chairs (one less than the number of players)
- "Theme Party Animal Stickers" (page 87, 164 and 272)
- Copier paper or copier card stock (white or bright colors)
- Scissors

HOW TO PLAY:
Before the party:
1. Make 4 photocopies of the "Theme Party Animal Stickers" onto copier paper or copier card stock and cut out individual stickers.

During the party:
2. Set chairs in a large circle in party area.
3. Select one player (birthday child first) to be "It," and ask rest of children to sit on chairs.
4. Divide children into groups of two or three.
5. Give each member of group the same animal sticker, and place one complete set of stickers (one sheet cut up) in a hat or box.
6. Explain to children that "It" will pick a sticker from hat or box and hold up a sticker. When animal sticker is shown, every player having same animal sticker must get up and change seats. During the scramble, "It" tries to sit in a vacant chair.
7. The one child who is left without a chair, becomes "It" for next round, and gives his/her sticker to child that took his/her place.

 BEAN BAG TOSS

Recommended age: 3 years and older

Here's a chance to use up all those one-of-kind (unpaired) socks, as well as any outgrown baby socks—and have fun at the same time!

WHAT YOU NEED:
- "Theme Photo Backdrop" (located in each chapter)
- Dry beans (at least 1 pound)
- Children's socks (8–12 individual socks)
- Wide-tipped, permanent ink marker (black) ✿

✿ Optional

WHAT YOU DO:
1. Make "Theme Photo Backdrop."
2. To make bean bag, fill each sock half-full with beans, and tie a knot at end of sock.
3. Depending on their age, children stand at a challenging distance from backdrop and toss bean bags into hole.
4. You may want to turn bean bags into theme-party animals by drawing "eyes" and a "mouth" on each bag with black marker.
5. To keep game non-competitive, have children play several rounds and try to beat their own performance.

BLINDMAN'S BUFF

Recommended age: 5 years and older

WHAT YOU NEED:
- Blindfold

HOW TO PLAY:
1. Blindfold "It" (birthday child first), and spin "It" around several times.

2. Have other players move around "It," making loud noises (appropriate for the theme of the party), like "wild animal sounds" for the "Jungle Party".
3. "It" tries to locate the players by sound, and tag the closest one.
4. Players bait or tease "It" with their noises, while trying to avoiding being tagged.
5. The first player that is tagged becomes the next "It."

BLOB

Recommended age: 5 years and older

HOW TO PLAY:
1. Have children spread out in party area.
2. Select one player to be "The Blob" (birthday child first).
3. "The Blob" tries to tag other players.
4. The first player tagged becomes part of "The Blob," and he or she must hold hands with "The Blob."
5. While holding hands, both players of "The Blob" try to tag other players. "The Blob" continues to grow as each newly-tagged player holds hands with the other members of "The Blob" and tries to tag other players.
6. Game is played until all players are tagged, and the last player to be tagged starts the next "Blob" in the new game.

CATCH THE TAIL

Recommended age: 5 years and older

This is an excellent game to teach group cooperation and to focus everyone's efforts on one goal.

HOW TO PLAY:
1. Children stand in single file, holding each other's waists.
2. Player at head of line (birthday child first) tries to catch player at end or "tail" of line.
3. When player at head tags player at tail, the "head" becomes the "tail," and everyone in line moves up one place in line.
4. Continue playing until everyone gets a chance to be the "head."

DROP THE CLOTHESPINS IN THE BOTTLE

Recommended age: 4 years and older

WHAT YOU NEED:
- Empty bottle or jar (wide-mouthed is preferred for younger children)
- 5–10 clothespins (or small objects to drop into bottle, like peanuts or buttons)

HOW TO PLAY:
1. Children form a single line.
2. Each child (birthday child first) stands over bottle, holding arm out at shoulder height.
3. Children take turns dropping clothespins into bottle.
4. To keep game non-competitive, have children play several rounds and try to beat their own performance.

DUCK, DUCK, GOOSE!

Recommended age: 4 years and older

HOW TO PLAY:
1. Have children sit in a circle. Select one child to be the "duck" (birthday child first).
2. The duck walks around the outside of the circle, tapping each child on the head or shoulder lightly, saying, "Duck!" When duck wants someone to be "It," duck taps that child and says the word, "Goose."
3. The goose gets up and chases the duck around the circle. If the goose tags the duck before they make a full circle (from the goose's original spot), the goose becomes "It."
4. If the duck outruns the goose, he/she remains playing the duck, and the game continues.

EGG RELAY RACE

Recommended age: 6 years and older

WHAT YOU NEED:
- 2 spoons
- 2 boiled or plastic eggs

HOW TO PLAY:
1. Divide children into two relay teams, and give each team a spoon and an egg.
2. Mark a start/finish line for relay race and a turn-around point (like a tree or a chair), between 15–20' from start/finish line.
3. Explain to children that each player must place the egg on the spoon, and walk, as fast as he/she can, to the turn-around point and back, balancing egg on spoon.
4. Make sure children understand that they cannot hold egg while they walk. If egg falls, they must stop, place egg back on spoon, and continue race. Anyone caught holding egg will have to start his/her turn all over.
5. The first team to have all players complete the race, wins.

FREEZE TAG

Recommended age: 5 years and older

HOW TO PLAY:
1. Have children spread out in party area.
2. Select one player to be "It" (birthday child first).
3. "It" tries to tag other players.
4. When tagged, players must "freeze."
5. Other players (who have not been tagged) can "melt" frozen players by touching them. "Melted" players can continue playing the game.
6. The first player to be "frozen" 3 times becomes the next "It."

FUN TIME MUSICAL CHAIRS

This is a non-competitive version of the standard game, "musical chairs." Since no one is eliminated, everyone has fun.

Recommended age: 4 years and older

WHAT YOU NEED:
- Chairs (one for each child)
- Source of music

HOW TO PLAY:
1. Set chairs in two rows, back-to-back, in middle of play area—one chair for each player.
2. When music plays, children walk in a circle around chairs. When music stops, children sit on nearest chair. After the first round, everyone gets up and one chair is taken away.
3. In the next round, when music plays, everyone walks around chairs. When music stops, children sit on nearest chair, even if it means sitting on the same chair that someone else is sitting on. Game continues in this way until everyone tries to sit on the same chair.

HOT POTATO

Recommended age: 3 years and older

WHAT YOU NEED:
- Potato (or theme object)
- Cassette tapes, records or compact disc recordings of (theme-related) music
- Cassette tape, record or compact disc player for music

HOW TO PLAY:

1. Children sit in a circle.
2. Give one child (birthday child first) the potato and tell children it is "hot."
3. Explain that the only way he can avoid burning himself is to pass it on (quickly) to the child next to him/her in the circle (right or left) when the music starts.
4. Continue passing potato until music stops. The person holding the potato is "It."

I SPY

Recommended age: 6 years and older

HOW TO PLAY:

1. Establish a "home base." (This could be a theme-related area of the party.)
2. "It" (birthday child first) covers his/her eyes at "home base" and counts to "60" aloud as other players hide.
3. Then "It" leaves home base and tries to find the other players.
4. When "It" spots another player, he/she says who is spied and where. For example: "I spy Natalie under the table."
5. Spied players are then sent to home base.
6. Other players, who have not been spied, can return to home base and can free any spied players by tagging them. However, if these players are spied in the process, they must stay in jail and anyone they freed must return to jail.
7. The last player to be spied is the next "It."

MEMORY GAME

Recommended age: 8 years and older

WHAT YOU NEED:

- One serving tray
- 12–15 small household (or theme-related) objects to fit on tray
- Pen/pencil (one for each child)
- 3" x 5" index card (one for each child)

HOW TO PLAY:

1. Before party, select objects you want to use and place on a tray. Cover tray and store out of view of party area.
2. To start game, have children sit in large circle.
3. Carry tray to game area and slowly show each child objects on tray. Give every child the same amount of time to view objects.
4. Tell children to try to remember the objects on the tray.
5. Take tray into another room and then pass out one pen/pencil and one index card per child.
6. Tell children they have 3 minutes to write down the objects they remember.
7. Child with the most items listed, wins.

PARTY GAME TOSS

Recommended age: 3 years and older

WHAT YOU NEED:

- 1 large-sized bowl
- 1 medium-sized bowl
- 1 small-sized bowl
- 1 bag of peanuts (in the shell) or individually wrapped candies
- Card table

HOW TO PLAY:

1. Children line up behind a line (single file).

2. Hand each child three peanuts or candies.
3. Place three bowls (in a row) on card table 3–6 feet away. (To test the skill level of your child prior to party to determine comfortable playing distance.)
4. Children take turns throwing peanuts or candy into each bowl: one peanut into the large, one peanut into the medium and one peanut into the small bowl.
5. To keep game non-competitive, have children play several rounds as they try to beat their own performance.

PIÑATA FUN

1. If you stuff the piñata with loose prizes and candy, make sure children have been given a loot bag to gather up their "loot." On the other hand, you may want to stuff the piñata with tightly-sealed, individual bags of loot so that there is one bag for each child. (Make sure you tell children that they are only getting one bag each.)
2. Use a safe bat to hit the piñata. Store-bought plastic bats work well, or you can make your own bat by following these simple directions:
   - Take a broom handle (preferably without the broom) or 3/4" dowel about 3' in length and slide an empty 2-liter bottle over one end;
   - Tape the bottle in place with duct tape.
3. Have children wait their turn by standing behind a line, several yards out of the bat's range.
4. Blindfolds should only be used on children 5 years of age and older, as younger ones tend to become frightened.
5. Prizes for children 3 years and younger should be large enough to avoid choking.

QUICK CHANGE RELAY RACE

Recommended age: 6 years and older

WHAT YOU NEED:
- 2 boxes or baskets
- 2 hats
- 2 coats
- 2 dresses
- 2 shirts/blouses
- 2 skirts
- 2 pairs of pants
- 2 pairs of shoes

   [NOTE: Clothing should be large enough to fit easily over what children are already wearing. If possible, choose clothing that matches the party theme.]

HOW TO PLAY:
1. Divide children into two relay teams.
2. Mark a start/finish line for relay race and place both boxes (one set of clothing in each box), 15'–20' from start/finish line.
3. Explain to children that each team has its own box of clothes. The first player from each team starts the game by racing to the box and putting on all of the clothes from his/her box.
4. That player then races back to the start/finish line, quickly takes off the clothes and hands them to the next player.
5. The next player rushes to put on the clothes, then races back to the box, and quickly removes the clothes and puts them back in the box.
6. That player then races back to the start/finish line, tags the next player, who runs to the box and quickly puts on the clothes.
7. The first team to have all players complete the race, wins.

RED LIGHT, GREEN LIGHT

Recommended age: 5 years and older

HOW TO PLAY:

1. Establish a start line at one end of the party area and a finish line at least 15–20 feet away.
2. "It" (birthday child first) stands at the finish line.
3. Other children line up along start line.
4. "It" starts a race among children, from start line to finish line, by saying "Green light."
5. "It" can stop the race, or "freeze" the children at anytime during the race by saying "Red light."
6. Any player who moves while he/she is supposed to be frozen is sent back to the start line.
7. The first player to cross the finish line is the next "It."

SARDINES

Recommended age: 5 years and older

This is a game of "hide-and-seek" in reverse.

HOW TO PLAY:

1. Select one child (birthday child starts) to be "It."
2. Give "It" 2–3 minutes to hide somewhere in party area while rest of children stay in one location.
3. At end of allotted time, release children to look for "It."
4. As each child finds "It," he/she hides along with "It." One by one, children will "disappear" from party area.
5. The last child to discover the hiding place is "It" for the next game.

SAVE THE PRINCE/PRINCESS FROM THE DRAGON

Recommended age: 5 years and older

HOW TO PLAY:

1. One child (birthday child) plays the prince/princess and another child plays the dragon.
2. Remaining children hold hands and make a circle around prince/princess, forming protective "wall," while the dragon roams outside the wall.
3. The wall tries to keep the dragon away from prince/princess. Children hold their arms tight to keep dragon from breaking through the wall.
4. If dragon does break through the wall, he/she tries to tag prince/princess. Children can allow prince/princess to escape by raising their arms and keep the dragon "trapped" by lowering their arms. If dragon does tag the prince/princess, dragon becomes the new prince/princess.
5. The old prince/princess takes his/her turn as part of the wall.

SEARCHING FOR BURIED TREASURE

This game is ideal for those who already have a sandbox.

Recommended age: 3 years and older

WHAT YOU NEED:

- Sandbox
- Plastic "Theme Party" toys (at least 5 for each player)
- Small bags

HOW TO PLAY:

Before the party:
1. Hide plastic toys in the sand.

During the party:
2. Start game by having children line up around sandbox and give each child a small bag. Tell children that buried beneath the sand are treasures just waiting to be discovered. Then, let the children dig for their theme party "treasures."
3. Have extra toys on hand for those who don't find any toys (or limit everyone to finding five toys).

THE EXTRA TOUCH

• If you want to have children search for "shiny coins," here is a way to turn those old pennies into "treasures."

WHAT YOU NEED:
- Pennies (at least 10 for each player)
- 1/2 cup of vinegar
- 4 Tbs. salt
- Small bags

WHAT YOU DO:
1. Before party, soak pennies in a solution of vinegar and salt for 10 minutes to make them bright and shiny. Rinse with water and let dry on paper towel.
2. After pennies have dried, hide them in the sand. (Keep a few pennies in your own pocket to give to those who don't find any coins.)

 # SQUIRT BALL

Recommended age: 4 years and older

WHAT YOU NEED:
- 1 card table
- 5 empty soda bottles (2-liter)
- 5 ping pong balls ❀
- 1 squirt gun
- Bucket of water

❀ Used ping pong balls
will work fine for this game.

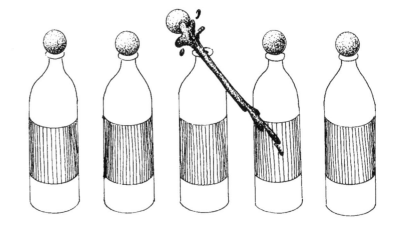

HOW TO PLAY:
Before the party:
1. Set bottles on table in a row, with caps off.
2. Place 1 ping pong ball on top of each bottle.
3. Set bucket of water next to player's line.
4. Have birthday child use squirt gun to knock ping pong ball off top of bottle Establish a comfortable "playing distance" for your child's age group.

During the party:
5. Have children form a single line, with birthday child first.
6. Each player takes a turn squirting ping pong balls off tops of bottles until their squirt gun is empty.
7. To keep game non-competitive, have children play several rounds and try to beat their own performance.

STEPPING STONES

Recommended age: 6 years and older

WHAT YOU NEED:
- 4 carpet squares or 4 paper grocery bags

HOW TO PLAY:
1. Divide children into two teams, and give the first player on each team two carpet squares.
2. Mark a start/finish line for relay race and a turn-around point (like a tree, box or chair), 15'–20' from start/finish line.
3. The first player on each team places one carpet on the ground in front of him/her and steps on it with both feet. The player then places the other carpet in front of him/her and steps on that with both feet. Player continues to move to the turn-around point and back in this manner throughout the race, children's feet must never touch the ground as they walk on their "stepping stones."
4. The first team to have all players complete the race, wins.

TAG

Recommended age: 6 years and older

HOW TO PLAY:

1. Establish a "home base." (This could be a theme-related area of the party.)
2. "It" (birthday child first) covers his/her eyes at "home base" and counts to "30" aloud as other players hide.
3. Then "It" leaves home base and tries to find the other players to tag.
4. Players try to run back to home base without being tagged.
5. The last player to be tagged is the next "It."

TRAMPOLINE

Recommended age: 2–5 years of age

WHAT YOU NEED:

- 1 bed sheet or blanket (at least full size)
- 1 stuffed "Theme Party" animal or doll

HOW TO PLAY:

1. Lay sheet in middle of play area, with animal/doll in center.
2. Have children take their places around sheet, and with both hands, grab on edge of sheet.
3. Children lift sheet together, and bounce animal/doll up and down.
4. Children must work together to keep animal/doll bouncing and to prevent it from falling off trampoline.

WHO HAS IT?

Recommended age: 5 years and older

This game requires children to concentrate and practice skills of observation.

WHAT YOU NEED:

- 1 "Theme Party" toy

HOW YOU PLAY THE GAME:

1. One child sits in middle of a circle of children and plays "It." (The birthday child should be first.)
2. Remaining children are seated with their hands behind their backs.
3. While "It" keeps his/her eyes closed, adult leader gives one of the children a toy to hold behind his/her back.
4. "It" opens his/her eyes and adult leader says, "Who has the toy?"
5. "It" gets three chances to guess who is hiding the toy.
6. If "It" guesses correctly, then the child holding the toy becomes the next "It."
7. If "It" does not guess correctly, then he/she stays in the center of the circle and the adult resumes the game, starting with Step #3. (After three unsuccessful turns, "It" is retired, and a different child is chosen as the next "It.")

Hit of the Party

INDEX

-D-

–H–